# CHILDREN'S LITERATURE

AN ILLUSTRATED HISTORY

# CHILDREN'S LITERATURE

## AN ILLUSTRATED HISTORY

*Edited by*

PETER HUNT

*Associate editors*

DENNIS BUTTS, ETHEL HEINS,
MARGARET KINNELL, TONY WATKINS

Oxford    New York

OXFORD UNIVERSITY PRESS

1995

Oxford University Press, Walton Street, Oxford OX2 6DP
Oxford  New York
Athens  Auckland  Bangkok  Bombay
Calcutta  Cape Town  Dar es Salaam  Delhi
Florence  Hong Kong  Istanbul  Karachi
Kuala Lumpur  Madras  Madrid  Melbourne
Mexico City  Nairobi  Paris  Singapore
Taipei  Tokyo  Toronto
and associated companies in
Berlin  Ibadan

Oxford is a trade mark of Oxford University Press

British Library Cataloguing in Publication Data
Data available

Library of Congress Cataloging in Publication Data
Data available
ISBN 0–19–212320-3

1 3 5 7 9 10 8 6 4 2

Printed in Great Britain
on acid-free paper by
The Bath Press
Bath, Avon

Endpapers: by kind permission of the Royal Mail.

# CONTENTS

# CONTRIBUTORS

EDITOR

**Peter Hunt** is a Senior Lecturer in English at the University of Wales, Cardiff.

ASSOCIATE EDITORS

**Dennis Butts** was formerly Head of the English Department at Bulmershe College of Higher Education, Reading.

**Ethel Heins** was formerly Editor of the *Horn Book Magazine*, and an adjunct Professor teaching Children's Literature at Simmons College, Boston.

**Margaret Kinnell** is Professor of Information Studies and Head of the Department of Information and Library Studies at Loughborough University.

**Tony Watkins** teaches in the English Department at the University of Reading. He developed the first Masters degree in Children's Literature in Britain.

CONTRIBUTORS

**Gillian Avery** has written widely on children's literature, and has written novels for children.

**Julia Briggs** is a Fellow of Hertford College, University of Oxford.

**Betty Gilderdale** lectures on children's literature at the University of Auckland.

**Peter Hollindale** is a Senior Lecturer in English at the University of York.

**Anne Scott MacLeod** is a Professor of English at the University of Maryland, College Park.

**Roderick McGillis** is a Professor of English at the University of Calgary.

**Michael Stone** lectures in the School of Education, University of Wollongong, New South Wales.

**Zena Sutherland** was formerly Professor in the University of Chicago Graduate Library School and children's book editor of the *Chicago Tribune*.

EDITORIAL ADVISERS

**Louisa Smith** is a Professor of English at Mankato State University.

**C. W. Sullivan III** is a Professor of English at East Carolina University.

# LIST OF COLOUR ILLUSTRATIONS

# EDITOR'S PREFACE

'There's an old saying', observes the villainous Mr Jemmerling in Arthur Ransome's *Great Northern?* (1947), '"What's hit's history; what's missed's mystery"', and the history of children's literature, full of colour and interest as it is, can be singularly mysterious on occasion for several reasons.

The first is a practical one. Children's books are possessed in a way that few adult books are: they are, quite literally, read to pieces. One of the most remarkable features of one of the greatest British collections of children's books, the Opie collection, is that among its 20,000 volumes there are as many as 800 published before 1800—as Iona Opie has said, this is 'a staggering number, considering the odds against their survival'.

The second reason is a little more philosophical: that nobody is quite sure what children's literature *is*, and therefore constructing its history is at best a contentious business. Ultimately most people take either the approach of Pontius Pilate on Truth or Dr Johnson on Poetry: if we stay for an answer, the answer is that we all *know* what it is, but it is not easy to *tell* what it is (or what it is not). As this book demonstrates—celebrates—it is everything from a sixteenth-century chapbook to a twentieth-century computer-based, interactive device. It is everything from the folk-tale to the problem novel, from the picture-book to the classroom poem, from the tract to the penny-dreadful, from the classic to the comic. It includes experiments in several media, metafiction, *jeux d'esprit* of major authors; we find links to the deepest human emotions, confrontations with virtually all aspects of human experience. And so if our eclecticism seems, as E. M. Forster said of his definition of the novel, unphilosophic, we wait upon a definition that comprehends this diversity.

For the definition of children's literature, unlike that of some other species of literature, depends on the involvement of its audience—which brings us to our third difficulty: children. The concept of childhood shifts constantly from period to period, place to place, culture to culture—perhaps even from child to child. The literature designed for childhood is going, therefore, to reflect this variety too. It takes a considerable mental leap to remember that the innocent schoolgirl intrigues of Angela Brazil or Enid Blyton in the 1940s were designed for the same age group as the sexually active and angst-ridden teenagers of Judy Blume in the 1970s. Just to add to our problems, children are notorious literary omnivores, and have always (initially perforce) read books not designed for them, while adult uncertainty about appropriateness has led to many books which were originally written for adults, such as Richmal Crompton's *Just—William*, 'becoming' children's books. Frances Hodgson Burnett's *Little Lord Fauntleroy* was originally written for the author's two

Iona and Peter Opie have had an outstanding influence on the study of children's culture and literature. Their collection of 20,000 children's books (begun in 1946) is now in the Bodleian Library, Oxford.

sons, and published in the children's magazine *St Nicholas*; and yet the irascible first Director-General of the BBC found it 'most affecting', and it now appears in scholarly editions for adults. Others, such as *The Wind in the Willows*, remain in eternal limbo. And so there is a two-way interaction which seriously blurs the already blurred boundaries.

Of course, all of this may simply go to prove what unsympathetic critics have often suspected, that what we are trying to write the history of is a sociological phenomenon, which can hardly be dignified by the name 'literature'. Literature, after all, requires a cultivated audience. As Henry James tartly observed in 1899, in dealing with 'the literature, as it may be called for convenience, of children . . . the sort of taste that used to be called "good" has nothing to do with the matter: we are so demonstrably in the presence of millions for whom taste is but an obscure, confused, immediate instinct'.

This is not the place to enter a Johnsonian debate on the definition of 'literature'—although one might think that any texts which so absorb their readers that they are read to extinction and inspire for life, and are passed tenderly or by familiar custom from generation to generation might well qualify. We are, rather, looking at a species of 'taste' that simply does not conform to the dominant literary-cultural concept. As a result, children's books have been marginalized; as Brian Alderson has observed, only minimal progress has been made 'in literary circles towards seeing children's books as having any cultural significance beyond quaintness'.

But this marginalizing does not take into account (at least, consciously) that most mysterious relationship between children and books and adults (who are, after all, child-readers grown up). To marginalize children's books may be to marginalize, and thus to escape from, childhood.

In short, the biggest hidden problem about children's literature is that nobody is sure *whose* it is.

Is it the children's? If so, the greatest writers are probably those with the largest output and the highest 'read-to-destruction' ratio: 'Peter Parley',

Charles Hamilton, the Stratemeyer syndicate, Roald Dahl, and that one-woman fiction factory, Enid Blyton. Such literature (if we can use the term, as I think we must, eclectically) certainly belonged to the childhoods it addressed. Or is it the property of adults? After all, with rare exceptions, such as S. E. Hinton in the USA or Pamela Brown in the UK, adults write children's books, market them, and to a large extent, buy them. (Daisy Ashford's *The Young Visiters*, sometimes cited in such debates, is probably unique as an adults' book written by a child.) They also read about them, and write the histories—which means that they also have strong feelings about what is good and acceptable. This applies to the writers as well as to the readers: what motivates them to write for children may well be the need to react to, to sublimate, to repair their own childhoods. Perhaps more than any other literature, it is the 'blindnesses' of, or the omissions from children's books—what they *don't* or *can't* say—which are important. The silences may speak to their primary audience, the children, as eloquently as the explicit meanings speak to their peers.

For the history reveals some common elements in what the adult sees as the essential children's book, and what the child sees. For the adult there is a potent mixture of nostalgia (often in the form of a rural or suburban arcadia); there are the learning of codes and initiation, group identification, and, strangely enough, retreat. For the child, the wish-fulfilment is forward-looking; it breaks the bounds, it is anarchic in that it has not learned taste and restraint, or has retained the spirit of rebellion, and of hope.

If this seems to be a preamble of unnecessary problems to a meal of remarkable delights, it is necessary because the writers of history have to make some decisions about the boundaries as well as the interstices of their subject. F. J. Harvey Darton, in the first authoritative account, *Children's Books in England* (1932), defined children's books as 'printed works produced ostensibly to give children spontaneous pleasure, and not primarily to teach them, nor solely to make them good, nor to keep them *profitably* quiet'. The words *ostensibly* and *primarily* are important here: unqualified adherence to the pleasure principle gives us a subject either too wide to be manageable or too narrow to be worth considering. Fortunately, Darton broke his own rule often enough for us to follow in his footsteps.

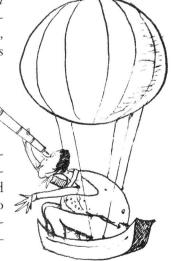

Books *for children* began early, when, if children were entertained (as it may be confidently inferred that they were) then they were very different children, with very different concepts of entertainment. These books give us a remarkable picture of how society wished itself to be (and to be seen to be), and thus, often inadvertently, give us a picture of how it actually was. As years go by, and as children's literature changes—and in a sense, blossoms—that picture of society becomes broader. Children's books—perhaps like children—see more, or at least, say more.

And if the history is sometimes mysterious, it is also far from simple. Not only does it parallel (and lag behind) other aspects of history, it moves between the two poles of adult responsibility and irresponsibility: between didacticism and control and *apparent* freedom.

The most common view of the history of children's literature is that the books have progressed steadily from didacticism to freedom, or from strictness to corruption.

Time was when the story was merely a cloak, at best a thin one, for the moral: its engaging qualities served as a means to an end, not as the reason for its existence. The standard, principle, or ideal was always unflinching, and everything else must be moulded to it. Now the ideal must be moulded to suit the child. Everything has to give way before the infallible instincts of childhood; it is the unfortunate outside influence which is looked on with suspicion.

It might come as a surprise to find that this somewhat wry account was written not in 1990 but in May 1906 (by Eveline C. Godley, in the *National Review*). But as history it is false because children's books can never be free of didacticism or adult ideological freight. Certainly the earliest writers for children were more obviously aware of their stewardship—children's books were part of God's work; but even the most modern, liberated book cannot escape the adult–child relationship. Adults know that they influence, they know that their readership is less experienced than they; they know that society is looking over their shoulders. The decisions that they make about content or balance of views vary between the 'mainstream' and the perhaps less scrupulous world of the 'manufactured' book: the dime novel, the penny-dreadful, the comic. But it is important to see children's books as the site of a good deal of anarchy, and therefore it would be a strangely unrealistic history which did not notice the less-than-respectable, whether it be a chapbook or a video-game (both of which may well be based on ancient legends).

This book, then, not only makes some theoretical decisions about the extent of its subject, but also reflects what has been taken to be children's literature—material which an impartial observer might marvel at ever having been associated with children at all. Take fairy-tales, the displaced persons of the literary world. As J. R. R. Tolkien pointed out,

the common opinion seems to be that there is a natural connection between the minds of children and fairy-stories . . . I think this is an error; at best an error of false sentiment . . . Actually, the association of children and fairy-stories is an accident of our domestic history. Fairy-stories have in the modern lettered world been relegated to the 'nursery', as shabby or old-fashioned furniture is relegated to the play-room, primarily because adults do not want it, and do not mind if it is misused.

If there are some arbitrary inclusions, then there are some equally arbitrary exclusions. This book does not deal with what might broadly be called 'non-fiction', however influential and imaginative, once fiction for children had become firmly established. It would be unrealistic not to notice the *McGuffey Eclectic Readers* in the USA, or Arthur Mee's part-works and magazines and encyclopedias in Britain, or the non-fiction that appeared in the *School Journal* in New Zealand, all of which has profoundly influenced several generations. But to do more than nod at, say, the remarkable graphics of David MacCaulay or the science writing of Millicent Selsam, would be to venture into densely populated regions that deserve their own detailed and specialist guide.

But perhaps the most obvious exclusion is the non-English-speaking world. This book is about English-language children's literature, in its several major dialects; it charts the interchange between Britain, the USA, Canada, Australia, and New Zealand, colonial and post-colonial. While both Britain and the USA have their own cultural spheres of influence, their impact in terms of children's literature on other cultures, as in India and Africa, and latterly in Europe, is not the business of this volume. For all the obvious differences between the USA and New Zealand, for example, there is a certain cultural cohesion. For example, British girls in the late nineteenth century may have looked enviously at their more independent cousins, the four *Little Women* or the *Seven Little Australians*, but the gap between them was small compared to the gap between European and African narrative norms.

While this book absorbs and acknowledges the latest research into children's books, its aim is balance rather than revolution. Children's literature has been fortunate in that the male hegemony exercised in 'adult' literary history has not established itself quite so strongly in this sphere. Women did, and do, have the major influence on the subject, and so revisionist readings are perhaps not quite so desperately needed as elsewhere—but that does not mean that the children's book world is in any sense a cosy or complacent one. Much 'criticism' of children's books has been marred by sentimentality and nostalgia, but the historian is confronted by such a wealth of innovation— and such energy where innovation is lacking—that complacency is a difficult position to sustain.

Equally, it has been well argued that the vast amount of material in libraries and archives still requires enormous amounts of scholarly work; we are a very long way from establishing the extent of children's book publishing and its influence, or putting children's literature on a bibliographic footing with its literary peers. But there cannot, of course, ever be an ultimate, definitive statement of such matters: each new discovery revises our views of literature as well as social history. What we present here is today's edition of a road-map (albeit on a very large scale) that might provide a fresh viewpoint for the social historian, or outline an immensely fascinating and influential body of texts for literary critics and other readers.

And not only for them. It would be a brave editor who missed Biggles or Simon Black or the Hardy Boys out of a book like this, who slighted Arthur Ransome without (or even with) weighty evidence, or who failed to mention the Christian name of one of the Bobbsey Twins (Freddie and Flossie, Nan and Bert). Feelings run high about those things that really affect us. Children's books are so personal, so enthusiastically taken over by their readers and preserved as part of their internal childhood that writers about children's books do well to take heed of Dorothy Parker, who wrote, in one of her skirmishes with A. A. Milne: 'There is a strong feeling, I know, that to speak against Mr. Milne puts one immediately in the ranks of those who set fire to orphanages, strike crippled newsboys, and lure little curly-heads off into corners to explain to them that Santa Claus is only Daddy . . .'

Just over a hundred years ago, in *The Parent's Review* of 1890, Edward Salmon wrote: 'Nothing surprises me more at times than the ignorance of parents on the subject of literature provided for their children.' He would perhaps be surprised at how little things have changed, but this history, by giving one reading of the way we have arrived at our present situation, may help to demonstrate the riches and the relevance of the subject, to childhoods past, present, and hidden.

P.H.

*January 1994*

# 1 THE BEGINNINGS OF CHILDREN'S READING

to *c*.1700

*Gillian Avery*

## FESCUE AND FERULA

I F one considers what British children read before there were recreational books designed specially for their needs, two things become immediately evident. First, that the children's book industry, which may be said to have had its beginnings in the 1740s but which did not really reach a significant number of child readers until the last century, is a very recent phenomenon; children of previous generations became literate—and often highly literary—without any such help. And secondly, that it says much for the conservatism and obstinacy of the British that, in the teeth of centuries of denunciation from preachers, moralists, and pedagogues, they clung to their 'fayned fables, vayne fantasyes, and wanton stories' (as Hugh Rhodes's *Boke of Nurture* put it in 1577), and produced a literature notably rich in fantasy and imagination.

But it was a long time before any of this was addressed specifically to children. In 1766 the Revd John Ash, adapting a manual of English grammar for children under 10, appended a reading list several pages long. The least weighty section is the one headed 'Books of Amusement and Imagination', but the titles suggested are as follows:

Mr Newbery's Books, viz Mosaic Creation, . . . New History of England . . ., Philosophy for Children, Circle of Science, Atlas Minimus . . . Philosophy of Tops and Balls; Robinson Crusoe; The Pleasures of Imagination, Spectator vol. VI; Dodsley's Aesop's Fables; Gay's Fables; The Moral Miscellany by W. Rose; Dr. Fordyce's Temple of Virtue.

But before we consider what children read for amusement before they had

I

A schoolmaster with his pupils, his birch rod bese him. Frontispiece and first page of a Latin grammar, *Informatio Puerorum*, printed by Richard Pynson *c.*1503.

their own books, we should look at their schoolbooks. Historians of children's literature customarily brush these aside, but this is to jettison much of what formed the literate adult, and is particularly obtuse if applied to the pre-eighteenth-century period, when children had little else. Thomas Lye in his *New Spelling-Book* (1677) reckoned that a fourth part of life was given up to the 'Fescue and Ferula' (pointer and rod), and there is much to be discovered about attitudes to the young, even in the preface to a Latin grammar.

What is certain is that pedagogues, though full of theory, were slow to change. From early days they preached mercy, but little was shown. A poem of *c.*1500, 'The Birched School-Boy' (included in the Early English Text Society's edition of *The Babee's Book*, 1868), ruefully describes how much pain attended the acquiring of education.

> I wold ffayn be a clarke
> but yet hit is a strange werke;
> the byrchyn twyggis be so sharpe,
> hit makith me haue a faynt harte.

The boy groans that he would rather trudge twenty miles twice on Mondays than go to school. When at last he slinks in with the admittedly impudent excuse that he has been 'milking duck'

> My master pepered my ars with well good spede . . .
> he wold not leve till it did blede.

From the earliest days of printing the elders take a poor view of the young. In 1483 Caxton prefaced his commentary on Cato's Distichs with much head-shaking about present decadence: 'I see that the children that ben borne within [the city of London] encrease and prouffyte not lyke theyr faders and olders.' In 1570 Roger Ascham had bitter things to say about contumacious modern youth:

Innocencie is gone: Bashfulnesse is banished; moch presumption in yougthe; small authoritie in aige: Reuerence is neglected; dewties be confounded: and to be shorte, disobedience doth ouerflowe the bankes of good order almost in euerie place. (*The Scholemaster*)

Nor had matters improved in 1693 when Locke wrote in his *Some Thoughts Concerning Education* that 'the early corruption of youth is now become so general a complaint', while in 1622, John Brinsley, a Puritan schoolmaster, made observations about declining educational standards which may sound familiar.

For this is a thing notorious, that in the greatest part of our common schools . . . the scholars at fifteene or sixteene yeares of age haue not commonly so much as anie sense of the meaning and true vse of learning, for vnderstanding, resoluing, writing or speaking . . . That in respect of being fit to be sent to the Vniuersities with credit, that they may proceed with delight and vnderstanding, when they come there, they are commonly so senslesse, as they are much meeter to be sent home again. (*A Consolation for our Grammar Schooles*)

But first, how did children learn to read? The experiences of Adam Martindale, a Lancashire yeoman born in 1623, were probably the same as generations of children before his time and after. His godmother gave him an ABC when he was nearly 6, 'a gift in itself exceeding small and contemptible, but in respect of the designe and event, worth more than its weight in gold'. With the help of older siblings, and 'a young man that came to court my sister', he quickly mastered it, 'and the primmer also after it. Then of mine owne accord I fell to reading the Bible and any other English booke.'

The ABC of those early times could be a hornbook. This convenient and relatively indestructible form of presenting the alphabet (followed by a syllabary, invocation to the Trinity, and the Lord's Prayer) was in common use from the sixteenth century until well on in the eighteenth; in Boston in the 1680s little Joseph Sewall, aged 3, was sent to school with his cousin Jane

Two eighteenth-century hornbooks. In the lower one the printed paper is protected by a thin layer of horn.

carrying his. Alternatively an alphabet, syllabary, and spelling lists might be included alongside a church catechism in what was known as an 'abcie' book. From a manual of this sort the Tudor boy in his 'petty school' moved on to a primer. The early form of this was a liturgical book with the church calendar in it, psalms, a portion of church services, and prayers. After the Reformation the contents changed to conform with the Book of Common Prayer, and contained the calendar of the Church of England, catechism, prayers, and collects. *The New England Primer*, which originated late in the seventeenth century, still kept this shaping during the whole of its long life.

Out of the hornbook developed the battledore, popular until the mid-nineteenth century, a folded piece of cardboard with a more enticing appearance since the alphabet was usually illustrated.

Much of the elementary teaching must have been informal, as it was with Adam Martindale. Francis Clement, whose *Petie Schole* (1576) is one of the earliest books to attempt to teach the rudiments of English spelling and pronunciation, begins with some verse addressed 'To the litle Children'.

> Come, litle Childe, let toyes alone,
>   and trifles in the streete,
> Come, get thee to the parish Clarke,
>   H' is made a Teacher meete.
> Frequent ye now the Taylers shop,
>   And eeke the Weavers lombe;
> There's neither these, but can with skill
>   Them teach that thither come.

The 'Semstresse' is also recommended. In short, any literate person with a sedentary occupation would be suitable.

In 1570 John Hart (an early advocate of the rationalization of English spelling) produced a little manual, *A Methode, or Comfortable Beginning for all Unlearned*, to teach such people how to teach reading, using phonetic methods. It contains the first known printed picture alphabet. Edmund Coote addressed his *English Schoole-Maister* (1596) to 'men and women of trades . . . as haue undertaken the charge of teaching others'; 200 years later, Samuel Bamford, born in 1788, remembered that he had been taught his alphabet while his father, a weaver, sat at his loom, and had then been sent to the parish clerk (who had, however, taught him very little).

John Brinsley, headmaster of Ashby de la Zouch grammar school, in *Ludus Literarius; or, The Grammar Schoole* (1612), laid down a syllabus for those who were going to receive a more formal schooling. (This book was listed as among the books taken out to Virginia in 1635 by the Revd John Goodborne.) Brinsley said that children 'in our countery schooles' commonly started school at the age of 7 or 8, but that he would recommend the age of 5, when

*Facing*: the successors of hornbooks. A collection of printed paper battledores published by W. Davison of Alnwick, *c*.1830.

4

The first known
English use of a
picture alphabet. From
John Hart: *A Methode,
or Comfortable
Beginning for all
Unlearned* (1570).

they were more biddable and less reluctant to leave their play. After they had learned the alphabet and could read syllables, 'thus they may go through their Abcie and Primer'. Having mastered these they could progress to other English books, notably metrical versions of the Psalms. (Verse and metre were regarded as the way to tempt children along the path of learning, long before pictures were used for this purpose.) After the Psalms Brinsley prescribed the Bible, and then *The Schoole of Vertue*, versified maxims by Francis Seager, first published in 1557, and *The Schoole of Good Manners*, which, adapted by Eleazar Moody in 1715, was one of New England's first publications for children.

The rules for children's behaviour—or those that we encounter in print—changed remarkably little over some 300 years. In *Nurse Truelove's Christmas-Box*, a little book which the Newbery firm first put out *c.*1750 and went on reissuing until 1787, the same directions as Caxton gave in his *Book of Curtesye* (1477)—about piety, neatness, honouring one's parents, politeness—are being given:

When the Sun doth arise, you must get up each Day,
And fall on your Knees, and to God humbly pray;
Then kneel to your Parents, their Blessing implore;
And when you have Money, give some to the Poor.
Your Hands and your Face, in the next Place, wash fair;
And brush your Apparel, and comb out your Hair;
And wish a good Morning to all in your View,
And bow to your Parents and bid them adieu.

The main difference is that Newbery, typically, promises material rewards; little Master Friendly in the subsequent story follows all these precepts and 'God Almighty has blessed him . . . Why, you see he is a Parliament-Man already.'

The first aim of the early devisers of what later generations were to call 'Reading Made Easy' books was that children should read the Bible and study their catechism. The poet John Clare, born in 1793, thought the traditional method of setting village children like himself to read the Bible as soon as they knew their letters was wrong; especially as the school kept them 'clinging at it without any change till they leave it'. The Bible being the accepted goal, the vocabulary in these early reading books was often inappropriately complex. It is a long time before we find child-centred narratives. However, books such as *A Play-Book for Children* by 'J. G.', or *A Little Book for Little Children* by 'T.W.' (n.d., *c*.1704—not to be confused with Thomas White's religious manual of the 1670s which had the same name) attempted to illustrate their sometimes arcane vocabulary with sentences dealing with material within the children's experience, and birds and animals.

Despite the efforts of John Hart to teach phonetics by means of a picture alphabet, illustrated alphabets are not often found before the eighteenth century. Comenius's *Orbis sensualium pictus* (first published in Nuremberg in 1658, translated into English in 1659) begins with a particularly delightful one, where the child is invited to make the sound of the animal shown, for example, 'the serpent hisseth SS'. But as its translator, Charles Hoole, pointed out, 'the alphabet is fitted for German children rather than ours', and though Comenius is a name that occurs in all histories of children's literature, he made curiously little impact on English schoolbooks.

John Amos Comenius (Jan Komenský) was born in Moravia in 1592 of Protestant parents. He had witnessed the appalling sufferings inflicted by religious persecution (his own wife and children died of privation; he himself had to flee from his native country), and he had a vision of a universal peace which might be achieved through a new system of education which he called 'pansophic'. He hoped that his *Janua linguarum reserata* ('The Gate of Languages Unlocked') would be an instrument to achieve this, but finding that it was too difficult for many children, he devised the *Orbis sensualium pictus*, an encyclopedic assemblage of labelled pictures designed to give a logical and pansophical view not only of the world but of learning. It begins with God, and finishes with the Last Judgement, with the natural world and human life displayed between.

For it is apparent that Children (even from their Infancy almost) are delighted with Pictures, and willingly please their eyes with these sights. And it will be very well worth the pains to have once brought it to pass, that scarecrows may be taken away out of wisdomes Gardens.

What strikes us now is the absence of all concession to childhood as some later generations came to see it—a time of innocence and make-believe, when children ought to be sheltered from harsh realities. Comenius's pictures show life as it is, and as his own children had experienced it—war, torture, death, disease, deformities.

Locke does not mention Comenius when he writes in *Some Thoughts Concerning Education* about the desirability of finding illustrated books for the

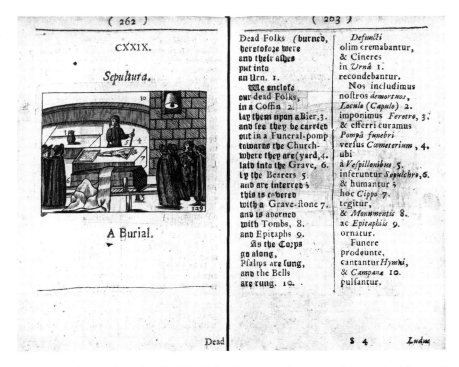

From Comenius'
*Orbis sensualium pictus*
(trans. Charles Hoole,
3rd edn., 1672), one of
the earliest 'picture-
books' for children.

young reader, and we find in English educational works of the period few references to him. John Evelyn in a sorrowful record of the short life of his 5-year-old son (*The Golden Book of St John Chrysostom* (1659)) says that the child had worked his way through Comenius (though this may have been the *Janua linguarum*), and the tutor in the Earl of Bedford's household at about the same time recorded that he bought Comenius for his younger pupils. With its many engravings it must always have been an expensive book; the illustrations related to German life, and where science and industries were concerned soon became out of date. In the English edition of 1777 the editor was lamenting that it is 'now fallen totally into disuse'.

There was one writer on education who, ten years before *Orbis sensualium pictus*, in some ways anticipated Comenius' ambition to present children with a broader-based education. This was William Petty, a man of many parts who later became professor of anatomy at Oxford, a founder member of the Royal Society, and a distinguished political economist. In 1648, when he was only 25, he published a short pamphlet, *The Advice of W.P. to Mr Samuel Hartlib for the Advancement of some particular parts of Learning*. He wanted children to be taught music, drawing, gardening, chemistry, anatomy, architecture, and technical skills, to study trade, all of which would come much more easily to them than 'a rabble of words'. He also gives a rare account of how children amused themselves then:

8

For we see Children to delight in Drums, Pipes, Fiddels, Guns made of Elder-sticks and Bellowes noses, piped Keyes &c. for painting Flags and Ensignes with Elder-berries and Corn-poppy, making Ships with Paper, and setting even Nut-shells a swimming, handling the tooles of workemen as soone as they turne their backs, and trying to worke themselves; fishing, fowling, hunting, setting sprenges and traps for birds, and other animals, making pictures in their writing bookes, making Tops, Gigs and Whirligigs, quilting balls, practising divers jugling tricks upon the Cards, &c. with a million more besides. And for the Females, they will be making Pyes with Clay, making their Babies Clothes, and dressing them therewith, they will spit leaves on sticks, as if they were roasting meate, they will imitate all the talke and Actions, which they observe in their Mother and her gossips, and punctually act the Comedy or Tragedy (I know not whether to call it) of a Woman lying in.

William Petty's emphasis on the importance of trade and industry and his concern that children should acquire manual skills, foreshadow the system of education that Richard Edgeworth was to devise with his daughter Maria al-most 150 years later.

But it was to take twice that time to effect much change in the education of the British male élite, and for centuries Latin dominated the curriculum. For the seventeenth-century colonists in Virginia and New England too the classics were the backbone of education and polite learning, and their sons were taught from the same books used by grammar schools in England. Locke looked upon Latin 'as absolutely necessary to a gentleman', but quali-fied his assertion by saying that it was ridiculous for tradesmen and farmers to make their boys struggle with the language when they would be far better served by learning to write a good hand and cast up accounts. This sound ad-vice was not heeded by Tom Tulliver's father and his kind, and George Eliot's description of Tom's uncomprehending flounderings in the sea of Latin acci-dence must represent the sufferings of countless schoolboys of an earlier age. 'Yet all men couet to haue their children speake latin', Ascham had said in 1570, and it is significant that Lily's *Latin Grammar* probably had the longest

The grammar school and song school at Durham, orginating in 1414, rebuilt 1666.

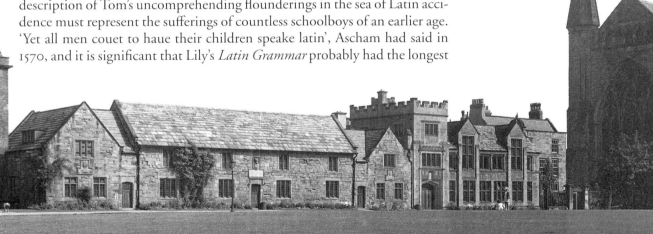

life of any book composed specifically for youth. Partly the work of William Lily, partly of John Colet, it was published in revised form in 1549, the year that Edward VI proclaimed its use mandatory in all grammar schools. It was to remain virtually unchanged for over 400 years and through some 350 editions.

The fundamental elementary Latin reading book of the Middle Ages was the *Catonis disticha de moribus*, a compilation of gnomic couplets, which although attributed to the moralist Cato (234–149 BC) was a far later work. It was one of the earliest and most popular books printed by Caxton (in a verse paraphrase by Benet Burgh). Francis Seager makes frequent reference to Cato in *The Schoole of Vertue* (1557), John Brinsley translated it for his school in the early 1600s, and versions were still being printed in the next century. It preaches foresight, prudence, circumspection:

Come not to pleade any matter in Law except thou be well instructed what to saie.
Giue thou place to a man that is of greater puissaunce and mightier than thou art.
A wise man chaungeth according to the qualitie of the tyme.

Its precepts were absorbed into many books of advice addressed to youth in the seventeenth century. Some, like Francis Osborne's *Advice to a Son* (1656), are worldly, some more spiritual, but all appear to be the work of writers reared on Cato. This essentially middle-aged rule of life was to linger on in the eighteenth century, in Lord Chesterfield's *Letters to his Son* (1774) and in the little moral fables—like William Darton's *First Book of Accidents*, and its two sequels, published in the early years of the nineteenth century—which warned children, especially boys, of the appalling dangers resulting from imprudence.

The aim of schoolmasters—and this was to remain true until very near our own times—was not to inculcate a love of literature when the classics were studied, but to drill their pupils in the language, using a very limited number of texts. To this was added moral teaching—even Lily's *Latin Grammar* was prefaced by *Carmen de moribus*. Moral maxims were culled from the plays of Terence, and John Brinsley's pupils and countless others read not the orations of Cicero, but such essays as *De senectute* and *De amicitia* (also published by Caxton).

What may surprise us now is the abstract nature of the texts used in schools, and their limited number. From Ascham onwards, though there was much theory about *how* children should be taught, the same few books by the same handful of Latin authors are named. It is rare indeed to find books in the vernacular recommended before the seventeenth-century Puritans began prescribing aids to conversion. It is thus very interesting to see what Caxton suggested in *The Book of Curtesye* for 'lytyll John's' reading: Hoccleve's *Regiment of Princes*, Gower's *Confessio amantis*, Lydgate, and *all* Chaucer, 'for his hole entente | How to plese in euery audyence'. Manuals of behaviour did not often suggest that there might be pleasure in reading.

Many enlightened educationalists in the sixteenth and seventeenth centuries were pleading for children to be treated with greater consideration, and for learning to be made a pleasure. One brave spirit even attempted to make a game of Latin. Despite the threatening sound of its title, Elisha Coles's *Nolens volens: Or You shall make Latin whether you will or no* (1675) tries hard to take the mystery out of Latin accidence, and it includes *The Youths Visible Bible*, where the key words in selected biblical texts, arranged alphabetically, are illustrated with a plate for each letter.

Thus when Locke set down *Some Thoughts Concerning Education* in 1693 he did not think of it as particularly innovative. Over 100 years before Roger Ascham, in *The Scholemaster*, had emphasized that 'the Scholehouse should be in deede, as it is called by name, the house of playe and pleasure, and not of feare and bondage'. Richard Mulcaster, the first headmaster of Merchant Taylors school, in *The Training up of Children* (1581) had echoed Ascham in emphasizing that learning should be a delight. He also said that laughing should be encouraged: 'the more children laugh for exercise, the more light some they be.' Over 100 years before Locke, he had stressed the importance of physical exercise and games, had devoted an entire chapter to tops, and had written of the need for games and gymnastics; Locke insisted that children should be free to choose how they played, '[so] that it will discover their natural tempers, show their inclinations and aptitudes, and thereby direct wise parents in the choice . . . of the course of life and employment they shall design them for . . .'. In this consideration for the child's individuality Locke differs radically from the traditionalists who asserted that children were entirely subject to their parents' arbitrary wishes, and from the Puritans who distrusted all leisure.

It was not Locke who had introduced the idea of the *tabula rasa*. Caxton, with the air of one uttering a truism, had prefaced his *Book of Curtesye* with the remark:

> But as waxe resseyueth prynte or figure
> So children ben disposde of nature
> Vyce or vertue to folowe.

Ascham too had likened the 'pure cleane witte of a sweete yong babe' to wax, and to 'a new bright silver dish neuer occupied, to reciue and kepe cleane, anie good thyng that is put into it'.

Nor should Locke be given the credit for the developments in children's book publishing in the eighteenth century. As has been described, the seventeenth century had seen a number of books designed to make learning a pleasure. J.G.'s *A Play-Book for Children*, published the year after *Some Thoughts*

*Concerning Education*, is much more likely to be an experienced teacher's independent reflections than an effort to jump on the Locke wagon, and Mary Cooper, Boreman, and Newbery would no doubt have put out the same books if Locke had never written.

Locke's treatise therefore is not a dramatic breakthrough after which everything changed; it is a reflection of changing attitudes. In the first half of the seventeenth century, child-slanted material can only be found in the dialogues composed for Latin speakers. But from the 1670s the mood was changing. James Janeway in *A Token for Children* (discussed later) devoted a whole book to narratives about godly children, addressing his readers as 'dear lambs'. And in 1712 William Ronksley in *The Child's Weeks-Work* is coaxing the child thus:

> Come, take this Book
> Dear Child, and look
>   On it a while, and try
> What you can find
> To please your Mind;
>   The rest you may pass by.

He includes verses for each day, riddles, jokes, and fables.

But we have to wait a long time before this gentle light-heartedness becomes commonplace. As can be noted from the Revd John Ash's reading list (cited at the beginning of this chapter) many people, even in the 1760s, expected children to be greybeards while they were still in petticoats.

## FAYNED FABLES

For centuries educators and moralists tormented themselves with the thought of the Pandora's box to which the newly literate had been given the key. Francis Clement in *Petie Schole* in 1576 warned children against books which were 'the enemies of vertue, nources of vice, furtherers of ignorance and hinderers of all good learnyng'. Ascham, in 1545, had associated such pernicious material with the bad old days, 'our fathers tyme [when] nothing was red, but books of fayned cheualrie'. These books, he asserted, were particularly dangerous to children, 'for surelye vayne woordes doo woorke no smal thinge in vayne, ignoraunt, and younge mindes'.

The seventeenth-century Puritans returned to the theme again and again. Cotton Mather spoke of 'Satan's library' (*Man Eating the Food of Angels*, 1710), and warned readers that they would be seized with loathing for the manna of heaven. Fiction to the Puritan mind was dangerous because of its addictive nature, and the way it deflected readers not only from contemplation of their latter end, but from more profitable occupations. To the strictly orthodox there was besides a far more serious objection; it was all a lie, and therefore damnably wicked. It was an attitude that took a far greater hold on New England Puritans and their descendants than in Old England, whose inhabitants have always been more resistant to preachers, and in the nineteenth century there was still much American heart-searching about whether or not children should be allowed fairy-stories. Many indeed would have liked to proscribe fiction altogether. '"Is it a true book, John?"' asks the grandmother in Charles Dudley Warner's *Being a Boy* (1877). '"Because if it isn't true, it is the worst thing that a boy can read."'

There was one category of fiction, however, that appears always to have been unobjectionable. This was the corpus of tales traditionally known as Aesop's *Fables*—'the only book almost that I know fit for children' said Locke in 1693. (We find them, together with Gay's fables and *Robinson Crusoe*, as the only fiction on Ash's 1766 reading list.) But until the eighteenth century they were not so much recreation as part of the classroom experience, read in Latin, very often in the verse adaptation made by Phaedrus in the first century AD. Long before Locke, Luther had given them his imprimatur in *Colloquia mensale.* Together with Cato there was nothing more suitable for schoolchildren, he said.

Caxton made the first English translation in 1484, when the fables would have been very familiar to his public. They had been used in Greek schools of rhetoric, in Roman schools, and then in Christian schools throughout Europe. Even more than Cato's 'Distichs' they were constantly modified, added to, edited, and rearranged, so that the Aesop of the Middle Ages was no classical work but a medieval creation resting on an ancient basis.

The Aesop 'umbrella' came to shelter many fabulists, and one of the few to admit the complexity of the situation was Thomas Blage, who in 1569 published *A Schole of Wise Conceytes, Translated out of Divers Greke and Latine Wryters.* In addition to the fables traditionally ascribed to Aesop, he drew on nineteen authors, from Horace and the younger Pliny to Erasmus and the Italian humanist Poggio (1380–1459), and though he does not identify who wrote what, he speaks in the opening verse apologia of 'the falsly forged tales' that attach themselves to the name of Aesop. By 1692 Roger L'Estrange, whose collection included some 500 fables (approximately three times as

The Famous and Renowned HISTORY OF Sir Bevis of Southampton GIVING An Account of his Birth, Education, Heroick Exploits and Enterprises, his Fights with Giants, Monsters, Wild-Beasts and Armies, his Conquering Kings and Kingdoms, his Love and Marriage, Fortunes and Misfortunes, and many other Famous and Memorable Things and Actions, worthy of Wonder; With the Adventures of other Knights, Kings and Princes, exceeding pleasant and delightful to Read.

Licensed and Entred according to Order.

Printed for *W. Thackeray* at the *Angel* in *Duck-Lane*, and *J. Deacon* at the *Angel* in *Gilt-Spur-street*, 1689.

One of the 'fayned fables' abhorred by authority. *Bevis of Hampton* was a popular verse-romance from the late thirteenth or early fourteenth century, based on a twelfth-century Anglo-Norman *chanson de geste.*

The first English translation of the *Arabian Nights*. The stories captivated the European imagination.

ARABIAN Nights **Entertainments:** CONSISTING OF One Thousand and One **STORIES,** TOLD BY The Sultaness of the *Indies,* to divert the Sultan from the Execution of a Bloody Vow he had made to marry a Lady every Day, and have her cut off next Morning, to avenge himself for the Disloyalty of his first Sultaness, &c.

Containing A better Account of the Customs, Manners, and Religion of the Eastern Nations, *Tartars, Persians,* and *Indians,* than is to be met with in any Author hitherto published.

Translated into *French* from the *Arabian* MSS. by M. *Galland,* of the Royal Academy; and now done into English.

In Two Volumes.

Vol. I.

*London,* Printed for *Andrew Bell,* at the Cross Keys and Bible in *Cornhill,* 1706.

many as Caxton), felt that it was impossible to distinguish 'the Original from the Copy. And to say, which of the Fables are Aesop's, and which are not.'

The ethic of the older beast fables is pre-Christian, and the unanimous approval given to it by churchmen of every cast, from medieval abbots to Puritan divines, seems strange: 'The fables of Esop have always been esteemed the best lessons for youth, as being well adapted to convey the most useful maxims, in a very agreeable manner' is a typical comment, this time from the Dodsley brothers' *Select Fables of Esop and Other Fabulists* (1761)—the edition recommended in the Revd Mr Ash's reading list.

But the main thrust of the teaching contained in Aesop is worldly wisdom—presence of mind, trimming one's sails to circumstance, and above all caution. And, as in the beast legends of most cultures, cunning and guile play a prominent part. 'Good night, Uncle, this is the fashion of the World; some go up and some go down,' the fox calls out to the drowning wolf whom he has tricked into saving him (Nathaniel Crouch, *Delightful Fables in Prose and*

*Verse*, 1691). (The same spirit is to be found two centuries later in 'Uncle Remus'.)

Caxton had kept the moral comment brief and crisp; many later compilers appended ruminations which were wearisomely prolix. The Revd Samuel Croxall was one such. He designed *Fables of Aesop and Others* (1722) to supplant L'Estrange, whose 'pernicious principles' he attacked with much passion (Croxall was a Whig, L'Estrange a Tory). Despite the ponderous wordiness of his 'applications', his version went through some 200 editions, retaining its popularity well into the Victorian period.

Few of the many later compilers appeared to recognize that most of the fables require adult experience to interpret. One of the more curious versions was Walter Crane's *The Baby's Own Aesop* (1887). Crane put the fables into limerick form, which left no room for a moral and emphasized their harshness:

> A poor half-blind Doe her one eye
> Kept shoreward, all danger to spy.
> As she fed by the sea
> Poor innocent! she
> Was shot from a boat passing by.

Crane surrounded his brief text with inappropriately lavish, eye-teasing decoration—Aesop has always had a very strong appeal for illustrators. One of the rare efforts to adapt Aesop to a young child's comprehension was made by William Godwin in *Fables Ancient and Modern* (1805). He pointed out that in their original form fables are far too terse for children, and end either unhappily or abruptly and unsatisfactorily. Godwin clearly felt that the young reader should be presented with a gentler view of the world and its ways than the adult knows is so—an instinct which was by no means universal even at that date.

The Bidpai fables, deriving from the *Panchatantra* and other Sanskrit or Hindu tales, reached English readers by a more labyrinthine route even than Aesop. They had first been translated into English by Sir Thomas North in 1570, and were put out in editions for young readers in the eighteenth century, usually under the title of *The Fables of Pilpay*. They are ingeniously linked, often subtle stories supposedly told by an Indian sage (named variously Bidpai, Pilpay, Vishnucarman, or Sendebar) to his king to

Aesop's fables are here used to give children practice with handwriting.

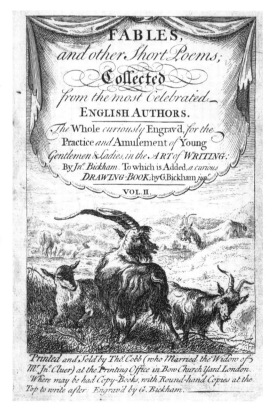

FABLES, and other *Short Poems*; Collected from the most Celebrated ENGLISH AUTHORS. The Whole *curiously* Engrav'd, *for the* Practice *and* Amusement *of* Young Gentlemen & Ladies, *in the* ART *of* WRITING: By *Jn.º Bickham.* To which is Added, *a curious* DRAWING-BOOK, by G. Bickham jun.<sup> r.</sup> VOL. II.

Printed and Sold by Tho.º Cobb (who Married the Widow of M.<sup>r.</sup> Jn.º Cluer) at the Printing Office in Bow Church Yard London. Where may be had Copy-Books, with Round-hand Copies at the Top to write after. Engrav'd by G. Bickham.

The History of *Tom Thumbe*, the *Little*, for his small stature surnamed, King ARTHVRS *Dwarfe*:

Whose Life and aduentures containe many strange and wonderfull accidents, published for *the delight of merry Time-spenders.*

Imptinted at London for *Tho: Langley.* 1621.

Title-page of the earliest surviving text of one of the most popular of all English folk-tales.

incite him to virtue. They never approached the popularity of Aesop though they are more satisfying narratives.

Some of them indeed were absorbed into the late thirteenth-century *Gesta Romanorum*, an extraordinary hotch-potch of legends of the saints, classical stories, tales of the chroniclers, oriental fables (often strangely incorporated into a background of feudal Europe), and all with some form of moral exposition attached. The *Gesta* was originally designed, it seems, for monastic communities, and for preachers to draw material for sermons, but in chapter 155 of the printed Latin versions of the *Gesta* we find the whole family gathering round the fire on winter evenings after the evening meal, and passing the time, as was the custom in the higher classes, by telling stories.

Sir Thomas North in the preface to his translation of Plutarch's *Lives* in 1579 recognized this need for stories: 'stories are fit for euerie place, reach to all persons, serue for all times.' And this was the attitude of the clerics who had compiled the *Gesta* and of their contemporaries; stories were for everyone, young and old. In 1477 Caxton, for instance, presented his *History of Jason*—a combination of classical legend and medieval romance, with a strong love interest—to the 6-year-old future Edward V. Edward IV, the little prince's father, had instructed the child's governor that during dinner he should listen to 'such noble stories as behoveth a prince to understand and know'.

But the Reformation brought a new moral earnestness about the purposes of literacy, and Protestant authority abhorred stories such as Caxton had been publishing. To Ascham and his kind they were emblematic of the bad old days 'when Papistrie, as a standyng poole, couered and ouerflowed all England'. How little heed was paid to this sort of denunciation can be gathered from the fact that 1590 saw the publication of such chivalric works as Sidney's *Arcadia* and Spenser's *The Faerie Queene*, and in the same decade, though for a wholly different readership, *The Seven Champions of Christendom*, Richard Johnson's extravaganza about the deeds of St George and others. Plenty of writers recorded what these stories had meant to them as children. Richard Baxter, author of many Puritan classics, spoke in his *Reliquiae Baxterianae* of the sins of his youth; in addition to the 'excessive gluttonous eating of Apples and Pears', he had been 'extreamly bewitched with a Love of Romances,

Fables and old Tales'. Bunyan, his contemporary, made a similar confession in *Sighs from Hell; or The Groans of a Damned Soul*. In his youth, he said, he had heard many a warning from the preachers, but had rejected them.

> The Scriptures, thought I, what are they? a dead letter, a little Ink and Paper, of three or four Shillings price. . . . Give me a Ballad, a Newsbook, George on Horseback, or Bevis of Southampton. Give me some book that teaches curious Arts, but for the holy Scriptures I cared not.

But more people remembered those ancient stories with tenderness. Wordsworth, for instance, in Book V of *The Prelude*, writes nostalgically of Fortunatus, Jack the Giant-Killer, Robin Hood, and St George. Among Coleridge's favourite boyhood heroes were Tom Hickathrift (a legendary English Hercules) and Jack the Giant-Killer. Thomas Holcroft, born in 1745, was given *Parismus* and *The Seven Champions* by Dick, his father's apprentice, when he was very young, tales which 'were soon as familiar to me as my catechism. . . . Oh how I loved poor Dick.' Touchingly, he also remembered that he had modelled his behaviour on 'the renowned heroes of fable', 'and to be a liar, a rogue, and get hanged, did not square well with the confused ideas I had either of greatness or goodness, or with my notions of a hero'.

At that time, he said, books were hardly seen except in the houses of the most well off. Thomas Carter, a generation younger than Holcroft, recalled in *Memoirs of a Working Man* (1845) that the only books his parents possessed were two Bibles, the Book of Common Prayer, a spelling book, Watt's *Divine and Moral Songs*, 'and some tattered volumes of theology'. Both Carter and Holcroft devoured the few stories that came their way, ancient romances which centuries before had had a universal appeal but which were now only to be found in chapbooks. For, Holcroft said, 'that love of the marvellous which is natural to ill-informed man, is still more lively in childhood'. It is interesting that in 1743 when Mary Cooper published her spelling book, *The Child's New Plaything*, she included as 'stories proper to raise the attention and excite the curiosity of children' St George and the Dragon (from *The Seven Champions*), Guy of Warwick, Fortunatus, and Reynard the Fox— which with its twelfth-century French origins was older than any of them.

In America these stories never had the same hold; they belonged to a past which the colonists had left behind them. From invoices of the 1680s we know that Boston booksellers imported

a handful of items like Valentine and Orson, Fortunatus, and Reynard, among the catechisms, schoolbooks, and theological works that were their standard requirements. But we find little evidence that children knew and loved them as they had done in England. However, Caleb Bingham, author of many schoolbooks, included a satirical account of a little boy's reading in *The Columbian Orator* (1797). The lad boasts that he is 'a monstrous great student'.

There is no telling the half of what I have read . . . The Arabian tales, Tom Thumb's Folio through, Winter evening tales, and Seven Champions, and Parismus, and Parismenus, and Valentine and Orson, and Mother Bunch, and Seven Wise Masters, Robinson Crusoe, and Reynard the Fox, and Moll Flanders, and Philip Quarle, and Conjuror Crop, and Aesop's Fables.

Once in this mood, he says, he can swallow anything—'my mind is capacious enough for a china-shop'.

It can now be seen how small a part fiction played in prescribed reading lists, and one is tempted to say that the young had to wait until the advent of Sir Walter Scott to find a novelist—as distinct from a writer of moral tales—acceptable to authority. ('Fling *Peregrine Pickle* under the toilet—throw *Roderick Random* into the closet,' says the frantic Lydia Languish to her maid in *The Rivals* when she hears her aunt on the stairs.) But there were palatable substitutes, and these did not have to be the books of advice that were so abundant from the seventeenth century onwards. (The two that Miss Languish substituted for her Smollett were Mrs Hester Chapone's *Letters on the Improvement of Mind* and Lord Chesterfield's *Letters*, both to become classics but in 1775 only a couple of years old.)

From *The Family Life of Ralph Josselin* we learn that young Ralph, in his boyhood (about 1630), was indeed much taken up with 'histories' of the sort just described, and like Bunyan and Baxter, he remembered this fact with grief. But he was also 'much delighted with Cosmography', and this probably included Hakluyt's *Voyages*, first published in 1582, and his *Principall Navigations* (1589), found in many private libraries. History was also much read by the young, both then and for many years to come. John Adams, for instance, writing to his son John Quincy from Philadelphia in 1777, tells him to read Thucydides now that his country is at war.

Classical history was read by children far younger than the 10-year-old John Quincy Adams. Increase Mather, recording the life of his daughter Jerusha in 1711 (she was born in 1684 and died in childbirth in 1710), said that she had been a great reader ever since she was 4, 'in Historical Books, as well as Theological', and this no doubt included Plutarch, and perhaps the *Jewish Antiquities* of Flavius Josephus. Written in the first century AD, it was first translated into English in 1602. At least two seventeenth-century compila-

*Facing: A School for Boys and Girls*, Jan Havicksz Steen (1625–79).

18

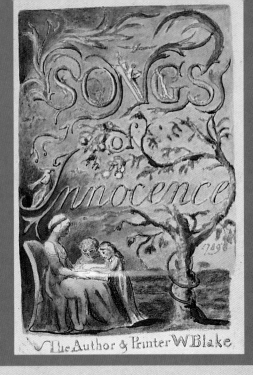

The Author & Printer W Blake

## THE·STAG·IN·THE·OX·STALL THE·DEER·&·THE·LION

SAFE enough lay the poor
hunted Deer
In the ox-stall, with nothing
to fear
From the careless-eyed men:
Till the Master came; then
There was no hiding-place
for the Deer.

FROM the hounds the swift
Deer sped away,
To his cave, where in past times
he lay
Well concealed; unaware
Of a Lion couched there,
For a spring that soon made
him his prey.

· AN·EYE·IS·
KEEN·IN·ITS·
OWN·
INTEREST·

·FATE·
CAN·MEET·
AS·WELL·AS·
FOLLOW·

44

tions quoted from it at length; it was studied in young ladies' seminaries; John Harris issued a version (which went through four editions)— *The Wars of the Jews,* 'adapted to the capacities of young persons'—in 1823, and as late as 1887 Warne published *Our Young Folks' Josephus.*

As in England, the libraries of many Massachusetts and Virginia colonists had included Ralegh's *History of the World* (this was the ancient world only), and Plutarch's *Lives of the Noble Greeks and Romans* in Sir Thomas North's translation of 1579. Plutarch made a profound impression on many children. (John Newbery, the foremost children's publisher of the eighteenth century, published an abridgement in 1762.)

Children enjoyed Plutarch's *Lives* not only because of the heroic past that they described, but also because of the vivid narrative, the anecdotes, and the deft choice of detail. We are told that Cicero had a wart on his nose, that Pericles is usually represented helmeted because his head was misproportioned, that Caesar, served at a friend's house with asparagus dressed with 'oil of perfume' instead of salad oil, 'eate it and found no fault'. One late instance of the effect that Plutarch could have is found in a memoir of the Victorian writer Annie Keary. The *Lives* (surreptitiously borrowed from her father's study) meant far more to her and her sister than the tales of Mrs Sherwood that they were expected to read, and such characters as Alcibiades and Pericles and Themistocles were not only shining heroes, but friends who walked and conversed with them in their nursery. It is yet another instance of how children's imagination could (and can) be set on fire without the aid of books written for them.

## BOOKES OF GODLY LEARNYNG

'When thou can read,' Thomas White told his readers in *A Little Book for Little Children* (1671?), 'read no Ballads and foolish Books, but a Bible, and the Plainmans pathway to Heaven, a very plain holy book for you; get the Practice of Piety; Mr Baxter's Call to the Unconverted; Allen's Allarum to the Unconverted; read the Histories of the Martyrs that dyed for Christ . . . Read also often Treatises of Death, and Hell and Judgement, and of the Love and Passion of Christ.' (*The Young Christian's Library,* a publisher's pamphlet of 1710, takes eight pages to list similar books.)

This advice fascinates the modern reader. Here in the 1670s is one of the first books ever addressed to young children—children so young that they cannot yet read for themselves; indeed may only just have learned to speak plain ('Thy Father and Mother loved to hear thee speak in thy broken language'). And yet they are being directed, as a matter of course, to adult theological and devotional works. Three were already Puritan classics. Arthur Dent's *The Plaine Mans Pathway to Heaven; wherein every man may clearly see*

*Facing, above*: a new version of childhood, both naturalistic and mystical. The symbolic title-page of William Blake's *Songs of Innocence* (1789).

*Below*: from Walter Crane's *The Baby's Own Aesop* (1887).

New Series.      Price One Penny.]

# HISTORY

## OF THE

# SEVEN CHAMPIONS

## OF

# CHRISTENDOM.

*(Illustrated with Coloured Plates.)*

*St. George encounters and kills a terrific dragon.*

LONDON:
Printed by W. S. FORTEY, Monmouth Court, Bloomsbury, W.C.

*whether he shall be saved or damned* had been published in 1610. The popularity of Lewis Bayly's *Practice of Pietie* (1613) in the seventeenth century went far beyond party, and it is interesting to see from records of early colonial libraries that it was a favourite choice of Puritan divines in New England and Anglican plantation owners in Virginia alike. Bayly's book was so venerated that one minister complained that his congregation thought it had almost the authority of the Bible. Richard Baxter, author of *A Call to the Unconverted* (1657) and other religious classics, enjoyed the same sort of popularity in both England and America, and *A Call to the Unconverted*, translated into the Massachusetts Indian language in 1664, was a very early New England publication. (In 1840, the Revd Heman Humphrey, Congregational clergyman and president of Amherst College, Massachusetts, in his *Domestic Education* censured the religious fiction provided in Sunday schools. Children no longer took up 'solid, practical doctrinal religious reading with anything like the same zest, with which young disciples of their age did, one third of a century ago'. Baxter was one of the authors he felt they should be reading.)

*Allarum to the Unconverted* by Joseph Alleine, published posthumously in 1671 (it was later renamed *A Sure Guide to Heaven*), would achieve the same classic status as the preceding three. Of the histories of the martyrs that died for Christ, the pre-eminent one was John Foxe's *Actes and Monuments* (1563), popularly known as the *Book of Martyrs*, much read by children, who were enthralled by the brisk narrative, the dialogue, and above all by the gruesome power of the woodcut illustrations.

It was probably books like Thomas White's *Little Book* that gave Janeway the idea for his more famous *Token for Children*, published in two parts in 1671 and 1672. It was subtitled 'An Exact Account of the Conversion, Holy and Exemplary Lives, and Joyful Deaths, of several [thirteen, in fact] young Children'. In it he was, like Alleine and the other writers recommended by White, striving to awaken his readers' hearts, to bring them to a sense of their total depravity, and thus to the 'early piety' which was the supreme aim of the responsible Calvinist preacher or parent. Alleine had written of the torments of hell that awaited the unconverted, of the fiends whose only music it was

to hear how their miserable patients roar, to hear their bones crack: 'Tis their meat and drink, to see how their flesh frieth, and their fat droppeth; to drench them with burning metal, and to rip open their bodies, and to pour the fierce burning brass into their bowels, and the recesses and ventricles of their hearts.

*Facing*: front cover of a nineteenth-century chapbook version of Richard Johnson's chivalric tale written *c*.1597.

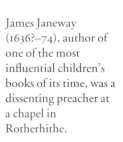

James Janeway (1636?–74), author of one of the most influential children's books of its time, was a dissenting preacher at a chapel in Rotherhithe.

21

White and Janeway pleaded in a gentler fashion. If only children would behave like those they showed them, 'then you shall be one of those sweet little ones that Christ will take in his Arms, and bless, and give a Kingdom, Crown and Glory to'.

Janeway did not believe that he was doing anything new. Others besides White had written about exemplary young people; indeed Janeway admitted he had lifted one narrative from the Presbyterian Isaac Ambrose's *Life's Lease* (which appears to be extant only in Ambrose's *Compleat Works* of 1674). But in that Janeway was focusing only on children of his own time his book was a completely new departure. The ordeals endured by White's young Jewish martyrs seemed remote beside the accounts of the everyday lives of Janeway's children, and their triumphant deaths surrounded by admiring onlookers had a profound effect on readers; his book was to be much imitated, well into the Victorian period.

Like White, Janeway had mentioned the *Book of Martyrs*—his John Sudlow was 'hugely taken' with it, and was always ready to leave his dinner to go to it. Foxe's place in Protestant culture cannot be overestimated. He lit an even brighter candle than Bishop Latimer, whose last words are always quoted from Foxe. Its light shone for centuries and affected much that was

'A Prospect of Popery, or a short view of the Cruelties, Treasons, and Massacres, committed by the Papists.' From an eighteenth-century edition of *The Protestant Tutor*, *c*.1720.

written for children. His book was begun when Edward VI was still king, and when most would not have foreseen the persecutions of the next reign. The first version, published in Strasburg in Latin in 1554, included a few foreign martyrs such as Huss and Savonarola, but dealt mainly with the English Lollards, and Wyclif especially. When Foxe returned to England in 1559 the full horror of what his contemporaries were suffering under the Catholic Mary Tudor was revealed. If anything could make England Protestant for ever it would be this, and he wrote to burn the memory into the minds of his countrymen.

In the event his book—the new version of which appeared in 1563—was more influential than he could have dreamed. 'No popery!' was a rallying cry in England for centuries, and could whip mobs into anti-Roman frenzy. Foxe's popularity increased dramatically, so that the nineteenth century saw some thirty different editions, including Sunday school versions. It was the first volume in Cassell's Penny Library in 1868 and as late as 1904 we find *Stories from Foxe's Book of Martyrs* for children's reading.

In Foxe's wake followed a long train of anti-papistical literature, much of it directed at the young. There was for instance *The Protestant Tutor* (1679), published and perhaps written by Benjamin Harris, a book of virulent anti-Catholic propaganda, while *The New England Primer*, throughout its long life and many variant versions, devoted a page to John Rogers, the first Marian martyr. Anti-Rome feeling inflamed many of the nineteenth-century writers for children—though more in England than America, where waves of immigrants from widely scattered cultures had brought more tolerance. One of the most violent was Charlotte Elizabeth Browne Phelan Tonna (who wrote under the first two of these five names); to her and her kind the Roman Church was the Babylon of the Apocalypse. Mary Martha Sherwood, very popular for Sunday reading, was also deeply conscious of the Roman peril, especially after the Catholic Emancipation Act of 1829. (This to 'Charlotte Elizabeth' had been the 'most hateful year in the annals of England's perfidy to her bounteous Lord'.)

But religious teaching in the form of fiction is a comparatively recent development, and one that was to cause both English and American tract societies much anguished debate. *The Pilgrim's Progress* (1678), which, especially in the nineteenth century, was widely read by children, was so manifestly allegorical as to be acceptable. So were poems such as *War with the Devil* (1673) by the Baptist minister Benjamin Keach. His laboured verse takes the same theme—conversion—as the manuals prescribed by Thomas White. Conscience, Truth, the Devil, and Christ all wrestle for the young man's soul, and Christ triumphs. (It was done more succinctly in 'A Dialogue between Christ, Youth and the Devil' in the *New England Primer* (1686–90), only there the Devil wins.) It is interesting chiefly because it is another instance of

Seventeenth-century fashions for aristocratic children. The children of Sir Lionel Tollemache, Bart, *c*.1600–10.

the new 1670s trend to try to adjust books for the young to a more youthful level.

The 1670s also saw a dawning realization that there was money in promoting piety. Nathaniel Crouch (alias R.B., or Richard Burton, becoming Robert Burton after his death), publisher, editor, and plagiarist, indeed boasted on the title-page of *Youth's Divine Pastime* (3rd edition, 1691):

> He certainly doth hit the White
> Who mingles Profit with Delight.

He worked on this principle so successfully that a contemporary gloomily described him as 'the only man that gets an estate by the writing of Books'—an estate acquired by pilfering from other writers. He began his career with *The Young Man's Calling* (1678), a rehashing of Samuel Crossman's *Young Mans Monitor* (1664) with added 'Remarks upon the Lives of Several Excellent Young Persons' which he had taken from other sources. These ranged from Josephus' seven young Jewish martyrs (lifted out of Thomas White) to the nonpareil Lord Harrington who died in 1613, aged 22, solitary, studious, and ascetic, an interesting example of what Crouch supposed would appeal to his contemporaries as a model youth.

Crouch's own ideals were flexible. He was an opportunist who adjusted to the mood of the times. As there were commercial possibilities in Puritan-slanted reading for the young he provided this. Anti-popery was always a good line, and in *Martyrs in Flames; or, The History of Popery* (1695), a popular work which went into three editions, he fed his public with much about the 'Bloody Beast of Rome' who grinds the bones of God's saints, and belches curses and excommunications.

From early times it had been held that verse was a way to tempt children into learning; the fifteenth-century *Stans puer ad mensam* ('The Boy Standing at Table') was in verse, as were other books of courtesy like *The Babees Book* and *The Book of Curtesye*.

24

Bunyan's *A Book for Boys and Girls* (1686) retains something of the saltiness of the traditional rhymes. He called these verses—later issued under the title of *Divine Emblems*—'country rhymes', and in them can be found descriptions of homely objects and everyday pastimes, such as no one hitherto had troubled themselves to set down for children. The boy chases a butterfly:

> He halloos, runs, and cries out, 'Here, boys, here!'
> Nor doth he brambles or the nettles fear:

There is of course a lesson; the boy symbolizes unthinking humanity, and the butterfly the things of this world.

> I do't to shew them how each Fingle-fangle,
> On which they doting are, their Souls entangle,
> As with a Web, a Trap, a Ginn, or Snare,
> And will destroy them, have they not a Care.

But even if the symbolism seems laboured there is a freshness about the rhymes that was something new in 1686.

We have to wait for nearly a hundred years before there is anything comparable in verse for children, with the work of Christopher Smart.

There were, then, glimmers of light amongst the Calvinist gloom, but it took the slow emergence of a new concept of childhood, and the more rapid development of commercial publishers to move children's literature closer to what we now understand by it.

# 2 PUBLISHING FOR CHILDREN

## 1700–1780

*Margaret Kinnell*

### TRANSITION

IT was common to see large numbers of children in Puritan families; they were the expression of God's blessing on the faithful and their care and education was a sacred trust. The family stood under God's special protection so that the very first words taught to children had to have religious significance: phrases like 'God alone can save me' or 'learn to die'. The first words read by the child were also permeated by religious significance. Writing in 1706 about the education of his children, Cotton Mather noted how he began 'betimes to entertain them with delightful stories, especially scriptural ones. And still conclude with some lesson from the story.' As we have seen, primers and story-books to feed this need to teach children their religious and social obligations were published on both sides of the Atlantic and became an important element in the development of the children's book trade. Puritan absorption in educating children for an early death had wonderfully concentrated the minds of publishers and booksellers in the production of 'plain holy' books during the late seventeenth century, books which tapped the growing market for child-centred material.

Chapbook merchants like John Marshall were issuing in a more accessible format items which first appeared during the latter part of the seventeenth century: John Bunyan's *Divine Emblems; or, Temporal Things Spiritualized*, previously published as *A Book for Boys and Girls*, and Isaac Watts's *Divine Songs* were two examples of chapbook publishing. Chapbooks for children had their origin in the cheaply produced and widely disseminated folk-tales which the London publisher-booksellers around Aldermary Churchyard and Little Britain published in the mid-seventeenth century and continued to

issue in vast quantities right into the mid-nineteenth century. The chapbook, a slim pamphlet which was easily packed into bundles for distribution by pedlars throughout the country, was sold as the popular literature of the masses: adults, young people, and children alike. All kinds of subjects were covered, from romances and dramas to histories like those of *The Learned Friar Bacon* and *Tom Thumb*, moral and religious tracts such as *God's Just Judgement on Blasphemers* and *A Timely Warning to Rash and Disobedient Children*, and prophetic books which included *The History of Mother Shipton* and *The Old Egyptian Fortune-teller's Last Legacy*. Amongst them, increasingly, were items to amuse and divert children.

As a boy, Walter Scott relied for his reading on the contents of Allan Ramsay's Edinburgh bookshop with its 'specimens of every kind, from the romances of chivalry, and the ponderous folios of Cyrus and Cassandra, down to the most approved works of later times'. The chapbook romances, though, were what fired him most, as they inspired many other writers.

In contrast there is the gentle and unworldly Isaac Watts, author of the most famous Puritan classic of all, *Divine Songs, Attempted in Easie Language for the Use of Children*. This was first published in 1715, and some twenty

The importance of story demonstrated in the 'first English Novel': *Pamela or Virtue Rewarded* by Samuel Richardson. *Pamela tells a nursery tale*, painted by Joseph Highmore (1744).

editions appeared in Watts's lifetime alone. The verse is not distinguished; only the 'Cradle Hymn', which begins

> Hush! my dear, lie still and slumber,
> Holy angels guard thy bed!

approaches poetry. In some thirty-odd lyrics (more 'Moral Songs' were added later), he set out children's duty as Puritans saw it—to read their Bibles, think on death and hell, avoid idleness and evil company, obey their parents. Advice in rhyme, he thought, might be remembered in times of temptation. *Divine Songs* became a part of English-speaking childhood for nearly two centuries—learnt as a Sunday task, recited in schoolrooms and Sunday schools on both sides of the Atlantic, anthologized, included in hundreds of tracts, and surviving in the English hymnals. The 'Cradle Hymn' appeared in many later editions of the *New England Primer*. Watts had set himself to write for everyone: 'you will find here nothing that savours of party; the children of high and low degree, of the Church of England, Dissenters [he himself was one], baptized in infancy or not, may all join together in these songs.' In this he succeeded brilliantly, but although his popularity was so widespread, there are many reminders in *Divine Songs* of his Calvinist outlook (the emphasis on the achievement of 'early piety', the torments of hell that await those who delay). His influence echoes through the century, notably in the work of Anna Laetitia Barbauld, Dr John Aikin, Hannah More, and the Tractarians.

But this was also the period when the 'literary' fairy-tale came to England by way of the French court, through the *Histoires ou contes du temps passé: avec des moralitez*, which were written down by Charles Perrault and published in Paris in 1697. Translated into English by Robert Samber, they were published as *Histories, or Tales of Past Times. Told by Mother Goose* (1729). John Newbery and his associates took up the tales and they were published in popular versions for children, although it was not until a sixth edition of 1772 that they were issued simply for children's delight, without the French alongside the English to serve as a token lesson book. After this, chapbook versions of

*One of the less tortuous 'comparisons' or morals from the first extant illustrated edition of John Bunyan's* Divine Emblems *(1724).*

DIVINE EMBLEMS for YOUTH. 51

XXXI.

Upon the Frog.

THE frog by nature is both damp and cold,
Her mouth is large, her belly much will hold;
She fits somewhat afcending, loves to be
Croaking in gardens, tho' unpleafantly.

COMPARISON.

The hypocrite is like unto this frog;
As like as is the puppy to the dog.
He is of nature cold, his mouth is wide
To prate, and at true goodnefs to deride.
He mounts his head, as if he was above
The world, when yet 'tis that which has his love.
And though he feeks in churches for to croak,
He neither loveth Jefus, nor his yoke.

the fairy-tales were common, but it had taken more than half a century for the fairy-tale to reach the mass of children.

The period 1700–50 was a transitional one, during which the momentum of this market developed, the child population began to grow, and education became a pressing concern. The amount of educational material available grew in response, and there was also a veritable explosion of material to encourage young readers to exercise their imaginations.

## A GROWING MARKET

A major reason for the expansion of the book trade for children in the eighteenth century was the increasing number of children as a proportion of the population. Low fertility in England at the end of the seventeenth century had meant that the population was an ageing one. This began to change around the beginning of the next century, and from 1770 English annual population growth rates began to outstrip those of other European countries until, by 1826, the number of children under 15 reached its peak at 1,120 for every 1,000 adults, a trend which had been evident from around 1750.

More children were also surviving as inoculation became possible for smallpox, one of the greatest scourges of children and young adults; in 1721 Lady Mary Wortley Montagu decided to have her daughter inoculated and this drew attention to the procedure, although the widespread adoption of vaccination with the cowpox virus did not

'Fun at Bartholomew Fair, 1721.' Drawings on a fan of toys, a peep-show, and other children's and young people's amusements.

begin until 1796. There were many other childhood deaths from tuberculosis, which remained a killer disease until the 1920s, and measles, scarlet fever, and whooping cough also claimed their victims. Nevertheless, there was a decline in infant deaths during this period, especially in rural areas, although the poor suffered most. Thomas Malthus, looking back in 1798 over recent population trends, noted how 'this mortality among the children of the poor has been constantly taken notice of in all towns. It certainly does not prevail in an equal degree in the country.' Jonas Hanway, the philanthropist and protector of sweeps' apprentices, had similarly drawn attention to the unequal survival chances of pauper children in the urban parishes of London: 'in the whole year, 1763, of the capital parishes, under 12 months old and remaining under the care of the parish officers at the end of the year 1765, there were living, at most, not above 7 in 100; in many parishes, as you have seen, not one remained alive.' It was the country-bred and middle-class children in particular (and despite increasing urbanization most children's experience was of a rural environment) who were growing up in communities dominated by the presence of other children. Significantly, too, these were the children whose parents had more reason to expect they would survive into adulthood.

Coinciding with this rise in the child population there was a very rapid growth in educational provision. In Leicestershire, for example, at least twelve new schools were established between 1700 and 1736 and a further twenty-six received fresh endowments from local benefactors. Village schools like these were often rough and ready

Discipline in eighteenth-century schools. An engraving by Faber (1739), after Mercier.

and presided over by a motley crew of teachers: the 'deaf, poor, patient widow' described in Crabbe's retrospective poem *The Borough*, or the ill-prepared schoolmaster identified by Goldsmith, who had been a quartermaster under Marlborough, read only 'tolarably [*sic*] for an Irishman', and was rewarded for his service through the post of 'country schoolmaster to a country parson'.

Village dame schools were one product of many generations of parochial concern for educating the local poor, and by the mid- to late eighteenth century all the parish children were being encouraged to attend. In Dorothy Kilner's *The Village School* (*c.*1783) there is an equal provision of schooling so that the children of clergymen, farmers, and even labourers sit down together to their lessons. 'Roger Riot', the squire's son, is the tearaway character, while 'Frank West', son of a humble cobbler, is a model pupil. In the most famous of all the early children's books describing village education, Newbery's *The History of Little Goody Two-Shoes* (1765), Margery Meanwell advances from 'trotting tutoress' to village schoolmistress under the squire's patronage. We read how 'all those whose parents could not afford to pay for their education, she taught for nothing', and how 'she not only taught the children in the day time, but the farmer's servants, and all the neighbours, to read and write in the evening'. This microcosmic depiction of rural education describes not just a preoccupation with teaching the youngest children their letters but an equal concern for illiterate servants who made up an adolescent underclass.

During the early part of the century the charity school movement had provided for small schools like that of Margery, schools which contained no more than twenty to twenty-five children. In contrast, around 1780 the

31

*The History of Little Goody Two-Shoes*. The first edition (1765), in characteristic Newbery style. This book inspired a whole genre.

THE
HISTORY
OF
Little GOODY TWO-SHOES;
Otherwife called,
Mrs. MARGERY TWO-SHOES.
WITH
The Means by which fhe acquired her
Learning and Wifdom, and in confe-
quence thereof her Eftate; fet forth
at large for the Benefit of thofe,

Who from a State of Rags and Care,
And having Shoes but half a Pair;
Their Fortune and their Fame would fix,
And gallop in a Coach and Six.

See the Original Manufcript in the *Vatican*
at *Rome*, and the Cuts by *Michael Angelo*.
Illuftrated with the Comments of our
great modern Critics.

LONDON:
Printed for J. NEWBERY, at the *Bible* and
*Sun* in St. *Paul's Church-yard*, 1765.
[ Price Six-Pence. ]

*Little Goody Two-Shoes*

The frontispiece from Mrs Sherwood's revised edition (1820) of *The Governess* by Sarah Fielding, with additional moralizing material.

average Sunday school, which catered for a wider age range of pupil, including those older children employed in factories, had an enrolment of about eighty. It has been estimated that by 1818 450,000 children were being educated in these Sunday schools, which arose out of local needs and interests and from a recognition of the problems posed by the poorest children in towns and villages. Robert Raikes accounted for his establishing one in Gloucester: 'I was struck with concern at seeing a group of children wretchedly ragged, at play in the street . . . and lamented their misery and idleness.' While Raikes was not the orginator of the Sunday school idea—Hannah Ball described to John Wesley in 1770 her efforts with the 'wild little company' she taught on Sundays and Mondays in High Wycombe—he was the first to publicize the system, through his newspaper the *Gloucester Journal*. The range and reach of schooling was therefore widening during this period.

Aspiring artisans could now afford books and offer their children a superior education, while the growing provision of elementary education to the working classes caused literacy levels to rise rapidly; a readership was being created which was hungry for popular reading. Higher up the social scale, where basic literacy had not been a problem, private academies set new demands for reading as the curriculum expanded to take account of the eagerness of middle-class parents for their children to have a classical education and for social accomplishments like drawing, music, and French. In the city of Chester alone, thirty-six such schools were started between 1747 and 1800, although some were probably very short-lived and—like the village schools—run by masters and mistresses who were not necessarily of the best. In recalling his aunt's childhood, Robert Southey describes a girls' school of the time—run by a butcher's wife—who 'was a handsome woman, and her children were like the Harleian miscellany, by different authors. This was notorious; yet her school flourished notwithstanding, and she retired from it at last with a competent fortune, and was visited as long as she lived by her former pupils.' Sarah Fielding famously wrote of such a boarding school in *The Governess; or, The Little Female Academy* (1749), in which her Mrs Teachum was of unimpeachable, if single-minded, character: the first in a long line of teacher role models. (She was possibly an influence on the description of a rural school dame

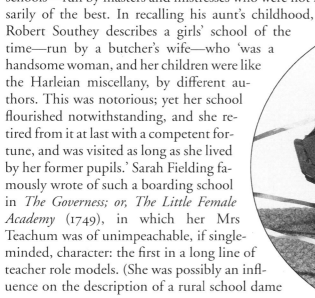

A toy stage-coach of wood, leather, and metal. The toy trade became increasingly important as the children's market grew.

in *Goody Two-Shoes*.) Exhorting her girls that 'the true use of books is to make you wiser and better', she nevertheless allowed of some fairy-tales, and so acknowledged the growing movement towards a softer approach to children's reading needs in and out of school. Also, children were for the first time offered realistic characters placed in a recognizable setting, children with whom readers could identify. When Mrs Sherwood rewrote *The Governess* for a nineteenth-century audience in 1820 she jettisoned all but one of the fairy-tales (and this she 'edited' herself into a suitably moral story) 'since fanciful productions of this sort can never be rendered generally useful', but by then the damage was done: a more light-hearted literature was available and being read by children.

## A BUSINESS OF IMPORTANCE

John Newbery has often been credited with originating the publication of children's books; in reality, though, his role was even more important: he began the serious *business* of publishing for children. Apart from the chap-book producers there had been publishers before Newbery who published books that were bought for and read by children, such as Thomas Boreman, who put out his set of ten miniature books, the *Gigantick Histories*, between 1740 and 1743. The illustrations, particularly those of animals, his use of Dutch floral binding, and the amusing tone adopted—down to the tongue-in-cheek subscription lists—mark them out as early examples of a child-centred literature which married teaching and entertainment. Isolated instances exist of even earlier attempts such as: 'T.W.'s' *Little Book for Little Children*, which contained for the first time in print 'A was an Archer and shot at a frog'. Mary Cooper published *The Child's New Plaything* in 1742 and Benjamin Collins of Salisbury, who was later to collaborate with Newbery, issued the first edition of *A Pretty Book for Children* in 1743—a second followed in 1746. Publishing recreational reading for children was, however, still something of a gamble, as Boreman obviously considered when he begged that would-be purchasers of his *Histories* 'bring or send their names to Thomas Boreman Bookseller in Guildhall and . . . pay down six-pence a set in part at subscribing, it being a large and expensive undertaking'.

John Newbery, who started out as a provincial bookseller, newspaper proprietor, and general dealer and became a purveyor of patent medicines—

[ 62 ]
dead : This is the fierceſt beaſt in the Tower ; her name is *Nanny*.
    Third, the young he *Tiger*, nam'd *Dick*, ſon of Will and Phillis ; deſcribed in pag. 44, 45.
    Fourth, a *Porcupine* in an iron cage. This is one of the ſtrangeſt animals in the world ; its back, ſides and tail, are guarded with ſtrong quills, each a foot and half long, all pointed
as

[ 63 ]
PORCUPINE.

Thomas Boreman's *Curiosities in the Tower of London* (1741). Description of one of the 'strangest animals in the world' with a relatively accurate woodcut.

especially the renowned Dr James's powders—ventured into children's books as only one of many business opportunities. In his will he makes plain that children's publishing was by no means the most important of his undertakings; his newspaper interests and patent medicines were more lucrative. Newbery's significance lay in developing the children's side of his publishing business to such an extent that this class of book could be seen as worthy of the kind of artistic and financial investment reserved for adult books. He was the first publisher-bookseller to recognize the potential of producing games on a commercial scale, the first to pay real attention to the growing economic importance of children as the social base of the book market widened.

Newbery's publishing for children coincided with the increasing preoccupation with educating children for social accomplishment in addition to teaching them moral precepts and religious principles. His series of lesson books, *The Circle of the Sciences* (1745–8), fashionably deferred to Locke's recommendation of grammar, arithmetic, geography, and chronology in the curriculum, although he also included elements from a past era, with volumes on rhetoric and logic. Even his more light-hearted items had a considerable didactic purpose and amusement was always linked to instruction. The emphasis, however, was changing. Alongside the lesson books were those which acknowledged and accepted play as an important element in children's lives; play was becoming respectable. In his very first children's book, *A Little Pretty Pocket Book* (1744), published soon after his move from Reading to

35

London, the frontispiece shows a boy and girl being taught by mother or governess, with 'Instruction and delight' as a caption. Intended for 'the instruction and amusement' of children, the book was sold with a ball or pincushion at 8*d*., or 6*d*. without, a marketing ploy which indicates the tone of the whole production. Light-hearted throughout, the book is mostly pictures of children at play: games which included chuck-farthing, kite-flying, maypole dancing, blind-man's buff, and 'boys and girls come out to play'. The verses accompanying the blocks are short, descriptive instructions with the 'morals' offering a mix of advice, some of it deriving directly from John Locke. Play is encouraged, but directed, a nice compromise which suited both parents and their children. A successful book which continued in print after Newbery's death in 1767, it became, like *Goody Two-Shoes*, one of the best loved of the early children's books.

Newbery's literary connections—he had Dr Johnson, Oliver Goldsmith, Christopher Smart, and Tobias Smollett working for him—were important for another arm of the business, the periodical and adult book publishing; Goldsmith in particular, though, contributed to the children's side. Certainly, he wrote *An History of England, in a Series of Letters from a Nobleman to his Son* (1764) and there is good reason to suppose that he also produced *Goody Two-Shoes*. What these connections also offered was a certain re-

*The Lilliputian Magazine* (1772). A later edition, demonstrating the rivalry between Newbery's successors.

spectability and authority in the production of material for children. Children's books were part of the mainstream of literary output for the first time in publishing history, issued as they were by the publisher of *The Idler*, *The Vicar of Wakefield*, and such an immensely popular and profitable production as the *Ladies Complete Pocket Book*. It is impossible now to identify all of the influences on Newbery's children's output, but certainly the impact of his position at the heart of literary London may have been undervalued.

One of his most interesting innovations, *The Lilliputian Magazine* (1751–2), originally designed to be published as a periodical at 3*d.* a time, is an example of this link with the mainstream. Probably intended to exploit his journal and newspaper interests, it did not meet with the success that he hoped for and ended up as a composite volume rather than a journal. The lack of response was surprising, as it is a light-hearted mix of tales, letters, jests, songs, and riddles with neat engravings in the text, bound in Dutch paper boards. Perhaps there was not enough of the schoolteacher in the work to encourage parents, despite his attempt to moralize from the tales and encourage further purchases:

How master Hiron improved the arts and sciences in Lilliput, and taught even little children to become polite gentlemen and ladies, will be shown in the future parts of this work; which all our society are desired to learn, for by learning of that account perfectly, they will also learn the arts and sciences.

Or perhaps he was targeting the wrong age group. A slightly later attempt to imitate the adult literary journal compilation, Madame Le Prince de Beaumont's *The Young Misses Magazine*, first published in 1757 and profitably reissued by John Nourse and his successors, was aimed at 'the most dangerous of all the stages of life . . . about fourteen or fifteen'. Certainly Horatia Nelson's copy of the 1806 edition, which has her inscription on the fly-leaf, is well thumbed and bears signs of long use. A more traditional format of dialogues between a governess and her pupils, after the style of Sarah Fielding's *The Governess*, may have contributed to its success. Quality of production in *The Lilliputian Magazine*, as with all Newbery's books, was excellent and by advertising in the *Gentleman's Magazine* he might have expected a good following for his enterprise: unusually, on this occasion he was not as successful at reading the market as Nourse, who specialized in French-language books for the school market.

More popular, though, were the Newbery books, like *Goody Two-Shoes*, which caught the spirit of the times, a middle-class preoccupation with thrift, hard work, and moral as well as business certainties. It is this which sold so well and entered the popular imagination, so much so that Charles Lamb, when bewailing the current lack of books like *Goody Two-Shoes* when writing to Coleridge in 1802, overlooked the world-weary cynicism of some of the

Three wooden, English and Continental gingerbread moulds shaped like hornbooks. Diligent pupils were allowed to lick the gilt (gold leaf) off the gingerbread.

sentiments it expressed to children, such as: 'our relations and friends seldom take notice of us when we are poor, but as we grow rich they grow fond.' Coleridge's son Hartley grew up with the book and similarly recalled the enormous pleasure it gave him: 'the old wooden sculptures, rather symbolic than imitative—and the square-covers-gilt in tempting resemblance to gingerbread . . . What heart, what knowledge, what true piety there is in that little story.' Adaptations began early and continued well into the twentieth century. The first to emerge was John Marshall's version, *The Entertaining History of Little Goody Goosecap* (1780), a tale about one Frances Fairchild, who was left to the care of a wicked uncle. Like Margery, she overcomes her misfortune by learning to teach and subsequently, after many adventures, makes a profitable marriage. *The Renowned History of Primrose Pretty Face* (1785) follows a similar theme: the reward of virtue is a solid marriage, although Mrs Trimmer was later to criticize the book for teaching girls of 'the lower order' to aspire too high for a husband. Later, John Harris published *The Alphabet of Goody Two Shoes: By Learning Which, She Soon Got Rich* (1808) and Mary Elliott wrote *The Modern Goody Two-Shoes* (1815) and a book about her brother *The Adventures of Thomas Two-Shoes* (1818). This is altogether a more spirited tale of Thomas's adventures first as a sailor and then as a famous bird doctor who fitted wounded canaries with wooden legs. Goody's values were to inspire other spin-off works: notably *Dame Partlett's Farm* (1804) 'Containing an account of the great riches she obtained by industry, the good life she led, and alas, good reader! her sudden death . . .'. The Dame was said to have been 'a very near relation of that renowned person Goody Two Shoes, so well known to every good child who hath read those pretty books at the corner of St. Paul's Churchyard'—Newbery's premises.

Newbery also published one of the few poets who wrote for children in this period. Since Watts's time, there had been a theologically arid period so far as the Church of England was concerned, and Newbery's publications had a strong secular flavour, the dominant message being that good conduct will bring material rewards. There was, however, one exception, the Grub Street author Christopher Smart, who was associated with the Newbery firm from about 1750. He was permanently in debt and afflicted with periods of insanity; some of his poetry was written on the walls of Bedlam. Newbery admired his facility for light verse and worked him hard, but the only book issued under his own name was *Hymns for the Amusement of Children* (?1770); the title itself is evidence of his quirkish nature. Many of the hymns are reminiscent of Watts, but some have memorable life and spontaneity. There is a 'Hymn for Saturday', beginning

> Now's the time for mirth and play,
> Saturday's an holiday;
> Praise to heaven unceasing yield,
> I've found a lark's nest in the field.

It seems almost to foreshadow William Blake. We find the same child vision, the capturing of the undiluted joy of the moment, in the hymn to mirth. 'If you are merry sing away,' it begins, and continues:

> I give the praise to Christ alone,
>   My pinks already show;
> And my streaked roses fully blown,
>   The sweetness of the Lord make known,
> And to his glory grow.

It is all the more poignant when we remember that Smart, broken by physical and mental illness, was in a debtors' prison when the poems were published, and died a few months later.

Of Newbery's other books for children—about one-fifth of his total output—many were intended for schools or home tutoring. Only sixteen or so could be described as mainly entertaining. His *Account of the Constitution and Present State of Great Britain* (1759), priced at 2*s.*, was one of several substantial books intended to exploit the education market. The more light-hearted items cost less, and usually ran to several editions. 'Abraham Aesop's' *Fables in Verse* (1757) priced at 6*d.* 'bound and gilt' was in its sixth edition by 1768 and *A Little Lottery Book for Children* (1756), an amusing illustrated alphabet costing only 3*d.*, was similarly popular; the sixth edition appeared in 1767.

Newbery and his successors in the business were quick to realize the potential of these slighter items as well as the serious schoolbooks. Turning over volume was everything, hence the emphasis on wide distribution and advertising through the fast-developing provincial newspapers such as the *Gloucester Journal, Western Flying Post, Leeds Intelligencer*, and *Newcastle Courant*; in each he specified the retail outlets available to customers. One of his notices in the *Oxford Gazette and Reading Mercury* for 7 December

*A Little Lottery Book for Children* (1756). Alphabets were published and distributed widely across the UK by the chapbook printers.

1767, for example, recommends retailers in Oakingham, Windsor, Walling-ford, High Wycombe, Basingstoke, and Gosport, as well as the printer of the paper and the newsboys who distributed it. He perfected the advertising of children's books, in the provincial press with which he had many connections and in the books themselves: the 'puff' as a marketing technique was his par-ticular speciality.

CHAPBOOKS AND CRUSOES

The book-buying public of the late eighteenth century for the larger, more expensive items was, however, quite small. Even a popular novel such as *Pamela* only sold five editions a year, possibly a total of about 9,000 copies. The chapbook-reading public, on the other hand, was every large indeed if the quantities issued by successful chapbook publishers are any indication. The catalogue of Richard Marshall and Cluer Dicey (1764), who operated from Aldermary Churchyard, contained a list of 1,000 engravings, 3,000 bal-lad sheets, and 150 chapbooks. It has been estimated that as early as 1688 one of the specialist chapbook publishers had in stock one chapbook for every fif-teen families in England. By the early nineteenth century James Catnach, who was particularly famed for his ballads and chapbooks of murders, trials, and executions, was reputed to be able to sell two and a half million copies of

*Of Rush's Murder*. His halfpenny sheets for children were similarly popular. Included in his children's list were: *The Easter Gift, Being a Useful Toy for Little Miss and Master to Learn their ABC, The Death and Burial of Cock Robin, Jack and Jill,* and *Little Tom Tucker*.

John Clare, who was born in 1793, describes in his autobiography what such reading material meant to a child growing up in a poor rural home, with a barely literate father who was 'very fond of the superstitious tales that are hawked about the streets for a penny' and a mother quite unable to read a letter. From the most basic education, Clare developed a 'furious' taste and passion for reading, but all he could get was

gleaned from the sixpenny Romances, of 'Cinderella', 'Little Red Riding Hood', 'Jack and the Beanstalk', 'Zig-Zag', 'Prince Cherry', etc., etc., and great was the pleasure, pain or surprise, increased by allowing them authenticity, for I firmly believed every page I read and considered I possessed in them the chief learning and literature of the country.

Like so many others, John Clare's reading experience grew out of the storytelling he encountered round the domestic fireside. Henry Bourne, a curate, writing in 1725 of his experiences of country folk, noted that 'Nothing is commoner in country places than for a whole family in a winter's evening, to sit around the fire, and tell stories of apparitions and ghosts . . . Another part of this conversation generally turns upon fairies.' The phenomenal success—with adults and children alike—of the chapbooks depended on their closeness to the folk-tales of the people. They sprang from the myths and legends retold by generations of ordinary folk, with many of the tales available in print from the sixteenth century onwards. In his *Shepherd's Calendar* (1827) Clare recounted in detail what he had read as a child: a great mixture of romance, fairy-, and folk-tale, very reminiscent of Caleb Bingham's list of 1797.

The eighteenth-century chapbook was a crude piece of production, despite its popularity: sixteen pages was the common length, although thirty-two or sixty-four was sometimes seen. The sixteen-page format was the easiest to fold from a single printed sheet and hence the most popular with the chapbook publishers and the chapmen. Cluer Dicey offered his to the packmen by the ream: '48 to the Quire and 20 Quires to the Ream, per Ream 4 shillings . . . small histories or books of amusements for children at 100 for 6 shillings.'

David Love, a travelling chapman and patterer, who not only sold chapbooks but sang and sold his own verses, provides a fascinating account in his autobiography (1823) of the impact he made on rural communities in delivering reading-matter like this, at a time when access to printed materials of any kind was limited, and newspapers were expensive at 2*d*. or 3*d*. for four folio sheets:

In these days the visit of the travelling bookman often created quite a stir in country places. In fact, so far from requiring to seek out the customers at their dwellings, the customers came, cash in hand, to the traveller's lodgings . . . So eager were people to obtain the books that the traveller, having possibly lost time on the earlier part of his journey, sometimes endeavoured, and that successfully, to redeem part of his loss by sending out the town-crier to announce his arrival.

The success of the chapbook publishers largely depended on this distribution network of chapmen as well as the men and boys who carried newspapers. Several guides and road-books were produced for them, evidence of the extent of their penetration into rural areas. Provincial publishers were able to disseminate their chapbooks by this means, on equal terms with the London trade. Newcastle upon Tyne was an early publishing centre for chapbooks, and books for adults and children were published by Houlston of Wellington in Shropshire from 1820, Mulrose of Berwick from 1829, and in York, Banbury, Lichfield, and many other places.

What did this welter of materials offer children? The quality of production was poor, but the chapbook did provide them with illustrations which, although crude by modern standards, were graphic and boldly drawn, although, the same woodcuts were used over and over for different tales. Where the chapbook was dignified by a simple cover—of a plain rough paper—any available woodcut would be used as decoration. Otherwise, most commonly, there would be a block printed on the title page, with little else of

*William and George*, a Houlston chapbook, which continued the influence of Isaac Watts's *Divine Songs*. 'Healthful play' was encouraged.

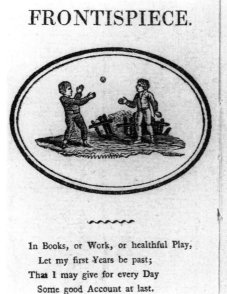

FRONTISPIECE.

In Books, or Work, or healthful Play,
Let my first Years be past;
That I may give for every Day
Some good Account at last.

William and George.

THE RICH BOY

AND THE

POOR BOY;

OR,

A Contented Mind is the

BEST FEAST.

Adorned with Cuts.

WELLINGTON:
Printed by F. Houlston and Son.

Price One Penny.

ornament inside. The chapbooks gave the traditional folk- and fairy-tales, ballads, collections of jests and riddles, and prophecies to children, and ensured their survival into the next generation of children's books.

Chapbooks also provided the principal truly popular vehicle for children's versions of works originally intended for adults. Defoe's *Robinson Crusoe*, first published for adults in 1719, is one of the most significant examples. Jean-Jacques Rousseau, writing in *Émile* (1762), his treatise on the education of youth, argued that *Crusoe* was a primary text for children: the one book to which they should have access so they could learn through the experience of living a hero's life:

Let him think he is Robinson himself; let him see himself clad in skins wearing a tall cap, a great cutlass, all the grotesque get-up of Robinson Crusoe, even to the umbrella which he will scarcely need . . . This is the genuine castle of the air of this happy age, when the child knows no other happiness but food and freedom.

Celebrating the individuality and freedom of the child as hero had little place in much of the literature provided for children at the time: *Crusoe* marked a new departure, and one to which children eagerly responded.

There were numerous abridgements for children, although of 150 or so which have been found dated between 1719 and 1819 only four basic texts have been identified. Chapbook publishers right across the country were involved: from Glasgow to Liverpool and Newcastle to Wrexham. Cheap editions were produced side by side with the better-quality productions of the mainstream London book publishers.

The Crusoe tale also had many imitators. Books on the heroic castaway theme were well known, but were hardly accessible to most children, given their generally extravagant production values. 'Edward Dorrington's' (Peter Longueville) *The English Hermit; or, The Adventures of Philip Quarll* was in print from 1727, but the 1751 edition was still a substantial octavo of 263 pages, hardly a book readily bought for most children. It was only when a pseudo-chapbook version was supplied at sixpence, bound in floral boards, in 1794, that it became more affordable—and readable—in its shortened form. Widely translated and adapted for children during the later part of the century, Joachim Campe's *Robinson der Jungere* (1779) was quickly translated into English (1781); John Stockdale's four-volume version, *The New Robinson Crusoe* (1788), was produced by John Harris in an abridged sixpenny version in 1808. Campe's hero was altogether more prosaic than Defoe's, the lessons taught rather less favourable to a state of nature. Nevertheless, the preoccupations of childhood, notably children's fascination at the preparation and devouring of food as part of open-air adventure (Arthur Ransome was to develop this theme to perfection in the 'Swallows and Amazons' adventures in the 1930s) are very much in evidence.

Benjamin Tabart's edition of *Gulliver's Travels* (1805). Stirring boys' adventure stories began with Crusoe and Gulliver.

Another lone hero appeared in Robert Paltock's *The Life and Adventures of Peter Wilkins* (1750), but he never became as popular as Crusoe or Quarll. One of the first fantasies about flying, this book failed to achieve such a significant readership as the Robinsonnades and was not taken up widely by the chapbook publishers. Instead, it won a largely cult following (Coleridge thought it 'a work of uncommon beauty'), and has continued in print into the twentieth century as an interesting oddity.

Another favourite of children, Swift's *Gulliver's Travels*, which first appeared for adults in 1726, and which was probably first abridged for children in an edition of 1727 by J. Stone and R. King, began to be published in chapbook editions at the end of the century. The best of the early versions for children did not emerge until 1805, when Benjamin Tabart issued his 'improved edition', in four parts, each of thirty-six pages with three hand-coloured engravings. The Lilliputian adventure has lasting appeal to children (as a friend of Thomas Holcroft remarked to him, 'boys and young people always prefer

44

the marvellous to the true'), and Newbery used the notion to full advantage, but even Gulliver did not match Crusoe for breadth of popularity across Europe as well as in Britain.

Much of the success of Crusoe during the mid- to late eighteenth century has to be attributed to changing attitudes towards childhood. Rousseau has been credited with—or blamed for—this. *Émile* expressed a distinct shift in sensibility from that of Locke's *Some Thoughts Concerning Education*, in which Locke continued to view the child as the *tabula rasa* of earlier centuries, a blank sheet upon which ideas could be impressed. This was countered by Rousseau with the idea that children learn best to be rational creatures through developing naturally at their own pace, and by exploring the world on their own terms: 'Childhood has its own ways of seeing, thinking, and feeling; and I should no more expect judgement in a ten-year old child than I should expect him to be five feet high.' The Crusoe legend admirably filled the need to allow children's imaginations full rein. Rousseau was not, however, as far from Locke as he himself believed. Both defined a system for delivering education, a system which saw the book as a means to an end, not an end in itself. Both were focusing primarily on the education of boys, not girls; there was little acknowledgement that schooling for girls really mattered other than as the means to preparing compliant and competent young women for lives as wives and mothers. While *Émile* was as confusing and contradictory in its way as Locke's essay, it provided a similar service in the later part of the century as had Locke in the earlier: highlighting the role of children's books in the creation of childhood.

One effect of this was that, as the eighteenth century progressed, the cheap and tawdry chapbooks for a mass readership began to develop into more clearly targeted publications, with children's chapbooks becoming recognizably distinct. The format began to change to the smaller three- by two-inch booklet, with coloured covers, a format which was commonly available up until around 1840 when journals and cheaper versions of mainstream children's books took over the role of the chapbook as purveyor of popular culture.

45

# 3 MORALITY AND LEVITY

## 1780–1820

### Gillian Avery and Margaret Kinnell

#### FICTION AND FEAR

As the numbers of books for children grew, so the content changed. There was, for example, much less insistence on the child's need to prepare for an early death, although the Janeway tradition continued to survive in books like George Burder's *Early Piety* (1777). Janeway himself was still being published: John Harris advertised a gift of 'pious little works in a box, in imitation of a bookcase' in 1804 of which *A Token for Children* was one. However, the emphasis was changing. Children were expected now to live as well as die in the fear of the Lord. A Houlston evangelical chapbook, *True Courage; or, Heaven Never Forsakes the Innocent*, begins with the sentiment that:

> 'Tis easier work, if we begin
> To fear the Lord betimes
> While Sinners that grow old in Sin
> Are harden'd in their crimes.

Children required schooling in order to fulfil a Christian life, as well as preparing for a good death: nevertheless, illness and early death continued to preoccupy writers. There were also descriptions of children's glorious deaths in chapbooks, but these were now competing with a flood of material which dwelt on children's amusement—fairy-tales, rhymes, riddles, games—or which emphasized their educational development and healthy physical growth.

Anna Laetitia Barbauld, writer of hymns as well as lesson books for children, was more typical of the mood of the times. In her *Lessons for Children* (1778) she acknowledged that it was worthwhile for a parent to invest in the education of even the youngest, 'from two to three years old'. Despite Rousseau's view that the possibility of his pupil's early death merited a tutor

46

Isaac Watts's *Divine Songs*, first published in 1715, was part of English-speaking childhood for nearly two centuries. From March's Library of Instruction and Amusement (*c.*1826–48).

**GENERAL SONG OF PRAISE TO GOD.**

How glorious is our heavenly King,
   Who reigns above the sky!
How shall a child presume to sing
   His dreadful majesty.

How great His power is, none can tell,
   Nor think how large His grace;
Not man below, nor saints that dwell
   On high before His face.

**AGAINST EVIL COMPANY.**

Why should I join with those in play
   In whom I've no delight?
Who curse and swear, but never pray,
   Who call ill names and fight?

I hate to hear a wanton song;
   The words offend my ears:
I should not dare defile my tongue
   With language such as their's.

being indulgent, this was not a view shared by writers, publishers, and, importantly, parents, who all considered children to be well worth a carefully judged and intensive education, with reading materials to match, from an early age. Mrs Barbauld and her brother John Aikin also brought disapproval upon themselves for their six-volume collection 'for the instruction and amusement of young persons', *Evenings at Home* (1792–6), from such defenders of Church of England orthodoxy as Sarah Trimmer. Mrs Barbauld and her brother were Unitarians, and their *Hymns in Prose for Children* (1781) was something new in religious writing for children. In the language of the Psalms they praise the beauties of the world as a child sees it, and God's loving kindness. Mrs Barbauld's teaching about death was at that time unique in its adjustment to a small child's comprehension.

I have seen the insect, being come to its full size, languish and refuse to eat: it spun itself a tomb, and was shrouded in the silken cone; it lay without feet, or shape, or

47

power to move. I looked again, it had burst its tomb: it was full of life, and sailed on coloured wings through the soft air; it rejoiced in its new being.

So shall it be with thee, O man! and so shall thy life be renewed.

It had taken a long time before fiction had become acceptable as a vehicle of religious teaching. Hannah More was one of the first to make use of it, and her Cheap Repository Tracts, published between 1795 and 1797, have never been equalled. She and her co-workers wrote to provide the literate working man with an alternative to bawdy and violent chapbooks and inflammatory political tracts, which, in the period of the French Revolution, were causing both social concern and governmental repression. Unlike Mrs Pardiggle and her kind, she recognized that the tracts must look as inviting as the literature they were intended to supersede. They were illustrated with woodcuts, and often given enticing titles. The stories were vigorously told in a simple and direct style, the background sharply observed, the dialogue convincing. The tracts were so popular that what had begun as a charitable venture ended by paying for itself.

Excellent though they were, they were very much of their time, supporting the social hierarchy as it was then (with a few swipes at farmers, whom Hannah More had found self-seeking and materialistic). Nor did the founders of the Religious Tract Society approve. At their first meeting, over breakfast, in 1799 they deplored the lack of evangelical principles in the Cheap Repository Tracts, and resolved that they themselves would do all they could to promote a new popular religious literature. But it was a quarter of a century before this took the form of fiction, and in the United States the American Tract Society in 1836 was still confident that the moral effect of fiction could only be injurious. In one sense they were right; the flood of religious fiction that washed over American and English Sunday schools alike in the nineteenth century was for the most part of a deplorably low quality and better forgotten. It lined the pockets of publishers, but it could have done little lasting good to any of its readers. Nor did the Sunday schools in general choose their books with much perspicacity. They tended to accept unquestioningly the wares offered by the particular publisher whom they had marked out because of his correct religious views.

But authority also, regardless of religious views, loyally clung to the names of the past. This is the only reason that can account for the lasting popularity of the Revd Legh Richmond's 'The Dairyman's Daughter' (*Annals of the Poor*, 1814), a lengthy account in the manner of Janeway of the death of a pious young parishioner. And it is the only explanation of the fact that Mrs Sherwood and in particular her *History of the Fairchild Family* was better known to young Victorians than perhaps any other author. Charlotte Yonge (b. 1823) said:

All the little Sunday books in those days were Mrs Sherwood's, Mrs Cameron's and

Charlotte Elizabeth's, and little did my mother guess how much Calvinism one could suck out of them, even while diligently reading the story and avoiding the lesson.

Some idea of how Mrs Sherwood's fame lasted can be seen from the fact that a London society hostess in the 1900s gave a party to which all her guests were bidden to come dressed as a Fairchild Family character. Mary Martha Sherwood (née Butt) and her sister Lucy Cameron were the daughters of an easy-going Anglican country clergyman. Her childhood reading seems to have been fairy-stories and *Robinson Crusoe* rather than theology, and her first two books were romantic novels. But her mood became far more serious after her marriage—the early years of which were spent in India, where her first-born children died—and *The Fairchild Family* (published in three parts between 1818 and 1847) shows a religious education very different from her own and more akin to the way Cotton Mather was bringing up his children in Boston over a hundred years before.

Mr Fairchild himself, being a gentleman of leisure, is able to preside over the education of his little family. As in the Puritan books on household and family management, he is the priest figure and in him rests supreme authority. The three parts of the book follow the same pattern: we have an account of the children's doings (and sometimes they are very naughty and require disciplining). This is followed by a hymn, and a lengthy prayer extemporized by Mr Fairchild. Sometimes a story is interpolated, supposedly read by a young Fairchild from one of their books. The whole is a curious medley of domestic detail, Calvinistic thundering about the depravity of the human heart and the exceeding sinfulness of sin, Georgian Awful Warning tales of Mrs Sherwood's childhood, and the Gothic tales that she read later. It is only fair to say that in parts II and III the ferocity of the Calvinism slackens. But the overall impression is that Mrs Sherwood, in attempting to deliver the same message as Joseph Alleine and James Janeway, has fettered herself by using fiction. Or alternatively, that Calvinism has spoilt what could have been a delightful domestic saga. There is evidence that some children enjoyed the book for the details

Mary Martha Sherwood, a prolific author of religious fiction and especially known to young Victorians for her *History of the Fairchild Family.*

49

*Facing, above*: an intricate example of the flourishing trade in games in the late eighteenth century. *The Game of Human Life* (1790) was published by John Wallis and Elizabeth Newbery, widow of the pioneer children's book publisher, John Newbery.

*Below*: a sheet with eight hand-coloured engravings, folded to form four leaves. One of the earliest types of moveable toy books.

about what the Fairchilds had to eat, and about deaths and corpses. But there is little testimony to any religious improvement that readers felt they had derived.

## THE AGES OF CHILDHOOD

Children's stages of development were being more clearly defined. Locke had made only an approximate distinction between the infant and the child, and had been vague as to when specific kinds of motivation and discipline should be used:

First children (earlier perhaps than we think) are very sensible of praise and commendation . . .

Whilst they are very young, any carelessness is to be borne with in children, that carries not with it the marks of pride or ill nature.

The age at which children should leave home he left similarly unclear, a lack of precision in defining when children reach adulthood very evident in early children's books. *The Top Book of All* (1760) was intended 'for little masters and misses' but with no indication of a particular age of readership. Equally, *A New Lottery Book of Birds and Beasts* (1771) 'for children to learn their letters by as soon as they can speak' offers no clue to a parent as to the age at which it might be used. Mary Cooper's *The Child's New Plaything* (1742), one of the earliest spelling books 'to make the learning to read a diversion instead of a task', is a little more helpful: 'I would have it made use of at home as soon as the child begins to form articulate sounds.' The alphabet is all that the very young could absorb from this book, as the rest is intended for a much older child, capable of reading and understanding moral and religious precepts and enjoying the old tales.

However, clearer distinctions of children's developmental stages were being drawn in child-care manuals, such as William Cadogan's *Essay upon Nursing and Management of Children from their Birth to Three Years of Age* (1748). James Nelson's *Essay on the Government of Children* (1753) identified the precise educational needs of children at various stages, with very little other than 'rote work' to be learned before the child reached 7, and that 'to be made as light, as easy and as pleasant as possible'. This concern that no stage or aspect of a child's growth should be left to parental conjecture also became very evident in children's books.

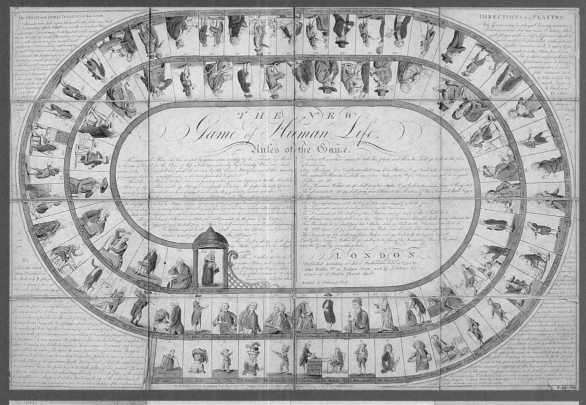

Anna Barbauld's *Instructive Lessons*, *Hymns in Prose*, *Lessons for Children from Two to Three Years Old*, and *Pastoral Lessons* all contain a selective vocabulary directed at a young child's developing language skills: 'The talk is humble but not mean; for to lay the first stone of a noble building, and to plant the first idea in a human mind, can be no dishonour to any hand' (*Lessons for Children from Two to Three Years Old*, 1778).

Ellenor Fenn used a similar, carefully judged vocabulary in her *Cobwebs to Catch Flies* (*c*.1783), with the first volume 'containing easy lessons in words of three letters' and the second offering more complex vocabulary and sentence structures. Her *Fables in Monosyllable* (*c*.1783) were composed for her own nephews and nieces—one was 3½ and another 5—and they were advertised as 'suited to children from 4 to 6 years of age'. The list of her books advertised by her publisher, John Marshall, specifies a clear readership age by each title, an indication that this was now an appropriate marketing ploy. In reviewing children's books, Sarah Trimmer's *Guardian of Education*, and the *Juvenile Review*, also attempted to assess their suitability for the various age ranges, as did Maria and Richard Lovell Edgeworth in their *Practical Education* (1798), where they made a point of criticizing Anna Barbauld's *Lessons*, which 'should, we think, have been lessons for children from four to five years old; few read or ought to read, before that age'.

COBWEBS TO CATCH FLIES. 21

*The* FAIR.

*JAMES* and *Edward Franklin* had leave to walk about, and amuſe themſelves in a fair. They ſaw a

B 3

Fun at the fair in Ellenor Fenn's *Cobwebs to Catch Flies* (*c*.1783).

*Facing*: Ann and Jane Taylor's father Isaac and grandfather were both distinguished engravers. The sisters were noted for their verses. In this portrait painted by their father in 1792, Ann is ten, Jane nine.

The idea that adolescence or 'youth' was distinct from both childhood and adulthood was also growing; children were educated for longer, and entered employment later. Lord Chesterfield had written to his son in 1741 that at the age of 9 'childish toys and playthings must be thrown aside and your mind directed to serious objects'. By 1761, in the *Parent's and Guardian's Directory and the Youth's Guide in the Choice of a Profession or Trade*, the youth seeking a job has already had his education and is aged about 14 before being apprenticed, some five years after the age at which Chesterfield's son was told to act like a man.

Transition from the early dame school to an academy appears to have been accepted as taking place at about seven or eight years: the time when Hannah More advised that children should resign their 'baby books'. The proliferation of lesson books for small children—those of Anna Barbauld, Ellenor Fenn, Dorothy and Mary Kilner, and Sarah Trimmer—and the increased availability of alphabets, spelling books, and chapbooks are evidence of parental interest in their children's early education as a preparation for later schooling.

Of course, all of this depended on class. In a chapbook published by Evans around 1820, *The Affectionate Daughter*, sending a 9-year-old down the mine to work on behalf of her family was positively encouraged: 'How different was the case of this numerous family from that of many others in the same humble situation of life. Mary and her brothers, so far from being a burden, were bringing a little fortune to their parents.' In *William and George*, a Houlston chapbook published *c.*1810, 8-year-old George 'in the summer mornings . . . got up with the sun, and in the winter with the first streaks of light; his breakfast was a bit of black coarse bread, and a draught of water, and then he went to assist his father in whatever his strength would permit'. Country girls were also expected to pay their way from an early age, as is demonstrated in the chapbook *The Amusing Story of Farmer Meanwell and his Daughter Sally* (*c.*1815), in which she 'assists her mother in her household concerns, and when the linen is washed, it is her business to hang it up to dry'. In one of Hannah More's Cheap Repository Tracts designed to help educate the rural poor, *The Shepherd of Salisbury Plain* (1795) describes the much-needed contribution that even the youngest of his children made to the family economy:

Though my wife is not able to do any out-of-door work, yet she breeds up our children to such habits of industry that our little maids, before they are six years old can first get a halfpenny, and then a penny a day, by knitting. The boys who are too little to do hard work get a trifle by keeping the birds off the corn; for this the farmers will give them a penny or two-pence.

Habits of work thus began early for the poor and continued into adolescence. The size of the domestic servant class was considerable in the mid-eighteenth century; Jonas Hanway estimated there were 50,000 servants in London, or one in thirteen of the population, with this number increasing by another estimate to around 200,000 by 1796. These young people had little chance of the kind of childhood experienced by the middle-class readers of lesson books and moral tales, but their reading needs were being recognized. Alongside the traditional chapbooks a new class of literature emerged which was designed as an alternative to the influence of the old tales. Sarah Trimmer provided the *Family Magazine* (1788–9), 'to counteract the pernicious tendency of immoral books etc., which have circulated of late years among the inferior classes of people', and her tale of *The Servant's Friend* (1787) was directed at a similar readership. Mary Sherwood, Mary Hughes, and Jonas Hanway all wrote for the servant classes who had left childhood far behind, young people undergoing very different life experiences from the readers of James Marshall's *Juvenile Magazine* (1788), which was aimed at 'young people from seven to fourteen years of age'; Mary Sherwood herself was still playing with dolls at the age of 14. While preaching the virtues of domestic service to the deserving poor, Sarah Trimmer was similarly confiding to readers of her *Guardian of Education* how she supposed 'all young gentlemen and ladies to be children till they are fourteen, and young persons till they are at least twenty-one'.

### THE NATURAL CHILD

Children were the grateful recipients of a new spirit in their literature as publishing for children flourished and a more child-centred literature emerged, with childhood being celebrated as never before. Children's writers were being touched by the new spirit of emotionalism which surrounded the subject of childhood; a lightness of tone crept into even the most moral of texts. Anna Barbauld, later to be so unfairly berated by Charles Lamb, captured this mood in one of her most celebrated books, *Hymns in Prose for Children* (1781): 'The birds can warble, and the young lambs can bleat; but we can open our lips in his praise, we can speak of all his goodness.' In *Evenings at Home* she continued to leaven the didactic intention with amusing tales. While many of the pieces in this collection were very ordinary, there were also items which

Mary Ann Kilner's *Memoirs of a Peg-Top*, an edition from *c*.1805 by John Marshall.

had the authentic ring of a folk- or fairy-tale. Children were being addressed with respect, and authors displayed an understanding of their reading tastes. Lady Ellenor Fenn, for example, had identified children's reading needs, and her desire to please and amuse as well as to teach is evident in her opening address to readers of *Cobwebs to Catch Flies*:

My dears, do not imagine that, like a great spider, I will give you a hard gripe, and infuse venom to blow you up,—No—I mean to catch you gently, whisper in your ear, Be good and you will be loved, Be good and you will be happy; and then release you, to frisk about in pursuit of your innocent pastimes.

She reminded parents that 'children, if you expect them to read with spirit and propriety must be supplied with lessons suited to their taste; that is, prattle, like their own'. The illustrations to the two small volumes are well realized, and complement the text.

Dorothy and Mary Ann Kilner also combined a didactic approach with the innocent pleasures of children at play. They used language and incidents to which children could relate. In *Dialogues and Letters on Morality, Oeconomy and Politeness, for the Improvement and Entertainment of Young Female Minds* (*c.*1780) Dorothy Kilner lamented the lack of childish pursuits in books—'almost the whole catalogue of entertaining books for children turn chiefly on subjects of gallantry, love, and marriage'. In *Memoirs of a Peg-Top* (*c.*1781) and *The Adventures of a Pincushion* (*c.*1780) Mary Ann Kilner (sister-in-law to Dorothy) provides evidence of the combining of uninhibited childishness with the need to control and contain. Her characters are comfortingly realistic. Miss Martha Airy, the exasperating 10-year-old depicted in *The Adventures of a Pincushion*, 'who had been for some time indolently lolling with both her elbows on the table', disputes fiercely with her sister over broken toys. Charlotte's violent and entirely understandable reaction, although strongly reproved by the author, is shown much more as the natural outcome of a squabble than as the kind of wicked or aberrant behaviour frowned upon by Puritan writers: 'Charlotte was so enraged at the loss of her play-things that without offering to help her sister, she gave her a slap on the face, and told her, she was very naughty to spoil things in such a manner by her carelessness; and that she would break her plates whenever they came in her way.' The subsequent making up between the sisters is truculent, in just the way that real children behave. No swift and easy reconciliations are offered to readers, for this is a normal children's quarrel which takes full account of natural aggression and stubbornness.

Much of this writing was undoubtedly influenced by Locke's view that children required a firm, if loving, parental hand, and a carefully judged literature to fit them for an ordered society. Ellenor Fenn referred directly to the ideas he popularized—'if the human mind be a *rasa tabula*—you to whom it is entrusted should be cautious what is written upon it'. Mary Pilkington, the author of around fifty books for children, took a similar line. The subtitle of her *Biography for Boys* (1799) is significant: 'Characteristic Histories Calculated to Impress the Youthful Mind with an Admiration of Virtuous Principles and Detestation of Vicious Ones.'

Not all of Mrs Pilkington's books were quite as intensely reasonable as the Biographies. Her *New Tales of the Castle* (1800), which followed from the Comtesse de Genlis's *Tales of the Castle* (1785), contrived to place moral tales in the unlikely framework of a French noble family fleeing the Revolution, taking up residence in a Welsh castle, recovering a treasure hoard, and returning it to the owner: a story-line worthy of any twentieth-century hack. Her poetry, too, has echoes of a more Romantic spirit. In *The Calendar; or, Monthly Recreations* (1807) her poem 'On the Recovery of a Young Lady of Seven Years of Age from a Dangerous Disposition' is thoroughly reminiscent of Coleridge's 'To a Young Lady on her First Appearance after a Dangerous Illness'.

The women writers who dominated the children's market at this time were themselves heavily involved in education, although the professional writer setting out to earn solely from children's books was some way distant. Hannah More retired from school-keeping in 1790 having made a comfortable living for herself; Anna Barbauld managed a boys' school in Palgrave; Mary Sherwood took in pupils alongside her own growing family; Sarah Trimmer ran three Sunday schools in Brentford, Essex; Mary Pilkington worked as a governess. She was probably one of the first children's writers to see herself as semi-professional; in a letter to a friend in 1807, she made it clear that writing had become her main source of income. Like Mary Sherwood, who had a similar need to earn money from her writing, she saw her children's books as serious projects.

Mary Wollstonecraft also made a considerable career out of her work; beginning first as a governess and then gaining the patronage of a publisher—Joseph Johnson, who treated her like a daughter and kept her comfortably on the books she produced for him. (Johnson also published Anna Barbauld, Sarah Trimmer, and Maria Edgeworth.) Closeness to the education of children and to the fashions in tutoring meant that writers such as these attuned their work to a conservative market. So it was that the otherwise radical and free-thinking Mary Wollstonecraft wrote the misnamed *Original Stories from Real Life* (1788). In this she expressed the unexceptional view that 'These conversations and tales are accommodated to the present state of society; which obliges the author to attempt to cure those faults by reason, which ought never to have taken root in the infant mind.' Mrs Mason, her uncompromising schoolmistress, was far removed from the gentler and more amiable creature in Sarah Fielding's *Governess*. (The 1791 edition was, however, distinguished by engravings from William Blake.)

These writers were attempting to integrate Locke's educational theories, the need to impress the 'right' attitudes upon children, and the importance of engaging a child in a reasoning dialogue with the teacher or parent, following Rousseau's philosophy of natural education. Allowing the child to learn

*Frontispiece.*

*Look what a fine morning it is.—Insects, Birds, & Animals, are all enjoying existence.*

Blake. inv. & sc.

Frontispiece for the 1791 edition of Mary Wollstonecraft's *Original Stories from Real Life*.

through experience—even when painful—was the means to true rationality. Maria Edgeworth and her father were two of Rousseau's staunchest disciples and Richard Lovell Edgeworth put his philosophy into practice by educating his own large family on that plan. He also read and applied Anna Barbauld's ideas, although neither approach appeared to have worked particularly well for his children. Coleridge, whose own ideas on education were implacably opposed to what he considered the unnatural strictness of Edgeworth's Rousseauism, was highly diverted to discover from one of Edgeworth's friends the failure of the system laid down in their *Practical Education* (1798): 'the Edgeworths were most miserable when children; and yet the father in his book is ever vapourizing about their happiness.' Undaunted by the problems they encountered, Maria and Richard Edgeworth adapted Rousseau's views for parents and tutors and laid about them with a will on such matters as toys for children: 'The glaring colours, or the gilding of toys, may catch the eye and please for a few minutes, but unless some use can be made of them, they will and ought to be soon discarded.'

Frontispiece from volume ii of Thomas Day's *The History of Sandford and Merton* (3 vols., 1783–9): 'Fighting the Bull'.

Maria became a successful writer of adult novels as well as of children's tales, some of which she wrote with her father. 'Dog Trusty' and 'The Orange Man', two of her earliest attempts in collaboration with him, appeared in *The Parent's Assistant* (1796) and its stories, notably 'The Purple Jar', continued to be popular well into the late nineteenth century. Less tolerable is the hero of *Frank* (1801), just enough of a real boy to show an insatiable curiosity about his surroundings, but painfully accommodating to his tiresome parents. They skilfully manipulate him into knowledge through defining every creature in sight (Dickens was to mock the method wonderfully well in *Hard Times*) and then have him fix the lesson by memorizing verse. '"Now, mamma, that I know what is meant by the bees in the waxen cells, may I learn those lines, and will you repeat them to me?"'

Other writers using this kind of approach to lesson books and tales were translated and widely read. *Conversations of Emily* (1787) by the

Marquise d'Épinay, Rousseau's friend, was modelled on similar lines. The Comtesse de Genlis was another imported author whose educational system followed *Émile*, although *Adelaide and Theodore* (1783) was at least applicable to girls as well as to boys. She also rounded on his notion that a tutor should have but a solitary pupil: 'Experience has proved to me that Rousseau opposes an opinion well founded: the deepest study of the human heart with every talent united, which is so essentially necessary in a Tutor will avail nothing without that experience which alone can be acquired by long practice.'

More in tune with an English readership was Thomas Day's *Sandford and Merton*, published in three parts from 1783 to 1789. As Darton observed, 'Day could tell a story', and his book was an attempt to present the spirit of *Émile* to English children in a series of stories about two children—Harry Sandford and Tommy Merton—which he struggles to string on a rational and moral thread. Day was popular, and the book went into many editions. It was abridged in 1790 by Richard Johnson and published by Elizabeth Newbery and continued a firm favourite well into the next century. Day's *Little Jack* (1788) is even more of a Rousseauist tale: the foundling hero's upbringing by a rustic who had built 'a little hut of clay' and his suckling by a nanny goat were the perfect embodiment of a natural education: 'It was wonderful to see how this child thus left to nature, increased in strength and vigour. Unfettered by bandages or restraints, his limbs acquired their due proportions and form; his countenance was full and florid, and gave indications of perfect health.' Simplicity, innocence, a state of nature, and all the attributes of a Romantic childhood were available in these Rousseau-inspired tales. What they lacked, though, was the story-telling art of Maria Edgeworth, or the directness in using language of Anna Barbauld. Crucially, too, they lacked any sense of fun or of the ridiculous.

## NEWBERY'S SUCCESSORS

Following John Newbery's death in 1767 there was considerable rivalry between the various factions in the family, confusingly led by two Francises, one the son, the other the nephew. The fruits of this were an increase in production, some of which comprised reissues of earlier titles, and a further exploitation of the marketing practices Newbery had begun. On the death of Francis the nephew in 1780, his widow Elizabeth took over this branch of the business and further developed the children's list. She published around 310 juvenile items and 210 adult books, a change in emphasis from the early Newbery days: her less catholic business mainly focused on selling to schools and parents, with the more expensive items a particularly significant element: *Geography for Children* (1787), in its fifteenth edition at 1s. 6d., *The Blossoms of Morality* (1789), at 2s. 6d., and Elizabeth Pinchard's *Dramatic Dialogues*

A trade card for Francis Newbery, nephew to John Newbery (1766). Patent medicines also made up much of his trade.

(1792) at 5s. for two volumes were clearly intended for use in the education and edification of the middle-class child.

*Blossoms of Morality* is an interesting example of the care that was now being taken over the production of more expensive books. It was first published with only an engraved frontispiece and title-page, but no woodcuts. However, what marks out this competent but unexceptional text in its second edition (1796) is the addition of some of the finest of John Bewick's illustrations. The wood engravings of the brothers Thomas and John Bewick transformed book illustration at the end of the eighteenth century. The early illustrations in children's books, even the engravings in some of John Newbery's most elegant productions, were crude by modern standards, and the woodcuts in cheaper books were often included simply because a block was available, with the text written to suit the pictures. Engravings, which were expensive to produce as they had to be printed separately from the text, were usually found only in the more costly items, so that basic wood block illustrations provided the visual stimulus for most children. Alphabet books particularly suffered from the confusing random illustrations which must have seemed very curious to the child learning its letters. The Bewicks perfected a new technique, the use of the end-grain of a hard wood block, which enabled them to produce a much finer line and greater variety of effects. Expressively drawn pictures at the beginning and neat, decorative vignettes at the end of each of the tales in *Blossoms of Morality* set a new standard for children's book illustration.

Heightened rivalry amongst children's publishers can also be seen in the widening range of their stock. Elizabeth Newbery continued to issue the more popular of her late husband's titles—*Mother Bunch's Fairy Tales* (1773) appeared again in 1790, 1795, and 1799—while adding other popular works, including *The Adventures of a Silver Penny* (c.1787) and an edition of *The Adventures of Captain Gulliver* (1782). She also collaborated with other publishers in the production of books and she co-operated in the publication of instructional games and jigsaw puzzles. These were somewhat dull affairs as games go, and all were aimed at the moral improvement and instruction of children, but they were neatly produced on cloth-backed paper, with bright colouring and instructions. *The New Game of Human Life* (1790), *A New Geographical Game* (1792), and *Chronological Tables of English History* (c.1796) were some early collaborations with John Wallis, the leading publisher of children's games at the time. The Wallis family continued in business with their 'dissected' maps, games, and puzzles into the mid-nineteenth century.

Links between this sector of the children's trade and the booksellers were common. The Darton dynasty, whose founder William Darton set up as an engraver, printer, and stationer in 1787, published a similar range to that of Elizabeth Newbery: schoolbooks, smaller, cheaper items, and a growing range of maps and games. Tempting children by devising more original ways of presenting material was necessary as the numbers of London booksellers specializing in the children's trade grew.

The harlequinade, a single sheet of paper, folded into four, with a picture divided horizontally to make two flaps, was one such means. It was a popular toy with young children and examples of home-made versions have been found. Robert Sayer, a map and print seller who published around fifteen of them between about 1766 and 1772, chose to depict the pantomimes or harlequinades at the London theatres of the time, hence the name for a simple but effective trifle. *Harlequin Cherokee; or, The Indian Chiefs in London* (1772), a sheet with eight hand-coloured engravings, is an example of Sayer's work. Other publishers took up this format and added it to their lists: Elizabeth Newbery issued the old favourite *Mother Shipton* (1800) in coloured and uncoloured versions and in the same year produced *A New Book of Emblems*. Both were co-ventures with other publisher-booksellers.

By the end of the eighteenth century a flourishing distribution network based on the newspaper trade was in operation, and London bookshops provided a good selection which could be purchased wholesale or retail through mail order. Elizabeth Newbery's catalogue for 1800 itemizes 213 'amusing and instructive books for young minds' and adds forty-eight

A price-list of books sold by Elizabeth Newbery. Many were chapbooks covering a wide range of interests.

### NEWBERY's New Publications.

Sold by E. Newbery, at the *Corner of St. Paul's Churchyard*, London ; where may be had the greatest Variety of Books, together with Dissected Maps of all Countries, Geographical Pastimes, Dissected Tables of the English and Roman Histories, and every Article for the Instruction and Amusement of young People.

| | £. | s. | d. |
|---|---|---|---|
| Chronological Tables of the English History, 4s. 6d. on a Sheet.—Dissected | 0 | 10 | 6 |
| Chronological Tables of the Roman History, 4s. 6d. on a Sheet.—Dissected | 0 | 10 | 6 |
| Youthful Recreations, or the Amusements of a Day | 0 | 0 | 6 |
| Life and Adventures of a Fly | 0 | 0 | 6 |
| Triumph of Good Nature | 0 | 0 | 6 |
| The Youthful Jester, or Repository of Wit | 0 | 0 | 6 |
| Anecdotes of a Little Family | 0 | 1 | 0 |
| The Entertaining and Affecting History of Prince Lee Boo, a Native of the Pelew Islands | 0 | 1 | 6 |
| The History of North America, by the Rev. Mr. Cooper | 0 | 1 | 6 |
| The History of South America, by the same Author | 0 | 1 | 6 |
| The Blossoms of Morality, by the Editor of the Looking Glass for the Mind | 0 | 2 | 6 |
| Holiday Entertainment, or the Good Child's Fairing | 0 | 0 | 1 |
| History of the little Boy found under a Hay-cock. | 0 | 0 | 1 |
| Hermit of the Forest and the Wandering Infants. | 0 | 0 | 1 |
| Foundling, or the History of Lucius Stanhope. | 0 | 0 | 1 |
| Rural Felicity, or the History of Tommy and Sally. | 0 | 0 | 1 |
| Lovechild's Golden Present, to all little Masters and Misses. | 0 | 0 | 1 |
| The Royal Alphabet, or Child's best Instructor. | 0 | 0 | 1 |
| The Father's Gift, or the way to be Wise and Happy. | 0 | 0 | 1 |
| The Sister's Gift, or the Naughty Boy Reformed. | 0 | 0 | 1 |
| The Brother's Gift, or the Naughty Girl Reformed. | 0 | 0 | 1 |
| History of Tommy Careless, or the Misfortunes of a Week. | 0 | 0 | 1 |
| The Holiday Spy. | 0 | 0 | 1 |
| History of Tommy Titmouse. | 0 | 0 | 2 |
| The Flights of a Lady-Bird | 0 | 0 | 2 |
| The Village Tattlers, or Anecdotes of the Rural Assembly | 0 | 0 | 2 |
| The Fortune Teller, by the renowned Dr. Hurlothrumbo | 0 | 0 | 2 |
| The History of Little King Pippin, to which is added the Story of the Children in the Wood | 0 | 0 | 2 |
| Virtue and Vice | 0 | 0 | 2 |
| The Entertaining Traveller | 0 | 0 | 2 |
| Tom Thumb's Exhibition | 0 | 0 | 2 |
| The Hobby Horse ; or Christmas Companion | 0 | 0 | 2 |
| Robin Goodfellow, a Fairy Tale, written by a Fairy | 0 | 0 | 2 |
| Little Moralists, or the History of Amintor and Florella | 0 | 0 | 3 |
| Little Wanderers | 0 | 0 | 3 |
| The Mountain Piper | 0 | 0 | 3 |
| False Alarms | 0 | 0 | 3 |
| The Adventures of Master Headstrong and Miss Patient | 0 | 0 | 3 |
| The Juvenile Biographer | 0 | 0 | 3 |
| A Bag of Nuts ready cracked, by Thomas Thumb, Esq. | 0 | 0 | 3 |
| The Puzzling Cap ; being a choice Collection of Riddles, in familiar Verse ; | 0 | 0 | 3 |
| Juvenile Rambles through the Paths of Nature | 0 | 0 | 6 |
| Adventures of a Silver Penny | 0 | 0 | 6 |

French books for schools and home tuition, not all her own products. At her bookshop could be found: 'a complete assortment, together with dissected maps and a variety of schemes in the form of games, calculated to make the road to knowledge pleasant and easy'. (By then, her business was being managed by John Harris, who was to take over the business completely in 1801 and go on to provide some of the most innovative of the early nineteenth-century children's books.)

The provincial emporia in which these children's books were found contained an odd assortment of goods: Coleridge's aunt kept an 'everything shop at Crediton', where he 'read through all the gilt-cover little books that could be had at that time'. Children would choose their books alongside the strangest mix of items. At the offices of the *Preston Journal* could be found: 'shop books, pocket books, china ware and all sorts of glasses, the best Poland starch, and blue smalt, fine wash balls and black balls, true spectacles for any age and great variety of toys'. Significantly, though, the children's book had arrived as a commodity, to be sold beside all of the other essential items for the eighteenth-century household.

The mainstream publishers did not entirely despise the cheaper end of the trade: Elizabeth Newbery's 1800 catalogue contained thirteen penny and fourteen twopenny items. The provincial publishers were printing large editions of their chapbooks in order to supply retail outlets; *The Young Child's Book of Instruction*, printed at Hereford by R. Elliott, was advertised as being sold both to hawkers and the trade; Houlston, of Wellington, sold series of tracts at 7s. a hundred, and Fordyce of Newcastle published a series of twenty-four-page chapbooks for sale 'wholesale and retail'. There were clearly close links between the London publisher-booksellers and the chapbook publishers, many of whom confined their activities exclusively to cheap printed items: chapbooks, ballads, ABCs, and so forth. Several collaborated with each other, or at any rate shared the same texts and woodcuts to produce virtually identical items. The text of the Newbery edition of *Robinson Crusoe* (*c.*1768) was taken up by Mozley of Gainsborough, Tregortha of Burslem, Johnston of Falkirk, and Lumsden of Glasgow, in addition to its use by other London printers. However, there was some disdain attaching to this end of the market. Thomas Gent of York wrote with pride in his memoirs of his histories of York and of Ripon, but made no mention of his lucrative, but much less prestigious, chapbook trade.

There were also those who unashamedly specialized in producing children's chapbooks, which by the beginning of the nineteenth century were becoming of a better quality. Another York publisher, James Kendrew, who began his business in Colliergate in about 1803, issued 'songs, pamphlets . . . lives and histories of celebrated and notorious characters, calendars and dying speeches of criminals, primers, battledores, 1/2d and 1d toy books for

A provincial bookseller. A plate from *A Collection of Entertaining Stories*, printed in Worcester in *c.*1785

children etc.' While much of his early work consisted of somewhat crudely printed broadsheet songs, by about 1808 Kendrew was specializing more and more in better-produced children's material: including *The Pleasant and Delightful History of Jack and the Giants*, *Ali Baba; or, The Forty Thieves*, *Farmer Thornberry's Mansion*, *Multiplication Table*, and *Useful Trades*. His little books made liberal use of woodcuts and coloured wrappers.

### NURSERY RHYMES AND POETRY

In his memoirs in 1856, Samuel Goodrich, the New England champion of rationality, triumphantly demonstrated (to his own satisfaction at least) how easy it was to compose rhymes for children. He took 'the very unpromising subject' of a toad.

> Oh, gentle stranger, stop,
> And hear poor little Hop
> Just sing a simple song,
> Which is not very long—
> Hip, hip, hop.

(And so on for eight more verses.) Verse such as this, he held, 'presenting rational ideas and gentle, kindly sentiments' should be used for young children

87

See-saw, Margery Daw,
Sold her bed, and lay upon straw.
Was not she a dirty slut,
To sell her bed and lay in the dirt?

What care I how black I be?
Twenty pounds will marry me.
If twenty won't, forty shall,
I'm my mother's bouncing girl.

*Left*: an unusual version of a familiar verse from *Mother Goose's Melodies*, published in Boston by Munroe and Francis, 1833.

*Right*: frontispiece from *The Entertaining Tales of Mother Goose* for the amusement of youth, published in Glasgow by Lumsden, c.1817. 'Mother Goose' was the storyteller associated with fairy-tales from Perrault's time.

instead of the 'coarse, vulgar, offensive' jingles that composed so much of *Mother Goose's Melodies*. He was attacking not only the book of that name which had been published in Boston in 1833 but the English revival of interest in the genre. Isaiah Thomas had been responsible for the first American appearance of Mother Goose. The date of the first edition of *Mother Goose's Melody* (taken from a Newbery publication) is conjectural; the second was published in 1794.

Goodrich was more successful with a contemptuous parody:

Higglety, pigglety, pop!
The dog has eat the mop;
The pig's in a hurry,
The cat's in a flurry—
Higglety, pigglety—pop!

(Perhaps to take revenge on an implacable enemy of Mother Goose, the Opies included these lines in the *Oxford Dictionary of Nursery Rhymes*.) But the fact is that the traditional rhymes 'stick like burrs', as Goodrich lamented, and the song of Hop has vanished, together with myriads like it. It is only very rarely that what is written *for* children survives into another generation. The appeal of the traditional rhymes is that, like fairy-tales, they were once part of a far more wide-ranging culture. They are fragments from the past, often the very distant past, their context and original meaning long ago forgotten.

The old rhymes are full of violence, disaster, and slapstick, all of which make a strong appeal to the juvenile mind: Cock Robin dies, Jack and Jill fall down the hill, a duck eats the love-sick frog. They reflect the real world; not a version of it filtered for juvenile consumption. Tabart's *Songs for the Nursery* (1805), in general a gentle collection which contains more rhymes about children than most, includes for instance 'Tom, Tom of Islington', a popular seventeenth-century jest about marriage, but its first appearance in a nursery collection. Tom takes a stick to his shrewish wife:

> Sick was she on Thursday,
> Dead was she on Friday,
> Glad was Tom on Saturday night
> To bury his wife on Sunday.

But there is far more to traditional rhymes than crude humour. Many of them have the ring of real poetry, like 'How many miles to Babylon?', 'Can you make me a cambric shirt?', 'I had a little nut tree', or a verse that may have Anglo-Saxon origins, the magical

> Gray goose and gander,
> Waft your wings together,
> And carry the good king's daughter
> Over the one-strand river.

Children brought up on the multi-stranded collection known as nursery rhymes have had, unawares, a bird's-eye view of centuries of popular literature. As a first literary experience they cannot be equalled and many poets have recalled what the old stories and rhymes meant to them. John Clare, for instance, said that long before he knew anything about Milton and Shakespeare they were the food of his winter evenings: 'I cannot help fancying that Cock Robin, Babes in the Wood, Mother Hubbard and her Cat, &c., &c., are real poetry in all its native simplicity and as it should be.'

The Opies have shown where the rhymes come from—barrack room and alehouse songs, bawdy ballads and ribald love songs, political squibs, stage plays, street cries, ancient rituals, proverbs, riddles. Much of the 'Mother Goose' corpus consists of verses wrenched out of context, thereby acquiring a teasing nonsensical quality or a mystery that the original never had. The rhyme that begins 'One misty, moisty morning' is the opening verse of an

( 8 )

Q. I sent a Token to my Friend,
It was a Pledge that had no End;
But when the same my Friend did get,
My Friend soon put an End to it.

*A. A Ring sent to an ungrateful Person,
who sold it.*

Q. One Mouth, one Nose, two charming eyes
Two Feet, two Hands, two Heads likewise.

*A. A young Virgin, whose Natural Head
and Maidenhead make two.*

Q. No Teeth I have, and yet I bite,
And when the Bite is seen,

According

( 9 )

According to my slender Might,
There are the marks of Spleen;
My Beard is red and green.

*A. It is a Nettle.*

Q. Two Brothers we are,
Great Burthens we bear,
By which we are bitterly prest,
In Truth we may say,
We are full all the Day,
But empty when we go to rest.

*A. A Pair of Shoes.*

Q. My Backside is Wood,
My Belly is as good,
My Ribs they are lined with Leather;
My Nose it is Brass,
With two Holes in my Arse,
And commonly us'd in cold Weather.

*A. A Pair of Bellows.*

Pages from *A New Riddle Book, or a Whetstone for Dull Wits*, printed at Derby for the benefit of the Travelling Stationers *c*.1790.

undistinguished seventeenth-century ballad called 'The Wiltshire Wedding', and the 'old man clothed all in leather' who sounds like a supernatural being is in fact only one of the guests. The old man 'who wouldn't say his prayers' in 'Goosey Gander' is part of a second rhyme, once recited by children as they pulled the legs off a crane-fly.

The brevity of the rhymes, the way in which the tragedies of, say, Humpty Dumpty, the three blind mice, and the maid in 'Sing a Song of Sixpence' are reduced to a few stark lines, gives infinite scope for individual interpretation. Generations of illustrators have brought their imagination to bear on them. Some have seen them as mysteriously beautiful; some as comic; some like Walter Crane used them as an opportunity for elaborate decorative detail, others—Kate Greenaway and Margaret Tarrant—made them gently pretty

64

and childlike. Randolph Caldecott added his own subtle subtext of pictorial commentary. It is rare indeed for the rhymes to be published without illustrations, and these have softened their original adult nature, and turned the violence and occasional terror into a joke.

With the exception of the alphabets, lullabies, and games, few of the rhymes were intended specifically for children, and one has only to look through the index of any collection to see how many feature adults—kings, queens, farmers, lovers, husbands and wives, old men and old women (especially the last). It is also noticeable if one studies the older compilations how a refining process has purged much of the original grossness. It was a long time before anybody thought of printing the rhymes and jingles with which adults amused or soothed the very young. The oldest surviving collection is *Tommy Thumb's Pretty Song Book Voll. II* published by Mary Cooper in 1744, of which one copy is known, in the British Library. (What 'voll. I' contained is a matter of bibliographic speculation.) The delicate copper engravings are at strange variance with the drinking and wenching songs and the coarse abuse. But even here there has been some bowdlerization. In 'Mistress Mary' it is cockle shells, not cuckolds 'all in a row'. The revolting habits of the old woman who sold puddings and pies—described with gusto in the original broadside—are omitted. *Nancy Cock's Pretty Song Book*, published by John Marshall *c.*1780, includes verses about children and their games. But there are cuckolds in Mistress Mary's garden; and, as in *Tommy Thumb's Pretty Song Book*, Little Robin Red-breast sits on a pole so that the last line can read 'Poop went his hole'.

*Mother Goose's Melody*, probably published at about the same time, is more decorous; society seems to be developing a new sense of what is appropriate to childhood. There are still robust drinking songs, and there are rhymes where one can suspect a lewd double meaning, but there is little which is overtly improper. This increasing refinement can be noticed in the various editions of James Orchard Halliwell's *Nursery Rhymes of England*. The original edition of 1842 was for scholars and antiquarians, and Halliwell printed the rhymes as he had found them. Thus 'William and Mary, George and Anne' ends 'And call'd their brother the son of a whore', which in subsequent, commercial, editions was altered to 'a shocking bad name'. Either Halliwell or his publisher also decided that the word 'kiss' was improper; lines were altered accordingly and kissing games were omitted. The book was reissued several times, always with added material, and formed the source-book for most Victorian

From *Tommy Thumb's Song Book* published by Isaiah Thomas in Worcester, Massachusetts, 1794 (2nd edition). Later versions amended the final line to 'dance' or 'stay' with your bride.

52 TOMMY THUMB's HARRY PARRY.

O RARE Harry Parry!
When will you marry?
When Apples and Pears are ripe;
I'll come to your Wedding,
Without any Bidding,
And lie with your Bride all Night.
SONG

JACK and Jill
went up the
hill,
To fetch a pail of
water;
Jack fell down,
and broke his
crown,
And Jill came
tumbling after.

JACK SPRAT
could eat no
fat,
His wife could eat
no lean;
And so betwixt
them both,
They lick'd the
platter clean.

KISS me asleep, and kiss me awake,
Kiss me for Dear Willie's sake.

compilations. Though Halliwell was slapdash in his scholarship, and wild in his assertions about the origins of the rhymes, he was the first editor to interest himself in their antiquity, and *Nursery Rhymes of England* was the main reference book until Iona and Peter Opie produced the monumental *Oxford Dictionary of Nursery Rhymes* in 1951.

The rhymes, as has been said, are mainly drawn from traditional sources; only a handful are by named authors writing for children, and these—'Mary had a little lamb' (Sarah Josepha Hale, 1830), for instance, and 'Twinkle, twinkle, little star' (Jane Taylor, 1806)—seem limp and pallid beside the vigour of the rest. These adjectives, alas, can be applied to the greater part of poetry written specifically for children. Goodrich in 1846 had composed for his juvenile magazine *Merry's Museum* a dialogue between 'Timothy and his mother'. Timothy has been rapturously chanting rhymes from *Mother Goose's Melody*; ' "I really do love poetry, because it is so silly!" ' Too late his mother realizes that the book is full of 'nonsense and vulgarity' and urges him to learn 'good, sensible things' instead, such as Watts's hymns. 'I hate 'em', says Timothy tersely, and goes on repeating 'Round about, round about, maggoty pie', a four-line glorification of drink.

Compared to this, most verse for children is milk and water; it is at its best when it is fantastic or nonsensical; for a long time it was admonitory or didactic.

In the 1780s and 1790s, when Mrs Trimmer and the Edgeworths were the voices respected by the educational establishment, Blake's *Songs of Innocence* (1789) seemed incomprehensible, even hallucinatory. But *Songs of Innocence* reached few if any children of the time; hand engraved and printed by Blake and his wife, they were never intended for the commercial market. Indeed, Harvey Darton, writing in 1932, said that it was only recently that Blake's spirit had become 'a living spark in poetry meant for children'. He foreshadowed much that was to come later, but at the time few if any understood what he was saying.

But the mildly moral versifying of Jane and Ann Taylor, whose *Original Poems for Infant Minds* appeared in two parts in 1804 and 1805, was wholly appropriate for their time. *Rhymes for the Nursery* followed in 1806, and *Hymns for Infant Minds* in 1810. The sisters, only in their early twenties themselves, penned their verse with 'a hearty affection for that interesting little race, the race of children'. Desiring to keep it within the comprehension of the youngest, they had thought it 'desirable to abridge every poetic freedom and figure' and to avoid all imagery, since children 'have few but literal ideas'. They wrote about good children and ones who needed to be mildly corrected; about being kind to the poor and the old; occasionally about flowers and animals. Their work is amiable but pedestrian, and wholly lacking in imagination; it opens no windows.

*Facing*: from Charles Bennett's *Old Nurse's Book of Rhymes, Jingles and Ditties* (1857). Bennett's illustrations convey the earthy humour of the rhymes.

Come take up your Hats, and away let us haste,

To the Butterfly's Ball, and the Grashopper's feast.

*The Butterfly's Ball.*

Come take up your hats & away let us haste
To the Butterfly's ball, & the Grasshopper's feast,
The trumpeter Gadfly has summon'd the crew,
And the revels are now only waiting for you

On the smooth shaven grass, by the side of a wood,
Beneath a broad oak that for ages has stood,
There the Children of earth, & the tenants of air
For an evening's amusement together repair

And there came the Beetle so blind & so black
Who carried the Emmet, his friend, on his back;
And there was the Gnat, & the Dragon-fly too,
With all their relations green, orange, & blue.

And there came the Moth with his plumage of down
And the Hornet, in jacket of yellow & brown;
Who with him the Wasp his companion did bring
But they promis'd that evening to lay by their sting

And the sly little Dormouse crept out of his hole,
And brought to the feast his blind brother the mole
And the snail, with his horns peeping out from his shell
Came from a great distance – the length of an ell

The Taylor style was often imitated, by, among others, Charles and Mary Lamb in *Poetry for Children* (1809) and Elizabeth Turner in *The Daisy* (1807) and *The Cowslip* (1811). Something of the sisters' reputation has survived; they still appear in anthologies (though Ann's once popular 'My Mother' has been so parodied as to be now unusable). They are usually held to be the first to write domestic verse for young children, but in fact a Newbery publication, very similar to their work in style and content, preceded them by over twenty years. This was *Little Robin Red Breast: A Collection of Pretty Songs for Children* (1782), which Isaiah Thomas published in Worcester, Massachusetts, four years later. There is much about sport and play, treats and red-letter days; correction is mild, and good humour seems to be the quality most desired. Play while you can, the unknown author urged.

> Do not ask about to-morrow,
>     Little wantons, revel still;
> Future times bring care and sorrow,
>     Soon, too soon, you'll have your fill.

As we would expect, there is no fantasy or nonsense; that was contrary to the spirit of the age. But with the new century the mood grew more light-hearted—at any rate so far as verse and picture-books went. William Roscoe's *The Butterfly's Ball*, which first appeared in 1806, had not a vestige of a moral, and so delighted readers that it was copiously imitated.

The surreal inconsequence of *Old Dame Trot and her Comical Cat*, a traditional rhyme, probably first published by T. Evans in 1803, was also imitated, notably by Sarah Catherine Martin in her *Old Mother Hubbard* (1805). Upwards of

68

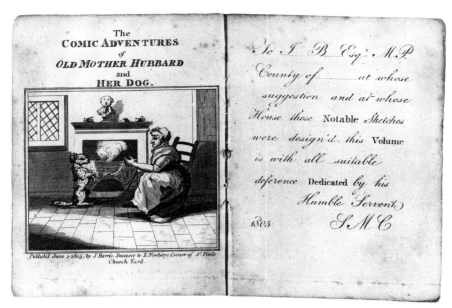

*Old Mother Hubbard* has been described as the most significant children's book ever published by John Harris.

10,000 copies of this were apparently distributed in a few months, and chapbook editions appeared soon after. Limericks made their first known appearance, in *The History of Sixteen Wonderful Old Women*, a Harris publication of 1820, but it was not until the Victorian period that nonsense became an accepted literary genre with Edward Lear's *Book of Nonsense* (1846). And until anthologies such as Coventry Patmore's *The Children's Garland* (1863) began to aim at literary rather than moral worth, the nursery rhyme collections were the best food for future poets.

## IMAGINED WORLDS

Evidence that fairy-tales as well as nursery rhymes were finding their mark can be seen in the alarm they aroused in critics. Sarah Trimmer, in her review of *Mother Bunch's Fairy Tales* (1773) (an early collection of tales taken from the original French version of the Countess d'Aulnoy), spoke against 'imaginary beings' for children. And in the *Juvenile Review* (1817) a similar view was expressed: 'Works of fancy highly wrought, such as *The Tales of the Genii*, *The Arabian Nights*, and the like, we would not put into the hands of young people till their religious principles are fixed.' Dorothy Kilner positively boasted to parents and tutors that her *Histories of More Children than One* (*c*.1783) was 'totally free from the prejudicial nonsense of witches, fairies, fortune-tellers, love and marriage, which too many are larded with'.

Interestingly, witches and fairies are equated here with the overtly adult preoccupations of love and marriage. Popular folk- and fairy-tales were

*Facing, above*: frontispiece to *The Butterfly's Ball*, published by John Harris (1807).

*Below*: manuscript copy of the beginning of *The Buttlerfly's Ball* by William Roscoe, to his son Thomas.

69

regarded as the preserve of adults, as well as of children. Such a sweeping dismissal of fairy-tales was not, fortunately, universal. Sarah Fielding had made them respectable in *The Governess*, and Lucy Aikin, niece to Anna Barbauld, writing in her introduction to *Poetry for Children* (1801), cautioned against jettisoning them altogether.

Since dragons and fairies, giants and witches, have vanished from our nurseries before the wand of reason, it has been a prevailing maxim that the young should be fed on mere prose and simple fact . . . the novel-like tales now written for the amusement of youth may . . . be productive of more injury to the mind by giving a false picture of the real world, than the fairy fictions of the last generation, which only wandered over the region of shadows.

Even then, as Dorothy Kilner witnessed, the chapbook tales contained references to more adult concerns. Burbage's edition of *The Sleeping Beauty in the Wood* (*c*.1800) has pithy comments on the current state of womanhood, and a 'new song, call'd poor Davy and Molly', which followed the tale, was all about the very adult subject of unrequited love. Fairy-tales appeared amidst a motley collection of folk- and moral tales in the lists of chapbook publishers. 'Cinderella' was almost submerged among the welter of rational tales, with no distinction as one of the oldest and most pervasive of fairy-tales.

Benjamin Tabart was the first publisher to produce a quite separate set of the tales in a format designed to attract children. Of these, his *Cinderella; or,*

*Blue Beard, or the Fatal Effects of Curiosity and Disobedience,* published by John Harris, 1808. Gruesome images were cheerfully presented to children in popular literature.

*The Little Glass Slipper: A Tale for the Nursery* (1804) was immensely popular and achieved sixteen editions in its first year. Tabart also published Perrault in the same year in his *Collection of Popular Stories for the Nursery*. The tales were translated and edited by Mary Jane Godwin, second wife of William Godwin; the three parts were 'adorned with numerous plates' and a fourth volume was added in 1809. The collection was later to be published by Richard Phillips in a single volume of *Popular Fairy Tales* (1818).

John Harris, whose coloured books set new standards of production for children, also published fairy-tales in a format designed to appeal to children. His *Cinderella* (1808), a sixteen-page booklet, was illustrated with 'elegant and appropriate engravings'. Even his version of *Bluebeard* (1808), with suitably horrifying illustrations of the hapless victims, was attractive, if somewhat grotesque, for children:

> The heads of six ladies,
> All lovely as life;
> With this writing on each,
> 'An inquisitive wife'.

The chapbook versions of Perrault continued to pour off the presses. In Warrington, the 'travelling stationers' were issuing *Bluebeard* around 1820 and J. Ross of Newcastle published a version at about the same time. There was, though, a distinct change in presentation from the early rough chapbooks in their buff wrappers. Coloured covers became common, and tales were often part of a distinct series, a 'Juvenile Library' or 'Juvenile Books' collection, to emphasize their separation from the adult or more overtly moralizing literature. Ross's list placed *Bluebeard* amongst *Nursery Ditties*—a collection of nursery rhymes—and *A New Riddle Book*. The fairy-tale had become the province of children, and furthermore was being separately presented from the clearly educational tales for children.

However, there was one element of the suspension of disbelief which was absent. Extensive fantasy narratives were not available, and while adults could relish the fantastic in a range of Gothic novels, there was no equivalent for children. One of the few early tales to include a fantasy of sorts in which supposedly lifelike characters took part was *The Picture Room at Benevolent Hall*, published by J. Evans around 1820. An intriguing, and so far as one can judge unique, exception to this absence of fantasy fiction was *Glenowen; or, The Fairy Palace*, by Eleanor Sleath, published by Black and Co. and John Harris in 1815. (Eleanor Sleath also wrote 'a romance' for adults—*The Nocturnal Minstrel; or, The Spirit of the Woods* (1810)—and showed herself capable of involving the reader in a romantic mystery.) The orphaned hero and heroine encounter a mysterious 'Fairy Peribanou', a veritable otherworld godmother, who fills their lives with delights and finally reveals herself as a family friend. She positively encourages the reading of fairy-tales as part of her spell, weaving

the stories of Cinderella, the white cat, the oger [*sic*] with his seven league boots and also an abridgement of two or three of the most popular stories from the Arabian Nights' entertainment, among which was the celebrated one of the Good Prince Ahmed and the fairy Peribanou . . . This was a kind of mental banquet new to Rosa. She was totally unacquainted with fiction.

Marjorie Moon, whose bibliographic research on early children's publishers uncovered this early gem, judged that 'she would not, one feels, have been one of Mrs Trimmer's circle'. Children would have to wait for *Alice's Adventures in Wonderland* (1865) before experiencing a similarly extended fantasy narrative written entirely with their pleasure in mind.

There were extensions of the anthropomorphism of *Aesop* in tales about animals, and these provided fantasies of sorts. Usually there was a strong moral principle to be conveyed which may have diluted the pleasure somewhat. However, even Sarah Trimmer acknowledged that children could learn best when helped to dream a few dreams. In her *Fabulous Histories* (1786), which Mrs Trimmer dedicated to the Princess Sophia and which later became better known as *The History of the Robins*, her birds speak English. However, she cautioned in her introduction that children should suspend their disbelief, although only for the purpose of the lesson. The book should be taken 'not as containing the real conversation of birds, (for that is impossible we should ever understand) but as a series of fables intended to convey moral instructions applicable to themselves'. Through writing for children in this way on the importance of treating the natural world wisely and compassionately, as part of God's will for creation, she nevertheless implicitly accepted their insatiable need for fantasy. Children's affinity and fascination with animals could be exploited to deliver homilies on man's duty towards them.

Identification between children and animals was explored in other narratives; animal 'biographies' proliferated. Of these, *Little Juba* (1807) was an abridged version for children of Francis Coventry's adult picaresque novel *The History of Pompey the Little* (1751). The adventures of lap-dog Pompey and his father, who contrived to remove poisoned sausages from the streets of Bologna during the 'sausage season', also included *risqué* descriptions of fashionable society which were less than suitable for the young, hence the adaptation. *Life and Perambulations of a Mouse* by Dorothy Kilner (1783), *Memoirs of Dick, the Little Poney* [*sic*] (1799), *The Dog of Knowledge* (1801), the charming *Felissa; or, The Life and Opinions of a Kitten of Sentiment* (1811), Mary Pilkington's *Marvellous Adventures; or, The Vicissitudes of a Cat* (1802), and Elizabeth Sandham's *The Adventures of a Bullfinch* (1809) similarly encouraged children to imagine themselves in the position of the animal heroes.

72

Animals had been recognized as an appropriate subject for children's amusement since Thomas Boreman's *Description of Three Hundred Animals* (1730), with its intention of 'engaging their attention'. There were numerous examples of animal fantasies masquerading as moral stories, and attractive factual accounts of the animal world reinforced the peculiarly English commitment to animal welfare. James Montgomery compared this unfavourably with their concern for children in his *Chimney-Sweeper's Friend and Climbing-Boys' Album* (1824): 'Were DOGS to be used in the same employment and the same manner as these poor climbing boys . . . an outcry would be raised.' Mary Elliott, in her *Book of Birds and Beasts* (*c*.1826), was typical of children's writers in commenting on the cruelties inflicted on wild creatures: 'I have seen a Goldfinch perform tricks that would surprise you; not that I should

Thomas Boreman's *Description of Three Hundred Animals* (7th edn., 1753). Exotic animals were of continuing fascination for children.

27    *A Description of* BEASTS.

40. AN APE (the moſt common Sort of which is that call'd *Smitten* ) is of a pale mouſe Colour, and grows to a wonderful Size, ſome of them being five Feet long. It is ſo bold and miſchievous, that it will attack a Man. The Negroes are ſo ſilly, as to believe theſe Apes can ſpeak, but will not, leſt they ſhould be ſet to Work, which, they ſuppoſe, they don't like. Baboons and Monkeys have Tails, but the Apes none.

41. THE BEAR-APE, a very deform'd Beaſt of *America*, has his Belly hanging very low, his Head and Face like a Child's; his Skin of an Aſh Colour, and Hair like a Bear's; he has but three Claws upon a Foot, as long as four Fingers, whereby he climbs up the higheſt Trees, and for the moſt Part lives upon the Leaves of a certain Tree common in thoſe Parts. It will not eat the Fleſh, nor attempt the Life of Man: But, when tam'd, is very fond of Mankind. He does not ſeem wet, tho' he has been long in the Rain.

42. THE FOX-APE is in the fore Part like a Fox, and in the hinder Part like an Ape. Under the common Belly it has a Skin like a Bag, wherein it keeps, lodges, and carries its Young, till they are able to provide for themſelves. Neither do they come out of that Receptacle,-except it be to ſuck the Dam, or ſport themſelves; ſo that it is the beſt Shelter againſt all its Enemies. For it is exceeding ſwift in running with that Load, as if it had no Burden at all.

43. THE

28

40

AN APE

41

THE BEAR APE

42

THE FOX APE

73

wish a bird of mine so taught, for I am aware in such cases, methods are used which I consider cruel, and why should we require more of a Goldfinch than its song—and such a song too!' Taken with the rhyming tales of *The Death and Burial of Cock Robin, The Comic Adventures of Old Mother Hubbard and her Dog*, and *The Butterfly's Ball*, animal biographies and juvenile natural histories provided a rich and varied menu of imaginative material for children. They also offered lessons on the treatment of animals and birds.

This juxtaposition of the imagined and the real, the never-land where animals by turns talked and danced like people and behaved as brute creation, was reflected in much of children's literature during this period. The theme is neatly caught in William Walker's version of *The World Turned Upside Down* (1820):

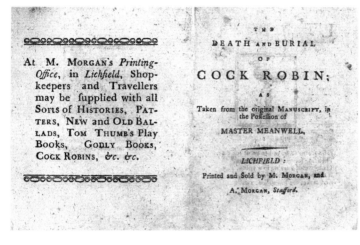

At M. MORGAN's *Printing-Office*, in *Lichfield*, Shopkeepers and Travellers may be supplied with all Sorts of HISTORIES, PATTERS, NEW and OLD BALLADS, TOM THUMB'S Play Books, GODLY BOOKS, COCK ROBINS, &c. &c.

THE
DEATH AND BURIAL
OF
COCK ROBIN;
AS
Taken from the original MANUSCRIPT, in the Possession of
MASTER MEANWELL.

LICHFIELD:
Printed and Sold by M. MORGAN, and
A. MORGAN, *Stafford*.

Title-page of a chapbook published between 1793 and 1802. The publisher's advertisement gives an impression of the stock carried by travelling stationers. *Cock Robin* was one of the most popular of all titles.

Our servants roasted rabbits once
Hanging them on hooks,
But in the picture, you perceive,
Rabbits roast their cooks.

But reality was always close at hand; the popularity of the tale of *Cock Robin* owing something, no doubt, to a continuing need to introduce the concept of death early to children. M. Morgan of Lichfield published a chapbook version around 1795, and both John Harris and William Darton issued their superior versions with coloured engravings in 1806. James Kendrew also issued an *Elegy on the Death and Burial of Cock Robin* in 1820, and Dean and Munday produced a broadside version at about the same time.

For the middle-class child many of the books about pauper children and the lives they led were equivalent to fantasies. In her *Family Tour through the British Empire* (1804) Priscilla Wakefield instructs her readers on the differences between them and 'the thousand children employed usefully and learning an early habit of industry' at the Cromford cotton mills of Sir Richard Arkwright which they 'visit' on their journey. Ann and Jane Taylor's *City Scenes; or, A Peep into London for Children* (1818) served a similar function: introducing well-to-do readers to the unimaginable lives of the deserving artisan classes. A companion volume, *Rural Scenes* (1806), had introduced them to the honest toil of country labourers.

As well as providing the modern reader with a fascinating contemporary outlook on working life, such descriptions offer an intriguing insight into their intended readership. The child is invited simply to *observe* the traders, crossing sweepers, and charity children. Readers are assumed to lead a totally different existence, dependent on the labours of others:

Do you know little reader, that you are indebted to a great number of persons for the conveniences and comforts by which you are surrounded, and that various manufacturers and arts are employed to provide you with food and clothing, and all the other necessaries of life? ( *The Little Tradesman; or, A Peep into English Industry,* 1824)

Pitying the poor was encouraged, but so too was an acceptance of the unbridgeable gulf between them and the more fortunate. The poet Robert Bloomfield, country bred but later a poor shoemaker in London, described the poverty in *The History of Little Davy's New Hat* (1815) and worried that he should be believed: 'Perhaps the characters are too good—too perfect for what we unfortunately see in real life; but that the poverty is not beyond truth, I am certain.' Maria Budden described the worst fate of the urban pauper in *Right and Wrong Exhibited in the History of Rosa and Agnes* (1822), with a 'spirit broken by constant repression . . . manners rendered savage by wretchedness and hopeless slavery'. Mary Sherwood, in one of her tracts for Houlston and Son, describes with vivid detail the closely packed yards of the new industrial cities which must have fascinated the better-off city children living close by:

A stout young woman, who had come to the door of one of the houses, with her hair in curl-papers, and an unfinished glove which she was stitching in her hand, throwing her work on a table just within the door, stepped up to the boy, and seizing his arms with a grasp he could not resist, was just whirling him round from the pump, when her mother, calling to her said 'Jenny, let the lad alone I say; do not meddle and make with other folks' quarrels.'

Life was harsh, and so too was punishment for pauper children. The reality of laws which publicly hanged children after the Gordon riots (1780) and transported others for their crimes—10-year-old Matilda Seymour was given ten years for stealing a shawl and a petticoat—would have been barely understandable to a wealthy child. The spectre of the gibbet, most vividly realized in *The Fairchild Family,* was equally a scarcely credible threat.

While the children of the middle classes enjoyed a more materially secure existence than the children of labourers, even they had few of the comforts associated with modern childhood. Reading was an activity that presented its own difficulties, as Sarah Tytler described when writing in 1877 about *Childhood a Hundred Years Ago*:

In what an absence of light, air, space, comfort and ease the child's business of learning lessons was accomplished . . . the nursery and the sitting room of a country house presented a mild darkness in which we struggled to attain our ends. Within my mother's memory, not even lamps were allowed to illuminate the great farm-house kitchen in the long nights of winter.

Life was spartan by today's standards, but the imagined worlds of many child-hoods—and not only those of the privileged—were widening to include the fairy-tale, new fictions, and embryonic fantasy.

# 4 THE BEGINNINGS OF VICTORIANISM

*c.*1820–1850

*Dennis Butts*

T HE years between 1820 and 1850 were years of turmoil, as Britain emerged from the Napoleonic wars into a world of industrial expansion and social and political turbulence. The Industrial Revolution, as well as producing economic prosperity for some, also brought distress and hardship, not only to such rapidly expanding towns as Birmingham and Manchester, but to agricultural regions in the south and west, and led to the violence of the agricultural 'Swing' riots and the great Chartist demonstrations. For many, the first half of the nineteenth century has indeed been justly named 'The Bleak Age'.

Yet this turbulent period was also one of industrial and technological progress. The years 1820–50 became an era of railways and steamships, and of important developments in manufacturing and mining. A new industrial society was rapidly establishing itself, and the achievements of Faraday and Brunel, Stephenson and Hudson have to be seen alongside those of the politicians Earl Grey, Lord Melbourne, and Robert Peel. The Great Exhibition of 1851 stands out as a fitting symbol of the success of their efforts.

Although the landowning aristocracy had survived the French Revolution, and an expanding urban class worked the factories and mills of the Industrial Revolution, the main thrust behind this movement towards improvement and progress was the ideology of the rising middle classes: Influenced initially by the Evangelical movement at the beginning of the century, they ardently embraced the Protestant work ethic, and transformed it into a gospel of work by the end of the period. The keynotes of this class were modesty and moderation, prudence and self-help, respectability and thrift. If its philosophical underpinning lay in the materialistic utilitarianism of Jeremy Bentham, its Bible came to be Samuel Smiles's *Self Help* of 1859.

The middle classes built their lives upon a combination of Puritan morality and economic aspirations. Weekdays were dominated by purposeful work and Sundays by attendance at church or chapel. Although family life had relaxed slightly from the severities practised at the height of the Evangelical revival, and continued to relax throughout the period, the father was still very much the head of the family, the role of the mother essentially supervisory, and the average family's four or five children were brought up on rigid gender-based lines, with the boys expected to follow their fathers into the world of business, and the daughters to become ladylike in preparation for marriage.

The first great age of Romantic literature was coming to an end. Keats died in 1821, Shelley in 1822, Byron in 1824, and Scott in 1832. Coleridge's and Wordsworth's best work was done, and the interregnum until the great novelists appeared was dominated by essentially minor figures—Ainsworth and Bulwer-Lytton, Philip James Bailey, the author of *Festus* (1839), Adelaide Procter, and Martin Tupper, whose *Proverbial Philosophy* of 1838 sold thousands of copies.

### MORAL TALES, PETER PARLEY, AND HARRIET MARTINEAU

It is tempting to see much of the children's literature of the period as equally disappointing. The tradition of the didactic moral tale, often fiercely evangelical, continued to flourish, with Mrs Cameron, Mary Belson Elliott, and Maria Hack being typical. Hack's *Harry Beaufoy; or, The Pupil of Nature* (1821), for example, tells how a mother teaches her son about natural phenomena, and encourages him to deduce the existence of God from them. Mrs Sherwood continued her prolific career.

Yet, although many writers of moral tales had roots in the Evangelical tradition and expressed a fundamental belief in the Christian faith and the needs of children to follow it or risk damnation, there were some signs that the Evangelical movement was changing character. The values of Bible-reading, church-attendance, and following a Christian sense of duty were everywhere asserted, but some writers were beginning to articulate their religious teaching within a denser social context than earlier writers had attempted. Though the daughter and wife of a clergyman, Alicia Catherine Mant is distinctly more secular than evangelical in *The Cottage in the Chalk-Pit* (1822), an account of a family's struggles after their father becomes destitute.

The anonymous *Life and Adventures of Lady Anne* (*c*.1826) combined praise of the young heroine's conduct under testing circumstances with a picture of the wretched treatment of orphans at the time, in order to impress upon the minds of young readers the need to show gratitude for the blessings of parents and to teach obedience to them. This lively picaresque owes something to Defoe's *Moll Flanders* (1722) and points forward to Dickens's *Oliver Twist* (1838), not least in its fortuitous denouement, and the story introduces the reader to a wide social range—clergymen, the school-mistress, gardeners, shopkeepers, pedlars—and also offers more than a glimpse of the Protestant work ethic. Not only is the reader assured that 'honesty is the best policy' and that kindness is right, but also that it is likely to be rewarded financially, for the Earl goes round at the end of the story giving handsome presents to the poor but sympathetic individuals who helped Anne in her distress.

Barbara Hofland had always displayed a social awareness in her simple moral tales, almost from the publication of her first story *The History of an Officer's Widow* in 1809. For this the vicissitudes of her long, hard, and ultimately heroic life are almost certainly responsible. Not surprisingly, her tales often depict a moving picture of family life; ordinary people, frequently children or adolescents, struggle in adverse circumstances (such as bankruptcy or the death of parents) to maintain their integrity and Christian values, and at the same time exercise all kinds of economic ingenuity to support themselves. *The Son of a Genius* (1812) and *The Blind Farmer and his Children* (1816) are earlier examples of Mrs Hofland's belief that the practice of Christian virtues in business affairs can lead to financial security, and later works, such as *Elizabeth and her Three Beggar Boys* (1833), have similar preoccupations.

When she writes of women and work she does so with real conviction and no little originality. A firm advocate of marriage, she often demonstrates in her stories how harassed wives and widows can reveal unexpected strength and ability at a time of crisis. In *Decision* (1824) Mrs Hofland came near to writing a feminist novel, for when Maria learns that her father has squandered his wife's fortune as well as his own, the teenage girl borrows £6 from a friend and sets herself up as an iron-merchant. Maria prospers and continues in business after she could have sold out and returned to her ladylike former way of life. She turns down two proposals of marriage, preferring to go on living with her mother and running the company on her own. For Maria is an early example of the career-woman, and *Decision* is almost a subversive book.

Mrs Tonna, who wrote under the name of 'Charlotte Elizabeth', was another author of moral tales whose work exhibits considerable social

Mrs Hofland was born in Sheffield in 1770. After her first husband died she married an impecunious artist, and often drew upon the hardships of her own life in her moral tales for children.

awareness. One of the major concerns of the Evangelical movement was the abolition of slavery, and when the transportation of slaves was abolished in 1807, debate turned to the question of how slaves were to be prepared for their freedom. In *Perseverance; or, Walter and his Little School* (1826) Charlotte Elizabeth tells the story of Mr Shirley, a wealthy West Indian planter, and his family. Despite the hostility of an older brother and the doubts of his father, 14-year-old Walter so successfully runs a school for the Christian education of negro children that he converts the critics and sceptics to the cause, and the story ends with an appeal for funds to open more schools. Though the author's motives are not entirely altruistic (she suggests that the education of negroes will not only be Christian but make them work more effectively for their masters), her book sounds a more radical note than many earlier tales.

By the 1840s several writers were beginning to develop the tract-like form of the didactic moral tale in the direction of the more complex and psychologically realistic novel. In the third volume of Mrs Sherwood's *History of the Fairchild Family* (published in 1847), for example, the mellower tone and the occasional vein of comedy are nearer to the domestic novels of Charlotte M. Yonge than to Mrs Sherwood's earliest books. Elizabeth Sewell spent her whole life on the Isle of Wight, where she taught and produced many devotional books and stories for children which were more strongly influenced by the Oxford Movement than by the early Evangelicals. *Amy Herbert* (1844) is one of her best works, illustrating the author's ideas of how the Christian faith was or might be practised in many middle-class homes. The story is scrupulously written and the remorse of Rosa's older sister and her responsibility for her sister's death are discussed with an almost Jamesian subtlety.

Harriet Mozley is even more remarkable. The eldest sister of John Henry Newman, she produced a number of children's books, including *The Fairy Bower; or, The History of a Month* (1841), *The Lost Brooch; or, The History of Another Month* (1841) and *Family Adventures* (1852), of which the first is the most rewarding. The title of the book suggests that it is a fantasy, but Harriet Mozley makes clear in her opening pages that she is in fact

*The Child's Companion.* Launched by the Religious Tract Society in 1824, this penny monthly was aimed mainly at Sunday-school children, and concentrated on stories about the apostles and Christian homilies, though it also contained some secular material.

THE

CHILD'S COMPANION;

OR,

*Sunday Scholar's Reward.*

No. 40.]    APRIL, 1835.    [VOL. 4.

See page 100.

ST. JAMES.

OF our Saviour's apostles, two bore the name of James, and they have been distinguished, probably on account of their age, as James

NEW SERIES.    E

trying 'to represent characters as they really are, [rather] than to exhibit moral portraiture for unreserved imitation or avoidance'. In this realistic domestic story the children are often left to their own devices, enjoying lots of jokes, skating, and frequently arguing over the rights and wrongs of their own behaviour. At the centre of the novel the children prepare for their Twelfth Night party, and Grace has the idea of decorating an ante-room in the house with plants and flowers to transform it into a 'fairy bower'. The 'fairy bower' functions rather like the performance of *Lovers' Vows* in *Mansfield Park*, exposing a variety of moral attitudes, and, although the story also discusses the question of the education of upper-class children, it is the sensitivity and intensity of feeling with which the vibrations of its delicate moral web are teased out that give the book its unique quality.

In the wake of the Evangelical movement, juvenile religious periodicals had appeared as early as 1815, and in 1824 two remarkable magazines began publication. The *Children's Friend* was started by an Anglican, the Revd W. Carus Wilson, who is often identified with Charlotte Brontë's portrait of Mr Brocklehurst in *Jane Eyre*. A stern religious tone pervaded this penny magazine. The early monthly numbers, with tales of children making pious deaths in the Janeway tradition, with prayers, and Christian poems, often quote Mrs Trimmer and Mrs Sherwood approvingly. Indeed the spirit of the Fairchild family walks through its pages.

When the *Child's Companion; or, Sunday Scholar's Reward* was launched by the Religious Tract Society, the Society already had ten years' experience of publishing tracts for children, and George Stokes, the first editor, brought a broadened perspective to the magazine: this penny monthly, as well as containing prayers, accounts of the apostles, and Christian homilies, also showed some signs of secular interest. Geographical and historical information is conveyed through an account of Tyre and Sidon, for example, while an article on 'Country Pictures' consists of a dialogue between a father and son on the techniques of drawing pictures of the countryside. The Christian tone continued to dominate, but it was less evangelical and less overtly didactic. Four years after it started, the *Child's Companion* had achieved a monthly circulation of 20,000 copies, and the magazine survived under various titles until 1932.

The *Youth's Magazine; or, Evangelical Miscellany* had been started in 1815 by the 18-year-old William Lloyd of the Sunday School Union. But, although Evangelical in origin and containing Christian homilies and information about Sunday schools, by the 1820s this monthly magazine also contained articles on classical mythology, poetry by John Clare, and a scientific account of conchology. Obviously aimed at an older readership than the *Children's Friend*, the *Youth's Magazine* faintly exudes the urbane and scholarly flavour of such adult periodicals as the *Gentleman's Magazine*.

The *Children's Weekly Visitor*, which began in 1832, is another sign of the way the religious climate was changing. Its first number describes the Beaumont family with six children ranging in age from teenagers to infants, and declares its intention of giving a weekly account of how these young people 'amused or instructed themselves during their leisure hours'. There are articles on how to draw on slate and on the importance of watering plants; Mr Beaumont tells his children something of the history of British rule in India, and Charlotte, the eldest child, submits a poem about 'The Snowdrop'. Although each weekly number ends with a specific religious item in which the parents usually explain an episode from the Bible to their children, the tone is more pedagogic and secular than other periodicals, as if reflecting the changes that were occurring in Britain in the 1830s.

Indeed by 1849 even the *Children's Friend* was changing. Influenced by the enormous expansion of missionary work overseas and by the growing interest in the British empire, it now published 'Anecdotes from Mrs. Ward's Travels in Kaffirland', 'The Way they Boil Kettles in Iceland', and an account of a British regiment's exploits in India. Little sermons and stories about pious children can still be found, but there are unmistakable changes of contents and emphasis: the essays on crocodiles, volcanoes, and 'whalefish' are less morally didactic and more secular than earlier items. An account of Chamouny in Switzerland, for example, in June 1849, is entirely descriptive and geological. 'Mary's Gleanings for the Sunday School' and articles on 'Little Sins' continue, but the influence of Samuel Goodrich, alias 'Peter Parley', the popular American writer, is apparent.

'Parley's' success did not pass unnoticed in Britain. Goodrich's work struck a deeply responsive note, and many of the American's works were published in Britain, with or without his permission. Indeed F. J. Harvey Darton identified no fewer than six different authors in England who issued books for profit under Goodrich's pseudonym—William Martin, George Mogridge, Thomas Tegg, Charles Tilt, Edward Lacey, and Samuel Clark.

One of the most striking aspects of Goodrich's impact upon British children's literature was the success of two periodicals—*Peter Parley's Magazine* and *Peter Parley's Annual*, although William Martin edited many numbers of the *Magazine*, and Goodrich was not directly involved with either. The *Magazine*, published monthly from 1839 to 1863, contained a mixture of articles about history, travel, and other factual topics, and the parts were bound together and later published as the *Annual*, usually bound in red cloth with attractive gilt decorations, which ran from 1840 to 1892.

The contents of both the *Magazine* and the *Annual* are strikingly varied. They usually contain a mixture of historical articles ('Tales of the British Navy'), natural history ('Martins and Swallows'), and moral tales about schoolboys, wicked uncles, and Cornish wreckers. But such tales usually in-

*Facing*: refinements in book design; an example of a decorated endpaper from 1763. *Little Red Riding Hood* (inset) is one of the stories collected by Perrault, and first published in English in 1729. This edition was produced in 1804 by Benjamin Tabart, who was responsible for versions of many fairy-tales aimed specifically at children.

MOORE Newgate Street LONDON

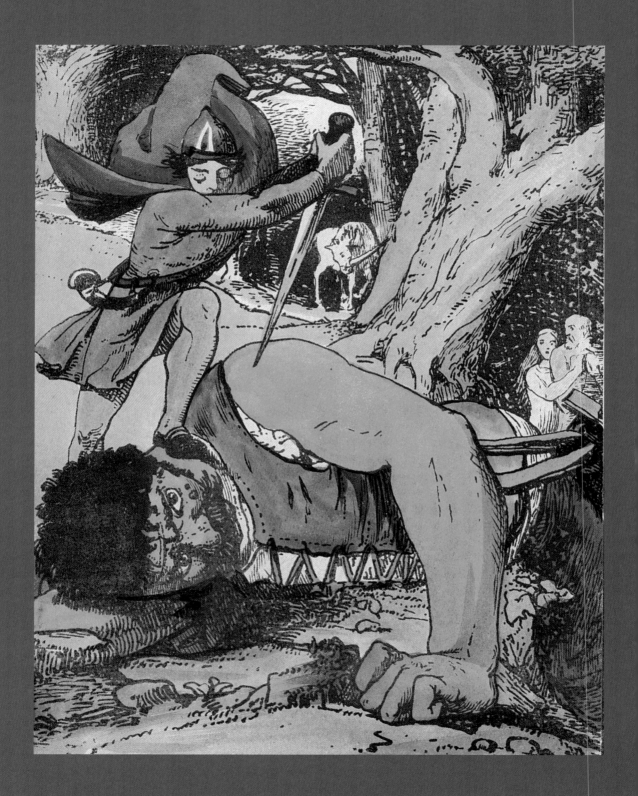

clude factual information often introduced in a laboured way. For example, 'A Tale of Youthful Courage', about two boys captured by Red Indians near the Hudson River (*Peter Parley's Magazine*, 1844), begins by comparing the Hudson with the rivers Thames, Loire, Tagus, and Ganges. *Peter Parley's Annual* can surprise us with the occasional poem or ghost story, and the Editor certainly hopes that children will read it 'with pleasure and profit', but the majority of articles assert the primacy of factual information. Essays about 'Uncle John's visit to the Polytechnic Institute, Regent Street' and on civil engineering in 'The Thames Tunnel' reflect the dominance of utilitarianism in an age which had seen the establishment of the Society for the Diffusion of Useful Knowledge in 1827 and the British Society for the Advancement of Science in 1831.

Juvenile books of instruction had always been popular. *Mangall's Questions* had been frequently reprinted from 1800 along with many similar books, but the works of Peter Parley and his imitators intensified that development, and shifted works of fact and information to the centre of publications for children. Catherine Sinclair was one of the first to rebel against this utilitarian tendency, and her revolt has given her story *Holiday House* (1839) an almost legendary status. In the preface she criticizes the way in which children have one side of their nature almost starved by an over-regard for instruction. 'In this age of wonderful mechanical inventions,' she says, 'the very mind of youth seems in danger of becoming a machine; and while every effort is used to stuff the memory, like a cricket-ball, with well-known facts and ready-made opinions, no room is left for the vigour of natural feeling, the glow of natural genius, and the ardour of natural enthusiasm.'

The daughter of Sir John Sinclair, Catherine grew up in Edinburgh in a large, well-informed family—most of whom became fervently evangelical—and began writing at an early age. *Holiday House* is much more conventional in form than its reputation as a literary milestone would suggest. It is really a very moral and religious tale about the maturing of two children, Harry and Laura Graham, finally achieved after the death of their older brother, which is described in the manner of many Victorian novels.

What gives the story its freshness, however, is the sprightly and sympathetic manner with which Catherine Sinclair describes the exploits of the children in the first half of the story. For the children are brought up by their grandmother and kindly Uncle David after their mother has died and their father has been sent abroad, and, although they get into various scrapes—breaking china, causing a fire, spoiling a dress—for which they are punished by their governess, their grandmother and uncle are remarkably forgiving, once they are satisfied that the children's behaviour is thoughtless rather than deliberately wicked.

The degree of toleration shown towards the children is truly astonishing,

*Facing*: in the 1840s hand colouring was being replaced by chromolithography, or, often more crudely, by wood blocking. This version of *Jack the Giant-Killer*–a story with ancient origins, but first printed in 1711–dates from 1845.

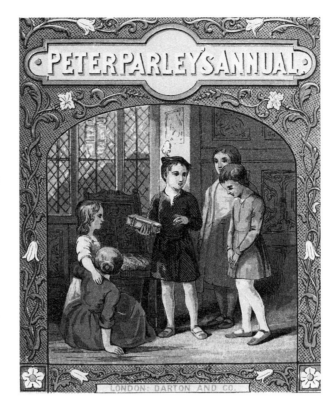

*Right*: *Peter Parley's Annual* (1849). Often attractively illustrated and colourfully bound, this annual was published in English from 1840 to 1892, but its aim was to instruct as well as to please children.

*Below*: *Something about Building*. This article from the British *Peter Parley's Annual* for 1849 illustrates the didactic and utilitarian features characteristic of 'Peter Parleyism'.

## Something about Building.

WHAT a strange thing it would be if we had no houses to live in, and were forced to sleep on the tops of trees, in caves, or among the clefts and crannies of rocks and mountains. Many ages ago, mankind, then in a savage state, were obliged to make use of such wild retreats. They had not learned to build houses, and were, in this respect, not so well off as the birds, which, you know, mostly manage to build a nice warm nest, in which they bring up their young.

The first houses were, in all probability, cut out of the sides of crags, or banks; after this, it was found, perhaps, more advantageous to build them of branches of trees, set up an end, and leaning together in a point at the top. Marabee houses were also made of the skins of beasts, stretched over a pole, of a similar form. These were the earliest tents; but how long it is ago since the eastern nations,

who were the first inhabitants of this earth, had such kinds of habitations, is not known.

We know that, at the present day, all savage nations have such houses. The Icelanders build theirs of snow; and the inhabitants of America, of the South-sea Islands, of the wilds of Africa, and New Holland, form their huts in the rudest manner. We know, also, that the Irish mud cabins, the Scotch hovels, and some of the English cottages, are not a great deal better than the huts of savages.

But if you look at such buildings as the one here represented, you will find them to be very different from the rude hut, wigwam, or snow house; you will observe that they are much larger, and of greater beauty. The finest buildings are temples, which are generally of larger dimensions than houses. The temples of rude nations were, however, as rude as their dwellings; for they sometimes consisted of a number of upright stones fixed in the ground, with another on the top, the whole enclosing an immense circle.

considering when the book was first published. (Would Mr Fairchild have been so understanding about the fire Harry starts by playing with a candle?) But the mood of the story gradually deepens from the accounts of the young children's high-spirited exploits in the first half of the book, especially when they encounter a soldier's widow and a poor beggar boy in the later chapters, even before the tragedy of Frank's death at the end.

Yet all this is a long way from the prosy and pedantic children's stories which dominated children's literature in the 1830s, and the gentle humour of Uncle David, when the children organize a disastrous tea-party or damage a table, is unexpectedly appealing. He even tells the children a deliberately nonsensical story about giants and fairies, though it has a moral point. In its combination of earnestness, high spirits, and tolerance of the nature of real children, *Holiday House* stands out as one of the first books to exhibit some of the characteristics of Victorian children's literature, and if Uncle David is not as witty as Lewis Carroll he is not unlike Albert-next-door's uncle in Nesbit's *The Treasure Seekers*.

Harriet Martineau's works for children also show how far tastes were beginning to change. Born in 1802, the seventh child of a prosperous Unitarian family, Harriet experienced an unhappy childhood, and suffered from deafness and other ailments for most of her adult life. A true child of the era dominated by utilitarianism and Useful Knowledge, Harriet first made her name with *Illustrations of Political Economy* (1832–4), a series of tracts designed to enlighten the poorer members of society about the principles of economics. A comparison with Hannah More's religious Cheap Repository Tracts shows how society had become more secular over three decades.

But there was always a degree of tension between reason and the imagination in Harriet Martineau's work, and, although her early children's stories, such as *Five Years of Youth; or, Sense and Sentiment* (1831), are rather diagrammatic moral tales, there are signs of a more imaginative treatment of children in them, especially of those in difficult circumstances, which were most successfully realized in *The Playfellow*.

*The Playfellow* consists of four stories, published quarterly in 1841: *The Settlers at Home*, *The Peasant and the Prince*, *Feats on the Fiord*, and *The Crofton Boys*. *The Settlers at Home*, a Robinsonnade set in seventeenth-century Lincolnshire, is about the ordeal of some young children when sudden floods separate them from their parents and maroon them on high ground. The situation is desperate and the baby dies, but the children cope with courage and ingenuity until they are rescued. *The Peasant and the Prince* really consists of two short stories of eighteenth-century France, one an anecdote about the young Marie-Antoinette, the other a bleak account of the short life of the Dauphin, who died aged 10 in 1795; there is more angry history than imaginative writing in these sad tales.

*Feats on the Fiord* is the imaginative *tour de force* of the series, however. Set in eighteenth-century Norway, the main story describes the adventures of Odda, a mischievous but brave herdboy, and Erica, a timid, superstitious maid, when Erica's lover Rolf disappears, and their small rural community is threatened by pirates. The landscape of mountains and waters is vividly realized, and in the treatment of Erica and her superstitious fears Harriet Martineau not only reveals her insights into endurance under stress, but also urges greater understanding and tolerance from more dogmatic believers.

*The Crofton Boys*, the last tale in the series, is an early example of the school story, about the exploits of 8-year-old Hugh Proctor when he joins his older brother Philip at Crofton School. A bright, lively boy, Hugh lacks concentration and purpose at first, and is easily led into mischief, but gradually learns to study and make good friends. As the result of an accident, however, Hugh's foot is badly crushed and has to be amputated, and the second half of the story focuses upon his struggles to become reconciled to his new situation. Though the tale is too explicitly didactic, and there is just a hint of the Protestant work ethic about Hugh's material reward at the end, George Eliot confessed to some 'delightful crying' over *The Crofton Boys*, and Elizabeth Barrett praised *The Playfellow* as a whole for its 'fine heroic child-spirit'.

### FAIRY-TALES, FANTASIES, AND HANS ANDERSEN

History, of course, is never quite so tidy as the telling of it, and despite the dominance of the moral tales or works inspired by Peter Parley during this period, works of the imagination including fairy-tales continued to be published. The brothers Grimm's folk-tales, first translated into English by Edgar Taylor and published as *German Popular Stories* in 1823, led to other publications such as T. W. Croker's *Fairy Legends and Traditions of the South of Ireland* (1825–8). The quality of the scholarship of Jacob and Wilhelm Grimm has been challenged in recent years, and some readers have found their material too disturbing for children, but the richness and variety of the brothers' collection, containing such tales as 'Rumpelstiltskin' and 'Snow White', has never been surpassed. Ironically the rehabilitation of fairy-tales was beginning at the very moment when children were being discouraged from reading them and being offered books of information in their place.

The great revival in chapbook literature encouraged by James Catnach had kept alive the tradition of fairy-tales and nursery rhymes at the beginning of the century, but later publications, such as those of George Mogridge, were little more than religious tracts. There is considerable evidence, however, that chapbooks, which carried on the tradition of romances, nursery rhymes, and fairy-tales, continued to be published, especially in the provinces. Houlston of Wellington, though mainly a publisher of evangelical works, advertised

*Rumpel-stilts-kin.* First translated into English by Edgar Taylor in 1823, the Brothers Grimm's *Popular Stories* were brilliantly complemented by George Cruikshank's black-and-white illustrations.

*Amusing Tales, Christmas Amusements,* and *The History of Sir Richard Whittington and his Cat* in 1825, while John Rusher of Banbury and James Kendrew of York both made determined efforts to improve the design and illustrations of chapbooks. Rusher, for instance, used George Cruickshank to illustrate his version of *Jack & Jill, and Old Dame Gill c.*1830. Kendrew's many publications between 1815 and 1841 include *Adventures of the Beautiful Little Maid Cinderilla, The Entertaining Story of Little Red Riding Hood, The History of Jack the Giant-Killer,* and *The Surprising Adventures of Puss in Boots.* Orlando Hodgson, active in London from 1832 to 1835, advertised among his penny publications for 'The Young Gentleman's Library' a version of *Robin Hood,* and in 'The Young Lady's Library' *The Children in the Wood,* a retelling of the very old story of 'The Babes of the Wood'. Although such publications tend to be bald, if robust, narratives, their publication suggests that

traditional folk-and fairy-tales continued to survive in the popular subculture of the 1820s and 1830s, even if the middle classes (ostensibly) concentrated upon more improving literature.

Catherine Sinclair was not the only rebel against the utilitarian tendency, however, for in 1842 Sir Henry Cole published his blast against Peter Parley and his monstrous regiment in the prospectus to *The Home Treasury*:

The character of most Children's Books published during the last quarter of a century is fairly typified in the name of Peter Parley, which the writers of some hundreds of them have assumed. The books themselves have been addressed after a narrow fashion almost entirely to the cultivation of the understanding of children. The many tales sung or said from time immemorial, which appealed to the other, and certainly not less important elements of a little child's mind, its fancy, imagination, sympathies, affections, are almost all gone out of memory, and are scarcely to be obtained . . . That the influence of all this is hurtful to children, the conductor of this series firmly believes. He has practical experience of it every day in his own family, and he doubts not that there are many others who entertain the same opinions as himself. He purposes at least to give some evidence of his belief, and to produce a series of Works, the character of which may be briefly described as anti-Peter Parleyism.

Peter Parley books were usually illustrated with competent but small wood engravings, the form which was often used instead of copper or steel. George Cruikshanks's etchings to the *Popular Stories* by the Brothers Grimm, and Newman and Dean and Munday's coloured editions of such works as *Dame Wiggin of Lee* (1823) were among the more attractively illustrated works of the period. But despite the steady improvement in book production in the 1830s and 1840s, the illustrated children's books of the period were distinguished more by technical proficiency than quality or style until the appearance of Sir Henry Cole.

Cole was a very remarkable man. For many years he worked as a civil servant in the Public Record Office, and later became involved with the creation of the Great Exhibition, the Albert Hall, and the South Kensington Museum. Deeply interested in art, and dismayed by children's books of the time, he developed a plan to produce books which would delight and amuse children. (He and his wife had three sons and five daughters.)

Under the pseudonym of 'Felix Summerly', Cole announced the publication of 'The Home Treasury of Books, Pictures, Toys, &c. purposed to cultivate the Affections, Fancy, Imagination, and Taste of Children', and, employing the best artists and printers he could find, he began issuing such stories as *Jack the Giant-Killer* and *Little Red Riding Hood* from 1843 onwards. Published by Joseph Cundall, the booklets sold separately at 1*s.* in plain or 2*s.* 6*d.* in coloured versions; the series also contained such delights as a *Colour Box for Little Painters* and a Box of Terra Cotta Bricks.

Cole considered the visual quality of the books most important and he employed such artists as William Mulready and John Linnell to illustrate them. After the first few titles were coloured by hand, the colour plates were printed, and were amongst the first children's books ever to have colour-printed illustrations. The stories themselves were attractively printed with coloured ornamental covers designed by Cole himself after patterns by Holbein. *The Home Treasury* series had the most distinguished design treatment ever given to children's books up to this time.

They are still a joy to look at, but it has to be said that Cole's retelling of the famous tales is rarely more than competent. Surprisingly, given the declared aim of the series, to appeal to the imagination rather than the understanding, many of the tales are prefaced by scholarly introductions explaining their historical origins, and a strong moral and didactic thread runs through many of the narratives. In *Jack and the Beanstalk*, for example, a fairy appears to Jack at the end to tell him that she made the beanstalk grow to such an amazing height to see if he would have the courage to climb it, or prefer to remain idle and lazy. In *Little Red Riding Hood* Cole stresses the little girl's moral and religious qualities throughout, and, telling the reader how much he dislikes the traditionally violent climax, offers an alternative happy ending in which the virtuous heroine is rescued by her father.

If the stories in *The Home Treasury* do not read today quite like the *jeux d'esprit* Cole intended, their publication undoubtedly made a welcome contrast to Peter Parley's works. Reprints soon followed and many of the original titles were collected together into larger volumes, selling at higher prices. *Popular Fairy Tales*, for example, which contained 'Jack the Giant-Killer', 'The Sleeping Beauty', and 'Cinderella', sold at 3*s.* 6*d.*

From 1845, furthermore, W. J. Thoms, under the pseudonym of 'Ambrose Merton', produced many versions of the old chapbook stories and ballads for children in a series entitled *Gammer Gurton's Story Books*. This series, which included such titles as *The Gallant History of Bevis of Southampton* and *The Sweet and Pleasant History of Patient Grissell*, was published by Cundall and printed by Whittingham, again in separate booklets with gaily ornamented stiff paper covers and coloured frontispieces by such artists as John Absolon and Frederick Tayler.

These booklets were republished as a bound volume called *The Old Story Books of England*, and various other collections of the stories followed, until in 1859 Sampson Low published *The Home Treasury of Old Story Books*, which claimed to contain all the fairy-tales from *The Home Treasury* and all the *Old Story Books of England*. Other scholars contributed to the process, such as J. O. Halliwell, who produced his *Popular Rhymes and Nursery Tales* in 1849, but it was mainly Cole and Thoms who rescued much of the material previously relegated to chapbooks, and restored fairy-tales and old stories to the

*The Sweet and Pleasant History of Patient Grissel.* Under the pseudonym of 'Ambrose Merton', W. J. Thoms published traditional stories for children from 1845 onwards. This dramatic frontispiece, with its emphasis on romantic adventure, promises something very different from Peter Parley's publications.

children of the middle classes. Thackeray's praise in *Fraser's Magazine* is eloquent testimony:

One cannot help looking with secret envy on the children of the present day, for whose use and entertainment a thousand ingenious and beautiful things are provided which were quite unknown some few score of years since, when the present writer and reader were very possibly in the nursery state. Abominable attempts were made in those days to make useful books for children, and cram science down their throats as calomel used to be administered under the pretence of a spoonful of current-jelly . . .

The mere sight of the little books produced by Mr. Cundall—of whom some thirty now lie upon my table—is as good as a nosegay. Their actual covers are as brilliant as a bed of tulips, and blaze with emerald, and orange, and cobalt, and gold, and crimson. I envy the feelings of the young person for whom . . . this collection of treasures is destined. Here are fairy tales, at last, with real pictures to them. What a library!—what a picture gallery!

The rise of Victorian fantasy, with its use of the supernatural and invention of secondary worlds, is clearly related to this revival of interest in fairy-tales and the Romantic movement's earlier unease at the primacy of rationalism.

90

The growing interest in modern fantasy can also be related to a number of other developments from the beginning of the nineteenth century, such as the popularity of Gothic novels—*Frankenstein* was published in 1818—and advances in visual technology which enabled the Strand theatre to offer such spectacular productions as *The Bay of Naples and the Recent Eruption of Mount Vesuvius*. The popularity of 'Toy Theatres' at this time with their sometimes dramatic stage effects may also have contributed to the process. The tradition of animal fantasies, stretching as far back as Aesop, had always been popular, as the success of *The Butterfly's Ball* and its imitations had shown, while Dickens's *Oliver Twist* (1838) and *A Christmas Carol* (1843) combined elements of the grotesque and supernatural and comic with a genius which swept Britain. Finally, recent archaeological discoveries of the remains of an iguanodon and a megalosaurus also aroused public interest in the existence of extraordinary, almost legendary, creatures.

Whether as a direct result of these developments or because the great interest in these events signalled a changing of consciousness, the Victorian public gradually became more sympathetic to works of fantasy. Not surprisingly, one of their earliest exponents was a genuine child of the Romantic movement. Sara Coleridge was the daughter of the great poet, and a remarkable person in her own right. A linguist, minor poet, and editor of her father's works, only poor health prevented her achieving a more substantial reputation. As it is, her one full-length fantasy, *Phantasmion* (1837), remains an extraordinary monument to her talent. This long and mysterious story about the adventures of Phantasmion, king of Palmland, and his search for Princess Iarnine from the neighbouring kingdom of Rockland, teems with romantic elements—rival lovers, wicked opponents, and supernatural spirits. The climax comes when Phantasmion confronts treacherous King Magnart and the evil counsellor Glandreth in a great battle. Magnart is killed and Oloola, goddess of the clouds and winds, strikes Glandreth with lightning. Phantasmion and his allies are victorious and the lovers are united at last.

Begun for Sara's 6-year-old son, the story is too labyrinthine and the language too elaborate for most children, even though Sara later suggested that it might appeal to teenagers. Owing something to Spenser and Milton and especially Sidney's *Arcadia*, it perhaps stands nearest to Keats's *Endymion*, particularly in its lyrical poems. Weak in characterization but strong in invention and atmosphere, the story hints at an allegorical meaning which Sara denied, though her tale constantly identifies virtue with nature and natural phenomena. 'If you ask me', she told her brother Derwent, 'what advantage a young person could possibly derive from such a tissue of unrealities, I should say that every work of fancy in its degree, and according to the merit of its execution, feeds and expands the mind; whenever the poetical beauty of things is vividly displayed, truth is exhibited, and thus the imagination of the

The title-page of *Phantasmion*. Sara Coleridge, daughter of the poet S. T. Coleridge, wrote this extraordinary fantasy for her 6-year-old son in 1837. The Bodleian Library copy bears Sara's inscription to William Wordsworth's daughter Dora.

youthful reader is stimulated to find truth for itself.' *Phantasmion* was a remarkable pioneering fantasy, and nothing like it was to appear until the work of George MacDonald.

F. E. Paget edited *The Juvenile Englishman's Library* published in twenty-one volumes between 1844 and 1849. *The Hope of the Katzekopfs: A Fairy Tale* appeared in 1844. 'The book was published', Paget wrote, 'to ascertain whether a race that has been glutted with Peter Parley, and Penny Magazines, and suchlike stories of (so called) useful knowledge, will condescend to read a Fable and its morals, and learn wisdom from a Tale of Enchantment.'

The story opens with a brilliant description of a royal christening, and the invention, light-heartedness, and authorial exuberance strike a truly fresh note:

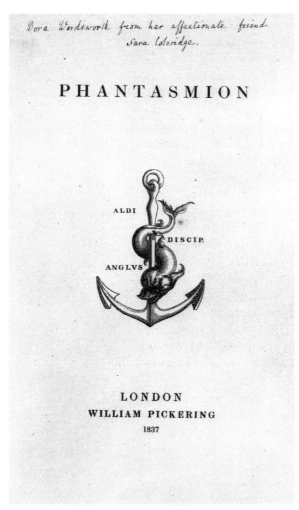

*Dora Wordsworth from her affectionate friend Sara Coleridge.*

PHANTASMION

ALDI

DISCIP.

ANGLVS

LONDON
WILLIAM PICKERING
1837

So when Queen Ninnilinda had an heir, the nation almost went beside itself with joy. The church bells rang till they cracked; the guns of the citadel were firing till they grew so hot they went off of themselves; oxen were roasted whole in the great square (my dear reader, never attempt to roast an ox *whole*, either on your own birthday or on that of anybody else; the thing is an impossibility, half the meat is sure to be raw, and the other half burnt, and so good beef is spoiled); the two chief conduits of the city no longer poured forth water, but one spouted out cowslip-wine, and the other raspberry vinegar; the lake in front of the palace was filled with small beer (this, however, was a failure, as it killed the fish, and folks said that the beer tasted muddy); an air balloon hovered over the principal streets, and showered down caraway comfits and burnt almonds; Punch was exhibited all day for nothing; the prisons were all thrown open, and everybody paid the debts of everybody else.

Unfortunately King Katzekopf and Queen Ninnilinda forget to invite great-aunt Lady Abracadabra to the christening, and she decrees that the baby prince shall be named Eigenwillig (self-willed) and be a wilful child. Brought up by his foolish mother and indolent father, the young prince's selfish behaviour is contrasted with that of Witikind, the modest and likeable son of Count Rodolpho.

As the story develops, it increasingly turns

into a didactic moral tale with more than a flavour of *Sandford and Merton* and *The Pilgrim's Progress*, particularly in the closing chapters when Eigenwillig begins to learn wisdom from an old man called Discipline and literally sheds a heavy burden from his shoulders. The prince reforms and, instead of being called the Hope of the Katzekopfs, becomes known as King Katzekopf the Good. Though a long way from *Alice*, the tone and invention of the early chapters gives Paget's book an honourable place in the history of Victorian fantasy.

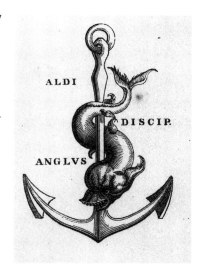

R. H. Horne, poet, journalist, and adventurer, was already collaborating with Mary Gillies on a series of small books for nursery children when, during the winter of 1844, he wrote a genial Christmas story, *The Good-Natured Bear* (1846), 'A Story for Children of all Ages'. Set in Germany, the tale takes on the flavour of fantasy when a friendly bear joins Doctor Littlepump and his children, and proceeds to tell them the story of his life. The comic mystery is only explained at the end of the tale, when the bear discards his disguise and reveals himself as the children's uncle, who had dressed up to woo their governess.

Horne's *Memoirs of a London Doll* (1846) is even more attractive, and in the autobiography of Maria Poppet, a jointed wooden doll made by Mr Spratt of High Holborn, Horne created a real character. A toy, except for her intelligence and powers of speech, Maria vividly describes her adventures as she passes from one owner to another through all London's social strata. Robert Browning admired Horne's talents—'He has unmistakable genius, and is a fine, honest, enthusiastic, chivalrous fellow,' he told Elizabeth Barrett. With its combination of imaginative invention, humour, and shrewd social observation *Memoirs of a London Doll* has deservedly become a minor classic. By comparison, Mark Lemon's *The Enchanted Doll: A Fairy Tale for Little People*, which appeared three years later, appears too grimly moralistic, although it is another indication of the way a fresh literary breeze was beginning to blow.

There was a great deal of pleasant, innocuous poetry written during the period, much of it of a quasi-pastoral kind in a line running from the Taylors via Elizabeth Turner to Sara Coleridge and William and Mary Howitt. This simple, unpretentious verse in its choice of diction and subject-matter at least reveals the new awareness of children in the nineteenth century, and it is hard to dislike such poems as Sara Coleridge's 'Trees' or the boisterous 'Wind in a Frolic' by William Howitt:

> The wind one morning sprang up from sleep,
> Saying, 'Now for a frolic! now for a leap!
> Now for a mad-cap, galloping chase!
> I'll make a commotion in every place!'

But most of the poems about wild flowers or birds or animals are remarkably unmemorable, usually working towards a well-worn moral conclusion. 'The Spider and the Fly' by William's wife Mary Howitt is one of the best-known exceptions. Mrs Alexander's *Hymns for Little Children* (1848) is uniquely successful in combining religious feeling with breath-taking simplicity:

> There is a green hill far away,
> Without a city wall,
> Where the dear Lord was crucified
> Who died to save us all.

Many poets were able to write comic verse, particularly in the field of nonsense. Richard Sharpe, said to have been a grocer in Bishopsgate, is sometimes credited with writing *Dame Wiggin of Lee and her Seven Wonderful Cats* (1823), an illustrated humorous verse-tale in the style of *Old Mother Hubbard*. Sharpe may also have contributed to the popularity of the limerick, for although, as we have seen, its first appearance had been in *The History of Sixteen Wonderful Old Women* in 1820, Sharpe reputedly wrote the *Anecdotes and Adventures of Fifteen Gentlemen*, published by John Marshall, *c*.1821.

This portrait of Edward Lear from the National Portrait Gallery was drawn by Wilhelm Marstrand when Lear was at his happiest while painting in Italy in 1840.

It was this book which inspired Edward Lear, while he was staying at Knowsley Hall, drawing the animals in Lord Stanley's menagerie, to write and draw for the children. Lear was a unique phenomenon. The twentieth child of a stockbroker, he had an unhappy childhood, and was subject to attacks of depression and epilepsy throughout his life. Despite poor eyesight, he was a talented artist, but it was his children's books, *A Book of Nonsense* (1846), *More Nonsense* (1872), and *Laughable Lyrics* (1877), which gave him lasting fame, particularly for such surrealistically absurd narrative poems as 'The Owl and the Pussy-cat' and 'The Pobble who has No Toes'. The rhythms of the verse, word coinages such as the 'runcible spoon', and Lear's use of extravagant imagery are wonderfully effective, even though a note of unease, almost panic, can often be felt even in the slightest lyrics:

There was an old lady of Chertsey,
Who made a remarkable curtsey;
She twirled round and round,
Till she sank underground,
Which distressed all the people of Chertsey.

Robert Browning's version of 'The Pied Piper of Hamelin', written in 1842 to amuse the son of his friend the actor William Macready, is a *tour de force*, and the tale of how an unfairly treated piper led away all but one of the children of Hamelin was soon established as a children's classic and reprinted in numerous illustrated editions.

The German writer Heinrich Hoffmann achieved a similar popular success with his collection of comic cautionary tales in verse *Struwwelpeter*, translated into English in 1848 as *The English Struwwelpeter*. Hoffmann wrote the poems as a present for his 3-year-old son one Christmas when he could find nothing to his liking in the bookshops, and produced a collection of comical awful warnings about children, such as silly Augustus who did not like soup, accompanied by his own exaggeratedly expressive drawings. But, though the book, sometimes retitled *Shockheaded Peter*, was im-

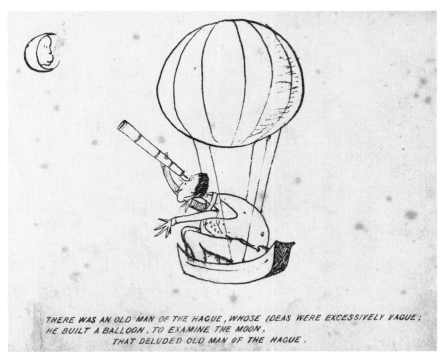

THERE WAS AN OLD MAN OF THE HAGUE, WHOSE IDEAS WERE EXCESSIVELY VAGUE;
HE BUILT A BALLOON, TO EXAMINE THE MOON,
THAT DELUDED OLD MAN OF THE HAGUE.

'There was an Old Man of the Hague'. Lear's limericks rarely preach Victorian morals but aim to make their readers laugh, while his black-and-white drawings often display adults as amusing eccentrics rather than figures to be respected. He presents himself as a figure of fun in the self-portrait above.

mensely popular throughout the century, inspiring imitations such as Belloc's *Cautionary Tales* (1907), there are readers who question its macabre quality, in the cruel deeds of the children and the violent ways they are punished. 'The Story of Little Suck-a-Thumb', for instance, describes how a long, red-legged scissorman cuts off little Conrad's thumbs because he will suck them against his mother's wishes.

By the late 1840s an even more remarkable writer had appeared on the English scene from Continental Europe, Hans Andersen. Born in Denmark, the son of a shoemaker who read him *The Arabian Nights* and of a mother who was deeply superstitious, Andersen had little formal education to begin with, but worked his way into the theatre and, after receiving some education through the patronage of friends, decided to become a writer and began producing plays, poetry, and travel books. In 1835 Andersen's first novel *The Improvisatore or, Life in Italy*, appeared, and later that year he published a small paperback booklet *Eventyr fortalte for Børn*, 'Tales told for Children', containing 'The Tinder Box', 'Little Claus and Big Claus', 'The Princess on the Pea', and 'Little Ida's Flowers'. The word *eventyr* means a short story of fantasy or adventure for any age, and Andersen later removed 'for children', calling them *Eventyr og Historier* (fairy-tales and stories without a supernatural element). For all that, it is as a children's writer that Hans Andersen's fame largely rests in the English-speaking world.

During a visit to London in 1847, Hans Andersen visited the Danish Minister Count Reventlow, where he read aloud after dinner. Carl Hartmann caught the situation in a drawing, which now hangs in the Danish Embassy in London.

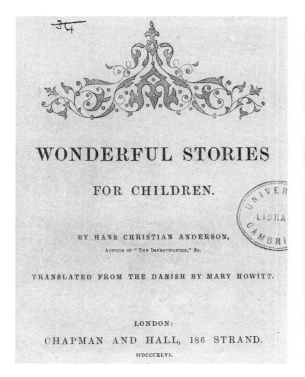

Mary Howitt translated the first selection of Andersen's tales into English as *Wonderful Stories for Children* in 1846, and three other selections followed in the same year: *Danish Fairy Legends and Tales*, translated by Caroline Peachey, *A Danish Story Book*, translated by Charles Boner, and *The Nightingale and Other Tales*, also translated by Boner. No fewer than twenty-one different collections of Andersen's tales were published by 1870, and his reputation was assured.

This was despite translations which often toned down Andersen's humour and the conversational touches characteristic of oral narrative, and concentrated on his more sentimental stories. There was even some bowdlerization; for example, the reference to babies was omitted at the beginning of 'Thumbelina'.

Andersen was a creative artist, not just a collector of folk-tales, and, though some of his stories such as 'The Tinder Box' were based upon tales heard in his childhood, Andersen adds wonderful touches in the invention of the three dogs and tells the story in a unique style. But many of Andersen's tales, such as 'The Nightingale' and 'The Ugly Duckling', sprang from his own imagination, and show him deliberately exploiting the form of the folk-tale. Despite the imperfections of the early translations, Andersen's genius still shone through. The narrative mastery, the social observation, the imaginative

*Above, left*: *Wonderful Stories*. A selection of Hans Andersen's tales were first translated into English by Mary Howitt in 1846. (Note the misspelling of the unfamiliar author's surname on the title-page!)

*Above, right*: 'The Tinder Box'. Charles Boner translated another selection of Hans Andersen's tales later in 1846 as *A Danish Story Book*. The illustrations by the Count Pocci often feature ingenious chapter-initials as here.

invention, the humour, the pathos, the poetry, proved irresistible, and Andersen became one of the immortals.

### ADVENTURE AND CAPTAIN MARRYAT

We have noted the popularity of chapbooks featuring folk-heroes such as Guy of Warwick, and the adventure story remained popular. The second edition of Joseph Ritson's great collection of Robin Hood ballads was deliberately published in 1820 in a single volume which could be read by young people. *The Swiss Family Robinson* by Johann Wyss, first published in Zurich in 1812, was translated into English in 1814. Other writers for adults rapidly adopted by children included Walter Scott, whose historical romances, from the publication of *Waverley* in 1814, showed that exciting adventures did not only occur at sea, and the American novelist J. Fenimore Cooper, who achieved great popularity with such stories as *The Last of the Mohicans* (1826), in which he wrote about the adventures of hunters and soldiers struggling against treacherous foes and natural hazards on the frontiers of North America.

Other writers were eager to provide similar stories specifically designed for the juvenile market. Agnes Strickland's *The Rival Crusoes; or, The Shipwreck* (1826) and Anne Fraser Tytler's *Leila; or, The Island* (1833) are just two examples of Robinsonnades. Mrs Hofland's *The Stolen Boy* (1830), the story of young Manuel who is captured by but escapes from Red Indians in Texas, is an example of the adventure story with an exotic background, while Harriet Martineau's *The Peasant and the Prince* (1841), and *Naomi; or, The Last Days of Jerusalem* (1841) by Mrs J. B. Webb, exploited the growing interest in tales set in the past.

This appetite for adventure stories developed at a time when Britain was emerging from the Napoleonic wars as a great naval and military power with an expanding empire. The exploits of Clive in India and Wolfe in Canada, and the more recent victories of Nelson and Wellington, had raised patriotic feeling to great heights, and it is not difficult to see the rise in popularity and to some extent the character of adventure stories as an expression of this feeling of patriotism.

Captain Marryat was the writer who played the decisive role in establishing the adventure story as a dominant form in nineteenth-century children's books. After an adventurous career as a naval officer in the war against Napoleon, he later saw service in the Atlantic, searched for smugglers in the English Channel, and took part in the Burmese war. In 1829 his first novel *The Naval Officer* took the public by storm, and soon afterwards he resigned from the navy and became a full-time writer, producing such novels as *Peter Simple* (1834) and *Mr Midshipman Easy* (1836).

He began writing for children when his own family asked him to write a story for them like *The Swiss Family Robinson.* Annoyed by its inaccuracies, Marryat produced *Masterman Ready; or, The Wreck of the Pacific* (1841–2), the story of a family marooned on a desert island who are attacked by savages but protected by the wise advice of an old seafarer, Masterman Ready. Despite some tendency to moralize, Marryat's otherwise brisk and imaginative narrative made the book a success and encouraged him to continue writing for children. He produced a Cooper-like tale *The Settlers in Canada* (1844), about the adventures of an immigrant English family, threatened by Red Indians and wild animals. Then in 1847 he produced his near-masterpiece *The Children of the New Forest.* This tells of the four Beverley children who are orphaned during the Civil War after their father dies fighting for the Royalists. Marryat vividly describes how the children are taken into hiding in a cottage in the New Forest, where a poor forester teaches them to survive by hunting and farming, and where they have dramatic adventures evading capture by Parliamentary troopers.

*Masterman Ready.* After a distinguished naval career, Captain Marryat wrote his first children's book when his own family asked for another adventure story about shipwreck like *The Swiss Family Robinson.*

Marryat's story-telling is not without faults. His account of the French political background in the last chapter is unnecessarily detailed, and his stereotyped portrayal of female characters is inevitably influenced by the historical situation when he wrote. But the tale contains less moralizing than his earlier books, as Marryat learned to express his ideas more dramatically through his characters. He also gradually gave his children more independence from the constraints of adult supervision in his stories. The Beverley children not only lose their parents, but soon lose their elderly mentor, Jacob Armitage. The children have to learn to stand on their own feet, and in the figure of Edward Beverley, a fiery, arrogant, gallant, persevering, sympathetic teenager, we may say that the nineteenth-century juvenile hero had arrived.

Marryat was clearly sympathetic to the Royalist cause in his story, but his treatment of the historical situation is rather more complicated than unswerving bias. Written at the time of the Chartists, when Britain threatened to become two nations, Marryat's story of young people caught up in civil war condemns the extremists on both sides, and the marriage of Edward with Patience, the daughter of a Parliamentarian, at the close vividly symbolizes the need for reconciliation.

In *The Children of the New Forest* Marryat wrote the first historical novel for children which has endured to the present day, and in his stories of shipwreck and of British settlers he laid the foundations of the nineteenth-century adventure story for children. Mayne Reid, Ballantyne, Kingston, and a host of others were soon to follow in his path.

### THE 1840s

Although the children's literature of the period between 1820 and 1850 was dominated by the utilitarian values which found clearest expression in the works of Peter Parley and his many imitators, when we look again at some of the books which appeared in the 1840s, we can see that the activities of this decade were decisive in the development of children's literature. *Feats on the Fiord, Masterman Ready*, and *The Children of the New Forest* reveal that the adventure story was establishing itself. The publication of *The Fairy Bower, Amy Herbert*, and the early works of Charlotte M. Yonge suggested how moral tales were beginning to develop into more realistic family stories. The success of *The Home Treasury, Gammer Gurton's Story Book*, and supremely of Hans Andersen signal the triumph of the fairy-tale, while such works as F. E. Paget's *The Hope of the Katzekopfs*, R. H. Horne's *Memoirs of a London Doll*, and Lear's *Book of Nonsense* show that the victory of fantasy was not far away.

Clearly something was happening. Changes in society had long been in the making, as the new Victorian age struggled to ameliorate the worst excesses of the Industrial Revolution. The great Reform Act of 1832 was followed by the state's increasing intervention into such matters as education and the Poor Law. Did the Chartist protests of the 1840s indicate that society was beginning to turn against the consequences of mechanistic utilitarianism? The 1840s saw crucial legislation on public health, on working hours in factories, and the repeal of the Corn Laws, which suggested that even more humane ways of thinking about society were asserting themselves. A new consciousness of childhood began to affect attitudes towards children and the family, led by Dickens above all, but not only by Dickens. The achievements of such men as Dr Arnold, the famous headmaster of Rugby School, opened up debate about the whole purpose of education in a Christian society. And reading of all kinds was increasing. As well as the Religious Tract Society (RTS) and the Society for Promoting Christian Knowledge (SPCK), such publishers as Joseph Cundall, A. K. Newman, and the firm of Longman began producing children's books.

Although the size of families had not changed significantly by the middle of the nineteenth century, and the hierarchical structure of family life continued, with obedience to parents regarded as divinely ordained, there were increasing signs of some relaxation of discipline in the treatment of children. At the beginning of the century, for example, play and games had been regarded as little more than childlike pursuits, but by the middle of the century many adults actively encouraged children to enjoy themselves—the cult of public school games was not far away—and in such books as *Holiday House* children's misdemeanours were regarded with much more tolerance than in earlier books.

The Romantic movement's rediscovery of the imagination was one of its most vital contributions to the development of nineteenth-century literature. The popularity of Scott's historical tales encouraged the great reawakening of interest in the Middle Ages that led to the Eglinton Tournament of 1839 and Tennyson's 'Morte d'Arthur' (1842), and Romantic poetry in particular emphasized the value of the imaginative exploration of the unreal and fantastic, in the dream-worlds of Xanadu and *Endymion,* to give two famous examples. In so doing, it pointed the way to the works of Sara Coleridge, F. E. Paget, and R. H. Horne, and ultimately to Kingsley and Carroll and George MacDonald. Confronted by the brutal realities of Britain's industrialized and alienated society, historical novels and fantasies may sometimes be regarded as escapist, but they can also be interpreted as imaginative ways of trying to grapple with reality in a manner which young readers find particularly accessible and attractive.

By the end of the decade a new kind of children's literature was beginning to appear—serious, but not as explicitly didactic as earlier writing, increasingly alert to the needs of the child, imbued with a sense of responsibility and duty, but with an increasing capacity for warmth and laughter and imaginative enjoyment, too. The structure of feeling, in Raymond Williams's phrase, was beginning to change and children's books reflected the cultural and moral history of the times.

# 5 CHILDREN'S LITERATURE IN AMERICA

## from the Puritan Beginnings to 1870

*Anne Scott MacLeod*

T<small>HE</small> story of children's reading in America begins with the Puritans. Although they were hardly the only settlers in a vast new land, the circumstances of their coming, the nature of their settlements, and the attitudes they brought with them had influence beyond their numbers on early American cultural history and on the development of an American literature for children. They were not adventurers, those Dissenters from England's established church, but families, intent upon forming a single-minded community in the wilderness. As Protestants, they read the Bible and sanctioned no priesthood between themselves and their God. As Dissenters and founders of a new society, they looked to their children to embrace their convictions and carry them forward into another generation.

It was imperative, then, that their children read and learn, from books as well as from parents, the intense theology that defined Puritanism. From the beginning, Puritans thought about children and provided for their schooling, at home and in the tiny settlements they called towns. By the 1640s, Massachusetts law required heads of families to teach their children and apprentices to read. No one, the law said, 'should suffer so much barbarism in any of their families as not to indeavor to teach . . . their children and apprentices so much learning as may inable them perfectly to read the english tongue'. 'Ignorance', wrote Increase Mather, 'is the Mother . . . of HERESY.'

Puritan doctrine took an anxious view of childhood, seeing the taint of Adam's sin in every infant. Puritan practice, however, was optimistic that even inborn depravity could be restrained, and natural ignorance cured by ceaseless education. Since so much depended on children's learning—the whole survival of a purified church—Puritans considered how best to teach them. They recognized that children could only receive 'that which is powred into them . . . by drops'. Cotton Mather, instructing parents on how to cat-echize their children as parental duty required, told them to 'Help their Un-derstandings, by breaking every Answer of the Catechism into little Parcels by Questions, whereto YES, or NO, or one word or two, shall be all the An-swer.'

And so it was that Puritans wrote literature for children. It was not what is recognized now as 'children's literature'; it was meant entirely for instruction, and religious instruction in a difficult doctrine at that. Yet it was written for children and designed to match children's capabilities and tastes as the au-thors understood them. Realizing how much more easily verse was memor-ized than prose, Puritans wrote doctrine in verse for the young. *The New England Primer*, most famous of all seventeenth-century books for American children, opened with the observation that 'in Adam's fall, we sinned all', and indeed, if we no longer accept the theology, we still remember the rhyme. *The New England Primer* was illustrated, since children were understood to like and learn from pictures. All editions had an illustrated ABC; most included the memorable woodcut of Mary Tudor's first Protestant martyr, John Rogers, surrounded by flames and watched by his wife, with nine small chil-dren, and a baby in her arms, with Rogers's advice appended, written in verse and addressed to his children. (The short account of his ordeal is derived from Foxe.)

Besides *The New England Primer*, a child of the Puritans might well have had a 'thumb Bible'—of hundreds printed, perhaps two or three remain— or John Cotton's *Spiritual Milk for Boston Babes in Either England: Drawn Out of the Breasts of Both Testaments for their Souls' Nourishment*. Many seventeenth- and eighteenth-century children read imported works along the same lines, among them James Janeway's *A Token for Children*. The first American edition of this famous book was published in Boston in 1700, and included an ad-dition by Cotton Mather, *A Token for the Children of New England*. Cotton Mather also published a sermon entitled 'The Duty of Children, whose parents have prayed for them' in the 1719 edition of Increase Mather's *The Duty of Parents to Pray for their Children*.

John Foxe's *Book of Martyrs*, though not origi-nally intended for children, was nevertheless fa-miliar to many, if autobiography is to be believed. Perhaps the best known of all Puritan books, John

*The New England Primer* was published from the 1680s to the eighteenth century. It appeared in many versions and editions, all of them illustrated with woodcuts.

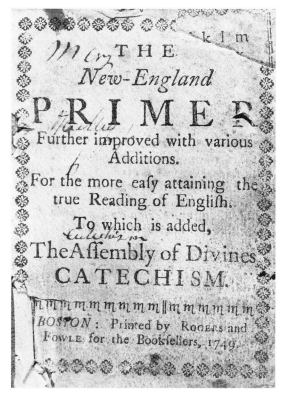

Bunyan's *The Pilgrim's Progress* was wholeheartedly embraced by American children for its strong narrative and memorable allegorical characters, and by 1830 fifty different editions had been published in America. As late as 1868, Louisa May Alcott's *Little Women* testified to Bunyan's place in the reading of American children, as *The Pilgrim's Progress* provides the framework for that book.

Not only in New England but elsewhere in the colonies, literacy rates were high by the standards of the time. John Adams claimed that 'a native American who cannot read and write is as rare as a comet or an earthquake'. Right or not for the native-born white male, the claim ignored the oppressed black population, the poorest immigrants, and the literacy gap between men and women. Until well into the eighteenth century, fewer women than men could read, and fewer yet could write. In the seventeenth century and for much of the eighteenth, literacy was a two-step process. Reading was learned at home, but writing was school-taught. Since girls were much less likely than boys to be sent to school, women who could read were not necessarily able to write. As girls gained greater access to schooling in the late eighteenth century, literacy rose above the basic level for many women, creating a whole new class of readers, one which would have enormous influence on nineteenth-century publishing, including that for children. By 1850, literacy rates for men and women are estimated to have been about equal.

Philadelphia was a publishing centre in the eighteenth century. This early Reader, *Peter Prim's Profitable Present*, published there at around the turn of the nineteenth century, wears an American air of independence.

ONE    TWO

Come buckle my Shoe.

You lazy Elf!

Pray do it yourself.

*Philadel.ª Pub. and Sold by W.Charles.*

While colonial America imported most of its books, usually from England, there was even before the mid-seventeenth century the beginnings of a publishing industry in Massachusetts, first in Cambridge, then in Boston. The products, like the readers, were mainly serious-minded: sermons, catechisms, doctrinal treatises, history, natural history, biography, and maps. The great majority of such publication still consisted of reprints or edited versions of English books, but from the beginning Americans also wrote in all categories. Boston was the home of the earliest newspapers in America. Philadelphia, though less prolific than Boston until the mid-eighteenth century, was the publishing centre for the Middle Atlantic Colonies. Between them, the two cities accounted for more than 60 per cent of American publishing before the Revolution. By the end of the eighteenth century, Boston had lost its leading position to Philadelphia, and New York had become a strong third centre of publishing, printing, and bookselling. The South was never a serious competitor to northern publishers, although Charleston was home to some small publishing concerns in the pre-war years of the nineteenth century.

Printing, publishing, and selling books were often the work of one person; outside the few cities, the colonial book trade was small and insecure. In general, the publishing business was hampered until the middle decades of the nineteenth century by underdeveloped transportation, inadequate supplies, and uncertain financial networks; nevertheless, it not only existed but thrived. Children's books were always an important part of the enterprise. Publishers' lists and advertisements suggest that school and other children's books were dependably saleable, since they often made up a goodly proportion of a bookseller's list, and usually of his income as well. James Bemis's

|   48        | BIRDS & BEASTS. |
|-------------|-----------------|
| a Yar-row   | Bit-tern        |
| a Yeo-man   | Black-bird      |
| a Za-ny     | Bramb-ling      |
| a Zea-lot   | Bunt-ing        |
| a Zea-bra   | Buſ-tard        |
| Ze-phyr     | Buz-zard        |

Schoolbooks, such as this *Book of Nouns* (1804), and other books for children were staples of the colonial book trade in America.

bookshop, established in 1810 on the frontier of western New York, printed and sold all kinds of books for children, many of them designed for American academies and common schools. Bemis advertised such standard school texts as Webster's *American Spelling Book*, *The Child's Instructor*, Isaac Watts's *Plain and Easy Catechism for Children*, and Wilson's *American Class Reader*, among others.

Neither Bemis nor any other bookmen ignored children's reading outside school. Itinerant booksellers always carried stock for children, often including some story-books; Parson Mason Weems's renown rests almost entirely on the fanciful biographies of famous Americans that he wrote himself and carried in his pack. Hugh Gaine, a New York printer of the later eighteenth century, both pirated and emulated John Newbery's books—as well as selling patent medicines. Isaiah Thomas, doubtless the most famous of early American publishers, also followed the example of Newbery in taking the children's book market seriously. From 1775 to the end of the century, Thomas's establishment at Worcester, Massachusetts, published more than a hundred titles for children, including *The New England Primer* and reprints of the best-known English children's books of the time: *Mother Goose's Melody*, *The History of Goody Two-Shoes*, Isaac Watts's *Divine Songs*, and *A Little Pretty Pocket Book*, all surely enjoyed by the relatively few American children lucky enough to see them. A more lugubrious eighteenth-century favourite, published for children under a variety of titles until well into the nineteenth

Early American children's fiction was strongly influenced by English examples. Maria Edgeworth's stories were favourite models. This elegant illustration, from *The History and Adventures of Little Eliza*, published in 1815, fits the pattern.

century, was the story of the babes in the wood. A Concord, Massachusetts, edition of 1831 called it *The Affecting History of the Children in the Woods* and underscored its message with a couplet:

Peruse this little book, and you will find,
How much the love of gold depraves the mind.

After 1785, American production of children's books increased, but remained largely reprints of English books, often those originally published by Newbery.

In the long run, however, it was not the cheerful, commercial-minded John Newbery, but Maria Edgeworth who had the strongest influence on the next period of American children's literature. The eighteenth century had seen a gradual shift away from the spiritual intensity of Puritan writings for children, toward a more generalized moralism. Newbery notwithstanding, Americans still looked on children's books as vehicles for instruction, not entertainment, though they were prepared to accept a moderate flavouring of fictional entertainment for the sake of more successful instruction. Moreover, as the children's book market expanded, publishers looked for material acceptable to all varieties of American Protestantism, which meant avoiding sectarianism. What both public and publishers wanted, in other words, was the kind of children's fiction Maria Edgeworth wrote: stories interesting enough to attract children and morally instructive enough to allay adult distrust of fiction. For, as Maria and her father Richard Lovell Edgeworth wrote in *Practical Education*, fiction for children should be 'the history of realities written in an entertaining manner'.

Reaction against imported books for American children set in after the war of 1812. A wave of nationalism easily permeated the literary field as a self-conscious new nation found foreign writings (particularly English) unsuitable for the children of a republic. Publishers of children's books began to encourage American writers for American children. When they responded, the pattern established by Maria Edgeworth (and, to a lesser extent, by her predecessor Anna Laetitia Barbauld) was at hand, attractive to most of them for both its rationalism and its high moral tone. Early in the 1820s, stories of wilful children learning to obey, of careless children learning to take care, of selfish children learning to 'live for others', started to flow from American presses, successfully achieving Edgeworth's rational tone, though rarely her sprightliness. Imitative as they were, these early American stories were quite distinguishable from their English counterparts. Few servants lived in them, and if class distinctions had by no means disappeared, there was much democratic insistence on the worthiness of every level of birth and work. And the characterization was identifiably American: the children of the fiction were serious, conscientious, self-reflective, and independent—testimony to the continuing dominance of the New England tradition in children's books.

There were some rare exceptions to the New England sobriety. Clement Moore's poem 'A Visit from St Nicholas' was published in a Troy, New York, newspaper in 1823. Better known now as 'The Night before Christmas', Moore's little fantasy in doggerel stands nearly alone as a survivor of this early literature.

No American writer wedded Edgeworthian philosophy to Puritan tradition more successfully than Jacob Abbott, which doubtless explains the wide popularity of his work in his own time. Abbott was a teacher, by all accounts a very good one, as well as a Congregational minister, who published his first fiction for children in 1835 in the form of two morally instructive tales about a little boy named Rollo. Taken together, the Rollo stories—there were twenty-eight of them, eventually—are a handbook of advanced American thinking on child nurture, educational method, and moral teaching in the early nineteenth century. The stories begin when Rollo is 5, and follow him as he grows, learns to read, learns to work and study, and travels to Europe. Like Rousseau's Émile, Rollo is accompanied at every stage by an adult who instructs him in the moral and, to a lesser extent, in the intellectual meaning of his experience. An American difference is that the adult is not a hired tutor, but a parent or another relative, or, sometimes, a schoolteacher.

Whoever instructs, the approach is the same: calm, rational, and heavily freighted with the conviction that all action—indeed, all thought, no matter how spontaneous—has moral meaning. The rationality, the grave but kindly lectures, and the transformation of experience into moral instruction echo the theories of Rousseau, Thomas Day, and the Edgeworths. The reliance upon self-contemplation as the means to inner change can be found everywhere in Puritan writing. Abbott wove these

Clement Moore's poem, 'A Visit from St Nicholas', was first published in 1823, a rare departure from the sober children's fare of the time. This edition, an accordian book, was published in 1864 by L. Prang of Boston.

A VISIT FROM St. NICHOLAS

PUBLISHED BY L. PRANG & Cº
159, WASHTºN ST BOSTON.

approaches together in more than 200 books for children, all of them well matched to the most thoughtful theorizing about children in his time. His description of his own stories would stand very well for most of the children's literature produced before 1850: 'They present quiet and peaceful pictures of happy domestic life, portraying generally such conduct, and expressing such sentiments and feelings, as it is desirable to exhibit and express in the presence of children.'

Even William Cardell's books, which seemed to promise exciting sea stories, held true to the pattern. *The Story of Jack Halyard* (1824), about a boy who went to sea, was subtitled 'The Virtuous Family' and was designed, as Cardell said in his preface, 'to give an account of one family of superior excellence, as a model to others'.

The testimony of an autobiographer of early nineteenth-century childhood suggests that American children did read and even enjoy these sober, preachy books, but not, usually, without a seasoning of something else. Lucy Larcom, born in Massachusetts in 1824, left an extensive record of her childhood reading in her memoir *A New England Girlhood*. She learned to read before she was 3 (early reading was not uncommon in the first decades of the century) and then read most of what came to hand, including *The Scottish Chiefs* at the age of 5. Larcom read a good many of the moralistic children's books of her time, most of them English. Her Sabbath-school library books were 'nearly all English reprints'; she thought them 'very interesting'. Among her favourites were Mrs Sherwood's *Little Henry and his Bearer*, *Ayah and Lady*, and *Infant's Progress*, the last based on 'the book that I loved first and best, and lived upon in my childhood', *The Pilgrim's Progress*. Everyday reading was likely to be English as well, especially Maria Edgeworth's tales, though Larcom also remembered Lydia Maria Child's stories in *The Girl's Own Book*. While she liked her English books, some of them were a little puzzling to a child of New England. References to servants had little meaning for her: 'Everybody about us worked, and we expected to take hold of our part while young.' And Lucy had never seen a beggar like those described in English stories, no 'ragged, half-clothed child' ever pleaded for charity in her village. On the other hand, she was shocked to learn from one of Samuel Goodrich's juvenile histories about the witch trials of Salem, the village next to hers. Mixed with the improving works intended for readers of her age were others Lucy borrowed from her older sisters: *The Vicar of Wakefield*, *Gulliver's Travels*, *The*

*Arabian Nights*, and 'some odd volumes of Sir Walter Scott's novels'. Besides all of that, little Lucy also 'devoured a great many romances' that she declined to list by name in her autobiography. Her sisters got them from a local circulating library, and Lucy read them, though as an adult she was sure that they were 'bad for [her] mind'.

Non-fiction in the form of school texts, histories, books of natural science, biographies, and the like also fed the ever-widening stream of books for children. The first half of the nineteenth century saw an increase in the number of common schools and consequently an increase in literacy, with a resultant expansion of publishing of all kinds. But if it is clear that more children went to school and for longer, it is less clear what 'increased literacy' really meant, for individuals or for society. Some historians say that literate Americans, from being a small minority, only became a larger one in the first half of the nineteenth century. All concede that literacy was uneven, with native-born whites having the highest rates, blacks, and immigrants from Ireland and Germany, the lowest.

And what 'literate' meant as a description of the reading public is even less certain. To be able to read was not necessarily to be a serious and thoughtful reader. Captain Frederick Marryat, travelling in America in the 1830s, balked at equating literacy with education. 'Is teaching a boy to read and write education? If so, a large proportion of the American community may be said to be educated.' He was willing to admit that education was 'more equally diffused' in America than in England, but the result, in his opinion, was nothing to cheer about. 'Every man in America reads his newspaper and hardly anything else.' Indeed, he thought that reading 'too often is the occasion of the demoralization of those who might have been more virtuous and more happy in their ignorance'. He had observed a 10- or 11-year-old boy 'reading a cheap periodical, mostly confined to the lower orders . . . called Penny Paul Pry. Surely it had been a blessing to the lad if he had never learnt to read or write, if he confined his studies, as probably too many do . . . to such an immoral and disgusting publication.'

Marryat's comments foreshadowed questions that would engage many American minds before the end of the century. A wider literacy quickly created a reading public neither as serious nor as homogeneous as it had been in the seventeenth and eighteenth centuries. From 1800 to the mid-century and beyond, as basic schooling reached a broader public, writing for publication became many-layered, catering to a variety of tastes and levels of interest and comprehension. The enormous multiplication of newspapers was the beginning, quickly followed by the other periodical forms: monthlies, weeklies, annuals, journals and magazines, and papers of every kind and quality.

Except for newspapers, publication for children followed the adult pattern, though on a smaller scale and at a slower pace. The first periodical for children, called the *Children's Magazine*, was put out by a Hartford, Connecticut, printer in 1789. It lasted only three months. The second venture, the *Youth's News Paper*, launched by a New York printer ten years later, was a weekly which survived for only six issues. The first decades of the nineteenth century saw several more children's periodicals come and go, but by the end of the 1820s, marketing and distribution systems had developed sufficiently to sustain new efforts to reach a growing audience. *The Juvenile Miscellany* was founded in Boston in 1826 and published until 1836. The list of the *Miscellany's* contributors includes some of the best-known (though now mostly forgotten) American women writers of the age: Lydia Maria Child, founding editor of the magazine; Lydia Sigourney, 'Sweet Singer of Hartford'; and Sarah Josepha Hale, who succeeded Child as editor and eventually went on to a long career as editor of *Godey's Lady's Book* and is famous for 'Mary had a little lamb' (1830). One of the longest-lived of all American periodicals was *The Youth's Companion*, established in 1827, also in Boston, by Nathaniel Willis. *The Youth's Companion* prospered until 1929, largely because, as one chronicler has noted, it was 'uncannily successful in reflecting the dominant trends about the sort of literature children should read'. In the early years, the *Companion's* religious emphasis was strong and overt; but as time went on, religion shaded into moralism, which in turn gradually gave way to less didactic efforts to attract and divert child readers.

The 1830s and 1840s produced new crops of periodicals, some of them tied to social issues of the time. Two antislavery periodicals aimed at children lived and died in the 1830s, *The Slave's Friend*, published for two years, and *The Youth's Emancipator*, which lasted less than a year. The American Temperance Union founded *The Youth's Temperance Advocate* along the lines of Sunday school publications (of which more later) and distributed it through the Sunday schools. The project was well funded and publication continued until the early 1860s. Some of the sturdier contenders in the periodical market were both more general and more frankly entertaining, though of course all maintained a high moral tone. *Parley's Magazine*, begun in 1833, merged with *Robert Merry's Museum* in 1844. As *Merry's Museum*, the magazine lasted until 1872. The years just after the Civil War produced more, and more distinguished, magazines for children. *Our Young Folks* in 1865, the *Little Corporal* and the *Children's Hour* in 1866, *Riverside Magazine for Young People, Frank Leslie's Boy's and Girl's Weekly*, and *Oliver Optic's Magazine*, all in 1867, were among the most successful. The creative burst culminated in 1873 with the best-known, best-loved children's periodical of all, the famous *St Nicholas* magazine, whose founding editor, Mary Mapes Dodge, tended it with love, intelligence, and remarkable results for thirty years.

The founder of *Parley's Magazine* and *Merry's Museum*, Samuel Griswold Goodrich, personified many aspects of the publishing history of his time. His career as a writer, publisher, bookseller, and entrepreneur for more than forty years illuminates both cause and effect of many developments in children's literature from the 1820s to the 1850s. Goodrich was born in Connecticut in the late eighteenth century, in a time, he wrote, when 'books and newspapers—which are now diffused even among the country towns . . . were then scarce, and were read respectfully . . . They were not toys and pastimes . . . Even the young approached a book with reverence, and a newspaper with awe.'

The reading Goodrich described—intensive rather than extensive, for information more than for entertainment—was characteristic of pre-nineteenth-century American reading, and reflective both of the scarcity of printed matter, and of pre-revolutionary attitudes toward the purposes of literacy. Goodrich recalled from his memoirs the paucity of what he considered acceptable literature for children. 'It is difficult now [in 1856] . . . to conceive of the poverty of books suited to children in [my youth.] Except for *The New England Primer* . . . and some rhymes, embellished with hideous cuts of Adam's Fall, in which "we sinned all" . . . I remember none that were in general use.' He heard traditional fairy-tales, but he found them even worse. As a child, Goodrich remembered, he was appalled by the violence of '*Little Red Riding*', '*Blue Beard*', '*Jack, the Giantkiller*', and other 'tales of horror'. Though in his case the conduct and example of his parents 'offset the influence' of the stories, he was 'convinced that much of the vice and crime in the world are to be imputed to these atrocious books put into the hands of children'.

Goodrich entered upon his long career in book publishing in 1816, at first mostly reprinting works of English origin, following common American practice. Soon, however, ambition, national pride, and a shrewd market sense persuaded Goodrich that he should publish books about America written by Americans, and he began to do so. As he prospered, he expanded both his business and his horizons. During a lengthy trip to Europe in 1823, he arranged to visit Hannah More, and their conversation solidified Goodrich's ambition to make 'a reform—or at least an improvement—in books for youths'. But where Miss More's moral reformism was designed 'chiefly for the grown-up masses; I had in contemplation to begin further back—with the children'.

PREFACE.

It might be supposed that I had written books enough to satisfy reasonable people, but the booksellers of London, not content with publishing what I have written, have published several under

Samuel Goodrich created 'Peter Parley', an old man with a lame leg who narrated many of Goodrich's books. To Goodrich's annoyance, English publishers 'borrowed' the Parley name for their books, as old Peter is telling the children in this illustration.

Throughout the thirty years that followed, Goodrich wrote often and much for children, every word reflecting his commitment to the kind of moral teaching Hannah More had practised. In books, magazines, and school texts, from the many tales in the 'Peter Parley' series, and the histories of the United States, Latin America, and Europe, Goodrich made children's literature the instrument of Protestant religion and the moral convictions of his Connecticut up-bringing. In this, he was entirely representative of the era and of its approach to children's reading. Even as the literature grew and as custom let down the barriers to fiction, the principle remained constant that all of a child's reading must be morally instructive. Authors might (and often did) characterize their work as entertaining, but never without also underscoring its moral purpose. And since the great majority of writers and publishers were Protestant, white, middle-class, and born in New England or the Middle Atlantic states, they agreed, by and large, on the moral framework that enclosed literature for children.

Samuel Goodrich was one of the most prolific and successful publishers of children's books before the Civil War.

Goodrich also represented the ambition and enterprise that propelled American publishing into a period of enormous growth. He rode the crest of a wave, furnishing the children's market with quantities of material, none of it exceptional, most of it hastily produced. He was successful, prolific, prosperous, and something of a hack, as he himself admitted toward the end of his life: 'I have written too much and done nothing really well.' Although by 1857 he had written and edited about 157 volumes selling 7 million copies, nothing in the 'long catalogue' of his work, he added regretfully, would give him 'a permanent place in literature'. In this, too, he was not unlike the majority of his published contemporaries. Certainly, many of the women writers and editors who found in the children's market an opportunity for self-support unavailable elsewhere wrote for the most practical of reasons—to make a living. What they wrote was rarely original or individualistic.

Besides the secular publishers doing a thriving business in children's books, there was another major presence in the juvenile market of the second quarter of the century. The American Sunday School Union (ASSU) was formed in 1824, though Sunday schools themselves long preceded the interdenominational Union. Sunday schools had a tremendous influence in a country where some outlying regions had no other schools and where most places had no other libraries. For many children of the early nineteenth century, Sunday schools were the sole source of reading materials more or less geared to their understanding.

The ASSU aspired to national influence; it wanted to speak for the various denominational groups then dwelling, not always harmoniously, in the house of Protestantism and to establish Sunday schools 'without distinction of sect, or creed, or custom'. The ASSU's first foray into the children's periodical market in 1824 was successful, according to the organization's figures: the *Youth's Friend*, a non-sectarian Sunday school paper, attracted 60,000 subscribers in four years. The ASSU was also ambitious to become a major publisher of children's books written by American authors. By the 1830s, however, when the ASSU undertook its juvenile book publishing effort, the conflict over slavery was growing harsher by the day, and national acceptance for any publication had become problematic. The fate of Lydia Maria Child was instructive. Child was an admired author of both adult and juvenile books and founding editor of *The Juvenile Miscellany* when she joined the abolition cause and wrote *An Appeal in Favor of that Class of Americans Called Africans*. Her calm, reasoned dissection of every pro-slavery argument roused fury and alarm, not just in the South but in Boston, where she lived and worked. A promising career quickly collapsed. Every national publisher read the lesson. The ASSU had already created an interdenominational Committee of Publication to ensure that books published by the national Union sidestepped 'all unnecessary controversy', but after both the Massachusetts Sabbath School Society and the Methodist Episcopal Sunday School Union took antislavery stands, the Committee had express orders to avoid 'studiously and constantly . . . the subject of slavery, abolition and every other irritating topic'.

By most measures the ASSU's children's publications were successful. The fiction was sober, moral, and, in accord with union policy, more than a little bland—but blandness was not usually reckoned a fault in children's literature before the mid-century. The books were well made, often well illustrated, and well-nigh ubiquitous. Many a child unlikely otherwise to actually own a book could and did win an ASSU publication for faithful Sunday school attendance or a good memory for Bible verses. Autobiographers who grew up in the *ante bellum* years, however, cast some doubt on children's enthusiasm for Sunday school books. They remembered them, but they often remembered even better their joy when they found alternatives to the fiction the ASSU described as 'wholesome reading matter . . . [written] to

*Facing*: entertainment for the whole village. The *Punch and Judy Show* by John Fuller (1821–67). Punch first appeared in England in the 1660s.

impress and improve morals and manners'. All the same, in spite of many obstacles, including the insistence of many denominational Sunday school unions on publishing their own Sunday school materials, the ASSU was a major publisher of children's books until the Civil War.

The growth in publishing was, then, very rapid, but changes in the content of books came more slowly. The conventions that dictated the attitudes and purposes of literature for children remained remarkably stable, especially considering the changes in the society around them, and the range they dictated was fairly narrow. Most controversy was excluded, not only in Sunday school books, but generally. Rationality was favoured over sentiment for young readers, though their elders were increasingly well acquainted with melodrama and the sentimental novel. Children's reading was emphatically not intended to encourage fantasy or imagination; the standard children's story before 1850 was domestic and undramatic, focused on the development of moral character, rather than on overtly public issues. Even non-fiction was at least as concerned with values as with fact; there was no great reverence for objectivity. *Parley's Universal History on the Basis of Geography*, written by Nathaniel Hawthorne and published by Samuel Goodrich in 1837, casually dismissed the non-Protestant, non-western world, telling young Americans that 'no country has ever been happy or well governed where Mohammedanism prevailed' and that 'the Chinese are great fibbers'. In fact, Hawthorne concluded, 'Nearly the whole of Asia is involved in darkness as to the character of God.'

Writing for children began to change about the middle of the century when some of the literary conventions already well established in popular adult fiction began to appear in children's fiction. Old styles persisted for a long time, of course, but a new kind of writing, sentimental and wildly overwrought by older standards, also took hold. The most obvious change was stylistic. Early nineteenth-century writers favoured literary restraint in writing for children. They were not given to vivid descriptions, whether of landscape or characters. Even less were they likely to describe or depict strong emotion since they believed that 'passions', as they called them, should be governed, not indulged. New writers, on the other hand, brought enthusiastic writing to children's books, the more feeling the better. The matter-of-fact deathbed scenes of early literature gave way to vivid—and lengthy—accounts, and melodramatic grief, an indulgence deplored by earlier standards, penetrated even Sunday school literature. *The Angel Mother*, published in 1854 by the Massachusetts Sabbath School Society, described in dramatic prose a mother's death ('even now the silver cord is loosening!') and the prolonged mourning of her children. Nature, too, turned romantic with 'shady nooks', 'lovely glades', and water that sparkled, unsurprisingly, 'like diamonds'.

THE HOME TREASURY

TOYS

FABLES

BALLADS

TALES

The Sisters,
and
Golden Locks.

JOSEPH CUNDALL

1. SHOCK-HEADED PETER.

Just look at him! There he stands,
With his nasty hair and hands.
See! his nails are never cut;
They are grim'd as black as soot;
And the sloven, I declare,
Never once has comb'd his hair;
Any thing to me is sweeter
Than to see Shock-headed Peter.          (2)

Nathaniel Hawthorne's *Wonder Book* (1851) and *Tanglewood Tales* (1853), though certainly not the first American books written especially for children (as is sometimes claimed), were nevertheless influential. Hawthorne's re-workings of legend and myth did not have immediate impact (although in Britain they provoked Charles Kingsley to counteract their 'vulgarity' by writing *The Heroes* (1856) ), but by the 1870s they inspired many others authors.

Even more striking was a new taste for romantic descriptions of children in children's books. Early nineteenth-century children's authors gave scant attention to appearance; they were interested in moral qualities. At most, a child might have 'frank' or 'honest' looks; an occasional writer might bend so far as to call a child's face 'interesting'. At the mid-century, however, popular sentimentality invaded a previously austere literature. In Francis Forrester's *Guy Carleton* (1859) such effusions as 'A little blue-eyed maiden, with plump cheeks and rich clusters of golden ringlets' and a baby 'pure and almost holy in his baby innocence' testified that the romanticized child of adult literature had found its way into the juvenile field.

Not only children, but other characters began to reveal their moral status by their appearance. *Boy of Mt. Rhigi* (1848) by Catherine Maria Sedgwick contrasted the 'Noble features, expressive of truth, decision and good temper' of the worthy, with the coarse features, shambling gaits, and crooked teeth of the wicked and derelict. The literature of the mid-century described the world in new ways, many of them more realistic and ambivalent, all of them less morally confident than those of earlier juvenile fiction. Social reality penetrated children's literature, blurring the old, clear moralities. The new fiction reflected contemporary society more directly than did the old, both by the greater degree of reality it admitted and by the doubt and confusion it exhibited in the face of social change.

By 1850, America was a society under strain. Although it was drawn to calm the slavery controversy, the Compromise of 1850 in fact settled nothing; the political and social struggle over slavery sharpened, rather than subsided, as the middle ground between the extremes narrowed to vanishing point. At the same time, the dislocations of industrialization and urban growth bore hard on Jacksonian optimism. Heavy waves of immigration in the 1830s and 1840s had filled East Coast cities with new arrivals too destitute to move on, too unskilled for any but the lowest-paid labouring jobs. Although factories absorbed (and exploited) some of the immigrants, many were without work or means to live at the most basic level; urban poverty was a demoralizing, increasingly visible problem.

Many of the new writers for children were city dwellers, who turned their attention to the world around them, creating a picture of urban life altogether missing in earlier juvenile literature. William Taylor Adams, Sara Par-

*Facing, above left*: the polymath Sir Henry Cole (1808–82) as 'Felix Summerly' began to produce his *Home Treasury* series in 1843, partly in reaction to the utilitarian texts of the American Samual Goodrich ('Peter Parley') and his imitators.

*Above, right*: in 1844 Hoffmann, who could only find 'long tales, stupid collections of pictures (and) moralising stories' for his son produced his own parodies of the 'cautionary tales'. The naïvety of the drawing is deliberate. *The English Struwwelpeter* appeared in 1848.

*Below*: water-coloured toys and tricks from the 1820s.

ton, and T. S. Arthur, among many others, wrote of shops and shopkeepers, newsboys and clerks, illiterate Irish urchins, Italian boys selling plaster casts of saints or singing on the streets for pennies; they mentioned ostlers, aldermen, and beggars. Fiction was suddenly precise about streets, stores, factories: a South Boston pier where 'a motley group of youngsters' came to fish, and the notorious Five Points slum, 'but a step or two from the famous Broadway'. As the city came into focus, so did the shocking poverty of the city's poor and a degree of social criticism, direct and indirect, that was unprecedented in older literature. Alice B. Haven's *Nothing Venture, Nothing Have* (1854) described a tenement 'crowded with families as poor, and as squalid as want could make them . . . Dirty children were sitting on the front steps, and forlorn-looking women looked out of the open doors. . . . The very walls had cracked and settled, leaving great chinks and crevices, gaping wider every day, in the black, smoked-stained plaster.'

Authors of children's books quite naturally tended to concentrate on the children of the poor. And indeed, they were hard to ignore. Filthy, ragged, barefoot even in winter, often abused at home, sometimes without any homes at all, the children of the urban poor haunted the juvenile writing of the 1850s. In editorials and stories throughout the decade, *The Youth's Companion* championed the 'little blue-lipped and barefooted children on the pavements' of New York, appealing to more fortunate children to support the Children's Aid Society with their pennies. Sara Parton, who as 'Fanny Fern' produced an immensely popular column for the *New York Ledger*, was a lively social critic. She lambasted the rich for ignoring 'the squalid poor of whom they never think' and wrote sentimental tales addressed to her 'dear little readers' about the fate of poor children in a society bent on pleasure and success. Parton's little stories, like many after mid-century, drew on the literary tradition that made suffering children vehicles for social protest. It was a tradition already well established in adult literature, but a startling change in children's fare.

Such writing mixed sentiment and reality in nearly equal measure. Parton wrote of children who had 'drunken parents, and the place which should be their home is made the scene of dreadful wickedness and cruelty'. She spoke of physical cruelty toward children, of parents who beat their children and sent them into the streets to beg or steal. Authors glimpsed the sociology of poverty, seeing that poverty often begot more poverty and that misery could induce not the effort to improve but the lassitude of hopelessness, and so perpetuate itself. 'Cousin Alice' (Alice B. Haven) described a slum mother as 'slatternly, heavy-eyed and drooping, like a person who had lost all pride, and energy of character'. She neglected her home and children, Haven explained, which so discouraged her husband that he spent his wages in bar rooms, and thus 'things had gone from bad to worse . . . [and] neither husband or wife

*Facing*: Nathaniel Hawthorne, who had once written on commission for Samuel Goodrich, published two volumes of Greek myths rewritten for mid-nineteenth-century children. Intended as money-makers, the books succeeded and were reissued in many different editions.

Many Americans at the mid-century regarded drink as the curse of the working classes and the enemy of the family. The Temperance Movement published stories for children urging Cold Water Clubs and temperance pledges.

tried to do better'. The poor and the wicked, observed another author, 'grow poorer and wickeder as the long days go by'. The literature often alluded to the moral corruption surrounding a slum child. Sara Parton remarked in her column that a street boy was all too often 'a boy in years, but a man in vicious knowledge'.

What could be done about these problems was no clearer to authors than to the society at large; responses ranged from helpless to institutional to sentimental. *The Youth's Companion* often reprinted stories and articles from other periodicals, many of which simply described the children's desperate state as affectingly as possible and closed the subject with pious reflections on their own good luck or with prayers that 'God, who feeds the ravens and clothes the lilies of the field, would guard and guide them'. Others directed attention to the relatively few social institutions that might deal with the destitute. T. S. Arthur recommended the almshouse for a woman begging on the streets of New York with her three children. For children left on their own by the death of their parents, Arthur, 'Aunt Friendly', 'Aunt Abbie', and some anonymous *Youth's Companion* authors suggested that orphan asylums were not only available but highly desirable solutions. Some writers joined *The Youth's Companion* in trying to acquaint the public with the work of the Children's Aid Society. An anonymous novel, *Harry Lee; or, Hope for the Poor* (1859), followed a poor boy from the city through the whole of the Society's scheme for rehabilitating the young victims of urban poverty: Harry is sent west to Ohio, where he works on a farm, rebuilds his moral character, marries the farmer's daughter, and gets his own land.

Sentimentality, however, was the last, best refuge for writers bewildered by the miseries they deplored. Sentiment softened the contradictions between the high hopes (and claims) of Jacksonian society and the clear evidence that American society had created an impoverished class as desperate as the despised poor of European cities. Sentiment could pretend that personal charity was an adequate answer to the human costs of industrialization. Sara Parton used her considerable command of sentimentality to accuse New York society of heartlessness toward the little starvelings of her stories, but she had no solutions to offer. Her pathetic Bennies and Jennies and Claras were rescued by benevolent strangers, or they died.

The mid-century also saw children's literature splinter along class lines as adult literature had done before it. A broader literacy had created new audiences for print while improved technology and better transportation made it possible to reach readers with cheaply produced books and periodicals. The expansion of the railways between 1850 and 1860—railway mileage tripled in that one decade—had an immense influence on the production and marketing of print. Publishers bid, successfully, for new readers at every level of sophistication.

The 1860s launched the juvenile series book, which soon became a staple of the children's market. Books sold in series were not a new idea; Jacob Abbott's 'Rollo' books can be considered a series; so can his 'Franconia' stories, published from 1850. The great house of Harper had discovered in the 1830s that books, children's or adult, could be arranged in series not necessarily related by subject or author, and marketed at modest prices as 'libraries'. In the fiercely competitive book market of the *ante bellum* period, Harper more than once salvaged its place by selling this kind of series. During the Panic of 1837, when publishing houses were falling fast, Harper created the Harper School District Library, a boxed set of fifty volumes, sold with its own pine cabinet for $20.00. It is unlikely that Harper made much money on this enterprise, but his company survived when many others succumbed to bad times.

But the series books that were to prove so enduringly popular with the young were of a different stripe. A species of formula literature, not necessarily (in fact, not often) well written but skilfully tailored to the tastes of a young audience, series books were long on action, if short on credibility, and

*Below, left*: in the 1860s and 1870s, improved technology made good illustration both possible and affordable for books and periodicals. This illustration is by Winslow Homer, one of many artists of the time to get his start in illustration.

*Below, right*: one of Horatio Alger's aspirants.

offered a welcome change from the quiet domestic tales that otherwise dominated the children's market. However repetitive and predictable, they were adventure stories, and they caught on quickly, especially with boys.

Nor had it escaped the notice of publishers that boys read adventure tales not specifically written for them, including, of course, those of James Fenimore Cooper. Cooper's frontier novels were less lurid and more complex than the pulp literature of later decades, but the tradition he founded, of lone, stoic heroes, noble, stoic Indians, and women whose only function was to be pure and in need of rescue, persisted in many a lesser frontier tale.

William Taylor Adams, writing under the pseudonym 'Oliver Optic', was one of the first, and arguably the most influential, of the middle-level series authors. Adams was as much an entrepreneur as Samuel Goodrich, founding and editing a number of magazines for children, including *Oliver Optic's Magazine, Our Boys and Girls, Our Little Ones*, and several others. He also wrote a number of works of fiction, mostly for boys, during the 1850s. *The*

# Jack's Ward

## HORATIO ALGER, JR.

*Boat Club*, published in 1854, was so popular that Adams wrote five more books, creating a series successfully aimed at middle-class readers. From this satisfactory beginning, he went on to more exciting stories of boys performing high-minded deeds in dramatic situations, all of which earned him lots of money and the scorn of genteel writers.

While Adams is often credited with developing the formula for boys' series books—a momentous event in the history of juvenile publishing—by rights he should be better remembered for his part in launching the career of Horatio Alger. It was Adams who found a publisher for the Alger story now famous as the very prototype of the 'rags-to-riches' novel, *Ragged Dick* (serialized in *The Student and Schoolmate*, edited by 'Oliver Optic', 1867; book form 1868). Nothing speaks more eloquently of a whole layer of nineteenth-century American society than Horatio Alger's clumsy, optimistic, repetitious tales of aspiration and achievement. Operating on a scale well within the comprehension of his young working-class readers, boys less privileged than Adams's readers, Alger married the American dream of social and economic advancement to the rules of a newly industrializing mass society. The old virtues of honesty, hard work, and general respectability provided an Alger boy with the basic qualifications to 'rise in the world'—to use Alger's signature phrase. If he then learned to be thrifty, punctual, regular in his habits, and dedicated to his employer's interests, Alger's hero invariably found the opportunity to recover the stolen money or rescue the capitalist's drowning daughter and so prosper all the rest of his days. Alger, like Adams, found little favour with genteel, mainstream writers and critics of children's literature, but he was the author of some 120 books which were best sellers in his lifetime and for nearly twenty years after his death.

As series books and rags-to-riches novels extended the definition of children's literature, so did the dime novel. Dime novels were not originally aimed at the young reader, nor were they invented by the house of Beadle and Adams, though form and publisher eventually became more or less synonymous. As early as the 1830s and 1840s, cheap and lurid novels were being produced for popular consumption with considerable success. In 1860, Beadle and Adams applied mass merchandising methods to the marketing of an equally sensational and even cheaper product, and struck gold. Oddly enough, the first of 'Beadle's Dime Novels', a melodramatic tale of mixed white–Indian marriage, *Malaeska, the Indian Wife of the White Hunter*, was written by an author quite like those who wrote for children. Ann Sophia Stephens was a New England woman, 29 years old when she wrote the story, but 50 when it was reprinted by Beadle and Adams. Success came swiftly— 65,000 copies sold in a matter of months—and it was soon followed by other novels equally dramatic and equally successful, some of them written by the same woman. Romance had some place in dime novels, but adventure was

American families by the hundreds travelled West in the 1870s and 1880s. Although they carried few books with them, their experience would be remembered in children's books many times over in the years to come.

the mainstay. Hack writers mined the country's history for stories of the Wild West, gold-hunting, wars with British, Mexicans, and Indians, sea adventure, and crime. Anything with enough blood and action was grist for the mill.

Dime novels went with soldiers into the military camps of the Civil War, providing escape literature for men who were actors in the greatest drama of their country's history. Between 1861 and 1866, the publishers sold more than 4 million Beadle's Dime Novels. Success, of course, attracted competitors. Publisher after publisher began to produce cheap novels in series, using the postal service and the railways to reach vast new audiences of readers. Writers likely and unlikely profited, including Louisa May Alcott, who as A. M. Barnard wrote tales of violent death, opium addiction, deception, and disguise.

Not surprisingly, boys younger than the reading soldiers found such books irresistible, with their non-stop action and wildly dramatic writing. They bought and traded and read dime and 'half-dime' novels published by Beadle and Adams and their competitors until the genre was thoroughly identified with boy readers. Like Alger's tales and most series books, dime novels were highly moral, but they were also—as Alger and series books were not—surpassingly violent, the more so as time went on. When parents objected to dime novels, and they did, increasingly, in the 1870s and 1880s, it was because of their violence and sensationalism, more than because they in any way openly assaulted conventional morality. As Louisa Alcott wryly observed in *Good Wives* (or *Little Women Part 2* (1869) ), 'in those dark days, even all-perfect America read rubbish'.

The Civil War slowed publishing in most of the United States and destroyed it entirely in the South, not for lack of demand but because supplies were hard to get. Patriotic fervour burned, of course, on both sides, but it was more easily transformed into publication in the North. The Boston firm of Walker, Wise developed a line of material known as the *Popular War Series*, which constituted, they said, 'a three-sided presentation of the new experi-

Dressed in their best and posed against a typically ornate background, Ulysses S. Grant's brother and sister, Nellie and Jesse Grant, were photographed in the Civil War period.

ence which the Rebellion has afforded'. Walker, Wise included children in their audience of patriots, publishing William Thayer's *A Youth's History of the Rebellion* and a four-volume Union Series as well as the *Child's Anti-Slavery Book*, which they sold with other juveniles designed for Sabbath school libraries. The firm's extensive catalogue of juvenile books underlines the triumph of the series concept. For middle-class children whose parents could spend more than a nickel or a dime, it offered the *All the Children's Library* (50c. a volume); the *Silver Penny* series, which promised to meet the 'demand for good but cheap juveniles' at 25c. per book; the *Pioneer Boy* series; and the *Home Story Books*. In fact, a number of publishers concentrated on the lucrative children's market during the war. The publishing house of Lee and Shepard began business in the inauspicious year of 1862. Their early publications, all reprints of existing books, were mostly for children. The first book issued under their imprint was John Ruskin's *The King of the Golden River*, which was followed by more children's books, including reprints of two Oliver Optic sets: the well-known *Boat Club* series (six volumes) and the *Riverdale Story Books* (twelve volumes). There was also a curious sequel to *The Swiss Family Robinson*, called *Willis the Pilot*, a book whose heavy moralism apparently surpassed even that of the original. The tireless William Taylor Adams, who became one of Lee and Shepard's most rewarding authors, turned his hand to making boys' adventure stories out of the war. In 1864 he produced *The Soldier Boy* and *The Sailor Boy*. 'Twin Boys—Twin Volumes' said the advertising. They sold well and, of course, Adams promptly added other volumes to the series. These tales abandoned most of the conscientious moralizing of earlier Optic stories in favour of 'thrills' almost competitive with those of the dime novel. Not until 1869 did Lee and Shepard publish any fiction for adults.

After the Civil War, American literature at last achieved the economic and social solidity it could not manage in the *ante bellum* years. The literary scene in the United States was both lively and distinguished before the Civil War, but it was also precarious. An American author found it difficult to make a living entirely as a writer; few could do it by writing for adults, fewer yet by writing for children. Jacob Abbott and Samuel Goodrich are the only two authors whose profession might be called writing for children, but neither made his living exclusively from children's books.

It was apparent by 1865 that there was beginning to be a public large enough and literate enough to transform American writing and publishing into a stable economic enterprise. The phenomenon of the domestic novel, written by women authors for women readers, reflected cultural developments that would make the middle-class domestic audience central to the literary history of the rest of the nineteenth century. The best sellers of the middle of the century were all domestic novels; their sales were phenomenal. Of them, perhaps *The Wide, Wide World* by Susan Warner ('Elizabeth Wetherell') is best known. No novels, not even Scott's or Dickens's, had ever sold in such numbers. Warner's readers, who read other, later domestic novelists just as avidly, together with the thousands who devoured dime and rags-to-riches novels, made up an audience that put American literary production on a firm footing. Technological improvements in printing and reproduction

*Facing*: though her fame now rests almost entirely on her children's books, Louisa May Alcott was a sometime editor and a prolific writer of adult novels and short stories, including sensational stories published under her pseudonym, A. M. Barnard.

125

and greatly expanded transportation networks ensured that these eager readers could and would be served. By the late 1860s it had become possible for successful American authors, whether of high-, low-, or middle-brow fiction, to support themselves by their writing.

Children's literature belongs in this picture, though it is often considered separately. Young readers and popular literature are never far apart; cheaply produced series and sensational stories in both book and periodical form had great appeal for children. Publishers knew it and produced vast amounts of pulp literature for children to consume—which they did. Some of it was frankly low, like the 'boy's storypapers'; more was middle-level formula fiction, Optic's or Alger's for boys, Sophie May's *Little Prudy* and *Dotty Dimple* for girls. None of it was acceptable to the genteel literate adult, but if genteel children's literature was to stand against the flood of what many adults considered egregious trash, it had to adapt. It was finally understood that literature for children must entertain, whatever else it might be expected to accomplish. While young readers might accept (or ignore) lessons carried along by an interesting story, if the lessons stifled all else—well, there were alternatives: *The Black Avenger*, *The Mysteries of Udolpho*, *Alonso and Melissa*, and countless more. Even the upright Thomas Wentworth Higginson recalled with affection 'those precious books that throve under shelter of school-desks'. Looking over the heads of his readers to their parents, Oliver Optic frankly acknowledged his double-edged task: 'The author . . . has endeavored to combine healthy moral lessons with a sufficient amount of exciting interest to render the story attractive to the young; and he hopes he has not mingled these elements of a good juvenile book in disproportionate quantities.' The right proportion was crucial to success in the new middle-class market.

Mainstream children's books, in other words, followed the adult market as it developed in its many-layered variety. If boys were eager to read lurid adventure novels produced for a non-genteel adult readership, then genteel writers would learn to write exciting adventure tales more in harmony with middle-class values. If domestic novels attracted enormous audiences among literate middle-class women, then surely the domestic tale could be adapted to serve the reading tastes of middle-class girls.

*The Wide, Wide World* was published in 1850. A domestic novel and an evangelical tract, its story is of a girl's growing up, but it was written and marketed as an adult novel. Seventeen years later, in 1867, when evangelical novels were a dead letter in the adult market, Martha Finley published *Elsie Dinsmore*, a girls' novel suffused with evangelical messages. The ghost of Susan Warner's peculiar masterpiece haunted *Elsie Dinsmore* on every page, but Finley's novel was more than a simple imitation. Hugely sentimental and overdrawn, full of dramatic scenes of emotional martyrdom and forgiveness, it was well tuned to adolescent fantasies. Elsie's Christian self-abnegation, far from making her invisible to those around her, gives her a power over adults that must have caused many a young girl to sigh with envy. Predictably, perhaps, the book was a great popular success, in England as well as in America, inspiring Martha Finley to write twenty-seven more 'Elsie' stories, taking her from girlhood all the way to grandmotherhood.

Popular as it was with adolescent readers, *Elsie Dinsmore* was not a book the adult of genteel sensibilities could embrace: it was too evangelical, too emotional, and far too sensational. In 1868, however, the novel that would be welcomed by girls and their parents alike, the story that became a model for all children's family stories, was published to general acclaim. Louisa May Alcott was unenthusiastic about writing 'a girls' book', but her own description of *Little Women* sums up exactly the difference between her work and Finley's. 'Lively, simple books are very much needed for girls', she remarked in her journal, and after she saw the proofs, she wrote, 'It reads better than I expected. Not a bit sensational, but simple and true, for we really lived most of it.'

*Little Women* was the book, and Alcott the author, that the mainstream children's market had been waiting for. Here was a girls' book that brought tradition and change together in a 'simple and true' story with both sound moral messages and enormous appeal for girls. Its values were familiar, its

An illustration from an early edition of *Little Women.* Alcott's famous 'girls' story' established her as the best loved of all American children's writers in her time.

narrative intimate and entertaining. On the one hand, Maria Edgeworth's voice could be heard throughout in Marmee's firm, rational (and constant) moralizing, reassuring the adult that a child would be improved by reading the book. The characterization, on the other hand, moved children's literature a giant step away from the purely instrumental role of instructor and into the realm of 'real' literature. If the adult figures are fairly stock, the fictional children are more consistently individual, interesting, and convincing than any in American children's fiction up to that time. Much as she might have preferred writing adult novels and much as she apparently did prefer writing (pseudonymously) the 'sensational' stories she deplored in her children's books, with *Little Women* Alcott found her niche in literary history. The family story in children's literature parallels the history of the domestic novel in adult literature; as successful, as central, and as enduring.

The domestic novel and its close relative, the children's family story, were both by-products of much broader social and economic changes. Industrialization, immigration, and urbanization had combined to sharpen the distinctions among classes. Captain Marryat, when he travelled the country in the 1830s, found 'no laboring class here', but that situation had changed by the middle of the century. In Eastern cities, at least, and in other places as well by the 1860s, there was an underclass of the truly poor and a working class employed in factories or as hired farm labour as well as a large middle class divided into many levels by education, wealth, and occupation. Although class lines were still flexible, the fact that classes existed in America was indisputable from mid-century on.

Economic and social changes altered middle-class family ways. More men worked away from home; as in England, children went to school more months in the year, and more years altogether. The culture exalted the mother's role in children's lives and a woman's role in making home the emotional centre of life. By the same token, children had entered upon a long process of separation from adult life. While rural and working-class children retained a working role within the family, most middle-class children did not; their lives were increasingly set apart from adult responsibilities. A romantic view cherished children as children and gave childhood a value in and by itself, rather than as a preparatory school for adult life. In practical terms, it was an attitude that required a modicum of economic ease. Poor families, whether urban or rural, could not dispense with their children's labour, but the middle classes, flushed with post-war prosperity, could and did.

An idealized perception of children and childhood had only gradually seeped down from adult to children's literature. In 1850 it expressed itself in the extreme sentimentality toward children which was often put in the service of some social purpose; but by 1870 the shift had been made from instruction barely disguised as fiction to novels that served up the genuine attractions of narrative fiction in a dish wholesome enough for the young. The major juvenile novels of the post-Civil War period clearly reflected a changed perception of childhood. Just as important, a new generation of authors, many of whom were respected editors or writers of adult literature, brought greater literary attention to writing for children, ensuring that children's literature would be part of the flowering of American literary culture in the last quarter of the nineteenth century.

For more than two hundred years, then, children's literature in America followed the evolution of its society. It absorbed and recorded the major changes in the American outlook: a slow shift from the Puritan preoccupation with spiritual meaning, to a more generalized Protestant concern for personal morality, and from that moralism to a largely secular interest in social behaviour. The literature changed as American attitudes to children and childhood changed, though more slowly; children's literature is usually conservative. Nevertheless, the cultural attitudes that shaped adult literature inevitably transformed children's as well.

The publishing history of children's literature is also inseparable both from the general history of publishing in America and from the economic and social developments that affected American culture at all levels. Children's books were always a reliable source of income for publishers, the more so as fiction became increasingly acceptable in the children's market. Reading was central to American cultural life in the nineteenth century, for the young as much as for their elders, and as the reading public grew, publication for every kind of reader flourished. By the 1870s mainstream writing for children, responding to competition from many sides, was more sophisticated, more varied, and more important to the publishing business than ever before. Children's literature was poised to enter its first golden age.

Typical nineteenth-century depiction of Father Christmas or St Nicholas.

# 6

# THE EMERGENCE OF
# FORM
## 1850–1890

*Julia Briggs* and *Dennis Butts*

### EVANGELICAL WRITING AND THE CHILDREN OF THE POOR

THE year 1850 can be seen as a watershed in the history of the book trade as a whole, and of children's books in particular. During the second half of the nineteenth century publishers competed to produce cheaper reading for an expanding market, and to improve the quality of popular reading matter. The development of publishing for children reflected economic and demographic growth, as well as a society more sensitive and responsive to children's needs. Middle-class children, who had once had books bought for them, were now allowed to choose their own, and they had a wider choice as adventure stories, school stories, nonsense, fantasy, and fairy-tales all became available. At the same time, older traditions of writing for children were adapting to changing conditions. In the first half of the century, the Evangelical movement had tried to reach the children of the poor, teaching the Christian message through Sunday schools; later, a series of education acts helped to extend literacy down the social scale. The Sunday schools had offered their pupils a system of 'reward books', cheap but attractively covered, usually published by the Religious Tract Society, or the Society for Promoting Christian Knowledge, and intended as prizes. 'Rewards' coated moral teaching with a fictional sweetener, but, as the century wore on, the tone of threat or admonition that had characterized the work of Mrs Sherwood, for example, gradually gave place to more hopeful and empowering examples that appealed to the idealism of the young rather than playing on their fears.

Mrs Charlesworth's *Ministering Children* (1854) was a Sunday school novel that, without ever questioning the justice of the social system, invited children to respond to the needs and sufferings of others, and to feel that each had something to contribute to the reduction of suffering, whether they were rich

130

or poor. Set in an old country town, the book has a large cast of children from a variety of different backgrounds who establish a network of 'little deeds of kindness'; even the neglected orphan Patience learns what it means to minister to others, reading to the children in the workhouse and teaching them the word of God. These high-minded children are clearer-eyed and more altruistic than the book's wary or cynical adults. As the romantic view of childhood as a state of innocence 'trailing clouds of glory' took hold, so a sentimental conviction of the child's innate virtue gradually came to replace the earlier emphasis on original sin. While both conceptions were inclined to produce explicit moralizing, that of the childish paragon offered a more inspiring and encouraging model for the young reader.

In the idealized society of loving children portrayed by Mrs Charlesworth, privileged and underprivileged children met as equals: 'The child of rank put her arm around the child of poverty, pressed a kiss of tenderness upon her forehead, and putting the half-crown in her hand, turned away.' The children of the poor—large-eyed, barefoot, and undernourished—growing up in rural or urban slums, were one of the most painful and unignorable facts of Victorian life: as cheap labour, they could be employed in factories, down mines, in the fields, or in the home, but when homeless and orphaned they

The 'street arabs' of Victorian London. 'Brenda' (Mrs Castle Smith) reminded her readers that 'they are our brothers and sisters'.

131

'Now Sir! Gi' us a Ha'penny, or I'll stand on my Nose.' In this cartoon the beggar children who worked as crossing-sweepers are regarded as a comic nuisance, but for Dickens, Hesba Stretton, and George MacDonald, they were the tragic and invisible victims of a thoughtless society.

*Below*: Jessica's first prayer is answered when Daniel's heart is softened by her plight. *Facing*: she gazes longingly at the Victorian middle-class family going to church.

were regarded as a burden on the economy, and consigned to the workhouse. Many died or resorted to crime. Increasing awareness of their plight resulted in a series of government acts that gradually limited the number of hours they were allowed to work and required them to attend school, but child poverty, labour, prostitution, and crime remained major social problems. The culture of the streets created children prematurely knowing, homeless vagrants, the little tribe of 'street arabs'. George E. Sergent's *Roland Leigh: The Story of a City Arab* (1857) relates the adventures of a small boy in the London underworld, abandoned even by the church, which he is too ragged to enter. The hungry heroine of *Jessica's First Prayer* (1867), another 'ragged little heathen', is also turned away; yet, drawn by her single 'peep into fairy-land', she returns unobtrusively each Sunday until the minister notices her and befriends her.

The story of Jessica, the beggar-child whose instinctive piety converts Daniel, the suspicious old pew-opener, was a best seller, and it is easy to see why: written in a simple, direct style, with a Dickensian insight into slum life and child behaviour, it depicts Jessica's faith without moralizing about it. Its author 'Hesba Stretton' (Sarah Smith) vividly recreated the quality of life among the poverty-stricken, down to such telling details as the emotions invested in outgrown clothes, or the satisfaction of meat pies after a diet of bread and oatmeal. She was at once a gifted story-teller and a realist: *Meg's Little Children* (1868) describes a 10-year-old's exhausting struggle to bring up two younger siblings after their mother's death, while *Alone in London* (1869) is the story of a small girl and her grandfather who are 'taken up' by another street arab.

For Hesba Stretton, as for Dickens, children were society's victims, struggling, often against hopeless odds, for physical and spiritual survival. Her observant presentation of them helped to change the ways in which the children of the poor were perceived. Of course, she idealized and sentimentalized them, and was probably responsible for the widespread popularity of 'baby talk' ( ' "Dolly vewy seepy," she lisped, "but must say her prayers always" '), but her narrative skills and her effect on public opinion as well as on later writers are easy to underestimate. Her tender accounts of children starved of food and affection were widely imitated, notably by Mrs Walton in *Christie's Old Organ* (1874), the tale of a young vagrant who drew others to the church, and by 'Brenda' (Mrs G. Castle Smith) in the notorious tear-jerker *Froggy's Little Brother* (1875): 'they may be street arabs, but they have immortal souls, and they are our brothers and sisters, though we may not own them.'

## THE ROMANCE OF THE FAMILY

Hesba Stretton and her successors sought to extend the sympathies of the middle-class child, at the same time appealing and offering hope to the underprivileged. Anna Sewell's *Black Beauty* (1877) tackles the subject of cruelty to animals; it takes the form of the autobiography of a horse, dragged down by the relentless brutality of city life, harsh or neglectful masters and vain mistresses. Written to draw adults' attention to the plight of cab horses, it has been enjoyed by children ever since. But for Charlotte M. Yonge life within the middle-class family itself might be as eventful and exacting as a voyage into the unknown or an adventure in the city's darkest alleys. The domestic sphere had its own particular trials to offer, tests of patience, generosity, and altruism that were no less significant for taking place in a familiar setting, in the garden, the parlour, or the schoolroom. She herself had passed a rather lonely childhood in the Hampshire parish of Hursley, where the young John Keble, leader of the Oxford Movement, was appointed vicar. She

133

revered him, adopting his High Anglican ideals of spiritual self-cultivation and service to the community, and making them the focus of her fiction.

Her first great success, *The Heir of Redclyffe* (1853), was to influence a generation of undergraduates that included William Morris and Edward Burne-Jones through its portrait of the young aristocrat Guy Morville, a man of passionate feelings who disciplines himself to live according to the noblest ideals of charity, courtesy, and consideration for others. Charlotte Yonge's several historical romances achieve a comparable blend of the recognizable and the romantic: *The Little Duke; or, Richard the Fearless* (1854), originally serialized in her Sunday magazine the *Monthly Packet* (1851–90), is the tale of a boy growing up amidst the political violence of tenth-century Normandy, learning when to fight for his rights, and when to forgive his enemies. Christina, the gentle heroine of *The Dove in the Eagle's Nest* (1866), is carried off by a young baron to Schloss Adlerstein, high upon its crag, where her firm faith comes to be loved and valued by the wild and warlike inhabitants.

The bearing rein was designed to force the horse's head up and back in order to make it look fashionable and well-bred. Ginger, the sensitive mare in *Black Beauty*, demands 'What right had they to make me suffer like that?'

In the English edition of Louisa M. Alcott's *Little Women*, Jo March retreats to the garret to eat apples and weep over *The Heir of Redclyffe* (in the American edition she was reading *The Wide, Wide World* ). Jo herself owes much to Yonge's Ethel May, the sympathetic, impetuous, and untidy heroine of *The Daisy Chain; or, Aspirations* (1856). This, her best-loved book, was described by its author as 'a family chronicle, a domestic record of home events during those years of life when the character is chiefly formed'. Charlotte Yonge was concerned above all with character formation, and her magazine, the *Monthly Packet*, was specifically addressed to young people between the ages of 15 and 25, and intended to help them 'perceive how to bring your religious principles to bear upon your daily life'.

When Dr May's wife is killed in a carriage accident, his eleven children must learn to grow up without their mother's guidance, for the mother was the moral focus and natural arbiter of Victorian family life. The two eldest children, Margaret, badly injured in the same carriage accident, and Richard, who has been called to the ministry, help and advise the younger ones. The family's varied and lively adventures are framed by a clear sense of where duty lies, and in what small but significant ways they may have failed to fulfil it. Ethel must surrender her ambition to study Greek to become a schoolteacher, working for the good of the community as a whole and accepting that she will not marry. Charlotte Yonge's central characters are dedicated to acquiring patience and serenity of spirit, yet what they display in the process of learning is high spirits, impulsiveness, or enthusiasm; her ability to value these qualities, at odds though they are with her moral teaching, sets up a high degree of tension and psychological conflict.

Among the best-known of the contributors to Yonge's *Monthly Packet* were a mother and daughter, Mrs Gatty and Mrs Ewing: Margaret Gatty had brought up a family almost as large as that of the Mays in a Yorkshire parsonage. Like many Victorians, she was fascinated by natural history and wrote a series of *Parables from Nature* (1855–71) in which the life cycles of butterflies, bees, and plants were made to yield simple moral lessons. In 1866 she started *Aunt Judy's Magazine* with her second daughter Juliana (later Mrs Ewing) who had shown herself a gifted story-teller from childhood. The magazine, 'intended for the use and amusement of children', included stories, poems, serials, articles on history and natural history, reviews, and letters. Mrs Ewing herself wrote a great deal for it, including fairy-tales, but her most characteristic work engages with the everyday experiences of childhood.

*Mrs Overtheway's Remembrances* (1869) brings together a lonely child and an old lady who relates stories of her own childhood. There is little plot, but remembered excitements and disappointments are wonderfully evoked: as a child, Mrs Overtheway had longed to see Mrs Moss in her rose brocade, trimmed with green, and is shocked to discover that she is now an old lady, dressed in 'feuille-morte' satin. The rapid telescoping of time that turns an old lady back into a small girl anticipates Philippa Pearce's *Tom's Midnight Garden* (1958). Mrs Ewing's great strength is her understanding of children's feelings, their pleasures and pains, their closeness to one another and to their animals. Stories that were particularly popular in her lifetime, such as *Jackanapes* (1883) or *The Story of a Short Life* (*Laetus Sorte Mea*) (1885), in which a young soldier and a heroic child make good deaths, conform to the expectations of her day rather than our own, but in *Jan of the Windmill* (1876), *Mary's Meadow* (1886), or *A Flat-Iron for a Farthing* (1872) she calls up the forgotten delights of childhood, its adventures, discoveries, and imaginative games: 'I imagined myself another Marquis of Carrabas with Rubens [the dog] in boots. I made a desert island in the garden . . . I planted beans in the fond hope that they would tower to the skies and take me with them.'

Although Mrs Ewing wrote in several different modes, she set a high value on 'strict fact and genuine feeling', so that fantasy and realism remained separate in her work. Mrs

A drawing of Juliana Horatia Ewing, 'Aunt Judy' of *Aunt Judy's Magazine*. She began her career by telling stories to her brothers and sisters in the Yorkshire parsonage where they grew up.

135

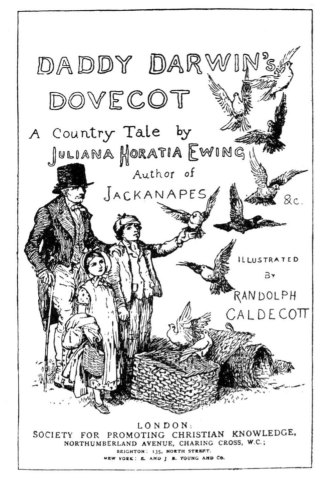

'A yellow sixpence, oh, how nice!' Carrots finds the lost sixpence which will get him into so much trouble, in Walter Crane's illustration to Mrs Molesworth's nursery story.

Randolph Caldecott illustrated several of Mrs Ewing's stories for children. Though brilliantly designed and drafted, his work had a natural and unaffected air that matched her style.

Molesworth often brought the two together, but she wrote for a similar middle-class readership, in which the family unit, with the wise and loving mother at its heart, provided security, companionship, and love. Parents who died or travelled abroad, as they increasingly did in real life as well as in fiction, were desperately missed, and the lonely child among strange adults yearned for a friend. *The Carved Lions* (1895) begins with the happy family unit of Geraldine, her brother Haddie, and their parents, an idyll that turns into a nightmare when her parents are posted abroad and she is exiled to boarding-school.

By the 1890s, families were growing smaller, but Mrs Molesworth's first great success, *Carrots—Just a Little Boy* (1876), is the story of the youngest child in a large Victorian family, bullied by an older brother but protected and cherished by his nearest sister. Mrs Molesworth shared with Mrs Ewing the happy knack of making stories out of the daily events of the nursery, but she is chiefly remembered today for *The Cuckoo Clock* (1877) and *The Tapestry Room* (1879), tales in which children undergo nightly adventures that may or may not be dreams, in which they find themselves conducted by talking animals into fantasy worlds. It is difficult to do justice to the large and varied output of Mrs Ewing and Mrs Molesworth, but their engaging child characters and narrators, and their diverse adventures, in both familiar and fantasy worlds, provided a repertoire of voices, plots, and situations which their successors, notably Frances Hodgson Burnett and E. Nesbit, drew on extensively.

## FROM FAIRY-TALES TO FANTASY

Wordsworth and Coleridge saw childhood as characterized by freedom and vitality of the imagination as it instinctively recognized its affinities with the natural world. Only too often, growing up diminished this capacity, and conventional education frequently hastened the process of loss. Writing that stretched the imagination—fairy-tales or the *Arabian Nights*—was thus more nourishing for the child reader than facts or tracts. In 1823 the Grimms' *German Popular Stories* greatly extended the existing nursery repertoire. This selection, with George Cruikshank's unforgettable illustrations, was clearly designed to appeal to children, but the collection had sprung from a serious and scholarly concern with the German language and national identity, and the original two-volume edition came with annotations. German Romantic writers such as Clemens Brentano, Ludwig Tieck, and Novalis had found in traditional folk-songs and *Märchen* an uninhibited imaginative power, and their re-evaluation and rewriting of fairy-tales was to alter the perception of them substantially and permanently.

Invented fantasies reworked motifs from legends and folk-tale: Friedrich de La Motte Fouqué's *Undine* (1811) and *Sintram and his Companions* (1814) were widely admired and imitated, as were the tales of E. T. A. Hoffmann, such as 'The Golden Flower Pot' (translated by Carlyle), 'The Sandman', and 'Prince Nutcracker and the Mouse King' (the last two now more familiar to us in their ballet versions, *Coppelia* and *The Nutcracker*). The greatest and most original of all those who drew on and reworked traditional fairy-tale, fable, and allegory was Hans Andersen. As Mrs Molesworth observed, his *Wonderful Stories* (1846) inaugurated 'a new era in child literature'.

The Romantic debate as to whether traditional fairy-tales really constituted suitable reading for children returned in the 1850s when George Cruikshank published his own versions of favourite nursery tales, with added warnings against the evils of alcohol. His friend Charles Dickens denounced these as 'Frauds on the Fairies', and burlesqued them by turning Cinderella

'And away they went over stock and stone till their hair whistled in the wind.' Describing Cruickshank's illustrations to Grimms' Fairy Tales, William Roscoe wondered 'Who else would have dared to make a man ride on a fox as he does, sitting firmly on the outstretched tail? It is the only way, when you come to consider it, a man could ride on a fox.'

into a member of the Juvenile Bands of Hope, dressing her in sky-blue satin pantaloons, and sending her to the ball in 'a virtuously democratic vegetable'. While Cruikshank's 'improvements' were absurd, his anxiety about the cruelty, violence, and amorality of fairy-tales was more justified than Dickens would admit: the counter-claim that these were 'harmless little books', inculcating gentleness and mercy, is, in its way, equally reductive. As it was, the versions of fairy-tales that reached Victorian children were already more mediated than their defenders supposed, pre-selected and often strategically cut and bowdlerized; and though they were seldom explicitly didactic or religiose in the way that so much evangelical writing had been, they commonly warned against the failings typical of childhood—greed and selfishness, curiosity and disobedience.

During the nineteenth century, the world of the fairy-tale became a familiar setting for children's stories. It was treated with varying degrees of seriousness, though some element of moral teaching was usually present. The earliest works written in this convention were F. E. Paget's *The Hope of the Katzekopfs* and John Ruskin's *The King of the Golden River* (written for Effie Gray in 1841, but not published till 1851). Both show a marked German influence, and Ruskin's tale is strongly coloured by his childhood delight in Grimms' tales, and Cruikshank's illustrations to them, as well as by his love for the Alps. This is a traditional tale of three brothers, the two eldest being selfish and greedy, while the natural kindness of the youngest brings unexpected rewards, but it is told with unusual humour and eloquence.

Three translations from Andersen in 1846 encouraged writers to draw on the rich repertoire of folk and nursery tales available. Sometimes an old tale was simply reworked, as in Mrs Ewing's version of the old Irish legend of 'Wee Meg Barnilegs', 'Amelia and the Dwarfs' (*The Brownies and Other Tales*, 1870), or as in Mrs Molesworth's adaptation of her Scottish grandmother's tale, 'The Brown Bull of Norroway', related during the course of *The Tapestry Room*. Sometimes the gap between far away and long ago and contemporary life was exploited for comic effect, as Dickens was to do in his tale of 'The Magic Fishbone' (*A Holiday Romance*, 1868), where a well-used wish brings King Watkins the First's quarter-salary rattling down the chimney. A similar blend of incongruous discourses had animated Thackeray's *The Rose and the Ring* (1855), where the Princess Angelica is shown to be a nicely brought-up young lady who 'could play the most difficult pieces of music at sight . . . [and] answer any one of Mangnall's Questions'.

*The Rose and the Ring* occasionally indulges in gentle moralizing ('now you see what I said from the first, that a little misfortune has done you both good'), but, like Dickens's stories for children, it is essentially an entertainment, with jokes for parents as well as children, appropriate to the pantomime structure that frames it. More typical of their period, though by no

*[Handwritten manuscript text in the image, reading:]* This is Valoroso XXIV, King of Paflagonia, seated with his Queen and only child at their royal breakfast table; and receiving the letter wh announces to his Majesty, a proposed visit from Prince Bulbo, Heir of Crim Tartary. Remark the delight upon the Monarch's royal features. He is so absorbed in the perusal of the King of Crim-Tartary's letter that he allows his eggs to get cold and leaves his august muffins untasted. ... What that wild wicked brave delightful Prince Bulbo! cries Princess Angelica ...

The first page of the manuscript of Thackeray's *The Rose and the Ring*: King Valoroso XXIV of Paflagonia sits down to breakfast with his Queen and that paragon of learning, the Princess Angelica (her hair is still in curl-papers).

means lacking in charm, are the stories in *Granny's Wonderful Chair* (Frances Browne, 1857), where the characters' names—the fishermen Sour and Civil, King Winwealth, Princess Greedalind—define their nature, and all receive their just deserts at the end. Most of the reworked or invented fairy-tales reiterated the kinds of moral or prudential lessons embedded in the folk-tales themselves, but occasionally such lessons became punitive, as in Lucy Clifford's 'The New Mother' (*Anyhow Stories for Children*, 1882), where the children's desire to be naughty replaces their own loving mother with a horrible new one, who has glass eyes and a wooden tail. But they might also be consolatory, as in Mrs Craik's delicate story of *The Little Lame Prince* (1875), in which the disabled child, confined to Hopeless Tower, learns to fly away on a magic travelling cloak that represents the power and freedom of the imagination.

Towards the end of the century, when the use of fairy-tale conventions was well established, the parodic treatment earlier employed by Dickens and Thackeray itself became a familiar mode. Inspired in part by Thackeray's Paflagonia, Andrew Lang's Chronicles of Pantouflia comprised the story of *Prince Prigio* (1889), cursed by a bad-tempered fairy to become too clever by half, and that of his son *Prince Ricardo* (1893), who has read too many fairy-tales. Largely depending on the skill of the narrative voice, this mode was used with great brilliance by E. Nesbit in *The Book of Dragons* and *Nine Unlikely Tales*, and by Kenneth Grahame in 'The Reluctant Dragon'. Lang also edited an original and highly influential series of anthologies of folk-tales, beginning with *The Blue Fairy Book* in 1889, and ending in 1910 with the *Lilac*, twelfth in the series. While the first volume included many classic tales, Lang later sought out stories from many countries, commissioning translations or adaptations, though hardly ever rewriting them himself, as he explained in the introduction to *The Crimson Fairy Book*: 'The Fairy Books have been almost wholly the work of Mrs Lang. . . . The reputation of having written [them] . . . weighs upon me and is killing me.' They were illustrated in line, and later in colour by H. J. Ford, achieved great popularity, and were many times reprinted. Lang himself had no patience with tales that dealt 'in allegory or in little episodic sermons', believing that 'We want *story*, and human beings and human interest', yet the recognition that fairy-tales might yield deeper meanings continued to attract serious artists to the form.

In *The Happy Prince and Other Tales* (1888) Oscar Wilde used fairy-tales in 'an attempt to mirror modern life in a form remote from reality—to deal with modern problems in a mode that is ideal and not imitative'. These fables, strongly influenced by Andersen, include not only selfish giants and delicate mermaids but also the brutal contrasts that make up life in the modern city: 'the rich making merry in their beautiful houses, while the beggars were sitting at the gates . . . the white faces of starving children . . . two little boys . . . lying in one another's arms to try and keep themselves warm.' Wilde's elegantly wrought stories, both here and in *The House of Pomegranates* (1891), play out the conflict between the Paterian desire for beauty and fine feeling and the impulse to pity and intervention on behalf of human suffering. Like all the best fairy-tales, these speak to children at the same time as they speak over their heads.

### INTO OTHER WORLDS

Nothing—not the jaunty narration of Thackeray in *The Rose and the Ring*, nor the surreal verse of Edward Lear—prepares us for the shock of Lewis Carroll's *Alice's Adventures in Wonderland* (1865), the most brilliant and original children's book of the century and perhaps of all time. Carroll, or more properly Charles Lutwidge Dodgson, was not a professional writer but a tutor in mathematics at Oxford, a bachelor don afflicted with a bad stammer. He was obsessively interested in little girls, and kept small toys and games about him as well as funds of stories as conversation openers. He also liked to photograph them, dressed up and even undressed. In his masterpiece, this habit of seduction rises to the heights of artistic intensity. The story of Alice was originally made up for Alice Liddell, the 10-year-old daughter of the Dean of Christ Church (Dodgson's own college), and her two sisters. According to legend, it was first told on a summer's day outing on the river, on 4 July 1862. At Alice's request Carroll later wrote up and illustrated the story as *Alice's Adventures Underground*. He then expanded it and added the episodes set in the Duchess's kitchen and at the Mad Hatter's tea party.

Like its sequel, *Alice's Adventures in Wonderland* may be read as a profound scrutiny of systems, including those of social behaviour, logic, and language. Carroll's oddities conferred on him an outsider status that enabled him to identify with the child's sense of puzzlement at the elaborate codes of the adult world. Alice's constant interrogation of the creatures she meets reflects her childish ignorance of widely accepted rules, while their interrogation of her may reflect Carroll's own search for greater intimacy with the object of his desire. These exchanges also reflect the contended-for and shifting dynamics of power between adult and child, controller and controlled: although full of self-doubt ('I'm not myself, you see'), Alice finds herself surrounded by strange and often childishly atavistic creatures. She is generally willing to take on adult responsibility (for example, for the pig-baby), resists intimidation, and gives as good as she gets conversationally, recognizing that 'they're only a pack of cards, after all. I needn't be afraid of them!' But she is also the child as victim, cross-questioned, bullied, and lectured by the Wonderland inhabitants, required to play croquet with a flamingo, summoned to give evidence at the trial, and then summarily dismissed on the grounds that she is a mile high.

Such violent alternations reflect the asymmetries of power between grown-up and child derived from differences in knowledge and size (Alice finds her knowledge—in this case, her school lessons—as elusive as her sense of self). When she is small, she is humiliated by a caterpillar, menaced by a puppy, and

*Above*: a page from *Alice's Adventures Underground*, written and illustrated by Charles Dodgson for Alice Liddell, and the earliest version of her *Adventures in Wonderland*.

*Facing*: Charles Dodgson photographed Alice Liddell many times, and in a variety of different costumes and poses.

John Tenniel's illustration of the Jabberwocky anticipates science-fiction's monsters. Originally intended as the frontispiece to *Through the Looking-Glass*, it was later replaced by a less alarming picture of Alice walking beside the White Knight.

almost drowned by her own tears, yet this vulnerable state also confers entry into the magic rose garden, the garden of lost delight. The child's desire to grow up and stabilize her relation to the world about her here encounters the adult's desire to re-enter the secret world of childhood, a desire to 'go small' which occurs elsewhere in children's fiction (for example in Masefield's *The Midnight Folk* and *The Box of Delights*, or in M. R. James's little-known story *The Five Jars*).

*Through the Looking-Glass* (1871) is that rare thing, a sequel which develops and extends the scope of its original. The episodic character of *Wonderland*, with its mixture of animals real and invented, people, and playing cards, is replaced by the tighter rules of a chess game and the reversed logic of the mirror image. Death, generally treated unseriously in the earlier book, has grown more threatening: Tweedledee reduces Alice to tears by telling her that, if the Red King awoke, she'd 'go out bang! just like a candle!' Her existence depends on his continuing to dream her. Difficult metaphysical considerations of this kind, which acknowledge the narrative as fiction and Alice within it, become more explicit in *Looking-Glass*, but the arbitrary nature of social and linguistic rules is a theme common to both books; it is evoked, as in Dickens, through the defamiliarizing eyes of the child. Carroll constantly parodies the logic of social structures—tea and dinner parties, games of croquet or chess, the protocols of polite conversation ('Curtsey while you're thinking'), revealing them to be as provi- sional as semantic difference: things are done like this, because this is how they are done.

Behind Alice's puzzled efforts to come to terms with her world lies Carroll's own professional scepticism about systems, whether of law, social conduct, education, or games, since the slightest change of terms, or even of individual letters (the Mock-Turtle's school teaches reeling, writhing, and fainting in coils), exposes their instability. Carroll's perception that all communication and negotiation depends on a shared, but ultimately provisional, system of meanings partly derived from his work in mathematics, since algebra continually adjusts given propositions; but the book's comprehensive exploration of semiotic systems and their clear connection with the subject self brings together the inexperience of the child and the speculations of the don, conferring on both a contemporary, even a postmodern flavour.

Following the pattern of many other Victorian stories for children, the 'Alice' books were interspersed with verse, though invariably parodic or nonsense verse, structural experiments in the nature of poetic language. The most original of these is 'Jabberwocky', the poem in mirror-writing that is also an archetypal quest poem, since its hero searches out and slays the monster of the title. *The Hunting of the Snark* (1876) was, Carroll acknowledged, in some sense a sequel to it. It too is a quest poem, but this time a doomed quest, played out in an atmosphere of metaphysical dread that includes a Kafkaesque nightmare of a trial, a recurrent motif. His last work, the two parts of *Sylvie and Bruno* (1889, 1893), includes sparkling flashes of speculation about the nature of time and space, and some entertaining verse, but it is deeply flawed by sentimentality: Bruno's baby-talk anticipates that of S. R. Crockett's *Sir Toady Lion* (1897), while Sylvie, dream-child and object of unacknowledged desire, sets the stage for Barrie's *Peter Pan*.

Carroll had mocked the didactic element in so much writing for children through characters such as the Duchess, who proffered implausible morals for every occasion. His intellectual robustness countered the age's tendency to indulge in over-explicit preaching, and his inventive and inconsequential scenarios offered new possibilities of fictional freedom. Imitations proliferated, but two books that adapted the model to their own purposes deserve to be singled out: both were by women poets. Jean Ingelow's *Mopsa the Fairy* (1869) is a fantasy of some subtlety and psychic inwardness: out walking with his nurse, Jack finds a hollow tree with a nest of fairies inside it. Pocketing them, he is carried off to Fairyland, where he wakes the tiny Mopsa by kissing her. After a number of adventures together, she becomes queen and he flies back to the security of his old life at home. The writing is always sensitive and imaginative, while the inset poems comment on and enhance the action.

Christina Rossetti, author

Tender-hearted Sylvie turns over a beetle lying on its back. Harry Furniss's illustration captures the combination of absurdity (the beetle is wearing boots) and sentiment characteristic of Carroll's last book.

Charles Dodgson photographed the Rossetti family. *From let to right*: Dante Gabriel, Christina, their mother Frances Mary, and William Michael.

of 'Goblin Market' and *Sing-Song*, also wrote a fantasy 'in the Alice style': in *Speaking Likenesses* (1874) three little girls undergo strange ordeals in which they confront surreal versions of their sins or weaknesses, memorably illustrated by Arthur Hughes. Spoilt Flora, who misbehaves at her own birthday party, is victimized by a party of monstrous children who torment and play games with her, rather as the goblins had harassed Lizzie in 'Goblin Market'. Edith, inclined to think herself more capable than she really is, spends a frustrating afternoon trying to light a fire underneath the kettle, while Maggie goes on a Little Red Riding Hood journey, but manages to preserve herself and her gifts from the fairy children who assail her. On her return, she finds in their place a dove, a kitten, and a puppy, and brings them home to a warm welcome. Rossetti's stories starkly contradict developing ideas of childhood innocence or wisdom: Flora is punished for her dissatisfaction, and all three are menaced and cowed by situations that they cannot control. As in Lucy Clifford's 'The New Mother', Rossetti threatens the naughty child with fantasy punishments where earlier writers would have invoked divine retribution.

Rossetti's wilful Flora and Carroll's dream-child were stereotypes reflecting antithetical views of childhood, yet some fantasy writers saw the exercise of

144

active Christian virtue as a possible form of negotiation between the two. Norman MacLeod's allegory *The Gold Thread* (1861) teaches faith and duty through the figure of the clew that Prince Eric must recover and pursue through a series of dangers and temptations, learning in the process that 'he would always be in the right road, so long as he did not trust mere appearances, but kept hold of his thread'. Allegory of this type, with its roots in the parables of the New Testament and *The Pilgrim's Progress*, was first used by Samuel Wilberforce in *Agathos, and Other Sunday Stories* (1840) and it was the preferred mode of Charlotte Tucker, who always wrote under the acronym ALOE (A Lady Of England). In *The Claremont Tales, The Giant Killer, The Young Pilgrim*, and their successors, faithful knights overthrew giants that were also vices, and a magic mirror clouded over when its user had sinned. The magical episodes took the form of dreams, or were narrated to the listening family, and sometimes a fantasy narrative ran parallel to a tale of nursery life, as in *Wings and Stings* (1855), where the alternative world is that of bees, and the lessons are inspired by natural history.

The clergyman and writer Charles Kingsley was similarly fascinated by what nature could reveal: *Glaucus; or, The Wonders of the Shore* (1855) was inspired by nature walks with his own children, and he wrote to his friend F. D. Maurice that in *The Water-Babies* (1863) he had 'tried . . . to make children and grown folks understand that there is quite a miraculous and divine element underlying all physical nature'. *The Water-Babies* brings together Kingsley's social criticism (Tom is a climbing-boy, cleaning the chimneys of rich men's houses partly with his own underfed body), natural history, moral allegory (the fairies, Mrs Doasyouwouldbedoneby and the harsher Mrs Bedonebyasyoudid), with Rabelaisian lists and hectoring attacks on aspects of contemporary life and institutions that made him impatient. The whole richly indigestible mixture is held together by the narrative voice: 'And now, my dear little man, what should we learn from this parable?'

Although *The Water-Babies* begins with

'She was the most nice, soft, fat, smooth, pussy, cuddly, delicious creature who ever nursed a baby; and she understood babies thoroughly.' Noel Paton's illustration for the first edition of *The Water-Babies* associates Mrs Doasyouwouldbedoneby with regressive pleasures.

Kingsley's own drawing of Danae and her child for *The Heroes* (1856), a collection of Greek legends.

*Facing, above, left*: an American version of a common ploy to heighten the task of learning: *The Infant's Grammer*, 1825.

*Above, right*: Maria Edgeworth's *The Birthday Present*.

*Below*: an illustration for Perrault's *Cinderella; or the Little Glass Slipper* published in Philadelphia, 1822.

the misery of the little sweep, his flight across the moors, and his death, as it seems, by drowning, it quickly moves on to describe the processes of purgation that Tom's soul, in the form of the small, newt-like water-baby, undergoes. The process mingles lessons in morality and marine biology, but Kingsley had come to regard the evolutionary workings of nature as the physical working-out of the aspiration to higher things, and thus analogous to the making of souls: when Tom is wicked he grows prickles, and an inset story records the fate of the Doasyoulikes, a race of human beings who degenerate into apes. At first Tom succumbs to various temptations, but he is gradually schooled by experience to altruism, 'fostered alike by beauty and by fear', as if Kingsley were taking Wordsworth's educative Nature literally. Most of the action takes place in the cleansing medium of water, and Tom's purgatorial trials are completed when he reaches St Brandan's Isle and recovers his beloved Miss Ellie (who has also died), and is permitted to go 'home' with her on Sundays. Mother Carey, the creative and guiding principle of the underwater world, dismisses them and we learn, surprisingly, that Tom 'is now a great man of science'.

The narrative bounces along, ignoring all such inconsistencies, yet its exploration of the margins and wastes of mid-Victorian society might seem more humane if it were less saturated with moral imperatives. A circularity in the narrative is reflected in the way in which the book's inconsistencies themselves engender a manic energy, and its power self-evidently springs from its gaping cracks and fissures. In addition to *The Water-Babies* and his natural history writings, Kingsley wrote two popular historical romances: *Westward Ho!* (1855), in which two young Elizabethans, Frank and Amyas, sail against the Spanish Armada, and *Hereward the Wake, Last of the English* (1866). His last book for children, *Madame How and Lady Why* (1870), explores the problems posed by geology, and was first serialized in the children's magazine *Good Words for the Young*.

This magazine was founded in 1868 with Norman MacLeod as editor (he also edited its adult counterpart, *Good Words*). The first episode of George MacDonald's *At the Back of the North Wind* appeared in the first issue (it was published in book form in 1871), and MacDonald subsequently took over the editorship, publishing in it *Ranalph Bannerman's Boyhood*, a vivid evocation of his own childhood in rural Scotland, and *The Princess and the Goblin*. The pressure to fill its pages produced MacDonald's best writing for children, his experiment in fantasy for adults, *Phantastes* (1858), having previously failed to sell.

George MacDonald was brought up as a Calvinist in Scotland, and for a

## THE PRONOUNS.

At this moment a bustle was heard at the door
From a Party of PRONOUNS, who came by the score.
And what do you think?   Why I vow and declare
THEY would pass for the Nouns who already were there.
And THEIR boldness was such, as I live IT is true,
ONE declar'd HE was I, and ONE call'd HIMSELF YOU.
THIS, THAT, and the OTHER, THEY claim'd as THEIR OWN,
But who THEY are really, will shortly be known.

THE BIRTHDAY PRESENT.

Why may not I try too, as well as the rest.     p. 15.

while he worked as a Congregationalist minister; but for most of his life he supported himself by his writing. Like Kingsley, he had been strongly influenced by the radical Christian thinker F. D. Maurice. He was also a close friend of Charles Dodgson, who had consulted the whole family as to whether he should publish *Alice's Adventures Underground*, and often photographed them. MacDonald wrote a great deal, in many different forms, including poetry, realistic and visionary novels, and the two fantasies *Phantastes* and *Lilith* (1895), now far more widely known and admired than they were in his lifetime, since he has come to be recognized as, in Auden's phrase, 'pre-eminently a mythopoeic writer'. For children, he wrote a number of fairy-tales ranging in mood from 'The Light Princess' (which begins with a christening that goes wrong, and ends in a troubling image of redemption) to 'The Golden Key' (in which Mossy and Tangle set out on a quest for a keyhole which eventually leads them home to God).

Kingsley's use of fantasy in *The Water-Babies* clearly influenced MacDonald's own writing for children, most obviously in *At the Back of the North Wind*. Yet many of the features that they have in common reflect contemporary cultural preoccupations rather than personal affinities. Like Kingsley, MacDonald was profoundly distressed by the condition of the poor: North Wind takes little Diamond to meet Nanny, the crossing-sweeper, and his concern for her and for others like her marks him out as belonging to the tradition of saintly children depicted by Dickens, Hesba Stretton, and others, a tradition exemplified in his novel *Sir Gibbie* (1879), the distressing story of a street arab.

Though little Diamond has an innate goodness lacking in Kingsley's Tom, both children undergo experiences that are in some sense purgatorial: Diamond's journeys with North Wind reflect the loosening bonds of his physical being, and he is finally released to join her for ever. It might seem theologically odd that the Broad Churchman Kingsley and the Calvinist MacDonald should adopt the figure of purgatorial suffering. One explanation lies in F. D. Maurice's influence on both writers, and his belief in salvation by love. Both of them represent suffering as a learning process administered by fairy women: these are at once versions of the mother as nurturer and moral guide of the family, and other-worldly creatures who display contradictory aspects of themselves, but are essentially as beautiful and sensuously comforting as North Wind herself, pictured by the illustrator, Arthur Hughes, as a mass of luxuriantly swirling hair.

Both writers are centrally concerned with the process of 'soul-making', and for both this involves the cleansing of the perceptions through washing or baptism. In both the child possesses a radical innocence which is at once blessed, and yet still requires to be educated in the forms goodness takes in

*Facing, above*: an American county school in 1871, Winslow Homer. The first grants of land for public education in 1802 were for 1/36 of the area of each township.

*Below*: *Under the Window* (1879) was Kate Greenaway's first major success. Although not distinguished as a figure drawer her original dress designs (which she actually made to ensure that they were practical) set a fashion. She worked closely with Edmund Evans, the most influential engraver and printer of the period.

this world. Loss, adversity, and even death must ultimately be recognized as aspects of the divine, punishments reluctantly inflicted by a loving mother who can see further than her children. North Wind reassures Diamond, 'I don't think I am quite what you fancy me to be. I have to shape myself various ways to various people. But the heart of me is true.' But whereas Kingsley found analogies in nature and evolutionary theory for the spiritual processes he represented, MacDonald's outlook was altogether more platonic and other-worldly: for him, the transcendent consisted in a beauty dimly reflected in mortal things. Little Diamond yearns for the country at the back of the North Wind, and eventually finds it: in the narrator's final words, 'They thought he was dead. I knew that he had gone to the back of the north wind.'

MacDonald's other two fantasies are set in a fairy-tale world, and both are quest narratives. In *The Princess and the Goblin* (1872), Curdie the miner saves Princess Irene from the goblins who are digging their way to her beneath her house, uneasily perched half-way up the mountain. In its attics lives her great-grandmother, whose magic aid includes a baptismal bath of roses and a thread that leads Irene to Curdie when he is lost in the mines. More than a

Princess Irene in *The Princess and the Goblin* tells her father about her discovery of her fairy grandmother. The illustrator, Arthur Hughes, has drawn the old king as a portrait of MacDonald himself.

decade later MacDonald wrote a sequel to it, *The Princess and Curdie* (1883), which reflects his growing disillusion with society. In this dark fable, Curdie saves the Princess's beleaguered father since he has learned to identify the beasts that lurk in men's souls. The two marry and rule the kingdom, but after their death greed causes the citizens to dig through their own foundations and the book ends on an apocalyptic note. 'One day at noon, when life was at its highest, the whole city fell with a roaring crash. The cries of men and the shrieks of women went up with its dust, and then there was a great silence.'

MacDonald described his approach to writing fairy-tales in an essay on 'The Fantastic Imagination' (*A Dish of Orts*, 1893). Fairy-stories may even convey divine truths if the writer has been dealing 'with things that came from thoughts beyond his own'. MacDonald thus gave the old neoplatonic arguments about the relative status of truth and fiction a further twist, even as he extended the Victorian sense of the weight and responsibility of fiction to include the old nursery tales.

MacDonald had wished 'to wake things up that are in [man]; or say, to make him think things for himself'. He succeeded in awaking at least two other writers to the possibilities of blending fantasy with Christian doctrine: in the matter of fairy-tales, both his precept and his practice were to influence J. R. R. Tolkien (notably in the goblin scenes of *The Hobbit*, the essay 'On Fairy Tales', and *Smith of Wootton Major*), but his greatest disciple was C. S. Lewis. For Lewis, the reading of *Phantastes* struck him as a revelation: 'It was as though the voice that had called me from the world's end was now speaking at my side.' The homeliness of the *Märchen* and the longing for a better world implicit in the fantasy of quest finally met and embraced in Mac-Donald's writing for children.

## EMPIRE AND ADVENTURE

During the second part of the nineteenth century Great Britain dramatically expanded her empire overseas, taking control of India after the Mutiny of 1857, annexing Burma, and acquiring vast parts of Africa, so that the area over which Queen Victoria ruled at the end of her reign was four times greater than at her accession.

Improvements in communications, together with the availability of cheaper newspapers, made the British public more aware of such dramatic episodes as the Zulu wars and excited a passionate pride in imperial events. Thousands of British subjects emigrated each year and many Victorian children shared their parents' interest in the empire, expecting to work there when they left school, in trade, the armed forces, or as public servants. Rudyard Kipling's own school, the United Services College in Devon, was actually founded to help boys pass the Army Examination and serve in such countries as India. It is not surprising then that this interest in exotic places overseas, offering the possibility of exciting adventure within the hegemony of British imperialism, encouraged boys and girls to read adventure stories describing similar events in which the heroes and (less often) the heroines were young people like themselves.

We have seen the importance of Captain F. W. Marryat in the history of the adventure story for young readers; other writers soon followed. Captain Mayne Reid, an Irishman who had served with distinction in the American army in the war against Mexico, produced such stories as *The Desert Home*, full of natural history and topographical information, from 1851 onwards. R. M. Ballantyne, after years working for the Hudson's Bay Company in Canada, began his series of adventure stories with *Snowflakes and Sunbeams;*

*or, The Young Fur Traders* in 1856, and published his extraordinarily popular Robinsonnade *The Coral Island: A Tale of the Pacific Ocean* two years later. W. H. G. Kingston, the third of Marryat's mid-nineteenth-century successors, specialized in sea-stories, such as *Peter the Whaler: His Early Life and Adventures in the Arctic Regions* (1851).

Kingston was succeeded as editor of the significantly named *Union Jack: Tales for British Boys*, a penny weekly devoted to adventure stories, by G. A. Henty, who became the most prolific exponent of the genre in the last decades of the century. A widely experienced war correspondent, Henty began writing full-time for children when poor health made strenuous travelling impossible. Soon he was producing four books a year, ranging from historical works such as *With Clive in India; or, The Beginnings of Empire* (1884) to stories about contemporary events, such as *With Buller in Natal; or, A Born Leader* (1901).

Henty was enormously popular, with sales estimated by his publisher Blackie at 150,000 annually. In view of his success, it is not surprising that by the end of the nineteenth century almost every publishing house—including Blackie, Nelson, Longman, Macmillan, and J. F. Shaw—was eagerly providing adventure stories for a young reading public.

The first and most important characteristic of the adventure story was its blending of the extraordinary with the probable, for if the events in a tale were too ordinary they failed to excite, but a sequence of completely extraordinary incidents failed to be credible. This sense of the probable was achieved by choosing as youthful hero a normal teenage boy, the son of a clergyman or innkeeper perhaps. Neither particularly clever nor stupid, but full of 'pluck', he usually leaves home at the beginning of the story as the result of a domestic crisis to seek his fortune elsewhere. After the death of his father at the beginning of R. L. Stevenson's *Kidnapped* (1886), for example, young David Balfour sets out in search of his other relations.

The settings are usually exotic; the young hero is sometimes accompanied by a companion, and often takes a special gift with him—a physical object like a map or weapon, or perhaps a facility for learning languages or for dis-

*The Union Jack: Tales for British Boys.* Begun by W. H. G. Kingston, the *Union Jack* ran for four years, G. A. Henty taking over when Kingston fell ill. The first issue opened with a typical adventure story by Kingston.

guise. Complications and difficulties arise—shipwreck, attacks by cannibals, treachery—and the narrative gradually rises to a great climax, which is often a fierce battle against powerful opponents.

Religious didacticism is not so prevalent in these stories as in earlier children's books, but their authors in a more secular age still took their moral responsibilities seriously. They tried to guide their young readers towards such virtues as honesty and loyalty, pluck and resourcefulness, and usually articulated the belief that the British possession of such virtues was unequalled, and that the British empire was an unrivalled instrument for harmony and justice. G. A. Henty was the most explicit exponent of late Victorian imperialism, often prefacing his tales with a letter to 'My Dear Lads', in which he drew attention to the heroic exploits of the story which followed and which helped to create the empire.

In their use of formulaic elements and stereotyped characters, adventure stories clearly owe a great deal to traditional folk- and fairy-tales, and the structure of the folk-tale clearly lies behind many of the adventure stories of Robert Louis Stevenson. Born in Edinburgh, Stevenson had a sickly childhood; he studied engineering and then law before deciding to pursue a full-

Robert Louis Stevenson seated on the steps of Vailima. Partly for reasons of health, Stevenson settled in Samoa in 1889, where he had a house built called Vailima, or 'the place of the five streams'. His wife sits on the right and his elderly mother second from the left.

The map of Treasure Island (the frontispiece of the book). Stevenson said that the idea for his story came to him one rainy afternoon in Braemar when he made a detailed map of an island in order to entertain his young stepson Lloyd Osborne.

time literary career. He travelled widely, often in search of better health, not only in Europe and North America, but in the South Seas, and finally settled in Samoa, where he was known to the natives as *Tusitala*, 'Teller of Tales'.

*Treasure Island* was first serialized in the boys' paper *Young Folks*, from October 1881 to January 1882. The folk-tale structure is immediately clear—hero, quest, struggles, and homecoming. But Stevenson varies and develops these formulaic elements with imagination and seriousness. In traditional tales the hero usually acquires some special gift, and Jim's discovery of the treasure-map is the equivalent here. Stevenson also introduces various complications into Jim's journey, such as the way the crew splits between loyal men and pirates, and the unexpected intervention of Ben Gunn. Indeed the story is full of wonderfully imaginative touches—the Black Spot, Jim's visit to the apple-barrel, and the dead man's song heard among the trees as the pirates near the treasure.

What gives *Treasure Island* its great originality, however, is the way Stevenson varies the expected pattern of the faithful companions and the stereotyped villains. For Jim's allies, especially Squire Trelawney and Captain Smollett, are not always sympathetic, while the villains combine vulnerability with their violence—Billy Bones with his nightmarish terrors, the blind beggar Pew, and Israel Hands, wounded but absolutely murderous.

Less interested in imperialism than other writers, Stevenson displays the most extraordinary development of the adventure-story formula in the character of Long John Silver and Jim's relationship with him. Silver is ostensibly the villain of the tale, but Jim immediately takes to him when they first meet, and they become—in the book's greatest irony—like father and son. Silver is the leader of the mutineers, but he consistently looks after Jim and shows him genuine warmth. Silver is a moral enigma.

Brought up by strict Presbyterian parents in mid-Victorian Edinburgh, where respectability and immorality flourished alongside each other, Stevenson became preoccupied with the problems of the ambiguity and duality of human nature. *Dr Jekyll and Mr Hyde*, his adult fable of 1886, dramatizes his sense of the paradoxes of human behaviour in their starkest form, but in *Treasure Island* and *Kidnapped* Stevenson showed how the adventure story, with all its opportunities for loyalty and treachery, could be a magnificent instrument for asking serious questions.

Challenged by the success of *Treasure Island*, Henry Rider Haggard combined memories of his years as a colonial administrator in Africa with a vivid imagination to produce *King Solomon's Mines* (1885). Haggard's story of big-game hunter Allan Quatermain's search for a missing Englishman and his eventual discovery of fabulous diamonds still holds readers by its narrative power, even if they cannot help noticing its quasi-imperialistic values. Its sequel, *Allan Quatermain* (1887), was even more admired by the young Winston Churchill.

The tradition established by Marryat and his successors continued to flourish in the final decades of the nineteenth century with George Manville Fenn and Gordon Stables, while Captain F. S. Brereton and 'Herbert Strang' produced similar tales well into the twentieth century. The only work of the genre which seems to have endured from the last decade of the century, however, is *Moonfleet* (1898) by John Meade Falkner. This is a tale of smugglers and treachery in eighteenth-century England, and Falkner reminds us of Stevenson more than the imperialist authors in his study of the relationship between his young hero, John Trenchard, and his friend, Elzevir Block.

New developments were beginning to appear. The naturalist Richard Jefferies produced a curious mixture of the animal fable, melodrama, romance, and realism in *Wood Magic* (1881), while his masterpiece *Bevis: The Story of a Boy* (1882), the almost autobiographical account of a boy's experiences sailing on a lake near his father's farm, successfully demonstrated how exciting adventures were possible within a realistic, domestic setting. *Bevis* has links with the imperial tradition, emphasizing home, manliness, and codes of behaviour, but at the time it was almost lost among the fanfares of imperial trumpets.

## SCHOOLS AND SCHOOL STORIES

From the middle of the nineteenth century Britain entered a period of prosperity. As the feudal and agrarian order of the past gradually gave way to an industrial and more democratic society, almost all sections of the community saw substantial gains in wages, rents, and profits. Many of the prosperous middle classes now sought a better education for their sons, and sent them away to boarding schools, which they expected to offer a more responsible upbringing than that enjoyed by the sons of the aristocracy in the unreformed 'public' schools, which were then often rather chaotic and brutal.

153

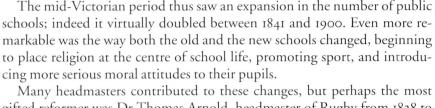

The mid-Victorian period thus saw an expansion in the number of public schools; indeed it virtually doubled between 1841 and 1900. Even more remarkable was the way both the old and the new schools changed, beginning to place religion at the centre of school life, promoting sport, and introducing more serious moral attitudes to their pupils.

Many headmasters contributed to these changes, but perhaps the most gifted reformer was Dr Thomas Arnold, headmaster of Rugby from 1828 to 1842. He attacked the bullying and drunkenness which then existed in many schools, and made Christian values central. Using senior boys as prefects, he practised corporal punishment only sparingly and encouraged games and sports for exercise and relaxation. Arnold's influence on his pupils was enormous. Some of them went on to become headmasters in their turn, and one, Thomas Hughes, commemorated the Doctor in *Tom Brown's Schooldays* 'by "An Old Boy"' in 1857. In doing so, Hughes popularized and largely defined the form of the school story, for the book was reprinted four times within its first year of publication, and has remained in print ever since, the most famous school story in the English language.

Of course, the way had been prepared for *Tom Brown's Schooldays*: school stories had appeared as early as Sarah Fielding's *The Governess* in 1749, and Harriet Martineau had produced *The Crofton Boys* in 1841. Charlotte Brontë's *Jane Eyre* (1847) and Dickens's *Dombey and Son* (1848) and *David Copperfield* (1850) had also contained scenes of school life which had attracted enormous public interest.

Hughes was born in Berkshire and was sent to Rugby in 1833, where he played football and cricket, suffered bullying, made friends, and came to revere his headmaster. After graduating from Oxford, he was called to the bar and became in due course a QC and Liberal MP. Under the influence of F. D. Maurice, he became a leading member of the Christian Socialist movement and devoted almost all his busy life to promoting good causes.

He wrote most of *Tom Brown's Schooldays* in 1856 in order to tell his 8-year-old son Maurice about school life, but completion of the story was delayed by the death of Hughes's eldest daughter from scarlet fever. For some readers this domestic tragedy explains a change of tone in the story. It has been suggested that, after the book's breezy introduction to school life, and Tom's encounters with East and the bully Flashman, the story rather loses its way amid all the moralizing and piety after Arthur arrives. But it seems clear that Hughes always intended a gradual change of mood in the novel, deliberately exposing Tom's animal high spirits and irresponsibility in the first part of the story before showing how he matures into a thoughtful and responsible young Christian under the Doctor's influence.

*Tom Brown's Schooldays* is a remarkable book; in its popularity it established a genre which later writers, influenced by its structure, were to develop.

More than this, Hughes also showed how an apparently limited form—restricted both because of the closed world of the school and the recurrence of formulaic elements—could actually be exploited. He not only described experiences with which many children would be familiar, but he also dealt with issues of immediate relevance to them: the fluctuating nature of friendships, the importance of peer groups, and the problems of dealing with adult authority. *Tom Brown's Schooldays* may have offered readers a picture of a small and even artificial society, but Hughes showed it was one in which real problems could be discussed.

F. W. Farrar's *Eric; or, Little by Little: A Tale of Roslyn School* (1858) resolves those problems with passionate intensity. Born in India in 1831, Farrar was sent to King William's College, the original of Roslyn School, on the Isle of Man, before studying at London and Cambridge. He was ordained, and taught for several years at Harrow, where he wrote *Eric*, before becoming headmaster of Marlborough College and eventually Dean of Canterbury. The author of various theological works, Farrar emphasized the religious aim of *Eric* in the Preface to the twenty-fourth edition published in 1889: 'The story of "Eric" was written with but one single object—the vivid inculcation of inward purity and moral purpose, by the history of a boy who, in spite of the inherent nobleness of his disposition, falls into all folly and wickedness, until he has learnt to seek help from above.'

Eric, the 12-year-old hero of Farrar's story, is truthful and honest when he starts at Roslyn School, but likes popularity and finds it difficult to resist cribbing and playing games in chapel. He gradually succumbs to other temptations, and begins to swear and to smoke. Though he tries to reform when his high-principled friend Russell dies, he soon resumes bad habits, and when he is found drunk in chapel is ordered to be expelled; he is only saved by the headmaster's forgiveness. Suspected of theft, he runs away to sea, but is cruelly treated by the captain and escapes to his aunt's home, seriously ill, and with evil cleansed from his heart. Then, in a final crushing blow, Eric learns that his mother's grief at his behaviour has killed her, and he himself dies.

Although a summary of the plot invites derision, Farrar's narrative proceeds with pace and contains powerful scenes, such as when Eric defies and breaks the cane of his favourite master, Mr Rose. *Eric* was enormously popular, in fact, reaching its thirty-sixth edition by Farrar's death in 1902. But though the conduct Farrar recommended is not so very different from that of *Tom Brown's Schooldays*, there is a pervasive, almost masochistic pessimism

*Facing*: Thomas Hughes (1822–96) was MP, lawyer, Christian Socialist, and the author of *Tom Brown's Schooldays*, as depicted by the cartoonist 'Spy' in *Vanity Fair*, in June 1872.

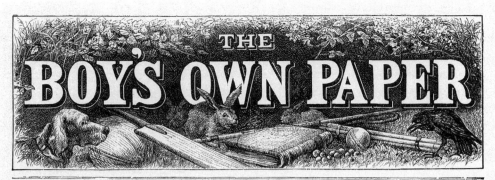

No. 1.—Vol. I.     SATURDAY, JANUARY 18, 1879.     Price One Penny.

## MY FIRST FOOTBALL MATCH.

### BY AN OLD BOY.

IT was a proud moment in my existence when Wright, captain of our football club, came up to me in school one Friday and said, "Adams, your name is down to play in the match against Craven to-morrow."

I could have knighted him on the spot. To be one of the picked "fifteen," whose glory it was to fight the battles of their school in the Great Close, had been the leading ambition of my life—I suppose I ought to be ashamed to confess it—ever since, as a little chap of ten, I entered Parkhurst six years ago. Not a winter Saturday but had seen me either looking on at some big match, or oftener still scrimmaging about with a score or so of other juniors in a scratch game. But for a long time, do what I would, I always seemed as far as ever from the coveted goal, and was half despairing of ever rising to win my "first fifteen cap." Lately, however, I had noticed Wright and a few others of our best players more than once lounging about in the Little Close where we juniors used to play, evidently taking observations with an eye to business. Under the awful gaze of these heroes, need I say I exerted myself as I had never done before? What cared I for hacks or bruises, so only that I could distinguish myself in their eyes? And never was music sweeter

"Down!"

present in *Eric*. It is not simply that Farrar gives an unrealistic picture of what boys were really like, but that his intense 'lachrimosity', to use Farrar's own word, led him to will Eric's decline too melodramatically.

Despite the success of *Tom Brown's Schooldays* and *Eric*, neither Hughes nor Farrar ever produced such popular school stories again. Hughes wrote *Tom Brown at Oxford* (1861), a conventional Victorian novel about university, love, and class, and Farrar also wrote a novel about college life at Cambridge in *Julian Home* (1859). *St Winifred's: The World of School* (1862), Farrar's other school story, lacks the intensity of *Eric*, and there is considerable dimming of the earlier novel's religious fervour and sentimentality.

Other school stories followed, such as *Schoolboy Honour: A Tale of Halminster College* (1861) by the Revd H. C. Adams and *Stories of Whitminster* (1873) by A. R. Hope, the pseudonym of Ascott-Hope Moncrieff. Young readers also enjoyed *Vice Versa* (1882), the comic adult novel by F. Anstey, the pseudonym of Thomas Anstey Guthrie. The passing of the 1870 Education Act, providing elementary education for all, also increased the potential number of readers of school fiction, and by the 1880s publishers were beginning to advertise some books as 'school stories', in fact, because both they and their readers had clear expectations of what such stories would contain.

School stories also appeared in various cheap and sensational boys' periodicals (often called 'penny-dreadfuls'), such as George Emmett's serial 'Boys of Bircham School', which opened in the *Young Englishman's Journal* in 1867, and the near-picaresque 'Tom Wildrake's Schooldays', which ran in *Sons of Britannia* (1870–7). Talbot Baines Reed was among many who were concerned about the popularity of the penny-dreadfuls—Emmett's tale is full of crude practical jokes—and it was this concern, perhaps almost as much as the works of Hughes and Farrar, which inspired Reed's most famous book, *The Fifth Form at St Dominic's*.

Talbot Baines Reed's work gave the school story its distinctive character in the 1880s. The son of an MP, Reed worked all his life in his father's typefoundry, and was actually educated at the City of London day school. But he had close connections with the *Boy's Own Paper*, started by the Religious Tract Society (RTS) as a counter to the popularity of penny-dreadfuls, and anonymously contributed 'My First Football Match' to its first issue in January 1879. Dismayed by the quality of the penny-dreadfuls, but wary of the fervour of much evangelical writing, Reed wanted his own sons to enjoy what he called 'manly reading', and he began to contribute regularly to the *Boy's Own Paper*.

His first serial, *The Adventures of a Three Guinea Watch*, began to appear in 1880, and *The Fifth Form at St Dominic's*, his first full-length story, was serialized in 1881–2 and published as a book in 1887. Reed's other school stories included *The Willoughby Captains* (published in book form in 1887), *The Cock*

*Facing*: started in 1879 by the Religious Tract Society to challenge the popularity of 'penny-dreadfuls', *The Boy's Own Paper*, with its mixture of adventure and school stories, soon became extremely successful. T. B. Reed opened its first number with his anonymous story about rugby football.

*House at Fellsgarth* (1893), and *The Master of the Shell* (1894). He also wrote historical novels, regular journalism, and a well-regarded history of old English letter foundries before, sadly, he died at an early age.

*The Fifth Form at St Dominic's* was extremely popular: frequently reprinted, it even sold 750,000 copies in a penny edition in 1907. The success was deserved, for it makes lively use of the conventions established by Hughes and Farrar, but with a significant change of tone. Though Reed's Christian values are clear, there is far less didacticism than in the earlier books, and there is much more humour and good-natured tolerance. Reed developed a story of some complexity by describing the first year of young Stephen Greenfield's career at St Dominic's and contrasting his naïve and amusing experiences with those of his fifth-form brother, Oliver. Reed intertwines the plots with considerable skill, linking them through the character of a corrupt sixth-former, and fluently moving from the serious accounts of Oliver's attempts to win the Nightingale Prize and cope with unjust accusations that he is a cheat, to Stephen's comic squabbles with his fellow-juniors.

Despite his popularity, Reed's quality has still not perhaps been sufficiently appreciated. Exploiting the ingredients of the school story, such as rivalry over games, with skill and zest, he brought a recognition of the real nature of schoolboys into his books. Even if there is some stereotyping, and a certain sentimentalism in his work, there is still much to admire, for Reed's account of school life, with its touching glimpses of schoolboy honour, is much more realistic, tolerant, and amusing than the insistently strenuous and occasionally overwrought stories of earlier writers.

Many girls read their brothers' stories, but they also began to look for stories of their own. The growth of secondary education for girls, with the success of the North London Collegiate School started in 1850, the foundation of public schools such as Cheltenham (1854), and the spread of the High School movement from the 1870s all helped to increase the readership for stories about girls' schools. But despite the fact that many of these newly established schools imitated boys' boarding-schools in the use of the house system and competitive team games, the most important writer of girls' stories in the period made surprisingly little use of such features.

L. T. Meade, the most prolific of girls' writers at the end of the nineteenth century, producing tales about street arabs and historical novels, as well as editing the magazine *Atalanta* from 1887 to 1898, is best known for such stories as *A World of Girls: The Story of a School* (1886). Her school stories are usually about girls from upper-class families who are sent away to rather small boarding-schools with no more than forty to fifty pupils and often run by rather motherly headmistresses. (Mrs Willis at Lavender House in *A World of Girls* treats the girls as her children and actually gives them 'a mother-kiss' on Sundays.) The ethos of the school is one of liberal Christianity. Girls should be trusted and, though their miniature world is full of temptations, L. T. Meade puts more emphasis on forgiveness than punishment. There is little interest in games or sport, and there is only a skeletal hierarchy of teachers and prefects in these schools. The plots often concern the arrival of a disruptive element in a previously harmonious school, and set up the mystery of identifying the culprit. But these are essentially stories about relationships—about friendships and loyalty, jealousy and misunderstandings. Hester initially dislikes Anne Forrester, in *A World of Girls,* but comes to love her; similarly, Star misunderstands Christian's true nature in *The Manor School* (1903). Discussion of characters' behaviour and motives lies at the heart of Meade's stories, expressed in a manner some way from Farrar's religious intensity or Hughes's muscular Christianity, but in describing all-female worlds where girls dominate the action as active decision-makers, not simply in passive roles, Meade clearly articulated the feelings of many adolescents of the time.

The rise of girls' school stories reflected what was happening more generally in society as girls and women began to seek education and more independence towards the end of the nineteenth century. But such moves threatened many Victorians' perception of women, and, although venturing out into the world of learning, L. T. Meade's girls are still essentially being prepared for the traditional roles of wives and mothers, and rarely question Victorian attitudes towards gender. None the less Meade's stories established a subgenre of children's books which was to be become enormously popular when developed by later writers such as Angela Brazil and Dorita Fairlie Bruce.

A much more disturbing writer of school stories was just on the horizon, however: in *Stalky & Co.* (1899) Rudyard Kipling produced a fiercely humorous account of life at a boys' school in which he made it crystal clear that, if the main purpose of education for British boys really was preparation for ruling the empire, then the most successful pupils were not necessarily those who played cricket, but those who subverted the system.

### THE POETRY AND THE POETS

The poetry of this period, it has to be admitted, is not impressive, except for three writers of rare and original talent. Charming and minor poets abound, of course, as they do perhaps in any age, and one would not willingly disparage the occasionally pleasant verse scattered amidst the prose writing of William Brighty Rands or of Jean Ingelow. Nor can one harshly dismiss Mrs Ewing's gentle 'The Burial of the Linnet' or the more robust, comic free verse of her 'The Doll's Wash'. But it is all a little too genteel, more the product of sentiment and restraint than of strong feeling.

A drawing of the young Christina Rossetti by her brother Dante Gabriel, founder of the Pre-Raphaelite Brotherhood and himself a poet.

There is certainly plenty of feeling in the verse of Lewis Carroll, even in such parodies as 'Speak roughly to your little boy', while a fascination with violence is never far below the surface in such poems as 'The Walrus and the Carpenter' or the linguistically extraordinary 'Jabberwocky'. Here is the unique voice of someone for whose expression of the tension between laughter and terror that overworked term 'black comedy' seems almost to have been invented.

At first glance, the poetry of Christina Rossetti might seem slight. But

'Goblin Market' (1862), the tale of Laura who becomes besotted with the mysterious fruit offered her by goblins until her sister saves her, powerfully depicts the lure of temptation beneath its fairy-tale narrative. Even *Sing-Song* (1872), which Christina Rossetti called 'a nursery rhyme book', contains much melancholy verse about dying children, such as 'Our little baby fell asleep'. The deceptive simplicity of the poetry combined with exquisite metrical skill raise questions, about childhood, time, and change in work which speaks to readers at many different levels. Among all the simple poems about the wind and the moon and the rainbow, one is always aware of the deep feeling beneath the apparently slight lyric grace:

A page from Christina Rossetti's *Sing-Song*. Arthur Hughes's illustrations and the page layout draw a touching analogy between the empty nest and the empty cradle.

> What are heavy? Sea-sand and sorrow;
> What are brief? Today and tomorrow;
> What are frail? Spring blossoms and youth;
> What are deep? The ocean and truth.

Hear what the mournful linnets say :
 " We built our nest compact and warm,
But cruel boys came round our way
 And took our summerhouse by storm.

" They crushed the eggs so neatly laid ;
 So now we sit with drooping wing,
And watch the ruin they have made,
 Too late to build, too sad to sing."

14

A baby's cradle with no baby in it,
 A baby's grave where autumn leaves drop sere ;
The sweet soul gathered home to Paradise,
 The body waiting here.

15

Robert Louis Stevenson's achievement seems even more remarkable: in *A Child's Garden of Verses* (1885) he produced the most important collection of serious poems for children of the century. The main body of the collection was composed in illness in 1883 when Stevenson was forced to spend hours resting and his mind went back to his sickly childhood in Scotland. He evokes the sights and sounds of childhood in winter and summer, indoors and outdoors, with great immediacy in such poems as 'My Shadow', 'The Lamplighter', and 'The Hayloft'. Even more originally, he valued and was able to recreate the imaginative experiences of children at play in such poems as 'Young Night Thoughts' and 'The Land of Counterpane', and to show, in the poem 'A Good Play', for instance, that complex state of childhood in which the child maintains total absorption in a game, while always recognizing that it is only a game:

> We built a ship upon the stairs
> All made of the back-bedroom chairs,
> And filled it full of sofa pillows
> To go a-sailing on the billows . . .
>
> We sailed along for days and days,
> And had the very best of plays;
> But Tom fell out and hurt his knee,
> So there was no one left but me.

### PERIODICALS, PUBLISHING, AND ILLUSTRATED BOOKS

The spread of literacy meant there was a growing readership to draw on, and the vigour of British publishing increased. In the 1830s books began to be steam-printed, new methods of binding with boards were developed, and cloth replaced leather; these factors not only helped to increase the number of books published, but also reduced prices in many cases.

As more publishers began to produce children's books—Macmillan (with Charles Kingsley and Lewis Carroll), Routledge, Ward, Lock, Nelson, Blackie, and Frederick Warne (in 1875 Routledge published a *Catalogue of a Thousand Juvenile Books*)—so the stratification of readership intensified. Publishers had always identified some books by gender as early as Benjamin Tabbard's *Presents for Good Boys* and *Presents for Good Girls* in 1804, and similarly writers such as Sarah Trimmer had produced stories deliberately aimed at the poor, such as *The Two Farmers*, rather than the middle-class readers of her *Fabulous Histories*, both in 1786. This process hardened in the later decades of the nineteenth century, particularly in relation to gender division, with adventure stories aimed at boys, though many girls also read them, and stories by such writers as Charlotte M. Yonge aimed more at girls.

The Religious Tract Society, founded to publish religious works at the end of the eighteenth century, clearly reflected changes in public taste in the second half of the nineteenth century. Although continuing to publish evangelical tales such as the enormously popular *Jessica's First Prayer*, it widened its appeal to keep up with the increasingly secular taste of the young, by also publishing such writers as Kingston and Ballantyne in its magazine the *Boy's Own Paper*. The SPCK (Society for Promoting Christian Knowledge) took a similar path, publishing stories by Kingston and Gordon Stables as well as by Mrs Ewing and Mrs Molesworth.

The contribution of periodical publishing to the growth of children's literature in this period cannot be overemphasized. As we have seen, many children's first encounter with Charlotte M. Yonge's *The Daisy Chain* would have been in her magazine the *Monthly Packet*, while Mrs Ewing's tales often first appeared in *Aunt Judy's Magazine*, started by her mother Mrs Gatty in 1866. Even *Treasure Island* first appeared in *Young Folks Magazine*.

The *Boy's Own Paper* was started as a weekly magazine costing a penny partly because the RTS felt that it should provide for a public made literate by the 1870 Education Act but only willing to read the sensationalist penny-dreadful magazines produced under the management of such men as Edward J. Brett, W. L. Emmett, and Charles Fox. Edward J. Brett dominated the field of cheap, juvenile fiction from the mid-1860s to the 1890s, with such serials as *The Dance of Death; or, The Hangman's Plot: A Tale of London and Paris* (1865–6), sometimes selling as many as 30,000 copies weekly, as well as launching the periodical *Boys of England* (1866–99). Brett mainly published tales of adventure, but he also serialized stories with school settings such as W. T. Townsend's 'The Captain of the School'. So successful was the *BOP*, with its mixture of school and adventure stories, that within five years the circulation had risen to nearly 250,000, and it ran until 1967. Its companion magazine the *Girl's Own Paper*, begun in 1880, with rather less robust mateial, ran till 1965.

Increasingly after 1870 one of the dominant features of children's publishing was 'Reward Books', prizes, often in gilt and decorated or pictorial binding, given to children for academic distinction, regular attendance at school, or good behaviour. Cassell, Nelson, Nisbet, and Ward, Lock all published Reward series in the last decades of the century, and, while Macmillan may have sold 86,000 copies of *Alice* by 1898, *Jessica's First Prayer*, an ideal gift for Sunday school pupils, sold two million copies by 1911.

One of the most remarkable aspects of publishing in this period was the extraordinarily high quality of book illustration. Artists such as Alfred Crowquill, the pseudonym of A. H. Forrester, and George Cruikshank continued to produce work of a high standard. W. M. Thackeray's illustrations added to the success of his pantomime-story *The Rose and the Ring*, while Charles Bennett's books, such as his wittily illustrated *The Nine Lives of a Cat*

'Holding his pocket-handkerchief/Before his streaming eyes.' Tenniel's carpenter, from *Through the Looking Glass* (1871).

A photograph of Kate Greenaway (1846–1901) in her studio in 1895.

(1860), were often reprinted. Although John Tenniel's illustrations to the 'Alice' books remain the best-known of this period, there are many who prefer Richard Doyle's illustrations to John Ruskin's *King of the Golden River* of 1851, or Arthur Hughes's Pre-Raphaelite drawings for George MacDonald's works, particularly *At the Back of the North Wind*.

For most of the early nineteenth century, colour book illustrations had meant colouring by hand, but the development of mechanical colour printing, especially by Edmund Evans, brought an immense improvement in coloured picture-books for children in the last quarter of the century. The practice of reprinting traditional tales and rhymes had been popular since the days of the chapbooks, but the emergence of toy books—picture-books in stiff paper covers, often of well-known poems or stories retold but reduced in size to provide more scope for pictures—revealed that Evans was more than a great colour-printer.

He employed the young Walter Crane to produce *Sing a Song of Sixpence* anonymously for Routledge in 1865, but from 1874 Crane, whose style was deeply influenced by Japanese art and the Aesthetic movement, began

164

producing a 'Shilling Series' for Routledge, including such titles as *Goody Two-Shoes* with his own name displayed to encourage sales. Crane did not confine himself to toy books. He worked with Evans to produce other important examples of colour printing, such as a song-book *The Baby's Opera* of 1877, and he also illustrated a number of Mrs Molesworth's books.

Kate Greenaway was earning a modest living designing Christmas cards as well as illustrating books for such publishers as Frederick Warne until Evans produced her collection of verses and pictures *Under the Window* (1879), which eventually sold 70,000 copies for Routledge. Further successes followed, notably an edition of *The Pied Piper of Hamelin* in 1888. Although Kate Greenaway has been criticized for her over-idealized pictures of children and her inadequate figure-drawing, John Ruskin was a great admirer of her work, and her popularity continues to inspire reprints.

The third of Britain's great children's illustrators, Randolph Caldecott, began sketching when very young and attended art schools for only brief periods in his career. His early work appeared regularly in magazines, but in 1878 he and Evans produced *The Diverting History of John Gilpin* for Routledge, and from then until his early death Caldecott and Evans published two picture-books each Christmas, usually based upon a comic poem or nursery rhyme, such as *The Queen of Hearts* (1881) or *Come Lasses and Lads* (1884). Caldecott's vigorous drawing, his use of colours, and his humorous observation have deeply impressed almost all his successors from Beatrix Potter to Maurice Sendak, and indeed it is not going too far to say that in his sense of the relationship between text and illustration he helped to create the modern picture-book.

The quality of such illustrators, the establishing of such genres as fantasy and the adventure story, and the development of them by such writers as Lewis Carroll, George MacDonald, and Robert Louis Stevenson, demonstrated that children's books had emerged from the nursery and the classroom. Discussion of children's books was improving in quality, too. Lady Eastlake's long and perceptive article on 'Children's Books' which appeared in the *Quarterly Review* in 1844, Charlotte Yonge's fine essays which appeared in *Macmillan's Magazine* in 1869, and Mrs E. M. Field's *The Child and his Book* of 1891 all showed that children's literature had become a subject for serious critical discussion. The Victorian age had established the legitimacy of children's literature as a form in its own right.

Randolph Caldecott (1846–86) began his career by contributing sketches to periodicals, but his most important work consisted of his famous series of superbly-illustrated children's picture-books, such as *The Queen of Hearts* and *Come Lasses and Lads*.

# 7 TRANSITIONS

## 1890–1914

*Julia Briggs*

## THE SECRET GARDEN OF CHILDHOOD

'For a century or more the progress of interest in and attention to the children has been steady and rapid. And now the best talent of the world is laid under contribution for the little ones,' wrote H. Clay Trumbull in 1891 (*Hints on Child-Training*). The nineteenth century saw a radical change in the depiction and position of the child in society, which was directly reflected in the range and variety of writings addressed to children, as well as less directly in the amount of writing centrally concerned with the nature and experience of childhood. Such alterations in consciousness had a variety of causes, some cultural (such as the creation of the romantic image of the child), some material (such as the demographic explosion of the first half of the century). The figure of the child lent itself to idealization, since it appeared to possess vitality and spiritual insight as yet uncontaminated by adult desires.

The retreat of Arnold's 'sea of faith' meant that, for some at least, marriage and the nuclear family had come to occupy the space left by the relationship with God, or with the Church as God's family. But, as marriage was increasingly regarded as a source of spiritual sustenance, its disruptive elements became more threatening, and were more anxiously concealed: notably sexuality. The figure of the child, on the other hand, possessed the energizing animal spirits and impulsiveness associated with sexuality, while not yet being driven by it. In this respect, the child occupied an Eden before the fall that was puberty. The proper place of the child was in the lost playground—an Arcadia not yet touched by mortality, a past not yet burdened by the guilts of adult sexuality, Alice's rose garden that all might find and enter, if only via the little door of the imagination.

For Carroll, by implication, and for later writers more explicitly, the unattainable rose garden was a place of desire: it held out the possibility of recov-

*Facing*: 'There were trees . . . and a large pool with an old grey fountain in its midst.' Charles Robinson's original illustration for Burnett's *The Secret Garden* (1911) delicately conveys Mary's melancholy and introversion, as she gazes at her own reflection.

ering the lost self, and promised the spiritual wholeness and insight found fleetingly in Elizabeth Barrett Browning's poem 'The Lost Bower'. Words from her poem are sung by the blind woman in Kipling's story 'They', a fable about a rose garden inhabited by lost (dead) children, while all these texts left their mark on the mystic rose garden in the opening section of T. S. Eliot's poem 'Burnt Norton', glimpsed through 'the door we never opened'. The garden also provided the central symbol of Frances Hodgson Burnett's story of social, physical, and spiritual healing, *The Secret Garden* (1911), where the lesson of Voltaire's Candide, 'il faut cultiver notre jardin', is therapeutically learned by two maladjusted children. The orphaned Mary Lennox, plain, sallow, and ill-tempered, returns to England from India. In a rambling house in Yorkshire she gradually cures herself and Colin, the sickly son of her guardian, through her discovery and gradual restoration of a locked and neglected garden. These two difficult children heal themselves by attending to the needs of other growing things; by turning their energies outward, they recover inwardly. Though the lesson looks back to Mrs Ewing, and the healing gardens of 'Reka Dom' and 'Mary's Meadow', the power of the story lies in the vivid characterization of Mary and Colin. 'This is a book for introspective town children,' wrote Marghanita Laski. 'I was just such a child myself, and it is therefore the most satisfying book I know.'

Frances Hodgson Burnett's work embodied fantasies of wish-fulfilment, consolation, or reconciliation often drawn from fairy-tales or popular romantic fiction. *The Secret Garden* charts the search for bodily and spiritual wholeness. In healing the hidden wounds of her own childhood, Burnett's writings afford solace to her readers as well.

## IMAGES OF CHILDHOOD

The need for healing, consoling, or reconciling myths that Burnett's work expresses is symptomatic, reflected in various ways in much of the writing for children of these years. Confidence in progress and expansion, whether at home or in the empire, faltered and by the end of the century narratives of self-division were proliferating: the splits in human nature so neatly epitomized in Stevenson's *Dr Jekyll and Mr Hyde* (1886)were also apparent in the several antithetical concepts of childhood.

As childhood came to be seen as a state distinct from and potentially opposed to being 'grown-up', so it came to be figured as 'other', with all the idealization, horror, and projection that such a status implies. For Wordsworth, 'Heaven lies about us in our infancy', yet for his contemporary Mrs

Sherwood the child's nature was determined by original sin. Later the theological doctrine of original sin came to be replaced by scientific theories of evolution which represented the child as biologically, intellectually, or socially primitive. Children were 'savages', awaiting the education that would transform them into civilized adults. The children of the poor, as we have seen, were referred to as 'street arabs', that is, alien and homeless wanderers who shared with the criminal classes 'degenerate' elements. And as such theories of origin began to take hold, the concept of 'recapitulation' became popular, the idea that childhood was a process during which different stages of animal or human development were progressively transcended, eventually reaching the evolutionary summit of fully formed adulthood. The uninhibited high spirits of childhood were equated with those of supposedly 'primitive' societies, and progress towards socialization was identified with progress towards civilization. Both the family and the extended family of empire required to be ruled with a mixture of kindness, firmness, and self-confidence.

Sexuality was another area where childhood experience was constructed as antithetical to that of the adult, the child being seen as innocent/ignorant, and the adult as guilty, if only in terms of conscious desires. Unlike women, who could be represented as dangerous temptresses, the Victorian child was more often perceived as the innocent object of desire. For reporters or reformers such as Mayhew or William Booth, the prostitution of children was a horrific fact, but in the world of fiction desire was invariably repressed, disguised, or displaced, as it is in the work of Lewis Carroll or James Barrie. The representation of the child as sexual innocent reflects that determination to separate sexuality from romantic love which is evident in the mythology of Victorian society as a whole (throwing up such oddities as Charles Kingsley's fantasy drawings of himself and his wife making love upon a cross). But if sexuality had no place in discourse intended for children, childish romance appealed

J. D. Batten's frontispiece to Joseph Jacob's *English Fairy Tales* creates a Gothic fantasy within an Art Nouveau frame. Attempts to protect children from the horrific elements in fairy tales had long since been abandoned, but adult sexuality was commonly modified, to become romance.

· Childe Rowland ·

to the more emotional writers of the period: Charles Dickens catches up the theme in several of his adult novels, and it is central to *A Holiday Romance*, where William Tinkling, Esq., aged 8, marries Nettie Ashford, and his 9-year-old friend Lieut.-Col. Robin Redforth is betrothed to Alice Rainbird, though their brides are unfortunately confined to school, from where their sweethearts plan to carry them off. Curdie'sreward, at the end of *The Princess and the Goblin*, is Irene's promised kiss; Kenneth Grahame's *The Golden Age* (1895) celebrates 'Young Adam Cupid', recalled in Hugh John's love for Cissy Carter in S. R. Crockett's *Sir Toady Lion* (1897). And, at once central and mystified, a troubled romance underpins Barrie's *Peter and Wendy* (1911).

## The Tiger

The Tiger on the other hand,

is kittenish and mild,

He makes a pretty playfellow for any little child ;
And mothers of large families (who claim to common sense)

Will find a Tiger well repay the trouble and expense.

BTB's illustrations to Belloc's *Bad Child's Book of Beasts* (1896) echo the comic indirection of the verse and are tellingly arranged inside it: neither text nor pictures spell out precisely why a tiger might make a useful pet, but the tiger's bulging stomach and the disappearance of the doll-like baby tell their own story.

That children are sexual beings, instinctively in touch with their bodily needs and pleasures, is obvious to those who care for them. Yet Victorian middle-class readers, the typical recipients of children's books, were brought up to think of sexual impulses as at best unclean, at worst wicked or depraved. The damage this could inflict was writ large in the work of the next generation: it was evident from Samuel Butler's *The Way of All Flesh*, and in the writings of D. H. Lawrence and Virginia Woolf (e.g. *The Years*, where Rose Pargiter is threatened by a sexual exhibitionist), as well as in the intense suffering and humiliation undergone by so many boys at public schools, as E. M. Forster and Hugh Walpole recalled. It was left to Sigmund Freud to point out to a disbelieving world the self-evident fact of children's sexuality: 'If mankind had been able to learn from a direct observation of children, these three essays [on the Theory of Sexuality] could have remained unwritten.' And it is no coincidence that he wrote them in these years, from 1890 to the 1920s, years in which children's literature was most heavily invested in denial.

If the nature of childhood sexuality was too threatening to be acknowledged, some at least of childhood's disruptive energies could now be safely released into literature, since Lear and Carroll had shown how this might be done. Victorian sentiment was now countered by a comic ruthlessness brilliantly exemplified in Hilaire Belloc's several books of verse for children, beginning with *The Bad Child's Book of Beasts* (1896). These were later collected as *Cautionary Tales* (1908), since they travestied the didactic tradition, but their Awful Warnings were often amusingly cruel, and occasionally directed over the reader's head. 'The Tiger', it is claimed, is:

> kittenish and mild,
> He makes a pretty playfellow for any little child;
> And mothers of large families (who claim to common sense)
> Will find a tiger well repay the trouble and expense.

The scratchy, eccentric illustrations by BTB (Basil Blackwood) precisely match the casual violence of the verse, written in strong and often highly memorable nursery-rhyme rhythms. These include 'Jim Who ran away from his nurse and was eaten by a Lion' and 'Matilda Who told lies and was burnt to death'. Belloc's sophisticated and often adult jokes appeal to young readers long before they actually understand them. His verses have always been more popular than Harry Graham's briefer and less culturally loaded *Ruthless Rhymes* (1899).

Belloc's verses belong to the tradition of nonsense, established by the end of the century as the most appropriate vehicle for subversive energies. It remained a popular mode not only for verse but also for fiction, partly because the episodic, improvisatory elements in *Alice* had always looked deceptively easy to imitate. This tradition is seen at its best in the work of G. E. Farrow (*The Wallypug of Why*, 1895; *The Little Panjandrum's Dodo*, 1899) where a free-floating and often highly inventive narrative line continuously exposes the illogicalities of the language from which it is constructed. Early in *The Wallypug of Why*, the puzzlingly named Doctor-in-law offers to take Girlie's watch in part-exchange for the (unwanted) advice he has inflicted upon her:

'Oh! My!' Another little monster, the tail-piece from Belloc's *Bad Child's Book of Beasts*.

> 'But it is worth a great deal more than sixpence,' argued Girlie.
> 'Not at all!' said the Doctor-in-law . . . 'mine only cost a penny.'
> 'Yes, but yours doesn't go,' objected Girlie; 'mine does, you know.'
> 'Oh well, then I don't want it,' said the Doctor-in-law hurriedly. 'I don't want a watch that will go, I want one that will stay . . .'

Here and in various sequels, Farrow created a series of fantasy adventures whose arbitrariness produces an exhilarating sense of the freedom and vitality of the imagination, a quality that had once been thought dangerous but was increasingly valued in children (and, by extension, in their authors). Such freedom is apparent in Edward Abbott Parry's stories, *Katawampus: Its Treatment and Cure* (1895), *Butterscotia; or, A Cheap Trip to Fairyland* (1896), and *The First Book of Krab* (1897). These are inevitably more structured and more didactic, even if jokily so, since they depend on a framework in which 'Pater' tells stories to his own four children. 'Katawampus' is a kind of childish disease, making its victims cross, contrary, or unhappy for no very evident reason; it may conveniently be cured by a visit to the Cave-man Krab, who specializes in repairing tempers ('Katawampus' is thus a less familiar precursor of

Kipling's 'camelious hump'). The topic of children's ill-temper, even when represented as amusingly as here, is inclined to promote myths that contrast the child's failure of self-control with that of the wise(r) adult. It was a rare writer who could confront the assumption of adult superiority with the scepticism of Dickens in 'Mrs Orange' or of F. Anstey in *Vice Versa* (1882).

### CHILD'S PLAY

Explicit moral lessons were rapidly becoming outmoded and the insistent moralizing of Victorian fiction for children had by the end of the century become a standing joke and an obvious target for parody. In *Cautionary Tales* Belloc had rewritten earlier lessons for children such as those of Isaac Watts or Ann and Jane Taylor, belatedly following the subversive treatment of such lessons in *Alice*, where contemporary educational models had provided a favourite target. By the end of the century, the use of parody was common in writing for children: the formula of the fairy court was one obvious source,

By the end of the nineteenth century, imaginative games were seen as necessary to the child's development. Many of these—dressing up, playing at soldiers, dolls' tea parties, or mothers and fathers—imitated adult behaviour, while other games acted out books and stories. Writers like Robert Louis Stevenson, Richard Jefferies, E. Nesbit, and Kenneth Grahame celebrated the pleasures of imaginative games.

drawn upon by Thackeray and Dickens and by Andrew Lang in *Prince Prigio* (1889), and E. Nesbit in *Nine Unlikely Tales for Children* (1901); something approaching self-parody is also apparent in the elaborately self-conscious narrative voices of Kipling's *Just So Stories* (1902), or of Barrie's *Peter and Wendy*. One vital source for parody lay in the power of imaginative play which the late nineteenth century had located at the centre of nursery life; by contrast, earlier ages had equated play with either idleness or mischief, believing that children needed to be kept occupied lest 'the devil find work for idle hands'. Its value had first been celebrated by Catherine Sinclair in *Holiday House* in the 1840s and it is implicit in the popularity of fantasy writing in the second half of the century. Middle-class children were now encouraged to exercise their imaginations both in reading and in the games they played, and play was recognized as an essential element in the learning process.

Shepherd's illustration of playacting from Grahame's *The Golden Age*.

Its full significance was first explicitly recognized in literature in two key texts of the early 1880s, written about, rather than for, children: these were Robert Louis Stevenson's essay on the subject in *Virginibus puerisque* (1881) and Richard Jefferies's novel *Bevis: The Story of a Boy*. Stevenson's essay, which also served as a starting-point for *A Child's Garden of Verses* (1885), describes the child's rapt absorption in imaginary games that continually transform his surroundings: 'In the child's world of dim sensation, play is all in all. "Making believe" is the gist of his whole life, and he cannot so much as take a walk except in character.' A vast difference in outlook divides children from 'such unthinkable deities as parents', but, sadly, 'they will come out of their gardens soon enough'.

*Bevis* could be seen as dramatizing Stevenson's insights into the nature of childhood; Bevis and his friend Mark are absorbed in an ongoing sequence of imaginative games around the farm and lake: ' "We ought to be something," said Mark discontentedly. "Of course we ought," said Bevis. "Things are very stupid unless you are something." ' So they become explorers on the Nile or the Mississippi, savages or Indians or Greeks (Pope's *Odyssey* is Bevis's favourite book). While Jefferies's writing constantly celebrates the beauty of landscape and living things, it also exemplifies Stevenson's point by showing how, for the boys, fantasy transfigures their surroundings, turning the Wiltshire meadows into jungles and deserts, possible settings for crocodiles, pythons, pumas, and kangaroos. In *Bevis* the Wordsworthian loveliness of real nature is distorted by the spectacles of books.

To represent the world of childhood as a self-sufficient and self-generated adventure was to find a new way of writing either *about* children, as did Kenneth Grahame in *The Golden Age* (1895) and its sequel *Dream Days* (1898), or *for* them, as did S. R. Crockett, E. Nesbit, and their successors. Grahame's two sets of stories combined aspects of the work of both Stevenson and Jefferies: they had shared the assumption that childhood involves a distinctive state of mind, from which adults are distanced: adults are 'bearded and petticoated giants . . . who move upon a cloudy Olympus, following unknown designs apart from rational enjoyment'. But while the five children of *The Golden Age* are as occupied with Indians and pirates, boating and the sources of the Nile as Bevis and Mark had been, Grahame's style is much closer to the formally discursive style of Stevenson's essay than to the more direct narrative that Jefferies generally used. With Grahame, we are in the presence of an adult, looking back nostalgically at his own past, and painfully aware of the distance between himself as child and adult, even while the self-as-child is conscious of the distance of the adult: 'The estrangement was fortified by an abiding sense of injustice, arising from the refusal of the Olympians ever to defend, to retract, to admit themselves in the wrong, or to accept similar concessions on our part.' This arch quality, a note of literary self-consciousness, an awareness of the adult reader over the shoulder, is also characteristic of Barrie (and, to a lesser extent, Nesbit). It took another generation and a substantial shift in attitude and style to produce the more direct narratives of Arthur Ransome.

*Bevis* had been slow to make its impact. It was reissued in 1891, abridged from fifty-two chapters to forty, though the third edition (1904) restored the full text. Grahame's *The Golden Age*, on the other hand, was a runaway success from the first and, with *Dream Days*, was initially preferred by critics to *The Wind in the Willows* (1908). Its influence was immediate and obvious in S. R. Crockett's *The Surprising Adventures of Sir Toady Lion*. Like MacDonald, Stevenson, and James Barrie, Crockett was a Scot, and the large Scottish contribution to writing for children from the 1860s might suggest that the concept of childhood north of the border was in key respects significantly different. 'Sir Toady Lion' is so named from Arthur George's lisped efforts to pronounce the name of his hero Richard Cœur-de-Lion, while his older brother Hugh John is self-styled 'General Napoleon Smith'. The brothers recall Grahame's Harold and Edward, while their sister Prissy combines elements of Grahame's Selina and Charlotte. Crockett reworks particular episodes from *The Golden Age* (notably 'Alarums and Excursions' and 'Young Adam Cupid'), though much of the story is taken up with a war of attrition waged against the local lads, and perhaps inspired by the equivalent episodes in *Bevis*. In *Bevis*, however, the war is treated almost as a team game, the boys taking on Roman roles and playing out 'Pharsalia', whereas in *Sir Toady Lion* there is a class distinction between the 'honourable' conduct of Hugh John and Arthur George, determined not to be 'dasht-mean', and their social inferiors, the 'smoutchy boys', sons of local shopkeepers who outnumber them but have no aspiration to behave like 'gentlemen'; they are the social equivalents of the Stoats and Weasels who would seize upon Toad Hall.

E. Nesbit's Bastable family made their first appearance in 1897, in an occasional magazine called *Father Christmas* (published as a supplement to the *Illustrated London News*) in a story entitled 'The Treasure-Seekers'. Ten further stories appeared in the *Windsor* and *Pall Mall* magazines, the latter illustrated by Gordon Browne (illustrator of *Sir Toady Lion*). There was some initial uncertainty as to whether these stories were aimed at children or adults, but this was becoming a less crucial distinction since middle-class magazines of this kind were largely intended for family reading. The problem in any case was one of address: the Bastables' adventures are implicitly narrated by Oswald, the eldest son, but mainly in the third person; they are thus free to compliment Oswald on his abilities and achievements whenever the occasion arises: 'It was Oswald who first thought of looking for treasure. Oswald often thinks of very interesting things . . .' The effect of this ingenious strategy is to produce two simultaneous viewpoints, that of the child and the adult, thus solving the difficult problem of self-positioning confronted by the adult talking to the child. It is a happy device to have Oswald try out his own narrative in the various different literary styles with which he is familiar, as if searching to identify the nature of the story he occupies: the narrator can thus convey the child's point of view with all the immediacy and lack of perspective that implies. As a child reader, Oswald considers *The Golden Age* 'A1 except where it gets mixed with grown-up nonsense'.

Yet beyond the child's limited viewpoint, the more sophisticated reader can distinguish different landscapes, and this double point of view, so brilliantly deployed by Henry James in *What Maisie Knew* (1897), adds richly ironic depths. Nesbit was less successful in her forays into fiction and verses for the adult market, but, like Kipling and Barrie, she brought to children's fiction a complexity of aim and execution that derived from her ambitions as a writer for adults; all three were experienced professionals who brought to children's writing what they had learned in writing for adults.

E. Nesbit had begun her career as a hack writer, turning out poems and

Edith Nesbit as a young woman in the late 1880s, before her career took off. She was already a socialist, a friend of Bernard Shaw and the Webbs, and a founding member of the Fabian Society. Her short hair was considered unconventional and indicative of 'advanced' views.

serials for women's magazines or socialist newspapers, but also colouring in Christmas cards for Raphael Tuck and writing keepsake verses and little tales to accompany the brightly lithographed books published by the German firm of Ernest Nister. Her first attempt at extended writing for children was a series of articles on 'My School-Days' for the *Girl's Own Paper* from October 1896 to September 1897. Here she described games with her brothers very much in the manner of *Bevis*, and several of these adventures later became part of the history of the Bastables. Writing them as memoirs enabled her to see their possibilities as fiction.

Nesbit wrote under pressure, to support a large household and her own extravagant tastes in entertaining. *The Story of the Treasure Seekers* (1899) and its sequels, *The Wouldbegoods* (1901) and *The New Treasure Seekers* (1904), often economize on pure invention by consciously reworking familiar texts from Burnett to Edgeworth for the structure and comic effects they afforded. She admired the toughness of traditional fairy-tales, and the Grimms' story of the three ill-chosen wishes provided the starting-point for *Five Children and It* (1902), in which the children's wishes, whether voiced accidentally or carefully thought out in advance, always bring problems. That getting what you want does not necessarily bring happiness was one of the lessons her own life had painfully taught her.

In the stories of the Bastables, the children act out their reading, while in fantasies such as *Five Children and It*, *The Phoenix and the Carpet* (1904), and *The Enchanted Castle* (1907) magically granted wishes come into conflict with everyday life, as they had done in F. Anstey's *The Brass Bottle* (1900), an important influence on Nesbit. In her work, imagination is closely and often specifically connected with books, and this is exemplified in two fables, one written towards the beginning and the other at the end of her career. In 'The Book of Beasts' (*The Book of Dragons*, 1900), little King Lionel discovers a volume whose pictures come alive and flutter from their pages into the actual world, with initially delightful and ultimately alarming consequences. The power of books to release their content into the world, thereby changing it, is also dramatized in her brilliant and neglected exploration of creativity *The Magic City* (1910), which culminates in a last battle between barbarian hordes and Caesar's legions, released from their respective books and animated by the genuine and transforming magic of the imagination.

## KIPLING AND SOCIETY

*The Magic City*, as well as incorporating a quest narrative, describes how children can construct their own miniature cities using building bricks, toys, books, candlesticks, finger-bowls, and other everyday household objects. Constructing imaginary cities and countries on the floor from bricks and books and cotton reels is also the subject of H. G. Wells's *Floor Games* (1911). These two books reveal the way in which, for Nesbit and Wells as adults, the impulse to reform society through Fabian socialism was closely bound up with the childish fantasy of creating imaginary worlds, and imaginary societies to people them. Their generation had been strongly influenced by the socialist utopias of William Morris (*The Dream of John Ball*, 1887, and *News from Nowhere*, 1890) and the impulse to reconstruct their world had begun at a very literal level in childhood and become an important commitment to them as adults. But their personal convictions in turn reflected a growing sense that the great hope for improving human life lay not so much in moral or religious reform as in better living and working conditions. The message of the Victorian reformers was beginning to be heard.

The search for the good society in Nesbit's work transports her child actors into the remote past as they pursue the missing half of *The Amulet* (1906), and into British history in *The House of Arden* (1908) and *Harding's Luck* (1909). Her use of time travel in children's fiction owed something to Wells's *The Time Machine* (1895), and was to influence more recent writers as Mary Norton and Penelope Lively.

Rudyard Kipling shared Nesbit's concern with society and history but started from the opposite end of the political spectrum. Unlike her, he knew the empire at first hand: his father had been Principal of a new art school in Bombay. Kipling like his sister had been brought up by an Indian ayah, and

Una shows Parnesius, the centurion of the thirtieth, how an elastic catapult works. In this illustration to Kipling's *Puck of Pook's Hill* (1906), H. R. Millar establishes the contrast between the Edwardian child and the Roman legionary by focusing on the details of their costumes.

felt exiled when sent back to England at the age of six. Although he went to an English public school, the United Services College, and he later married and settled in Sussex, he always felt that he had 'two separate sides to my head' and his most characteristic heroes—Kim in the novel of that title (1901) and Mowgli in *The Jungle Book* (1894) and *The Second Jungle Book* (1895)—feel simultaneously Indian and European, or torn between the jungle and the world of men. Kipling shared the ideals of empire, and his myths are not of emancipating social improvements but of reinforcing 'the law'. For Kipling, social structure is achieved by bringing law to the lawless, and protecting the vulnerable. Such myths are repeated in various ways in the 'Jungle Books' as well as in his later explorations of English history.

There is a striking contrast in the '*Jungle Books*' between the law of the

*Facing*: Walter Crane wrote that 'children . . . prefer well-defined forms and bright, frank colour, they don't want to bother about three dimensions'. This example from the 1870s illustrates *Goody Two-Shoes* in Routledge's Shilling Series. Margery teaches the village children on the village green how to read.

Jungle to which the animals conform, and the mistrust and suspicion of the villagers that causes them to drive out Mowgli's parents. This results in Mowgli 'letting in the jungle', a reflection, perhaps, of the fact that, as a child, Kipling had suffered greatly at the hands of adults in whose care he had been left (bitterly described in 'Baa Baa, Black Sheep'). The law of the Jungle represents both classical virtues and enlightened self-interest, just as the social structure of the wolf-pack suggests that of the army, and the jungle suggests that of the empire as a whole.

Mowgli, suckled by mother wolf, recalls Romulus and Remus and the foundation of Rome, the city that created its own empire committed to justice achieved through the law. Rome's significance for Kipling is also apparent in *Puck of Pook's Hill* (1906), in which Dan and Una (versions of Kipling's own children, John and Elsie) meet the old earth spirit Puck and embark on an exploration of the rise and decline of empire, British history, and human nature, beginning with the prehistoric pagan gods, and ending with the signing of Magna Carta. But whereas time travellers in E. Nesbit's books entered the past, Kipling summoned imaginary figures from the past into the present, and into the fields around his Sussex home, Bateman's: the Roman centurion Parnesius describes his experiences as a Captain on Hadrian's Wall, in the late days of the empire, when Roman Britain was threatened by Picts and Norsemen, his uneasy position inevitably recalling the difficulties of life on the North-West Frontier. Empire and conquest, law and order are predominant themes in this subtly constructed book; Sir Richard Dalyngridge, who comes

'O Beloved kids'— Rudyard Kipling telling one of the *Just So Stories* to a group of children, on board a liner bound for South Africa in 1902.

VIEW FROM THE HILL-TOP.

Page 68.

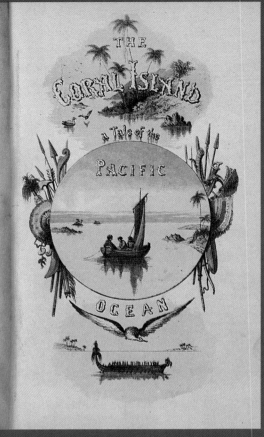

THE CORAL ISLAND

a Tale of the

PACIFIC

OCEAN

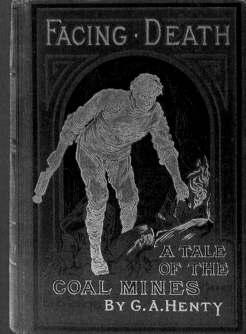

FACING DEATH

A TALE
OF THE
COAL MINES

BY G. A. HENTY

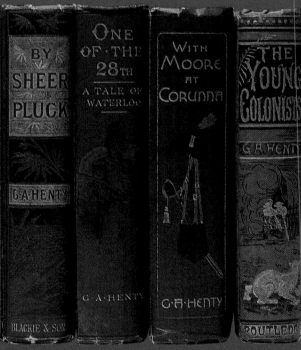

BY
SHEER
PLUCK

G. A. HENTY

BLACKIE & SON

ONE
OF THE
28TH

A TALE OF
WATERLOO.

G. A. HENTY

WITH
MOORE
AT
CORUNNA

G. A. HENTY

THE
YOUNG
COLONISTS

G. A. HENTY

ROUTLEDGE

over with William the Conqueror, has to learn how to govern his manor and reconcile Norman and Saxon to restore England. Kipling's view both of the inevitability of history and of the importance of individual responsibility in the creation of a just and democratic society is displayed in the final story, 'The Treasure and the Law'. Here an 'outsider', the Jew Kadmiel, casts away the treasure won by Sir Richard and his companions with the help of a sword forged by the god Weland, thus compelling King John to sign the Charter and bring law and justice to England. As Puck observes: 'It's as natural as an oak growing.'

Though Kipling's narratives reveal highly politicized subtexts, the combination of the children's games with historical, and sometimes fantastic, adventures (such as 'Dymchurch Flit') is simple and appealing, and the book is imbued with the exile's love of England, the island of 'oak and ash and thorn', the charm Puck uses to bring the past to the present. Its sequel, *Rewards and Fairies* (1910), is less concerned with social order and more with individuals— indeed the book as a whole is altogether closer to Kipling's short stories written for adults. As he wrote in his autobiography, *Something of Myself,* his 'underwood' or basic motif was the question posed in the short story 'Cold Iron', 'What else could I have done?' He added 'the tales had to be read by children, before people realized that they were meant for grown-ups'.

## ANIMAL LANDS

Kipling's *Just So Stories,* written for his daughter Josephine ('Taffy'), develop a tradition derived from Joel Chandler Harris's 'Uncle Remus' tales and perhaps ultimately from Aesop's fables. They explain how animals and men acquired particular characteristics—'How the Whale got his Throat', 'the Rhinoceros . . . his Skin', 'the Camel . . . his Hump', 'the Leopard . . . his Spots', and, more troublingly, how the Ethiopian came to change his skin from 'greyish-brownish-yellowish' to black. The stories are told in a highly stylized and rhythmic prose that often comes close to verse, full of private jokes and references. Kipling also provided a series of equally stylized illustrations, with elaborate commentaries ('The black thing in the water close to the shore is not a wreck at all. It is Strorks the Rhinoceros bathing without his skin. He was just as black underneath his skin as he was outside. I wouldn't ask anything about the cooking stove if *I* were you'.)

The interplay between Kipling's animal and human characters, and especially between the jungle animals and the man-child Mowgli, was to influence books as different as Edgar Rice Burroughs's *Tarzan of the Apes* (1914) and A. A. Milne's *Winnie-the-Pooh* (1926). The widespread use of animal characters in children's fiction is largely a twentieth-century phenomenon, although Mrs Trimmer's 'History of the Robins' (*Fabulous Histories,*

*Facing, above*: R. M. Ballantyne's *The Coral Island*, an immensely popular and much imitated book, was first published in 1858. Ballantyne himself illustrated the first edition.

*Below*: characteristic novels of G. A. Henty from the 1880s and 1890s, showing the fashionable embossed and coloured bindings and gilt lettering.

179

1786), Ballantyne's *The Dog Crusoe* (1861), Anna Sewell's *Black Beauty* (1877), and Richard Jefferies' *Wood Magic* (1881) are among the significant exceptions.

A very different, and far more anthropomorphic approach to animals is to be found in Kenneth Grahame's *The Wind in the Willows*, which owes something to Jefferies's detailed observations of the English countryside, as well as to his intense pleasure in water, boating, and woodland, but it is a book without a real child in it. Indeed, had the main characters been given human names instead of being called 'the Rat', 'the Mole', and 'the Toad', the book would have looked considerably more like such classics as *Three Men in a Boat* (1889), and less like a book for children. Toad himself, of course, provides the obvious link with the world of childhood, with his sudden, short-lived enthusiasms for boating or driving, his self-absorption, self-confidence, and lack of moral inhibitions, and his urgent and disruptive desires. He is a naughty child in a world of adults, carefree, irresponsible, and amoral. When his friends attempt to 'bring him to his senses' for his own good, he gives them the slip and sets off in search of further adventures, only to return to find his old home shut and held against him; in his search for an elsewhere, he loses what he has. The story of Toad provides the main impetus of the second half of the narrative, and was originally invented by Grahame to amuse his own small son.

Kipling illustrated the *Just So Stories* (1902) himself, each drawing being accompanied by a facing commentary. Here the parsee watches the rhinoceros bathing with a degree of evident complacency, since he has filled the rhino's cast-off skin with cake crumbs, in revenge for the rhinoceros eating up his fruit cake.

The movement towards and away from home provides one of the book's most fundamental structures and is another reason why it speaks so directly to child readers, despite never directly concerning itself with them. The desire for travel and adventure is contrasted with the reassuring familiarity of kitchen and parlour. Both Rat and Mole alternately desire to escape from and return home, and the chapter of Toad's homecoming takes its title from that of the weariest and most travel-worn of heroes, 'The Return of Ulysses'. Grahame's classical references usually carry a strong emotional charge, and this is particularly true of the unconsciously eroticized figure of Pan.

Both here and in *The Golden Age*, Grahame is concerned with character rather than appearance, and the relationship between the animal and human world is left less invitingly open than it had been in *Bertie's Escapade* (published posthumously in *First Whisper of 'The Wind in the Willows'* (1944)), where Mr Grahame's pig Bertie takes the two rabbits carol-singing and the animals return with the lift-man, Mole, to enjoy a champagne supper 'borrowed' from Mr Grahame, at the back of the pigsty. Of the animals in *The*

*Wind in the Willows*, it is only Toad who encounters the human world directly, but all the animals scull boats, wear clothes, live in holes by the river or underground in the wild wood. Toad himself condescends to a gaoler's daughter yet is flung in the river by an indignant washerwoman. Such uncertainties of size and status reflect the book's verbal rather than visual dimension. They create problems for illustrators, though E. H. Shepard's line drawings (1931) capture the idyllic quality of Grahame's imagination, and for many readers are inseparable from it. A. A. Milne's dramatization (*Toad of Toad Hall*, 1929) introduces the names and narrators so carefully omitted from the original: thus the play opens with the Alice-like Marigold on her daffodil telephone; the gaoler's daughter becomes 'Phoebe', the caravan horse 'Alfred'—a reminder, perhaps, that the animals' freedom from individualizing names was also a freedom from history. In *The Wind in the Willows* there are no prior or future events. The narrative begins at the moment when the Mole throws down his whitewash brush, and it surfaces with him, to live in the intensity of a holiday present with no backward glances. The book promotes a hedonistic delight in a world of long weekends, of leisurely summer days, and of male society. There is a scarcely mentioned yet ever present sense of threat, perhaps from the women and lower classes silently excluded from this arcadia.

*The Wind in the Willows* contrasts sharply with Walter de la Mare's neglected masterpiece *The Three Mullar-Mulgars* (1910; reissued as *The Three Royal Monkeys* in 1935 in an effort to find the wider readership it deserved). Writing originally for his own four children, de la Mare here created a quest narrative, a mythology, a language, and a landscape whose inventiveness and originality remained unchallenged until Tolkien published *The Hobbit* in 1937. The Mullar-Mulgars are princes of the blood, and when an unprecedented winter grips their forest, they set out to follow their father to the Valleys of Tishnar. The youngest, Nod, is the hero, and the guardian of the magic 'wonderstone' which helps all three of them through a series of perils before they achieve their quest. Among these is an encounter (inspired by the Elizabethan voyages described in *Purchas his Pilgrimes*) with the shipwrecked sailor Andy Battle, who finds it hard to recognize Nod's purposive intelligence and independence, and with the Water Midden, a fairy creature whose beauty almost persuades Nod to relinquish his quest.

Walter de la Mare also wrote outstanding short stories and poems for children. While his prose is often subtle and

E. H. Shepard's illustrations for *The Wind in the Willows* date from the early 1930s, but they respond fully to Grahame's nostalgia for the perfect summer's day.

sometimes elusive, his verses have the immediate appeal of nursery rhymes; yet though strongly incantatory and often mysterious, they differ in several respects from the nonsense verse of Lear or Carroll (whom de la Mare enormously admired). De la Mare is a poet of the inner eye, whether entranced—'Far are the shades of Arabia, | Where the Princes ride at noon', or alarmed—' "Grill me some bones," said the Cobbler, |"Some bones, my pretty Sue . . ." '. In his collections, *Songs of Childhood* (1902), *The Listeners and Other Poems* (1912), and, best of all, *Peacock Pie* (1913), he reproduced in poetry the kind of deep patterns and rhythms that appeal most strongly to children. Writing for them seemed to him 'ambitious and hazardous': 'Children are unflinching critics. They know usually beyond a doubt what they like, and make no allowances. And that is a chastening reflection.'

## PICTURES FOR WORDS

When *The Wind in the Willows* was first published, it appeared without illustrations; its publishers, Methuen, had approached the greatest illustrator of the day, Arthur Rackham, but he was 'too busy illustrating the *Midsummer Night's Dream*' and refused. He later came to regret his decision, and in 1940 provided a set of illustrations, but by that time Ernest Shepard's dreamier and less precise line drawings were well known and loved.

The period from 1890 to 1914 was unquestionably the golden age of children's book illustration, when colour printing reached new standards of accuracy. The bright, sometimes sticky process of lithography pioneered by Ernest Nister was now replaced by the more expensive four-colour process which reproduced water-colour painting particularly effectively, but required thin, glossy paper. The plates thus made were then tipped-in by hand on to the thicker paper of the rest of the book, and were often guarded with tissue. Using this technique publishers created luxurious gift-books, often heavily illustrated with line drawings, colour plates, and decorative endpapers, as was Rackham's *Midsummer Night's Dream*—objects to be treasured and enjoyed by the whole family. The power of Rackham's designs with their sharp delicate detail encouraged children to read pictures as well as text, as did the work of the age's other great colour illustrators such as Edmund Dulac and the Robinson brothers, Jessie M. King, and Kay Nielsen. The illustrated gift-book did not however survive for long in the straitened circumstances of the post-war world.

Rackham was a great original: for power and vitality of line, combined with an exact sense of colour, his work remains unmatched. It combines the idealization of the Pre-Raphaelites and their careful observation of the natural world with an almost Gothic delight in the grotesque, the gnarled and twisted, and displays a delightful sense of humour. Dulac's work, at its best in

*Facing*: 'Kensington Gardens . . . are in London, where the King lives.' After the success of his play in 1904, the six chapters of Barrie's *Little White Bird* concerned with Peter Pan were published separately as *Peter Pan in Kensington Gardens* (1906), an expensive gift-book, lavishly illustrated by Arthur Rackham. In this picture the dark and solid figure of Edward VII giving a salute is silhouetted against the animated and proliferating forms of the fairies, trees, and plants who make up his audience.

182

William Heath Robinson's drawing for his own *Adventures of Uncle Lubin* (1902) The propeller, mounted on its wooden board, anticipates the drawings of ingenious if fundamentally primitive contraptions that were later to make his name a household word.

*Facing*: Julius Stafford Baker's Tiger Tim and the Bruin Boys were among the earliest, and most enduring of strip-cartoons. They first appeared in the *Daily Mirror* in 1904, and after 1914 were featured in the children's comic, *The Rainbow*.

his illustrations for Hans Andersen and the *Arabian Nights*, was influenced by the art of the East, particularly Indian and Persian miniatures. Like Rackham, he was a great colourist, and his darkling blue seas and skies are particularly beautiful. Other artists who produced memorable work both in colour and black and white were the Robinson brothers, of whom William Heath Robinson is now best remembered for his drawings of absurd machines performing unlikely functions—but he was more versatile than these suggest, illustrating Poe, Shakespeare, and Andersen as well as his own charmingly whimsical *Adventures of Uncle Lubin* (1902). His brother Charles adopted a highly decorative art nouveau approach, which took into account every aspect of book production. He made his name with a new edition of Stevenson's *A Child's Garden of Verses* (1896), and he also illustrated *Alice in Wonderland* and the first edition of *The Secret Garden*.

The Robinsons worked in both colour and black and white, but many of the illustrators of this period were first and foremost line artists. The Brock brothers, Henry and Charles, were highly prolific over many years, using a traditional style and illustrating a wide range of books for adults and children: Charles illustrated many classics, among them a reprint of *Little Lord Fauntleroy*, as well as E. Nesbit's *The Railway Children*. Gordon Browne, son of Dickens's illustrator 'Phiz' (Hablot K. Browne), excelled at drawing children and figures in movement. He illustrated Hesba Stretton, Mrs Ewing, and Lang's *Prince Prigio*. Some of his best work is to be found in Crockett's *Sir Toady Lion* and, with Lewis Baumer, he illustrated Nesbit's *The Treasure Seekers*, although the artist most closely associated with her work was H. R. Millar, who made his name as an illustrator of fairy-tales and fantasy for the *Strand* magazine, where he had worked on Anstey's *The Brass Bottle*. He also illustrated Kipling's *Puck of Pook's Hill*, and assembled the *Gold* and *Silver Fairy Books*, collections in the tradition of Andrew Lang but using folk-tales previously published in the *Strand*.

The very excellence of these illustrators seems to have thrown up a few artists whose appeal lay rather in their clumsiness. One example is Helen Bannerman, whose *Little Black Sambo* (1899) and its sequels had a home-made air that appealed strongly to their earliest readers, though today their racial stereotypes are considered unacceptable. So too are those of another and far more gifted artist, Florence Upton, whose *Adventures of Two Dutch Dolls—and a Golliwogg* (1895) was the first of a series of large-format picture-books much loved in their day. Such series satisfied the child's most characteristic demand for 'more', and Upton's Golliwogg caught on immediately, rapidly becoming a favourite nursery toy.

Children's comics began in 1890 with *Comic Cuts* and *Chips*, and provided stories, illustrated jokes, and strip cartoons. One of the earliest was Julius Stafford Baker's Tiger Tim and the Bruin Boys, who appeared in the comic supplement *Playbox* in 1905, and from 1914 independently in the *Rainbow*, the first coloured comic for children. Animal characters like Tiger Tim or Charles Folkard's Teddy Tail began to make regular appearances in strip cartoons, and characters like them were later to

feature in animated films. The 'comic' behaviour of animals provided material for artists like Cecil Aldin, who specialized in drawing dogs, while Louis Wain's dressed-up cats were familiar from the mid-1880s. L. Leslie Brooke, who had earlier illustrated Mrs Molesworth's *The Carved Lions*, is now best remembered for his books of nonsense verse, *Johnny Crow's Garden* (1903) and *Johnny Crow's Party* (1907), with their line drawings of animals individualized by human traits.

Brooke's text was an old rhyme that his father used to recite and it is

*Above*: H. M. Brock's illustration for E. Hill's poem, 'When Father goes to town with me to buy my Sunday hat'. The firm and informative line is characteristic.

DR. HIPPO, THE NICEST DOCTOR IN THE WORLD, VISITS THE KINDERGARTEN SCHOOL

Beatrix Potter wrote this letter to amuse the 5-year old Noel Moore, when he was ill in September 1893. She later borrowed it back from him and used it as the blueprint for a little book, illustrated with ink and water-colour pictures. *The Tale of Peter Rabbit* was eventually published by Frederick Warne in 1902 in an edition of 6,000, which was entirely sold out before publication.

inevitably secondary to his drawings, but for many children's writers the text came first, and their drawings were supplementary. In the case of Beatrix Potter, one of the greatest of all animal artists, her pictures have traditionally been given precedence over her written texts, and she is sometimes regarded as an artist who invented stories merely to accompany her delightful water-colour pictures. Recent accounts of her work, however, have laid increasing emphasis on the elegance and wit of her prose, with its humorous understatement ('Quite the contrary; they were not in bed; *not* in the least' illustrates the kittens romping during Mrs Twitchit's tea party) and its balanced, almost biblical rhythms. Potter's correspondence with her publishers, Frederick Warne, and her corrections to galley proofs show that she was as much concerned for the precision of her texts as for the reproduction of her illustrations.

Her drawings have an accuracy and humour that avoids sentimentality—not such an easy task given that her characters are most commonly mice, rabbits, guinea pigs, and kittens—and a wonderfully tough outlook. Between Peter Rabbit's illicit excursion into Mr McGregor's garden (1902) and Pigling

'Now, my dears', said old Mrs Bunny 'you may go into the field or down the lane, but don't go into Mr McGregor's garden.'

ran straight away to Mr McGregor's garden and squeezed underneath the gate.

First he ate some lettuce, and some broad beans, then some radishes, and then, feeling rather sick, he went to look for some parsley; but round the end of a cucumber frame whom should he meet but Mr McGregor!

Flopsy, Mopsy & Cottontail, who were good little rabbits went down the lane to gather blackberries. but Peter, who was very naughty

186

Bland's bid for freedom in 1913, the year of her marriage, Potter published nineteen small-format books, each one wholly original. While the earliest warned against disobedience, Potter's sympathy with the adventurous/naughty child was such that any lessons were only of the most pragmatic and consequential kind, and there was more than a streak of subversiveness in her presentation of the impertinent Squirrel Nutkin, Tom Kitten, and the two bad mice. She begins with a forbidden paradise with its own avenging angel ('Don't go into Mr McGregor's Garden: Your father was . . . put in a pie by Mrs McGregor'), and her work takes in quest and escape (*Pigling Bland*), adventure (*Jeremy Fisher*), seduction (*Jemima Puddle-Duck*), while examining tidiness, class-consciousness, and bourgeois values with a considerable degree of scepticism (*Mrs Tittlemouse, The Pie and the Patty-Pan*, and *Ginger and Pickles*). Her work encompasses an astonishing range of themes, and the main sequence nears its end with the uncompromising *Tale of Mr Tod* (1912), a story of greed, violence, revenge, and murderous intentions which frightens many children and which, in its acknowledgement of hatred and anger as unresolved and unresolvable, marks the end of an era. 'Tod' is a dialect name for a fox, but it also means 'death' in German. Death threatens Pigling Bland and Pigwig; their escape 'Over the hills and far away' can be little more than a fantasized postscript to this, the sombrest of her tales.

## AN AWFULLY BIG ADVENTURE

It is, perhaps, significant that the sequel to H. G. Wells's *Floor Games* was *Little Wars* (1913); did the construction even of imaginary countries always have to end this way? There is a strong heroic ethos in much of the writing for children between 1890 and 1914, as if the generation doomed to die on the battlefield had been reared with exactly the ideals needed to persuade them to volunteer as soon as they could. To what extent did their childhood reading help to determine the fate of a whole generation?

For children, fighting is one of the primal pleasures, whether it takes the form of puppy tussles or the more organized structure of team games. Bevis and Ted choose sides and, in the guise of Caesar and Pompey, lead their men into battle. In Grahame's *The Golden Age*, a game of Knights of the Round Table is interrupted by the appearance of a troop of Horse Guards who 'acknowledged the [children's] salute with easy condescension'. The children are subsequently disappointed when the expected battle does not take place. This episode is reworked in *Sir Toady Lion*, where Hugh John finds, to his great delight, that his military salute is returned by the Scots Greys who even flourish their swords for him. E. Nesbit draws on this scenario in *The Wouldbegoods*, where the Bastables line up to salute a troop of soldiers from Chatham Barracks,

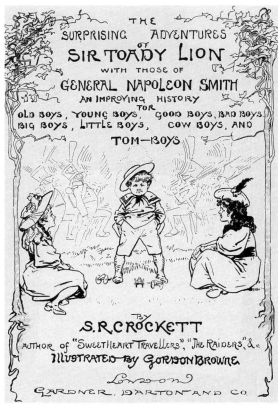

'As the highlanders had clung to the cavalry stirrups at Balaclava.' Gordon Browne's figures running out of the frame towards us anticipate the camera's ability to capture speed and movement, while neatly underlining the mock-heroics characteristic of S. R. Crockett's *Adventures of Sir Toady Lion* (1897).

though we had not read *Toady Lion* then. We have since. It is the only decent book I have ever read written by *Toady Lion*'s author. The others are mere piffle. But many people like them.

In *Sir Toady Lion* the officer salutes the child . . .

Nesbit begins disarmingly by acknowledging her precursor, but she takes the episode a stage further by establishing the connection between war and death when Mrs Simpkins learns that her soldier son Bill has been shot. Because this is a story for children, Bill is not really dead, but a shadow has fallen across the page: 'Et in Arcadia ego.'

The codes of public school and the ideals of empire combine disturbingly in Kipling's work, and most obviously in *Stalky & Co.* (1899). 'Stalky' employs the playful, aggressive, and competitive aspects of school as a preparation for life in the Indian army on the North-West Frontier—less purposely but just as effectively as Cormell Price, headmaster of the United Services College prepared his boys for the army. The book reveals Kipling's own boyhood fantasy, in which intelligence, as opposed to brute force, confers power in life. But *Stalky & Co.*, was perversely, reasserting the obvious point, that life at

188

public school was intended to train boys for their future roles as rulers of the empire. The later nineteenth century had seen a massive increase in writing for boys, school stories, stories of travel, quest, and adventure in far-flung places, and historical novels that perpetuated myths of heroism, male comradeship, and courage in the face of danger, and even death. Stories of this kind filled the 'penny-dreadfuls', but in more stylish and sophisticated versions they provided the staple for the family magazines that proliferated before the First World War. A series of writers emerged with extraordinary mythopoeic powers, who were as much enjoyed by children as adults: Kipling was foremost among them with *Kim* (1901), his novel about an Anglo-Indian child travelling along the Grand Trunk Road, his loyalty divided between the unworldly lama and the British Secret Service. Henry Rider Haggard also wrote many wonderful adventure stories, notably the African quest novels *King Solomon's Mines* (1885) and *She* (1887), and so did Arthur Conan Doyle, remembered for his tales of far-off times (*The White Company*, 1891), and places (such as *The Lost World*, 1912). But for his most popular hero, Sherlock Holmes, Conan Doyle returned to central London: Holmes's debut in *A Study in Scarlet* (1887) established a vogue for detective stories. Sexton Blake, who was even more popular, though much less intellectual than Holmes, first appeared in the pages of the *Marvel* in 1893. E. W. Hornung's *Raffles the Amateur Cracksman* (1899) was a gallant gentleman burglar, a sort of Holmes inside out. The imaginary mid-European state of Ruritania provided the setting for Anthony Hope's novels *The Prisoner of Zenda* (1894) and *Rupert of Hentzau* (1898), while John Masefield wrote two historical novels, *Martin Hyde* (1910) and *Jim Davis* (1911). John Buchan produced historical novels and spy stories of which *The Thirty-Nine Steps* (1915) is the best known. There were also supernatural tales, such as those of Lord Dunsany and the science fiction of H. G. Wells. All these were written for adults yet most of them have since become boys' books, inspired by noble ideals and moral simplicities.

But the ultimate expression of the boyish heroism that suffuses these years took a highly theatrical form: at the end of Act IV, Peter Pan stands on the rock in the Mermaids' Lagoon as the tide rises:

PETER [*with a drum beating in his breast as if he were a real boy at last*]. To die will be an awfully big adventure.

*Peter Pan*, first performed as a play in 1904, is at once a paradigm of children's adventure stories and a commentary upon them. Although James Barrie achieves his effect very differently, he shares with Nesbit and Grahame the ability to comment with amusement and irony on the state of childhood while simultaneously entering into it. In several crucial ways Peter is never an actual child, but the age's construction of the child, the sentimental or nostalgic memory of the little boy lost, purified and released from the less lovable or more troubling characteristics of childhood. He embodies the ideal boy's heroic aspirations to deeds of intelligence, daring, and courage, yet he is also magically exempt from fear and mortality, so that his courage is complicated if not compromised, at once performing and calling into question the clichés of heroism. His relationship with Wendy is not withoutsexual undertones (they play at being mother and father to the Lost Boys), and his anomalous nature generally works to justify a militant posturing and a sexual evasiveness that the text simultaneously invites us to judge and admire.

Both *The Little White Bird* (1902), the novel in which the story of Peter Pan first appeared, and the play of *Peter Pan* were inspired by Barrie's friendship with little George Llewellyn Davies, and subsequently with his younger brothers. The idea for the play came from the stories and games Barrie invented to amuse the boys, but it would never have been mounted at all had he not already established himself as the most successful dramatist of the day. As he worked on it, it became clear that it required a host of costly and complicated special effects, including the children flying, and the first night was postponed because of technical hitches. Even so, it was an in-

The American actress Pauline Chase played Peter Pan from 1906 to 1914. Frank Haviland has portrayed her at her big moment, when Peter faces death alone on a rock in the Mermaid's Lagoon.

stant and phenomenal success, becoming a national favourite, with Christmas performances in London until the 1970s. (In 1929 Barrie gave the rights to the Great Ormond Street Hospital for Children, in perpetuity.) Barrie attended rehearsals, rewriting, cutting, and adding to his original text, and the text as published represents only one of a series of different given performances. Its dialogue is fairly close to that of Barrie's prose version, *Peter and Wendy*. Like the 'Alice' books, it was rewritten by other hands in special versions for schools and younger readers.

In writing *Peter Pan*, Barrie was influenced by the main form of entertainment then available for children, the pantomime, and the play includes a number of traditional elements from it: a principal boy (Peter is normally played by a girl in tights), a villain whom the audience is invited to jeer at, a large number of parts for children (the Lost Boys are virtually dressed up as animals), transformation scenes, and audience participation (for example, when Tinker Bell is dying). But he was also very impressed by (and perhaps envious of) the success of Seymour Hicks's play *Bluebell in Fairyland* (1901 and revived thereafter), apparently the first full-length play to be specially written for children. Both *Bluebell* and adaptations for the stage of successful children's books (such as Burnett's *A Little Princess*) showed that children, accompanied by adults, could now be regarded as a commercially viable audience, particularly at Christmas time. The success of *Peter Pan* was followed by other plays for children, most notably *Where the Rainbow Ends* (1911) by Clifford Mills and John Ramsey, in which Rosamund and Crispian are helped by St George in their fight against the Dragon King. The play is full of patriotic sentiments and the book of it (1912) was dedicated 'To the children of the Empire'.

George Llewellyn Davies, like so many young men of his class and generation, volunteered in 1914 and was sent to France as a second lieutenant, taking with him a copy of *The Little White Bird*, the book that Barrie had written for him. He was killed in action the following year. That Christmas the Mermaids' Lagoon scene was cut out of *Peter Pan*—perhaps out of respect for George's death (Peter's words had originally been his), but more probably because, even if the approach of an inevitable death could still look like an awfully big adventure, it had now become shockingly commonplace.

# 8 RETREATISM AND ADVANCE

## 1914–1945

*Peter Hunt*

### THE CONTEXT OF CHILDREN'S LITERATURE

IN 1913, when 12,379 books were published in Britain (according to *The English Catalogue of Books*), 688 of them, or 5.6 per cent, were 'juveniles'; by 1938, while the overall output had increased by only 30 per cent to 16,091, the number of 'juveniles' had risen to 1,629—an increase of 137 per cent, and the proportion had nearly doubled.

These figures demonstrate how children's books had grown in importance, but they disguise the considerable contrasts in the types of books produced and the attitudes to them.

Although in the 1920s and 1930s children's books were, as the bookseller and publisher Eleanor Graham observed, 'by and large . . . regarded as trash' by reviewers, they were also gaining in respectability with the public. In 1931 the Library Association published a survey, *Books to Read*, and in 1938 the National Book Council brought out their first children's booklist, *Four to Fourteen*. In 1932 both F. J. Harvey Darton's standard work, *Children's Books in England*, and W. C. Berwick Sayers's *Manual of Children's Libraries* appeared; in 1936 the Library Association established the Carnegie Medal (the first winner was Arthur Ransome's *Pigeon Post*) and the first reviewing journal for children's books, *The Junior Bookshelf*, was published; the Association of Children's Librarians was formed in 1937.

However, Geoffrey Trease, who published his first children's book in 1934, felt that 'it was small wonder that so much of children's literature was hackwork', when copyrights were bought outright, and the writers were on a treadmill. The school story, the comic and the bulky anthologies known as 'rewards' and 'budgets' were virtually indistinguishable from the pre-1914 product: a new story was likely to be 'a fossil in which one could trace the essential characteristics of one written in 1880 or 1890'. But, in contrast, this was the period that produced characters as robust as Rupert Bear, Winnie-the-Pooh, the Hobbits, Biggles, Mary Poppins, William, Dr Dolittle, and the Swallows and Amazons; it was the period in which the progress made by Nesbit and Kipling and Ransome (with *Old Peter's Russian Tales* (1916)) in developing an unpatronizing mode of address to the child reader was gradually consolidated.

There were contrasts, too, between the rather sentimental and whimsical view of childhood typified by A. A. Milne or Rose Fyleman, and the quasi-realism of writers like Ransome or the extravagance of fantasists like John Masefield. But perhaps the single theme which unites these strands is a pervading quietism, a retreat from the realities of the world surrounding the child and the book.

For quite apart from two world wars, between 1914 and 1945 Britain changed almost out of all recognition. Extremes of wealth and poverty became more apparent; there was a general strike, a slump, the Jarrow marches, a series of inept governments, including a national government and the first Labour administrations. There was the abdication, the Wembley exhibition, the 'bright young things', the 'lost generation', Oxford bags.

Almost every fear that lay beneath the surface of Kenneth Grahame's *The Wind in the Willows* was realized. Women were awarded limited suffrage in December 1918; there was a huge growth in suburban building (along with hire purchase and electrical gadgetry). An act of 1938 gave 11 million workers the right to one week's holiday with pay (although by 1939 more than half the population still did not leave their homes for even one night each year) and one of the favourite destinations was the countryside, now invaded by the motor car. There were traffic lights (1926) and Belisha beacons (1934); the 'old' country ways were celebrated in books like A. G. Street's *Farmer's Glory* (1932) and A. P. Herbert's *The Water Gypsies* (1930), books which led, ironically, to the further 'invasion' of the country. The Youth Hostels Associations were founded in 1930 and 1931, and by 1931 nearly 300 hostels provided over 10,000 beds for ramblers and hikers. Both H. V. Morton in *In Search of England* (1927) and J. B. Priestley in *English Journey* (1934)—and other young men, including, less romantically, George Orwell—found in their journeys contrasts between urban poverty and a rural England that had not changed for centuries.

It was not only Britain that was changing. The first transatlantic flight was in 1919. In Europe, the frontiers that had been virtually open in 1914 became barriers both actual and symbolic. And yet, despite the Spanish Civil War, the growth of dictatorships, rearmament, the inexorable movement towards war (inevitable, in hindsight, since the Treaty of Versailles), and, further away, Japan's invasion of China, the mood of Britain was inward-looking. As

The large market for 'Books for Boys and Girls' is made clear in this advertisement for forthcoming titles, December 1924.

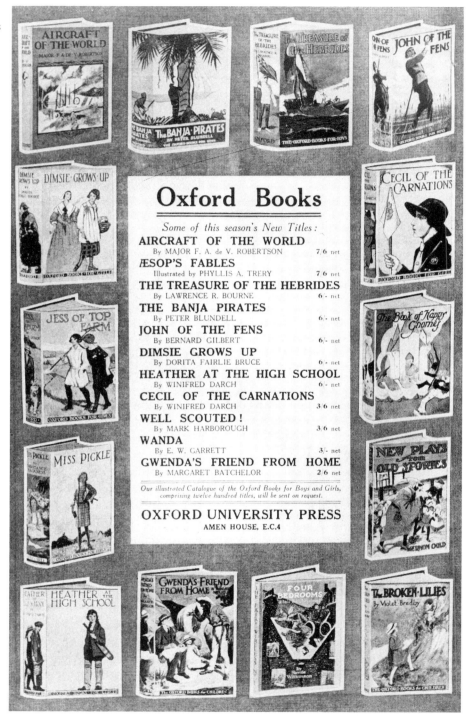

# Oxford Books

*Some of this season's New Titles:*

**AIRCRAFT OF THE WORLD**
By MAJOR F. A. de V. ROBERTSON                7/6 net

**ÆSOP'S FABLES**
Illustrated by PHYLLIS A. TRERY             7/6 net

**THE TREASURE OF THE HEBRIDES**
By LAWRENCE R. BOURNE                       6/- net

**THE BANJA PIRATES**
By PETER BLUNDELL                           6/- net

**JOHN OF THE FENS**
By BERNARD GILBERT                          6/- net

**DIMSIE GROWS UP**
By DORITA FAIRLIE BRUCE                     6/- net

**HEATHER AT THE HIGH SCHOOL**
By WINIFRED DARCH                           6/- net

**CECIL OF THE CARNATIONS**
By WINIFRED DARCH                           3/6 net

**WELL SCOUTED !**
By MARK HARBOROUGH                          3/6 net

**WANDA**
By E. W. GARRETT                            3/- net

**GWENDA'S FRIEND FROM HOME**
By MARGARET BATCHELOR                       2/6 net

*Our illustrated Catalogue of the Oxford Books for Boys and Girls, comprising twelve hundred titles, will be sent on request.*

**OXFORD UNIVERSITY PRESS**
AMEN HOUSE, E.C.4

L. C. B. Seaman observed of the 1920s: 'Since the struggles of the past decade had availed so little, the country was swept by a desire to ignore social and political problems altogether.' War, change, and the threat of war and change made nostalgia and retreat even more attractive and urgent than before, and it naturally found a place in children's books—at once a place of retreat for adults and of protection for children.

This retreatism was also intellectual. F. R. Leavis and the writers in the literary critical journal *Scrutiny* made great play of the idea of the 'golden age' which has haunted every generation to some degree. As Iain Wright observed of them: 'Just back around the last bend in the road, just out of sight over the last hill, there had apparently been a sort of happy Hobbit-land, the organic community, a golden rural world without class-conflict or exploitation.' D. W. Harding's shrewd comment in the first issue of *Scrutiny* in 1932 ('A Note on Nostalgia') is particularly pertinent to children's books: 'complete absence of nostalgia in a modern writer is suspect . . . [but] permanent, unresolved nostalgia is a failure too.'

And so, with very rare exceptions, the world of children's literature was the world of the comfortable middle class; it was not one in which there was a wide belief in the actively political function of literature. Children's literature did not register the attitudes of Auden or Caudwell, or notice the founding of *Left Review* (1934) or John Lehman's *New Writing* (1936), and it largely ignored class and political struggles until they were too overwhelming to be ignored.

What it could not fail to register was the impact of other media. At 6 p.m. on 5 December 1922, three weeks after national radio broadcasting had first begun, the British Broadcasting Company began its *Children's Hour* from its Birmingham transmitter. The programme lasted for fifteen minutes, beginning with a record of 'The Dance of the Goblins', and a story about two dwarfs called Spick and Span. The programme was so popular that other stations imitated the idea, and in 1924 a National Advisory Committee was set up, which advocated 'the creation of an atmosphere of a good home and the presentation of real beauty—in song, story, music and poetry on a plane attractive to the young'. *Children's Hour* developed into a mixture of serial readings, outside broadcasts, and plays, and among its most famous creations were S. G. Hulme Beaman's short plays about Larry the Lamb and his friends from Toytown. These were broadcast from 1928, and some appeared in book form in 1938. *Winnie-the-Pooh* was first dramatized in 1939. (*Children's Hour* survived until 1963.)

The link between broadcast media and print was immediate. Music-hall stars had long been featured in comics, and they were replaced by radio stars in comics like *Radio Fun* and books like *The Arthur Askey Annual* (1940), taken from radio's *Band Waggon*. Perhaps the most famous example of the link was Barbara Euphan Todd's *Worzel Gummidge*. The dedication of the first edition (1936) reads: 'Dedicated gratefully to Hugh E. Wright who played the part of Worzel Gummidge so successfully on the Regional programmes at Broadcasting House.' Another important programme of the period, reflecting the interest in the countryside, was G. Bramwell Evans's 'Romany' series, which became an equally successful series of country books beginning with *Out with Romany* in 1937. The series included a first-person narrative by 'Romany's' cocker spaniel Raq, in *Romany, Muriel and Doris* (1939).

For many years the presenters of *Children's Hour* were given honorary 'uncle' status, and perhaps the most famous, Derek McCullough ('Uncle Mac'), published a surrealist and very sophisticated collection of limericks and farcical tales in 1928, *Nonsericks,* with forewords by A. P. Herbert and 'Uncle Peter' and 'Colourlarfs by Earnest Noble'. (McCullough also wrote the book chosen by Eleanor Graham to be the second Puffin book, *Cornish Adventure* in 1941.)

And there was the cinema. 1919 saw 'Felix the Cat', whose stubbornly silent career (which lasted until 1933) led the way in merchandising; he appeared in his own annual in 1923. Walt Disney's Mickey Mouse came to fame with *Steamboat Willie* in 1928 (Mickey's third film)—although he was not the first mouse of that name: 'Mickey Mouse and his Jungle Friends' had featured in the *Wonderland Annual* of 1920 (for 1921). Disney's *Mickey Mouse Annual* appeared in 1930; Donald Duck joined him in 1934. In 1937 the immensely successful film of *Snow White and the Seven Dwarfs* with 'wild wood and old witch effects' by an artist from an earlier era, Arthur Rackham, demonstrated the universality and endless adap-tability of myth—as well as the importance of commercialism and the children's market. One small indication of the speed at which Mickey Mouse was absorbed into other cultures—and what would now perhaps be called his localization—is the bulky 'reward', *A Trip with Mickey Mouse*, almost certainly published in 1933. In this, Mickey tours England and *plays cricket*—and not only that, topically endures 'bodyline bowling', notoriously encountered in the 1932–3 test series in Australia. The British produced films as well; the *Sunday Express* cartoon strip 'Come on Steve' found its way into animated films from 1932.

As we have seen, children's literature often reflects adult literature: in this period, there was a contrast between how it reflected—or failed to reflect—serious and popular adult literture. Between the wars, as Peter Widdowson has noted, the novelists 'sought to engage with the social reality of their times', and wrestled with modernism and experiment. New forms were being explored by Joyce and others; there was also the anti-intellectualism of Lawrence, the latter-day liberalism of Woolf, the political involvement of Auden and Isherwood, the social comment of Waugh, Shaw, Huxley, and Wells. The Book Society was founded in 1928.

Little of this registered with children's writers, although the popular writers of adult romances were soon adopted by adolescent readers—Stanley Weyman, Jeffrey Farnol, Georgette Heyer (typically, *These Old Shades*, 1926), and Hugh Walpole with *Rogue Herries* (1930) and its sequels. Among the best sellers, from Sellar and Yeatman's *1066 and All That* (1930) to James Hilton's *Goodbye Mr Chips* (1934), there was a vein of escape to an idyllic past, or the distant romantic scene, or into an easy philosophy to solve current problems. This was also the period of Somerset Maugham, Priestley, Ethel M. Dell, Edgar Wallace, and Leslie Charteris.

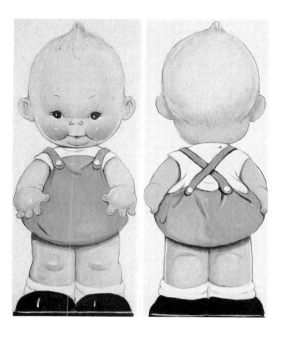

Mabel Lucie Atwell's designs for the 'Diddums' rubber doll.

And what of the readers? H. A. L. Fisher's Education Act of 1918 raised the school leaving age to 14—although at the price of huge classes: one-quarter had over sixty children in 1922—and the Burnham Committee was established to equalize teachers' salaries. The potential market for children's literature was perhaps greater than ever before.

The relationship between children's literature, adult literature, and society was neatly summed up by the British humorist Alan Coren, who in the 1970s imagined an interview with a geriatric Winnie-the-Pooh:

'It was,' he sighed, '1926. Jazz, short skirts, nightingales singing in Berkeley Square, angels dancing at the Ritz, know what I mean? A world full of excitement, sex, fun, Frazer-Nash two-seaters and everyone going to Le Touquet! And where was I? Hanging around with Piglet and passing my wild evenings in the heady company of Eeyore! *The Great Gatsby* came out that year,' said Pooh bitterly. 'The same year as *Winnie-the-Pooh*.'

## THE FIRST WORLD WAR

But before that there had been what one writer who survived it, A. A. Milne, described as 'that nightmare of mental and moral degradation', the First World War. If it was a rich subject for the magazines and comic papers, it found little place in 'mainstream' children's literature, and where it did appear there was a notable difference between what was thought suitable for boys and for girls. Generally, girls were exhorted to support the male cause,

*Facing*: Mabel Lucie Atwell's 'Fairy Tree'—money box and biscuit tin.

whereas the rollicking formulas of pre-war boys' stories were adapted to this new battlefield by writers such as F. S. Brereton (*Under Haig in Flanders*, 1917), 'Herbert Strang' (*With Haig on the Somme*, 1917), and John Westerman (brother of Percy F.).

In retrospect the gap between the heroics of the fictional characters and the horrors of the reality is grotesque. *Under Haig in Flanders* uses hoary devices of spying and the 'one English boy equals ten foreigners' formula, and has an officer describe the bombardment before the Somme offensive as 'There's never been anything like it before . . . this is really magnificent', before the heroes dash upon the craven enemy. If it is possible to make a literary judgement without compounding the offence (or offensiveness) it would be that no horror seems to be horrific enough to withstand popular literature. The power of nationalism and circumstance makes some fictional involvement, such as the boys of Greyfriars School facing firing squads, as inevitable as it now seems tasteless.

But the war was cheerfully fought by fictional characters of all kinds. Detectives from Sherlock Holmes to Sexton Blake and Nelson Lee were involved; and in the school story the likes of Angela Brazil and Bessie Marchant included war work and refugees: Brazil's *A Harum-Scarum Schoolgirl* (1919) features not only a visiting American, but Armistice Day, and middle-class dabbling at being land girls. In books such as Brenda Girvin's *Munition Mary* (1918) and *Jenny Wren* (1920), or Bessie Marchant's *A Transport Girl in France* (1918), patriotism was kept in line with suitable sex-roles. As Cadogan and Craig point out, 'the editorial policy of Lord Northcliffe's Amalgamated Press . . . was to involve its girl characters and readers unreservedly in the war' (*Women and Children First* (1978)). The war provided material for a new crop of adventure writers (although, it must be said, they were scarcely distinguishable from the old): Percy F. Westerman, for example, produced an air story, *Winning his Wings: A Story of the RAF*, in 1919.

## RETREATISM AND VERSE

After the war, writers for children, responding perhaps to an altered mood, turned away from social realism, often adopting—and distorting to the point of sentimentality—the 'beautiful child' cult. A precursor was A. A. Milne's pseudo-fairy-tale *Once on a Time* (1917), written 'for the amusement of my wife and myself at a time when life was not very amusing' and subtitled 'a fairy tale for grown-ups', which contrives to be ironic and whimsical by turns.

This approach to childhood, especially when blended with nostalgia, could be a potent mixture, and it can be seen at its best—or least objectionable—in the most distinguished 'annual' of the period. The publisher Basil

Blackwell, in one of several attempts to improve the standard of writing for children, produced *Joy Street: A Medley of Prose and Verse for Boys and Girls. Number One* (1923) set a high standard of design, although its bulk mirrored the cheaper 'rewards'. It had heavy paper, strong print, strong design, and tipped-in plates; but, rather than featuring the pre-war 'empire-building' writers, the 'new' generation was represented. *Number One,* dedicated to Rose Fyleman, began with Eleanor Farjeon's story 'Tom Cobble and Ooney' with its famous opening: 'When Tom Cobble of Southways was seven years old, he got stolen by fairies.' The volume also included one of Walter de la Mare's most famous stories, 'Miss Jemima', a sad tale by Laurence Houseman, 'The Open Door', and Hilaire Belloc's cautionary tale 'Maria, who made faces and a deplorable marriage'. Edith Sitwell's contribution, 'Death of a Gollywog', is, perhaps, a sign of the political incorrectness of the times: 'Sambo is dead, | Though he was black | He had, I said, | Of love no lack | . . . We'll bury him under | The cherry-tree | And the cherries darker | Than ever will be.' *Joy Street* ran for at least twelve volumes (to 1934), and later contributors included Lord Dunsany, A. A. Milne, and Barbara Euphan Todd.

Eleanor Farjeon's position at the beginning of *Number One Joy Street* is appropriate, for she was an important and prolific author; however, it is significant that she is very much of her time; with a few notable exceptions, her work (as opposed to her name and reputation) scarcely survived the second war. Her first book was a rather strained collection *Nursery Rhymes of London Town* (and *More Nursery Rhymes . . .*) (1916, 1917) the inventiveness of which was confined to exploring, often through puns, the names of London streets (Smithfield—'There was a Smith lived in a Field . . .'). From this inauspicious start, Farjeon went on to write over fifty books by 1945, many of them in the folk- and fairy-tale mode. Half of them were in verse, with titles such as *Singing*

A characteristic picture and verse from Basil Blackwell's *Joy Street* annual.

RESPECTABLE PEO

IT'S very nice to eat v
As Mother does, in
But oh, I think
To grab for jar
And if they
At least I

*Games from Arcady* (1926) 'with music by the author' and *Over the Garden Wall* (1933). She wrote in an unpublished memoir: 'What I did wasn't good enough; presently the effort to write [poetry] with a genius I didn't possess dwindled into using as well as I could such minor talents as were mine.'

Perhaps her most characteristic piece was, significantly, written for adults, *Martin Pippin in the Apple Orchard*, published in November 1921. This features a romantic, possibly medieval troubadour, in Adversane, deep in the deepest of literary Sussexes, who sings songs and tells stories to the six milkmaids who are guarding their virginal mistress. The book has, as Margery Fisher puts it, a 'febrile emotionalism' reminiscent of Georgette Heyer, and 'a faintly enervating atmosphere . . . which recalls *Restharrow* and Mary Webb and Quilter's Merrie England tunes' (*Who's Who in Children's Books*). The book went through many editions, the later ones being marketed for children: clearly fashions in romance changed. Its sequel, *Martin Pippin in the Daisy Field* (1937), is more obviously for children; and although there is still a touch of preciousness in the air, it contains some of her best work, including 'Elsie Piddock Skips in her Sleep'. Farjeon went on to win the Carnegie Medal for a collection of pieces, *The Little Bookroom*, in 1956, and the major British award for services to children's literature bears her name.

Farjeon's major contribution was undoubtedly in verse, and among her fellow contributors to *Punch* was a similarly skilled writer who had—although it is difficult to see at first glance—a rather less soft-centred view of childhood, Rose Fyleman. Fyleman published *Fairies and Chimneys* with Methuen in 1918, with the daunting dedication, 'To the *realist* fairy of my childhood—my mother.' The first poem in this collection, 'There are fairies at the bottom of my garden!', is possibly the most famous children's poem of all, and the manner and content were much imitated—for example, by the young Enid Blyton. Fyleman produced many examples of what later generations have seen as embarrassing whimsy, but she often approached a recognizable childhood, in verses that acknowledge the legacy of Robert Louis Stevenson:

> I wish I liked rice pudding
> I wish I were a twin,
> I wish some day a real live fairy
> Would just come walking in.
>
> I wish when I'm at table
> My feet would touch the floor,
> I wish our pipes would burst next winter
> Just like they did next door.

...se Fyleman, who, when she was editing *The Merry-go-Round* for
...ed a well-known playwright and ex-assistant editor of *Punch* to

contribute some verses. A. A. Milne had already written, for his wife, what was to become one of the most famous poems in the English language, 'Vespers'. As he was often at pains to point out, this was a poem that was 'sentimentalised over' rather than being sentimental. He went on: 'the spectacle in real life of a child of three at its prayers is . . . calculated to bring a lump to the throat. But even so, one must tell the truth about the matter' and the truth is that Christopher Robin is a tough little egoist, and the poem was a very sceptical, honest view of childhood. Nevertheless, Milne was unable to shake off the whimsical label attached to two of the most phenomenal best sellers in the history of publishing—let alone children's publishing—*When We were Very Young* (1924) and *Now We are Six* (1927). As Milne famously remarked in his autobiography, *It's Too Late Now*: 'whatever else they lack, the verses are technically good. *When We were Very Young* is not the work of a poet becoming playful, nor of a lover of children expressing his love . . . it is the work of a light-verse writer taking his job seriously even though he is taking it into the nursery.'

And there was a lot of it about. Not only were Rose Fyleman's long series of small collections, such as *Gay Go Up* (1929), very hard to distinguish from the much more famous verses of Milne, but there were very similar volumes by John Drinkwater—*All about Me* (1928) and *More about Me* (1929, both illustrated by H. M. Brock)—while Georgette Agnew's *Let's Pretend* was even more indistinguishable for being illustrated by Shepard. Even A. P. Herbert's Belloc-like *A Child's Guide to the Professions* (1922) had a similar look. In 1928 Kathleen Hale, whose fame rests on Orlando, the marmalade cat, illustrated Molly Harrower's *I Don't Mix Much with Fairies*. In the introductory note, the author acknowledges her debt to Milne, and hopes that her rhymes 'Which simply just came | Won't savour of cribbin'.' Others in the same tradition included E. V. Lucas's *Playtime and Company* (1925)—illustrated by Shepard—and Enid Blyton's *Real Fairies* (1923).

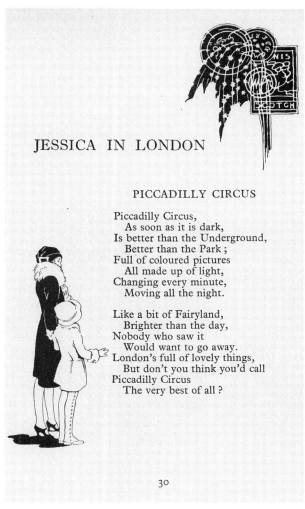

## JESSICA IN LONDON

### PICCADILLY CIRCUS

Piccadilly Circus,
    As soon as it is dark,
Is better than the Underground,
    Better than the Park;
Full of coloured pictures
    All made up of light,
Changing every minute,
    Moving all the night.

Like a bit of Fairyland,
    Brighter than the day,
Nobody who saw it
    Would want to go away.
London's full of lovely things,
    But don't you think you'd call
Piccadilly Circus
    The very best of all?

30

Rose Fyleman's *Gay Go Up* (1929), one of a long series of small poetry books, and there were many others like them.

201

Somewhat more problematical are Walter de la Mare's poems, which have little of the comfortable backgrounds of Farjeon or Milne. From *Peacock Pie* (1913) to *Poems for Children* (1930) and *Bells and Grass* (1941), his verses often seem slight, but there is no sentimentality, no compromise, and they very often have an unsettling and threatening feel about them. De la Mare produced two famous anthologies: *Come Hither* in 1923 and *Tom Tiddler's Ground* in 1932.

Other books of verse that stand out tend to be oddities, such as John Masefield's *Reynard the Fox* (1921), Humbert Wolfe's *Cursory Rhymes* (1922), and, most striking of all, T. S. Eliot's *Old Possum's Book of Practical Cats* (1939), a book seldom mentioned in studies of Eliot.

## BOOKS OF THEIR TIME

The successful playwright and children's author and his famous son. A. A. Milne and Christopher on holiday in Dorset.

A. A. Milne has, of course, become a national author, not principally from his verse but because *Winnie-the-Pooh* (1926) and *The House at Pooh Corner* (1928) have joined the very select company of national icons. There are many explanations for his success; Pooh Bear is the optimistic (or mystic) everyman, as well as the amiable child. The enchanted forest contains the whole of childhood (with a touch of Arcadian nostalgia), and there is a hierarchy of types of children to identify with—Piglet, Tigger, and Roo; the children are in conflict with the strange and pretentious adults—Rabbit, Owl, and the misanthropic Eeyore—but all is made safe by the presence of Christopher Robin. (Kanga, the only female, has a slightly ambivalent role.) It seems that this mixture is potent enough to transcend the precise class and period atmosphere of the books.

But it is sometimes forgotten—and Milne would have been the last person to wish it to be forgotten—that the children's books were only a small part of the author's output. He was the most successful London playwright of the inter-war years and a competent novelist (his *The Red House Mystery* ranks among the classics of detective fiction), and he always rather resented the fact that the children's books overshadowed the rest. For his relationship with childhood (and his own child) was at best ambivalent. When Dorothy Parker attacked him ('Mr A. A. ("Whimsy-the-Pooh") Milne') he replied that 'there is no artistic reward for a book written for children other than the knowledge that they enjoy it. For once, and how one hates to think it, *vox populi, vox Dei.*' That qualification is important, for it demonstrates that he was not the committed child-person that his admirers might wish him to be: the 'Pooh' books contain a lot of jokes directed at adults, just as the books of verse contain, as Milne admitted, 'some *for* children, some *about* children, some by, with or from children'.

But that slightly coy, rather comfortable, slightly retreatist, and whimsical tone that Milne often slips into exists in a great many books that have not survived the period. Some are famous by report; for example, J. R. R. Tolkien, in his seminal essay 'On Fairy Stories' (given as the Andrew Lang Lecture at the University of St Andrews in 1938), makes some interesting points which apply to the immediate post-war era, and which are, sadly, as applicable today:

It is true that the age of childhood-sentiment has produced some delightful books (especially charming, however, to adults) of the fairy kind or near to it; but it has also produced a dreadful undergrowth of stories written or adapted to what was or is conceived to be the measure of children's minds and needs. The old stories are mollified or bowdlerised, instead of being reserved; the imitations are often merely silly, Pigwiggenry without even the intrigue.

A book for its time: *The Wanderings of Mumfie* (1935), complete with philosophical signpost.

The reference is to Arnrid Johnston's lightly satirical *Pigwiggen: His Dashing Career*, published by *Country Life* in 1938, and using colour lithography with very colourful pages crowded with pictures and text. Pigwiggen, the flying pig, is taken on as deputy director of traffic and chief of police for the coronation of King Leo IX. King Leo's Queen to be, first encountered 'in the long gallery roller-skating with the Russian Attaché', suggests that he be given a knighthood. This causes a class problem. ' "But my dear," whispered the King. "Do you think he has been to a public school?" '

Characteristic fantasy of the period seems to have had a strong element of expediency, as in Eric Linklater's *The Wind on the Moon* (1944). Katharine Tozer's *The Wanderings of Mumfie* (1935) has shades of 'Alice' as well as of Milne: Mumfie wears his 'new pair of red leather boots because they made him feel superior about the feet'. Its mix, which includes policemen and trains and cabs, a scarecrow (who is not a patch on Worzel Gummidge, of whom more later), a dream factory, a witch, Father Christmas, and a golliwog called Nigger who has 'indifferently clean cotton gloves' and who says things like 'Sure a' has, boss', is reminiscent of C. S. Lewis's later uneasy blends. There were five sequels concluding with *Mumfie Marches On* (1942).

Among the most distinctive of the writers of the period was the eccentric short-story writer A. E. Coppard's *Pink Furniture: A Tale for Lovely Children with Noble Natures* (1930). Like *Mumfie* it is a rather ramshackle collection of fantasy incidents, mixed with some political satire along mildly Swiftian lines, as it follows Toby Tottel in his search for the Book of Wisdom and *real* pink furniture. Toby, having grown up through his adventures, comes home again to find the little girl who was his next-door neighbour has also grown up: 'And he knew then that what he had been seeking for the world over was here at his very home with his love beside him; it had never been anywhere else. Pride of youth had lured him and misled him . . . So he married Bridget, and they dwelt in a house full of *real* pink furniture.' *Pink Furniture*'s ending has a sentimentality and cosiness which undercuts the sharper tone of the rest of the book, and which is echoed in Nancy Bankart Gurney's illustrations. However, there was some satire around, notably in Archibald Marshall's *Punch* contributions published as *Simple Stories* and *Simple Stories from Punch* (1927, 1930), while Marshall's satire on nineteenth-century Puritan fiction also appeared in *Punch* and was published as *The Birdikin Family* (1932). It was, he observed, 'hardly a caricature, for it would be impossible to caricature some of the priggishness and snobbery of those old books'.

In any period, it is the books that did not survive, despite their popularity at the time, that give the truest feel. Such a book is Bernard and Elinor Darwin's *The Tale of Mr Tootleoo* (1925) (with its sequels such as *Mr Tootleoo and Co*, 1935), an affair of bright, crude lithographs, somewhat in the manner of Hugh Lofting, with serviceable couplets (Arthur Ransome had written a book in similar vein, *Aladdin*, in 1918). The same authors also wrote *Oboli, Boboli and Little Joboli* (1938).

One of the more accomplished of the books now largely forgotten was Esther Boumphrey's *The Hoojibahs*, illustrated by A. H. Watson, and published by Oxford in 1929. This is a piece of inspired nonsense, with a nicely muted satire behind it. The Hoojibahs, a vaguely defined nomadic race who don't quite know how to be human but want to be (and who are therefore ashamed of some of their own talents, like being able to fly), take over a village isolated because the lane to it has rolled itself up.

Other notable period pieces include Enid Bagnold's *Alice and Thomas and Jane* (1930), which was illustrated both by the author and by a young child, Laurian Jones; Vera B. Birch's *The Green-Faced Toad and Other Stories* (1921), illustrated very distinctively by Lois Lenski; and a series that acknowledged and made use of the war, M. Pardoe's 'Buncle' books (which were also adapted for *Children's Hour*), beginning with *Four Plus Buncle* (1939).

Buncle, so called because, as his brother Robin and sister Jill are inclined to chorus, 'he talks *such* a lot of bunk', is a somewhat deadpan bilingual prodigy, who gets involved with the secret service (of which their father is a member) and German spies. If the plots are outrageous, the intention generally comic, and the milieu middle class, the telling and the detail and the main characters come closer to naturalism than many books. As Lance Salway has observed, 'few authors of the time have conveyed so subtly and yet so vividly the gloom and austerity of wartime and post-war Britain'.

## ILLUSTRATION

Many of these books were illustrated, and the period saw much innovative work in the picture-book. The 'old guard', such as Leslie Brooke and Cecil Aldin, continued to publish, while W. Heath Robinson illustrated de la Mare's *Peacock Pie* in 1920, and produced some of his best work with a book tailor-made for his talents, Norman Hunter's *The Incredible Adventures of Professor Branestawm* (1933). Arthur Rackham was still working, illustrating Margery Williams's *Poor Cecco* in 1925, his last drawings being for an edition of *The Wind in the Willows* (published in a limited edition in 1940). Mabel Lucie Attwell's sentimental pictures of chubby children, which were in keeping with the view of childhood of the time, were extremely popular and influential, and her *Annual* ran for over fifty years from 1922. Artists like Shepard also caught this mood, although the unsentimental set of illustrations for Richard Jefferies's *Bevis* (1932) are thought by many to be his best work. There was an interest in wood engraving and techniques such as scraper board (Gwen Raverat for Kenneth Grahame's *Cambridge Book of Poetry for Children* (1933), Rex Whistler for de la Mare's *The Lord Fish* (1933)). Both Clifford Webb and Steven Spurrier contributed to the first illustrated edition of Arthur Ransome's *Swallows and Amazons* (1931), and Stuart Tresilian and C. Walter Hodges began their careers.

But perhaps the most striking and long-lasting influences on children's books came from those artists who were innovators in the picture-book, as opposed to illustrators. Sir William Nicholson illustrated his own *Clever Bill* (1926) and is perhaps best remembered for his illustrations to Margery Williams's *The Velveteen Rabbit* (1922). For this, as John Barr explains, Nicholson 'drew colour lithographs on the stone, from which transfers were taken and the book was printed, not entirely to his satisfaction, from zinc plates in the USA'.

When *The Story of Babar the Little Elephant* was published in English in

A self-portrait of one of the century's greatest illustrators: one of Edward Ardizzone's personal Christmas cards (*c*.1950).

1934, its bright colours and blending of text and pictures were very infl-uential, and a classic in the same style was Edward Ardizzone's *Little Tim and the Brave Sea Captain*. This was first published at the New York office of Oxford University Press by Geoffrey Cumberledge, with text lettering by Grace Hogarth (it was redrawn with letter-press text in 1953), and was one of the earliest books to be printed by photo-offset litho. The flow of the text may well come from the fact that Ardizzone first told the story to his two children, Philip (5) and Christianna (6), while some of the impact of the pictures may owe something, as Ardizzone said, to his early career: 'I started as a painter, and that's always my very first thing.' *Little Tim* also went some way to rehabilitating the 'speech-balloon' into mainstream texts.

Another startling talent was Kathleen Hale, whose *Orlando the Marmalade Cat: A Camping Holiday* (1938) began a long series in which the bold designs and flooding colour overwhelm the words both liter-ally and figuratively.

Possibly even more influential than *Babar* was the work of 'Lewitt-Him' (the Polish refugees Jan Lewitt and George Him), especially with *Locomotive* and *The Football's Revolt* (1939), and Diana Ross's *The Little Red Engine Gets a Name* (1942). Three outstanding books of 1939, all with very distinctive tech-niques, were Joan Kiddell-Monroe's panda story *In his Little Black Waistcoat*, H. V. Drummond's first book, *Phewtus the Squirrel*, and, perhaps most ec-centric of all, Mervyn Peake's *Captain Slaughterboard Drops Anchor*.

### 'POPULAR' LITERATURE

But this innovative group of writers and illustrators exists in the context of popular literature—the comic and the annual. Comic strips were becoming increasingly widespread. Tiger Tim, who had first appeared in 1904 in the *Daily Mirror* (and from 1914 until 1956 in the *Rainbow*), was the pioneer, and after the war *Tiger Tim's Annual* (1921 for 1922) sealed his popularity; at one point Tiger Tim was featuring in three comics (*Rainbow*, *Tiger Tim's Weekly*, and *Playbox*) and five annuals simultaneously.

Pip (a dog) and Wilfred (a rabbit), later joined by Squeak (a penguin), began their adventures in the *Daily Mirror* on 12 May 1919. Their success was consolidated by 'live appearances', and a children's 'secret society' called the

'Wilfredian League of Gugnuncs' was started in 1927, which developed a huge membership. The League included among its rituals the challenge 'Ick Ick Pah Boo?' to which the correct answer was 'Goo Goo Pah Nunc!'

One response to this success came from the *Daily Express*, whose Rupert Bear, drawn by Mary Tourtel, first appeared on 8 November 1920 and soon after in annual and 'Monster' book form. Albert Bestall took over the series in 1935 (until 1965). As Kevin Carpenter has observed, 'the pre-1935 Rupert lived in a sombre world where evil forces in the shape of ogres and witches constantly threatened to seize power. Bestall, however, changed Rupert from a frightened little bear into an adventure-loving and assertive boy-bear whose world became a greener and happier place.' Rupert is still with us, now in video and musical form.

The *Daily Sketch* in turn retaliated in 1921 with 'The Oojah' (an elephant), who ran in annuals until 1942. In the *News Chronicle*, another strip which probably had as much appeal to adults as to children concerned Mr Noah and his family's suburban ark (the series was variously titled 'The Adventures of the Noah Family', 'Japhet and Happy', and 'The Arkubs'). The *Japhet and Happy Annual* ran from 1933 to 1953, and the *News Chronicle* promoted the 'Grand United Order of Arkubs' with secret passwords and various circulation-promotions. The equally successful rival in the *Daily Mail* was the mouse Teddy Tail, with his attendant club, the 'Teddy Tail League'.

In separate comics, this was the era of the battle between the Associated Press and D. C. Thomson of Dundee. Among the famous long-running titles were *Chick's Own* (1920–57), *Rainbow* (1914–56), sold as 'the children's paper parents approve of', and which was claimed to have had royal readers, and *Sunbeam* (1922–40). D. C. Thomson's 'big five', established between 1921 and 1933—*Adventure, Rover, Wizard, Skipper, Hotspur*—were in direct competition with the Associated Press's *Champion* (1922).

For girls, there were *School Friend* (1919–29) and *Schoolgirl's Own* (1921–36), with annuals running to 1943; *Girls' Crystal* (under various minor changes of title) ran from 1935 to 1976, gradually taking on the comic-strip form. The Associated Press fought back with magazines such as *Modern Boy* (1928); *Film Fun* (1920) attempted to exploit a new market; and D. C. Thomson produced *Dandy* (1937) and *Beano* (1938), in direct competition to the long-running *Magnet* and *Gem*. Characters like Desperate Dan were illustrated by the visual equivalent of Frank Richards, Dudley Watkins (in 1,454 consecutive issues of *Dandy*).

The comics begot their own annuals, but vast numbers of other annuals and 'rewards' were produced. The 'rewards' (and their cheaper versions, the 'budgets') were heavily bulked out with thick paper. The *Giant Book for Girls* (undated), for example, was well over an inch thick for its ninety-six (unnumbered) pages. The annuals, like *Father Tuck's Annual* (1898–1935), the

Religious Tract Society's *The Empire Annual for Boys [and Girls]* (1909–33), and Oxford University Press's *Herbert Strang's Annual* (1911–27), *Mrs Strang's Annual for Girls* (1919–27), and *. . . for Baby* (1913–26), seemed to change little. In fact, 'Herbert Strang' (and the equally corporate Mrs Strang) was a creation of George Herbert Ely and James L'Estrange, and their annuals became the *Oxford Annual for Boys/Girls* (1927–41) until overcome by the paper shortages. 'Herbert Strang' wrote over 100 books and edited—at a conservative estimate—over 350 annuals, rewards, and series books, with very little differentiation of style, subject-matter, or indeed, presentation over thirty-five years. (In a piece of pseudonymity worthy of Charles Hamilton—of whom more later—the OUP series 'Great Books' (1925–30) was edited by 'Herbert Strang and Mrs Herbert Strang'.)

The years between the wars were also the 'era of the budgets': the 'budgets' with their matt boards rather than cloth binding, had begun in the 1890s and continued apparently timelessly. A typical example, *The Big Book for Boys*, edited for Oxford University Press by 'Herbert Strang' in 1923, had on its contents page, 'Jealous in Honour: A Story of the Civil War', 'A Knife and a Piece of String: A Scouting Story', by Lawrence R. Bourne, and school stories by Hylton Cleaver and Desmond Coke. At the other extreme in size were novelties like 'Mrs Herbert Strang's' *The Chubby Book of Animal Tales* which was 2 inches square ('Teenie-Weenie' books were popular).

Annual publishing boomed in the 1930s, until paper rationing in 1940 cut back a lot of the activities of the Associated Press and D. C. Thomson. Some of the market was taken up, prophetically, by the rather cruder magazines published by Gerald Swan, which had been stockpiled. Swan also produced American-style publications such as *New Funnies* (1940).

## ADVANCES AND GENRES

The two staples of the comics and magazines were the school story and the adventure story. The adventure story was still very much in the 'empire-building' mould, dominated by writers like Percy F. Westerman, Tom Bevan, Col. Brereton (who apart from war stories specialized in historical romances), and the ubiquitous 'Herbert Strang'. Few examples of that more respectable offshoot of the adventure story, the historical novel, have survived—Geoffrey Trease's *Cue for Treason* (1940) is an example; others, such as *Blow the Man Down* (1939) by Elfrida Vipont (writing as 'Charles Vipont'), deserve to. More conventional was 'Herbert Strang's' *Dickon of the Chase* (1931). Harriet Campbell's *A Royal Princess* (1934) was an adaptation of Margaret Irwin's *Royal Flush*, and C. Walter Hodges's *Columbus Sails* (1939) was distinguished for the artwork as well as the story-telling.

But there were changes in the wind, and one straw was Erich Kästner's highly original and ingenious *Emil and the Detectives* (1929, translated into English 1931). (Its sequel, *Emil and the Three Twins* (1935), was far less successful.) Basil Blackwell started an adventure series, 'Tales of Action', edited by L. A. G. Strong, with titles like Strong's *Fortnight South of Skye*, about a French trawler poaching in Scottish waters, and C. Day Lewis's historical novel *Dick Willoughby* (1933). Also included in the series was Rex Warner's *The Kite* (1936), one of the very few books that addressed the modern world—it was about drug-running in Egypt .

One book did, however, address contemporary political thinking, if not contemporary events. This was Geoffrey Trease's pioneering *Bows against the Barons* (1934), written 'in revulsion against the sentimental romanticism then pervading historical fiction', and its 'tushery' and thinly disguised didacticism. Robin Hood is portrayed as a democratic revolutionary fighting against explicitly brutal and corrupt aristocrats, and the book pulls very few punches. Significantly, Trease could not find a 'mainstream' publisher for his work, and it was taken by the 'left-wing' publishers Lawrence and Wishart.

This was also the era when the school story reached its peak in output if not in originality. As P. W. Musgrave noted in *From Brown to Bunter*, 'the life of the genre petered out in the inter-war years', prey to social change and stereotyping. But it was a remarkably sturdy plant for all that because it touched adults closely. Bernard Bergonzi sees the experience of (public) schools as 'both private and shared, a source of personal fantasies and public metaphors'. Never before or since have English writers 'been so heavily marked by the homogeneous educational formation of the English upper and upper-middle classes. It provided a potent source of myth and allusion, and . . . at a time of strong political passions, a tone and rhetoric in which it was very difficult to express political convictions seriously.' In adult fiction, schools appear in various guises in the work of Alec Waugh (*The Loom of*

C. Walter Hodges's illustration of Nottingham from the revised 1966 edition of Geoffrey Trease's *Bows against the Barons*.

*Facing*: Arthur Rackham's interpretation of 'Dymchurch Flit', the episode in Kipling's *Puck of Pook's Hill* in which the fairies or 'Pharisees', who have been hiding out on the Romney Marsh, insist on being ferried across the water to France.

*Youth*, 1917), Graham Greene (*Stamboul Train*, 1932, and *England Made Me*, 1935), George Orwell (*A Clergyman's Daughter*, 1935), Cyril Connolly (*Enemies of Promise*, 1938), Evelyn Waugh (*Decline and Fall*, 1928), and Christopher Isherwood (*Lions and Shadows*, 1938). But for adults as well as children perhaps the most influential and lasting school stories emerged in the pages of the magazines (scarcely comics in the modern sense). Some of the writers, such as Harold Avery, Herbert Heyens (with his 'Play Up' series), Gunby Hadath, and Hylton Cleaver, are still remembered by *aficionados*, but the stories in the *Gem* and the *Magnet* (founded 1907 and 1908) have lasted longest, and many are still in print. They featured the huge output of Charles Harold St John Hamilton, the man commonly credited with having written more published words (over 70 million) than anyone else. His 5,000 stories and over 100 fictional schools appeared under several pseudonyms, the most famous of which were Frank Richards and Martin Clifford. He also wrote annuals: *The [Greyfriars] Holiday Annual for Boys and Girls* (1919 for 1920) contained 360 pages, about 300 of which were written by Hamilton. The 'Greyfriars' saga was an intricate one; in the *Greyfriars Annual* for 1922 there is a complete guide to the school, with its daily routine and a list of all the forms, masters, and boys, with their ages, heights, and weights. Thus in the 'Remove or Lower 4th' we find Bunter, William George, aged 15 years and 1 month, height 4′ 9″ weight 14 st. 12½ lb.

George Orwell, famously, launched an attack (in *Horizon*, March 1940) on the political incorrectness of the stories. He accused Richards of snobbery, plagiarism, finding foreigners funny, being out of touch and out of date, and, in a frequently quoted phrase, concluded that boys' fiction 'is sodden in the worst illusions of 1910'. Hamilton's reply (May 1940) repays reading, if only because he expertly and urbanely demolished Orwell's argument by dissecting his considerable factual errors, inconsistencies, and prejudices. Orwell's case was somewhat undermined when he accused the authors of writing 'in a style that is easily imitated' because 'a series lasting thirty years could hardly be the work of the same person every week'. Hamilton, a remarkable man (whose life is not adequately portrayed in the anodyne *Autobiography of Frank Richards*), pointed out that misrepresenting the working classes 'would not only be bad manners, but bad business . . . If Frank Richards were the snob Mr Orwell believes him to be, he would still conceal the weakness very carefully when writing for the *Magnet*.' He summed up: 'Mr Orwell would have [the reader] told that he is a shabby little blighter, his father an ill-used serf, his world a dirty, muddled, rotten sort of show. I don't think it would be fair play to take his twopence for telling him that!'

And, of course, foreigners *are* funny. 'Take Hitler, for example, with his . . . fripperies out of the property-box. In Germany they lap this up like milk, with the most awful seriousness; in England, the play-acting ass would be

laughed out of existence . . . The fact that Adolf Hitler is deadly dangerous does not make him less comic.' It is hard to resist the conclusion that Hamilton, despite the lowliness of his profession, showed himself to be a thoughtful and urbane man who won this encounter by a large margin. As Mary Cadogan has observed, 'Hamilton's style is a highly individual blend of cosiness, satirical comment, and classical allusion that is deceptively difficult to analyse.' Writing school stories was clearly, even in its declining years, a more subtle business than Arthur Groom, advising in the *Writers' and Artists' Year Book* for 1932, would have us believe: 'bring your mind back to your own schooldays, and write of the things you always wanted to do but lacked the courage.'

Hamilton, and writers such as Richard Bird, wrote for the girls' market as well, but the books about girls' schools were dominated by female writers such as Christine Chaundler, Evelyn Everett Green, Dorita Fairlie Bruce, and May Baldwin. There was, however, a trio of writers for girls who stood out: Elinor M. Brent-Dyer, with *The School at the Chalet* (1925) and its fifty-seven sequels, Angela Brazil, whose *The Perils of Pauline* had come out in 1906, and whose last book, *The School on the Loch*, was published in 1946, and Elsie J. Oxenham, about forty of whose ninety books were about the 'Abbey girls' (the first was *Girls of the Hamlet Club* (1914)). Both Brent-Dyer and Oxenham, by following their heroines into adulthood, produced almost gothic sagas in the mould of *Little Women* and its sequels. During the Second World War, Oxenham wrote that 'I feel those early books are rather wordy and spun out', but she was not happy with later revisions and abridgements that changed the social milieu.

Typical of the lesser-known books is Dorita Fairlie Bruce's series about 'Dimsie', a girl in the tradition of Anne of Green Gables. As Cadogan and Craig observe, Bruce 'loaded onto Dimsie more instinctive goodness than she can comfortably sustain'. In *Dimsie Moves Up* (1921), for example, Dimsie nobly and successfully faces up to the school bully because her friend has been dropped from the junior cricket team. (The villainess, Nita, saves Dimsie from drowning at the school water sports in the last chapter.)

Some of Oxenham's books were devoted to the 'Camp Fire Movement' founded in the USA in 1911 (she objected to some of the militaristic overtones of the Girl Guide movement), but other authors saw Scouting and Guiding as a rich vein. The Boy Scouts were founded in 1908, and the Girl Guides in 1909. Dorothea Moore, who wrote *Terry the Girl Guide* in 1912, and a characteristic blend of genres in *Greta of the Guides: A Story of Wendover School* (1921), became a Guide Commissioner; other writers included Vera Barclay, Winifred Darch, Nancy Hayes, and Mrs Osborn Hann, whose *Peg's Patrol* (1921) had photographs as illustrations. Scouting stories were provided by Hayden Dimmock, John Finnemore, and Major Clifton-Shelton, while that

*Facing*: Edmund Dulac was one of the major illustrators and designers of the late nineteenth-century. His work was strongly imaginative, as can be seen from this fantasia of familiar characters from nursery rhymes and tales.

Note the collision, or collusion, of two genres in this 1936 edition of *The Magnet*.

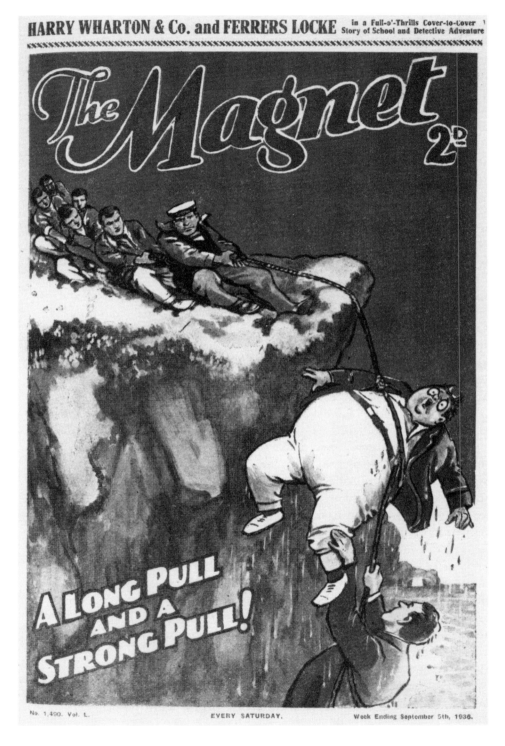

polymath of children's literature Rudyard Kipling, himself Commissioner for the Boy Scouts, produced *Land and Sea Tales for Scouts and Guides* in 1923, a volume that included the first, and previously unpublished, 'Stalky' story. The founder, Lord Baden-Powell of Gillwell, was more given to books like *Lessons from the 'Varsity of Life* (1933).

But it was in the apparently opposing fields of fantasy and realism that the inter-war years made their most lasting contribution.

## FANTASY AND 'REALISM'

Traditional and folk-tales did not find another reteller of the calibre of Arthur Ransome; *Old Peter's Russian Tales* was much helped in the telling by the setting of the snowbound forests and by Old Peter's narrative presence. In com-

parison, Walter de la Mare's *Tales Told Again* (1927) and *Broomsticks* (1925) are a little wooden. Other writers who contributed to the genre were Harcourt Williams (*Tales from Ebony* (1934) ), Amabel Williams-Ellis (*Fairies and Enchanters* (1933) ), and Angela Thirkell, with a collection of stories from the German, *The Grateful Sparrow* (1935); from the Irish tradition came Helen Simpson's *Mumbudget* (1928), and from the Scots Ann Scott-Moncreiff's *The White Duck* (1935).

Original work was far more striking. One of the earliest, first written as letters from the Flanders trenches in direct reaction to the horrors of the war—and particularly the horrors of animals in war—was Hugh Lofting's *The Story of Dr Dolittle, being the History of his Peculiar Life at Home and Astonishing Adventures in Foreign Parts, Never Before Printed* (published in the USA in 1920, and in Britain in 1922). Puddleby-on-the-Marsh, although sketched rather surrealistically, is an idyllic early Victorian village, and the story, although fantastic, is in a low key. The narrative device of Tommy Stubbins, introduced in the second volume, *The Voyages of Dr Dolittle* (1922), allowed an

One reaction to the First World War—the title-page of the first edition of Hugh Lofting's first stories of Dr Dolittle.

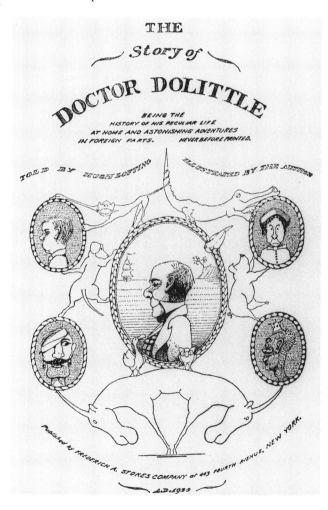

even better narrative contact between adult and child, and there is a sober compassion behind the fantasy that is accentuated through the series. Some of the episodes are racially offensive, although a good deal less so than the popular press of twenty years later, and modern editions have toned them down.

A similar quiet country wisdom pervades the long series that began with *The Squirrel, the Hare, and the Little Grey Rabbit* in 1929 (it ran until 1973) and *Tales of the Four Pigs and Brock the Badger* (1939–65). These stories, probably because of their format, are sometimes, unwisely, compared to Beatrix Potter's far more aphoristic books. But although they tend towards wordiness, these simple stories, which were told on country walks by Alison Uttley to her son John, reflect the love of the country that was shown in her autobiographical *A Country Child* (1931), which has been reprinted in editions for children. But for many her best book, while rooted in the country, moves far beyond the 'Grey Rabbit' books in terms of technical virtuosity: *A Traveller in Time* (1939). This fantasy involving a plot to rescue Mary Queen of Scots is a much more subtle and atmospheric book than its title suggests.

A rather less romantic view of the country is found in Barbara Euphan Todd's *Worzel Gummidge, or the Scarecrow of Scatterbrook* (1936), of whom

The world's best-known nanny makes her debut in 1934.

Marcus Crouch memorably remarked: 'This moody disagreeable boggart has developed a life independent of the books in which he has appeared. The books themselves, it must be admitted, have no great distinction in writing or invention.' This is, perhaps, a little harsh; Gummidge is a cheerfully irreverent original who has deserved his longevity if only for bringing the anarchy inherent in many children's books a little closer to the surface.

There is an ambivalence in his nature which is akin to that of the equally crusty and unpredictable Mary Poppins. The three main books in P. L. Travers's saga, *Mary Poppins* (1934), *Mary Poppins Comes Back* (1935), and *Mary Poppins Opens the Door* (1936) (there were other supplementary volumes, post-war), have a great deal more character and inven-

214

tion than is suggested by the Walt Disney film; the books are perhaps the apotheosis of the idea of magic in an everyday setting, helped a good deal by the humanly paradoxical central character.

But perhaps the most remarkable feats of the imagination came from John Masefield and J. R. R. Tolkien. Masefield, poet laureate from 1930, and a writer of prodigious output in novels, verse, and drama, crosses the boundary between adult and children's fiction with Smollettean adventure stories like *Dead Ned* (1938) and *The Bird of Dawning* (1933), which are now children's

The Hall at Bag-End. Residence of B. Baggins Esquire

The most famous book of a remarkable year in children's publishing—J. R. R. Tolkien's *The Hobbit* of 1937.

books in the same way that the work of John Buchan has moved into the children's sphere. But his lasting contribution to children's literature is *The Midnight Folk* (1927) and its lesser sequel (vitiated for some by its 'all a dream' ending) *The Box of Delights* (1935). But the title of the second book is the more apposite, for these are farragos with little to hold them to the earth, totally extravagant mixtures of talking animals, witches, highwaymen, the sea story, archetypal and legendary characters, grotesquely wicked governesses, and villains quite capable of kidnapping the Dean and Chapter of a cathedral. It is striking that *The Midnight Folk* has no chapter divisions—which is hardly surprising considering the breakneck pace of it all.

In contrast, *The Hobbit*, significantly subtitled *or, There and Back Again* (1937), was the precursor of one of the century's largest best sellers, *The Lord of the Rings*. The nostalgic country of the Shire is developed as a symbol of security and old values rather more in the latter book, but in *The Hobbit* it provides a base, a home for Bilbo, who in archetypal child-fashion ventures out on his circular adventure, gains in knowledge and skill, and then returns to the security of home. The story resonates with legend, and Bilbo succeeds as *guizer*, or trickster, within a highly coherent secondary world (in contrast to Masefield's highly incoherent primary one). One less celebrated fantasy, based on similar materials of legend and by another scholar, was W. Croft Dickinson's *Borrobil*, using a Puck-like figure (1944).

Other robust survivors include a series which originated on the radio and which ran into the 1980s, Norman Hunter's *The Incredible Adventures of Professor Branestawm*, and a *jeu d'esprit* by a distinguished scientist and popularizer of science, J. B. S. Haldane's *My Friend, Mr Leakey* (1937). Ursula Moray Williams's *Adventures of the Little Wooden Horse* (1938) remains popular with

Enid Blyton. The world's most popular children's author, with reader—a photograph from the collection of her daughter, Imogen Smallwood.

Enid Blyton began to edit *Sunny Stories for Little Folks* in 1926. When it became *Enid Blyton's Sunny Stories* in 1937 she was writing the whole thing, and she continued to do so until 1953 when it was replaced by *Enid Blyton's Magazine*.

younger children, and Patricia Lynch's Irish tales, particularly *The Turf-Cutter's Donkey* (1934) and *The Grey Goose of Kilnevin* (1939), have maintained an audience. And the ambivalent, eccentric T. H. White must be mentioned, for *The Sword in the Stone* (1938) is at least more for children than the revised version which appeared in *The Once and Future King* in 1958.

One of the most lasting and famous of children's book characters, the elephant intent on bringing middle-class western attitudes (and clothing) to Africa, Babar, found himself being 'retold' in *The Babar Story Book* (to the incredulity of critics) by Enid Blyton in 1941. Blyton, probably the most successful children's writer ever, had published her first pamphlet, *Real Fairies*, in 1923, and by the end of 1945 she had written over 100 children's books of fiction, and nearly 100 retellings and school readers. She was one of the few writers whose output was apparently unaffected by the war (between 1939 and 1945 she published at least 110 books); notably, her first 'Mary Mouse' stories (*Mary Mouse and the Doll's House* (1942)) were printed by Brockhampton Press on magazine offcuts to save the paper allocation (the series had sold 4.5 million copies by 1964). Blyton's output included a good deal of fantasy, the most famous from this period being her first full-length book, *Adventures of a*

*Wishing Chair* (1937). In the adventure story genre (another form of fantasy) she wrote *The Secret Island* (1938), and the beginning of what is one of the most successful series ever written, *Five on a Treasure Island* (1942). Blyton's contribution to the school story, and her use of a *state* school in *The Naughtiest Girl in the School* (1940) suggests that she was a far more original writer than she has been given credit for. Her circus story, *Mr Galliano's Circus* (1938), despite its anachronisms and the tendency towards animism, compares favourably with the Carnegie Medal winner for that year, Noel Streatfeild's *The Circus is Coming*.

If the cult of the beautiful child in the enchanted forest was a keynote of the 1920s, the antidote was at hand, in the form of that most unbeautiful of children, Richmal Crompton's insouciant William Brown. William first appeared in a story 'Rice-Mould' in *Home Magazine*—a magazine for adults— in February 1919. Between 1922 and 1940 (when the magazine closed) he appeared in *Happy Mag*, a more family-oriented affair. He appealed to children, as Mary Cadogan puts it, 'despite Richmal's satiric style and demanding vocabulary', and the first two volumes of stories collected from *Home Magazine*, *Just—William* (May 1922) and *More William* (June 1922), were marketed to juvenile readers. It was not, however, until the 1940s, when Crompton was writing directly for publication on children's lists, that William lost some of his narrational sophistication, and can be said to be genuinely directed at children.

Perhaps as a result of this, and because the books are essentially situation comedy, his status *vis-à-vis* the audience has remained ambivalent. Forty-two books (one full length, and the rest short stories) later William is still about 11 years old, but the world has changed around him. He begins in a world where there are servants, survives the war, and ends (*William the Lawless* (1970)) in one where there are pop groups (blackmailing, in passing, a Christopher Robin figure, 'Anthony Martin'). As in Antonia Forest's Marlow family series (1948–74), any correspondence between fictional and real time is abandoned—but that is irrelevant: all adult activity, in its endless oddity, is fair game to the irreverent child.

Curiously, just as Bessie Bunter was never as successful as Billy, so the nearest female equivalent of William, Evadne Price's Jane (from *Just Jane*

The un-beautiful child: the frontispiece to *Just—William* (1922), the first picture of William in hard covers.

WILLIAM, CLASPING AN EMPTY ACID DROP BOTTLE TO HIS BOSOM, WAS LEFT TO FACE MR. MOSS.

"*A happy snap at No. 1 One End Street*"

Eve Garnett's *The Family from One End Street* (1937)—a rare example of social realism.

(1928) to *Jane at War* (1947)), seems, for all her verbal energy, to have lacked archetypal qualities—as well as having certain lapses of taste.

Of social realism (even at this level) which looked outside the middle classes, there was little, which is perhaps why Eve Garnett's *The Family from One End Street* acquired its reputation (and its 1937 Carnegie Medal). These loosely constructed anecdotes have been seen by some critics as demeaning, by others as an unusually coherent portrait of family life. However, the period flavour is so strong that it is now very difficult to judge how far the Ruggles family are being patronized.

But the writer most credited not only with engaging children with the 'real' world, but also with inventing the holiday, was Arthur Ransome. He at once celebrated the codes and values of the family, and encouraged the independence of the children; he allowed his characters to escape the world of work, and yet, like Kipling, celebrates that too. With his books still in print, and the Arthur Ransome Society flourishing, he has some claim to be the writer from between the wars who has had the most long-lasting influence on the 'respectable' children's book.

*Swallows and Amazons* (1930), like its eleven successors, is firmly grounded in fairy-tale structures; the children develop skills which they use in practical circumstances. These structures help to universalize this secure, middle-class world (the Blacketts have a cook, the Walkers a nanny, at a time when about 5 per cent of private households had live-in servants) although Ransome used, unpatronizingly, working-class children as central characters (especially in *The Big Six* (1940)). Equally, although his children are well-behaved and supportive, with a strong adherence to social and moral codes, their characters are tested, and they are placed in real danger, as in the epic crossing of the North Sea in *We Didn't Mean to Go to Sea* (1937).

Ransome's books have an air of probability about them: like Defoe's (a writer he much admired), the 'impossible is caged by the calendar'. They are as Nicholas Tucker suggested, probably the best celebrations of play in the language, but they also link to the empire-building and sea-story traditions in which the children are steeped.

More broadly, they mirror that retreat from world-involvement which characterizes the 1920s and 1930s. *Swallows and Amazons* is set in '1929', and the series covers about five fictional 'years'; and so Ransome, while advised by his publisher to 'steer clear of the [second world] war' did not need to do so directly. However, the books written immediately before and during the war, *Secret Water* (1939), *The Big Six* (1940), and *The Picts and the Martyrs* (1943), and the fantasy *Missee Lee* (1941) can be read as allegories.

How far Ransome's books inspired later writers is not clear. Other books in the same field included M. E. Atkinson's long-running series about the Locketts, from *August Adventure* (1936) to *Steeple Folly* (1950), Elizabeth Yates's *High Holiday* (1938), and Francis Joyce's *Yes, Cousin Joseph* (1935). Kitty Barnes's *Easter Holiday* (1935, later retitled *Mystery of the Sandhills*) brought Buchan-like melodramatic devices to the genre. It may have been these that Geoffrey Trease was reacting against (he describes the literary situation in his 'early autobiography' *A Whiff of Burnt Boats* (1971)) in his down-to-Lake-District-earth post-war 'Bannermere' series, initially written at the request of a day-school child who thought he was socially ignored by writers. Other hearty and largely realistic work came from writers like Garry Hogg with his

The dust-jacket, by Stephen Spurrier, of the first edition of one of the landmarks—and benchmarks—of twentieth-century children's books.

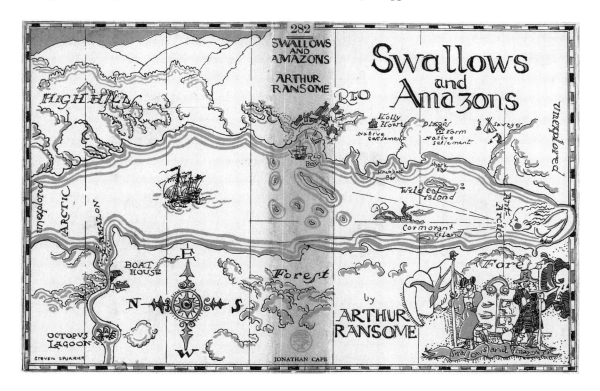

'Explorer' series, beginning with *Explorers Awheel* (1938) and *Explorers on the Wall* (1939), Conor O'Brien's *Two Boys Go Sailing* (1936), Lucy Bellhouse's *The Caravan Children* (1935), and Eleanor Helm's *Furlong Farm* (1938), published by the Young Farmers Club. Specifically about sailing were the books of Peter Dawlish (from *Dauntless finds her Crew* (1947) ) and Aubrey de Selincourt ( *Family Afloat* (1940) ).

Two books in this genre of 'realism' are worthy of more note. The first was one of the rare books for children written by children. Pamela Whitlock and Katherine Hull (16 and 15) sent Ransome a manuscript that he at first suspected to be a hoax: he then took it to his publisher Jonathan Cape with the words, 'I've got this year's best children's book under my arm,' to which Cape politely replied, 'When did you get it finished?' *The Far-Distant Oxus* (1937) (perhaps the best tribute to Matthew Arnold's *Sohrab and Rustum*) is, as Ransome astutely observed, 'exactly what its authors, being children, wanted to read'. It has all the Ransome strengths of a sense of place and an interest in expertise (ponies); and if it is rather more improbable, it is also a good deal more sensuous and spontaneous.

The second was written as an antidote to the wilder holiday and absent-parent stories, by someone who was far from being a literary innocent. Eleanor Grahame was one of the great influences on children's literature between the wars, as bookseller, children's editor for Heinemann and Methuen, and founder of the Puffin imprint. By the standards of the final decades of the century, *The Children Who Lived in a Barn* (1938) is mild and innocent, but it is rigorously practical, says a lot about family relationships, and portrays its slice of society very convincingly.

Although Noel Streatfeild now seems to epitomize the 'middle-of-the-road' writers, her first book, written after more than a decade of working in the theatre, *Ballet Shoes* (1936), was at the time seen as remarkable for taking the children's book into a professional world. She was amazed at its success, for, as she said: 'The story poured off my pen, more or less telling itself . . . I distrusted what came easily and so despised the book.' Streatfeild won the 1939 Carnegie Medal with the lively *The Circus is Coming*, using a subject well treated by Howard Spring in *Sampson's Circus* (1936).

The younger the audience, the more likely is any aspect of harsh realism to be edited out of their books, and, perhaps as a result, some of the 'younger' domestic comedies have survived very well, despite what might seem to adults to be a strong period flavour. Among these are the adventures of Ameliaranne Stiggins, which began with Constance Heward's *Ameliaranne and the Green Umbrella* (1920); unusually, the series was continued by several other writers, including Eleanor

The quintessence of inter-war domesticity. Milly-Molly-Mandy and family, and little-friend-Susan. (Joyce Lankester Brisley, 1928).

Farjeon. Joyce Lankester Brisley's unexceptional, but unexceptionable, series beginning with *Milly-Molly-Mandy* (1928) remains in print, portraying its Arcadian village and Milly-Molly-Mandy's 'nice white cottage with the thatched roof'.

One aspect of the rural dream that has not faded is the pony story, and the mother of this genre (in more ways than one) was probably Joanna Cannan. In *A Pony for Jean* (1936), Cannan moved the focus from the pony (where it had rested from *Black Beauty* to Allen W. Seaby's *Skewbald: The New Forest Pony* (1923) and 'Golden Gorse's' *Moorland Mousie* (1929)) to the rider, a rider who in this case is 'pony mad'. Its sequels (*Another Pony for Jean* (1938), *More Ponies for Jean* (1943)) demonstrate the strength of this particular formula, and the alternative plot, that of the ignorant girl who grows to respect the 'pony mad' group, was used by Cannan in *They Bought Her a Pony* (1944). Joanna Cannan was the mother of the Pullein-Thompson sisters, Christine, Diana, and Josephine, who have between them produced around 100 pony books.

Interest in the natural world was found in *Bambi*, which came into English in 1928, Henry Williamson's *Tarka the Otter* in Puffin Books in 1937 (it had been originally published for adults), and the 'Romany' books. 'BB's' questionable idyll *The Little Grey Men* (which Marcus Crouch described as 'a little better in conception than execution') won Carnegie Medal for 1942, which suggests both the enduring interest in nature and the nostalgia that we have seen before, emphasized in wartime.

### THE SECOND WORLD WAR

Indeed, with the approach of war, the stance of children's literature shifted. The *Girl's Own Paper*, for example, like many others, had seemed oblivious of European politics in the 1930s, and, as Cadogan and Craig have noted, 'published a surprisingly enthusiastic article about the girls of the Hitler Youth organization in a series "Schooldays at Home and Abroad"' in 1937. After the war started, it threw itself into the war effort, encouraging its readers to knit and grow vegetables, and began to recruit for the women's armed services.

Some writers began by ignoring the whole thing: Aubrey de Selincourt's *Family Afloat*, for example, published in 1940, features a peaceful visit to France. Others, like Ardizzone, who became a war artist and who described his experiences in the adult book *Baggage to the Enemy* (1941), stopped his work for children for the duration.

The popular press approached the second war in much the same spirit as it had approached the first; Angela Brazil with *Five Jolly Schoolgirls* (1941) weighed in with an evacuee story, and, until *Magnet* closed in 1940, the Greyfriars boys were again involved, although rather more circumspectly this time. Perhaps surprisingly, even Enid Blyton (who was engaged in a good deal of non-literary war-work) wrote a spies-and-submarines book, *The Adventurous Four*; and spies—always easy targets for children—were caught by Malcolm Saville's *Lone Pine Club* members and by veterans such as Dorita Fairlie Bruce's Dimsie. Even the Chalet School was forced to move from the Tyrol, and later from the Channel Islands.

Captain W. E. Johns, whose First World War flying hero Biggles had first appeared in *Popular Flying* in 1932, had been a vociferous supporter of a build-up in the RAF in the 1930s, and with the war he became a lecturer to the Air Defence Cadet Corps, later the Air Training Corps. He transferred Biggles to the RAF and began to write columns in the *Boy's Own Paper* and the *Girl's Own Paper* (from 1941 and 1942), and it is generally agreed that the Biggles books had a large influence on recruitment to the air forces. *Biggles of the Camel Squadron* was translated into Swedish in 1940 (as *Biggles Stridsfly-garen*). Such was his status that *Biggles Flies Again* was published by Penguin in 1941. Although Biggles degenerated after the war into a conventional tough thriller hero, in the early books he was portrayed as a sensitive, even neurotic, pilot, and his adventures in the First World War, especially, are if anything rather anti-heroic.

In 1941 Johns was asked by the Air Ministry for books which would help recruitment to the Women's Auxiliary Air Force, and *Worrals of the WAAF* appeared in the *Girl's Own Paper*. His portrayal of Joan Worralson and Betty Lovel shows his admiration of women pilots and in practical terms challenged sexist assumptions. The War Office also persuaded Johns to create a soldier for recruitment purposes, hence *King of the Commandos* (1943), featuring the very tough 'Gimlet' King, a figure rather more in the comic book mould.

During the war *Children's Hour* was moved to Bristol from London and was reduced to half an hour. In October 1939 a Sunday version was introduced, with notable contributions from Christopher Fry, and Dorothy L. Sayers who wrote *The Man Who Would Be King*, twelve plays on the life of Jesus. Many of Diana Ross's stories published in *The Golden Hen* (1942) were originally broadcast, while a 'purely' radio creation were the boy detectives Norman and Henry Bones, who date from July 1943.

The traditional British way of dealing with foreigners lives on in Captain W. E. Johns' *Biggles in Spain* (1939).

The approach of many 'mainstream' writers to the war was a little more circumspect than that of the writers of comics. The war impinged, of course, more directly on the home front, notably with evacuees. P. L. Travers's story *I Go by Sea, I Go by Land* (1941) described evacuation to the USA, and a domestic example was Kitty Barne's *Visitors from London* (1940), which walks between a studied realism and class-stereotyping. Her *We'll Meet in England* (1942) dealt with refugees. Although the best novels about the war were written at least two decades after the event (for example, Nina Bawden's *Carrie's War* (1973), or Robert Westall's *The Machine-Gunners* (1975) ), one of the better survivors is Mary Treadgold's novel about the Channel Islands, *We Couldn't Leave Dinah* (1941), where the Germans are portrayed with a certain sympathy. Certainly the sense of place is important here: as Mary Treadgold observed, a 'passion of recollection . . . in the unhealthy atmosphere of the [air-raid] shelter transmuted all to what, even in childhood memory, they had never quite been—islands of the blest . . . In that way nerves were steadied, and a peace unsteadily, inconstantly, but occasionally evoked.' Part of the longevity of *We*

'*I'll show ye what's the matter, ye spyin' rat*'

*Couldn't Leave Dinah* might well lie in its status as a pony book: more topical stories of the war such as Lorna Lewis's *Tea and Hot Bombs* (1941) and Eleanor Mordaunt's *Blitz Kids* (1941) have not survived even as curiosities.

The obvious question was, what role could a child play in wartime? Reality was all too harsh, fantasy too uncomfortable. William, naturally, provided an astringent viewpoint on adult behaviour with *William and the Evacuees* (1940), *William Does his Bit* (1941), and *William Carries On* (1942). Evadne Price's rather less well-measured Jane books included *Jane Gets Busy* (1940), although *Jane at War* was not published until 1947. Even Gwynneth Rae's small bear, Mary Plain, whose popularity was helped by BBC readings, did her bit in *Mary Plain in War Time* (1942) and *Mary Plain's Big Adventure* (1944)—not to mention Mumfie in *Mumfie Marches On* (1942).

And there were other notable books in different genres. In fantasy there was a neatly constructed parable, André Maurois's *Fattipuffs and Thinifers* (France, 1930, translated 1941), and a very loosely constructed story first told by Eric Linklater on a wartime walk in the rain—'to drown the loud, ill-tempered howling of my two small, rain-soaked daughters'—*The Wind on the Moon* (1944). Rowland and Mary Emmett produced the idiosyncratically illustrated *Anthony and Antimacassar* (1943) and a 16-year-old schoolgirl, Pamela Brown, published a very lively novel *The Swish of the Curtain* (1941).

Many thousands of books were destroyed in air-raids, while, as Geoffrey Trease observed, 'the economy standards of wartime book-production put an end to artificial bulking. Children's books underwent a healthy slimming process.' The 1944 Education Act, which abolished fees in state secondary education, gave at least a theoretical impetus to reading. By the end of the war, children's literature, now established as a respectable full member of the publishing world, was ready to enter an era of unprecedented richness and prosperity.

# 9 CHILDREN'S LITERATURE IN AMERICA

## 1870–1945

### CHANGING TIMES, 1870–1914

Between the end of the Civil War and the USA's entry into the First World War American literature as a whole changed radically, and children's literature changed with it. The best sellers of the 1850s (such as *The Wide, Wide World*), the growth of the 'dime novels', the predominance of women writers, and the development of the great 'monthlies'—*Atlantic, Harper's, Scribner's*—all pointed to the establishment of a commercially important literary culture.

In many ways the period between 1870 and 1914 can be seen as a golden age of children's books, parallel to that in Britain, but with very different characteristics. Jerry Griswold has observed that 'It was an era when "majors wrote for minors", when the very best authors on both sides of the Atlantic, writers with world-wide reputations, addressed themselves to juveniles . . . It was a time when Children's Books was not some satellite department, but the very center of publishing houses.' As in Britain, the threads of the past were drawn together and redirected, by writers like Alcott, Twain, and Hodgson Burnett; but both the 'domestic' tale and the boys' books had a far more independent tone, and the division between children's books and adult popular literature was much finer. Series books flourished under entrepreneurs like Stratemeyer; a new, American form of fantasy emerged with L. Frank Baum's *The Wonderful Wizard of Oz*. In a utilitarian atmosphere the traditional forms and materials which authors like Isaiah Thomas, Samuel Goodrich, and Jacob Abbott had campaigned against were beginning to be rehabilitated.

All this was achieved in a context of radical social change. The Civil War was over, but 4 million slaves were emancipated in 1865, immigration was

This chapter has been written with the advice of the Editorial Team, and with contributions from Gillian Avery, Louisa Smith, C. W. Sullivan III, and Zena Sutherland.

'The film of the book'—the most famous of all? Ray Bolger, Jack Haley, Judy Garland, and Toto thirty-nine years after the book came out.

increasing, and the USA was becoming an urban society: in 1920 the population living in cities passed 50 per cent for the first time. Reading habits were changing, even with the simple fact of electric lighting: in 1907 it was in 10 per cent of American homes; in 1929, nearly 70 per cent. Childhood was lived out not just in the culturally strong East, but in the farming communities spread across the great plains, and, as the historian Elliot West put it, 'Children did not see themselves as a "scattered people" since one must be scattered *from* someplace, and the West was the only place they had ever known first hand'. And yet, although the USA was becoming a multi-cultural, international power, literary inspiration was still drawn from Europe: it was not until 1894 that the number of American-producedchildren's books outnumbered European 'imports'.

Several children's books destined to become classics had already appeared in Britain, works as various as Lear's *A Book of Nonsense* and Thomas Hughes's *Tom Brown's Schooldays*. But even in 1865 observers could detect no glimmering of such an American Dawn, and Samuel Osgood, an Episcopal clergyman, lamented in the *Atlantic Monthly* (December 1865) that 'we have not yet apparently added a single [children's book] to the first rank of juvenile

226

classics'. Samuel Goodrich's 'Peter Parley' books and Jacob Abbott's 'Franconia' stories had certainly reached British readers in the 1840s and 1850s and Warner's chastely erotic *The Wide, Wide World* and its successors such as *Queechy* (1852) pleased emotional adolescent girls on both sides of the Atlantic. But none of these could be said to have much literary merit, although they were to be influential (and, Susan Warner's chastely charismatic female orphan was still making a strong appeal well into the twentieth century). The travelogue book, always a particularly American genre, reached its peak in the 1880s and 1890s when, for example, Hezekiah Butterworth was taking his Zigzag Club and Elizabeth Chamney her Three Vassar Girls on a different journey each year. (Between 1883 and 1892 they travelled to England, Russia, and Turkey as well as across the United States.)

Samuel Osgood in his article had gone on to try to account for the dearth of good children's books in his own country. American children grew up too fast, he thought: 'Our heads are apt to be much older than our shoulders, and English critics of our juvenile literature say that much of it seems to be written for the market and counting room rather than for the nursery and playground.' The Sunday school books with their stories of 12-year-old capitalists who accrue great material wealth by thrift and diligence and keeping the Sabbath—a theme still popular in the 1880s—would certainly seem to confirm this. (Mark Twain parodied the genre in his short story 'Poor Little Stephen Girard'.) Early numbers of *Oliver Optic's Magazine*, launched in January 1867, included articles on such subjects as how to make a will, and descriptions of the Paris morgue. American children, whether they grew up on farms or in cities, were expected to be purposeful, to understand money matters, and early to take on adult responsibilities. The fiction written for them reflected this, and contrasts with the fantasy and fairy-tales of England, where childhood, at least among the more prosperous classes, was prolonged and leisurely.

Fantasy did not make such a strong appeal to American readers. When the *Nation* reviewed *Alice's Adventures in Wonderland* in December 1866 it was the humour, the puns, and word-play that were praised (qualities that had not been much noticed by English reviewers).

Ideas of what was appropriate to young readers were changing; there was less moralizing, and it was no longer necessary that

'Educaton for the common people in the South' (undated).

An American family in the 1890s (from a cracked glass-plate negative).

parents be depicted as faultless although fathers had been very commonly represented as shiftless drones in comparison to the strong mothers of fiction. Some piety lingered on, with books like *Esther Reid* (1870) by 'Pansy' (Isabella Macdonald Alden), possibly because of the influence of Sunday school libraries, but, as in Britain, there was a parallel development of cheap popular literature.

The writer who stands at the turning-point of children's literature, Louisa M. Alcott, encapsulates these trends and in *Good Wives* provides us with an overview, as Jo March sets out to become a writer, as her creator had done. Her first efforts include moral reflections, 'which she had carefully put in as ballast for so much romance', which are struck out by the editor on the grounds that 'People want to be amused, not preached at, you know. Morals don't sell nowadays', to which Alcott (with a display of political correctness) adds: 'which was not quite a correct statement, by the way.' None the less, Jo's effort to produce a 'didactic gem' by emulating 'Mrs Sherwood, Mrs Edgeworth, and Hannah More' fails to find a market, while writing for children was either poorly paid or sectarian.

Then she tried a child's story, which she could easily have disposed of if she had not been mercenary enough to demand filthy lucre for it. The only person who offered to make it worth her while to try juvenile literature was a worthy gentleman who felt it his mission to convert all the world to his particular belief. But much as she liked to write for children, Jo could not consent to depict all her naughty boys as being eaten by bears or tossed by mad bulls, because they did not go to a particular Sabbath school.

Among publications for younger children the McLoughlin toy books should be mentioned. The firm had been founded in New York by John McLoughlin in the 1820s, but it did not acquire its distinctive character until his son, John II, had succeeded him and began publishing the brightly coloured picture versions of traditional rhymes and tales now associated with the McLoughlin name. Harry Thurston, writing in the *Bookman* (of which he was the editor) in December 1896, commended them warmly for continuing to put out 'those good old classics . . . which have long ago secured a glorious immortality'.

By 1894 children's books of all types represented around 12 per cent of all books published, but, equally, there was a major change in cultural influences on children. Films were becoming important. By 1910 it was estimated that over half a million children went to the cinema each day in the USA, despite the efforts of 'reformers'. As we shall see, children's books were quickly translated into film, while the line between adult and children's entertainment narrowed. For example, Edgar Rice Burroughs's serial *Tarzan of the Apes* (1914), which he wrote for the 'adult' *All Story Magazine* (it brought him $700), was filmed the same year—a monument of popular culture that crossed age ranges. There were twenty-four sequels and innumerable adaptations.

In this time of rapid social and literary change, children's literature found mentors in the form of librarians, a group that has had a great influence. Among major early figures were Caroline M. Hewins, who developed a children's library at Hartford, Connecticut, from 1875, and Anne Carroll Moore, who began the children's department at the New York Public Library in 1906. The American Library Association had been founded in 1886 (the School Library division was formed in 1915). Separate children's rooms were established in public libraries and high-school libraries and increasingly the libraries were staffed by trained librarians (at first, primarily women).

THE GREAT MAGAZINES

In the 1870s there were few children's books in public libraries and few school library collections; small wonder that children's magazines were popular—quite apart from the fact that they could be sent through the mail to be read by pioneering children. The magazines were particularly good barometers of social change. *The Youth's Companion* (1827–1929) began with an emphasis on religious and moral teaching that gave way, very gradually, to entertainment (at one point it carried the subheading *Sabbath School Recorder*). The level of contributions was high, including work by Harriet Beecher Stowe, Jules Verne, William Dean Howells, and Alcott. The magazine commissioned Thomas Hardy's only book for children, *Our Exploits at West Poley*, in 1883. Hardy wondered, in 1886, in a letter to the magazine, whether 'Our children here are younger for their age than yours; and possibly the story is too juvenile for your side of the sea'. For whatever reason, the story was not published in *The Youth's Companion*, but in an obscure magazine designed for housewives, the *Household* (1892–3)—without Hardy's knowledge.

The *Riverside Magazine for Young People*, whose first number appeared in January 1867, might be seen as the harbinger of the golden age, and a new recognition that there were now young readers with leisure to enjoy childhood. Distinguished in appearance and in contents, it had, unlike most of its predecessors and contemporaries (including *The Youth's Companion*), no didactic purpose, and carried no moral or religious message. Horace Scudder, its young editor (he was only 28 when Henry Houghton of the Riverside Press appointed him), believed passionately in the value of the imagination and his priority was literary excellence. At a time when fairy-stories were still regarded with some suspicion as a frivolous waste of time, he published new stories by Hans Andersen. Illustration was also taken seriously, and, instead of the usual practice of using blocks from stock, Scudder commissioned artists such as H. L. Stephens, F. O. C. Darley, John La Farge, and Thomas Nast. Houghton and Scudder undoubtedly took as their model *Our Young Folks*, which the Boston firm of Ticknor and Fields had started in 1865 (it ran until 1873). *Our Young Folks* printed Aldrich's *The Story of a Bad Boy* and Dickens's *A Holiday Romance*, but this with its mildly improving air and its quota of sentimental stories was made to look old-fashioned beside the newcomer.

The *Riverside* came to an end after only four years; there presumably not being enough demand for a quality journal for children. But *St Nicholas*, which Scribner's launched in 1873—building on the *Riverside*—survived until 1940. The difference was its informality, and the warmth communicated by Mary Mapes Dodge, whose editorship lasted from 1873 until her death in 1905. Dodge was already famous for *Hans Brinker; or, The Silver Skates* (1865) (which popularized the story of the Dutch boy who put his finger in the hole in the dyke wall). One reason for its success was undoubtedly her approach, expressed in an article in *Scribner's Monthly* (1873), when, talking of current magazines, she said:

We edit for the approval of fathers and mothers and endeavour to make the child's monthly a milk-and-water variety of the adult's periodical. But, in fact, the child's magazine needs to be stronger, truer, bolder, more uncompromising than the other

. . . Let there be no sermonising either, no wearisome spinning out of facts, no rattling of the dry bones of history. A child's magazine is its pleasure-ground.

For even though it lacked the aristocratic appearance of the *Riverside* its literary standards were just as high. Over the years many new American classics were first serialized in *St Nicholas*, and indeed its contents are an excellent guide to the writing of the time. T. B. Aldrich, Alcott (*Eight Cousins* (1875)), Baum, Burnett (*Little Lord Fauntleroy*), Coolidge, Palmer Cox, Mrs Dodge herself, Lucretia Hale, Joel Chandler Harris, Thomas Nelson Page (*Two Little Confederates*, which was partly anti-war and partly pro-slavery (1888)), Pyle, Scudder, Frank Stockton, John Trowbridge, and Mark Twain (*Tom Sawyer Abroad* (1893)) all wrote for it, as well as distinguished British authors such as Stevenson and Kipling (the first of the *Just So Stories* appeared in 1898). From the start it was outward-looking. There were certainly stories of frontier life, and of sturdily independent girls and boys, but it also presented information about foreign places, and it did so with a light touch. Frequently it was foreign and historical. John Bennet's 'Master Skylark', a poignant story of an Elizabethan singing boy (November 1896–October 1897), was a distinguished example.

24          THE STORY OF A BAD BOY.

A FRIENDLY OFFER.

The first train for Rivermouth left at noon. After a late breakfast on board the *Typhoon*, our trunks were piled upon a baggage-waggon, and ourselves stowed away in a coach, which must have turned at least one hundred corners before it set us down at the railway station.

*The Story of a Bad Boy*: Thomas Bailey Aldrich's lively, conversational anecdotes are based on his own boyhood.

## THE DIME NOVELS AND OTHER DELIGHTS

The 1870s were also the heyday of amateur publishing, a craze encouraged by the simple printing machine, the 'Novelty Press', which for under $20 set many young journalists and writers on the road to careers. Commercially, the steam-powered rotary presses vastly increased the output of books, especially the 'dime novels'.

After Ann S. Stephens's *Malaeska*, Beadle's Dime Novels series expanded eventually to 321 volumes, and was much imitated. (Beadle established his 'American Library' in Britain in 1861.) It was here that the new American folk-heroes such as Edward L. Wheeler's 'Deadwood Dick, the Rider of the Black Hills' (created for the first issue of Beadle's *Pocket Library* in 1884) were established. Real-life characters had been fictionalized as early as the 1840s—notably Kit Carson—and there was a certain amount of personal myth-making by men like William F. Cody (alias Buffalo Bill). Historical figures, including downright villains such as Billy the Kid or Jesse James, were elevated to the status of folk-heroes. The tales about Davy Crockett (who died, of course, a hero's death at the Alamo) sometimes took the form of a specifically American type of story, the 'tall tale', part fantastic adventure, part crude humour which appealed to adults and children alike. 'You had best to hoop your ribs before you reed 'em or you will shake your bowels out a Laffing', as Crockett's side-kick warned readers.

In 1883 books and papers of this kind were attacked, famously, by Anthony Comstock (who founded the New York Society for the Suppression of Vice): 'Trick and device, lying and deceit, dishonesty and bloodshed, lawlessness and licentiousness, is the lesson taught in much of these stories.'

Beadle died in 1894, two years before the appearance of the first 'pulp' magazine: Frank A. Munsey published the *Argosy*, 192 pages printed on 'pulpwood', the cheapest paper available, and selling at 10c., although children rapidly turned to the sixteen-page 5c. story weeklies.

This was the period of the first American comic books. Some had been produced before 1876 by Stroefer and Kirchner of Broadway, but the first full-colour comics came in 1888 from the Humoristic Publishing Company of Kansas City, Missouri—although they actually originated in France. The most famous comics first appeared in the New York Sunday papers comic supplements, and comic books proper started with reprints of these strips in 1902: 'Buster Brown' began in 1903, 'Mutt and Jeff' in 1910. In the USA, as opposed to Britain, these strips were for adults and children.

One step above the 'dime novels' were the 'series' books, and their most successful purveyor was Frank Stratemeyer, whose first story was published in 1890. Within a few years he was turning out at least a dozen titles per year, including the 'Rover Boys' (1899–1926) series (under the name of Arthur Winfield). Soon he was providing plot outlines for his hired writers, who produced around seventy different series under various pseudonyms. The name 'Victor Appleton' for some years disguised Howard Garis, whose *Uncle Wiggly's Adventures* (1912 and sequels) were very popular. 'Victor Appleton' wrote the 'Tom Swift' books, which first appeared in 1910. By 1935 Grosset and Dunlap had sold around 6 million copies of the forty *hardback* volumes. Another notable series was Leslie McFarlane's 'The Hardy Boys' (by 'Franklin Dixon'—from 1927), and Stratemeyer's daughter Harriet Adams (under the name of Carolyn Keene) began the saga of Nancy Drew in 1930 (she went on to write over 200 books).

## DOMESTIC FICTION

Although children's literature was diverse, with books such as Helen Hunt Jackson's frontier story *Nelly's Silver Mine* (1878) the classic books of the period connect both with the melodramatic side of the dime novel, and with the American concept of family and community. Their origins can be traced back to Catharine Maria Sedgwick (notably in *A New England Tale* (1822)), and they celebrate independence and self-reliance, both individually and collectively. The poor and the orphaned are virtuous, but they are not the objects of pity.

There are many examples, with various degrees of sentimentality attached to them. The foremost writer, as we have seen, was Louisa M. Alcott, whose *Little Women* (which she considered calling, at one point, *The Pathetic Family*) counteracted the mawkish sentimentality of many of its contemporaries. Her heroines are reluctantly moulded into domestic servitude; their appeal lies in their efforts to resist. Alcott continued the series through *Good Wives* (which was originally published as *Little Women Part 2*, and which was given a variety of other titles), *Little Men* (1871), and *Jo's Boys* (1886). Alcott was a practical writer, whose family books were designed as much as her dime novels to keep the pot boiling, but she was reflecting both the moral standards of the day and the more singular ethics of her father, notably in *Eight Cousins* (1875) and *Little Men*—in which Bronson Alcott's educational theories are partly demonstrated by Jo's Plumfield School.

From *The Peterkin Papers* (1880).

The older tradition held on, as readers wept their way through the books of Rebecca Clarke ('Sophie May') or Martha Finley. As M. Sarah Smedman (in the appendix to *20th Century Children's Writers*) observed of *Elsie Dinsmore*,

Finley's fiction is imbued with vulgar and pernicious attitudes: the subordination of women; the equation of blacks with servile, simple-minded, pious 'chilluns'; the snobbish conviction that wealth breeds gentility and refined spirituality . . . religious bigotry . . . For more than three generations *Elsie Dinsmore* outsold every juvenile book in America except *Little Women* . . . The influence upon millions of impressionable readers of the beautiful, lachrymose, righteous paragon is staggering to contemplate.

Elsie's relationship with her father might seem a little extreme today, not only for her affection, but for his attitudes: 'Elsie, I expect from my daughter entire, unquestioned obedience, and until you are ready to render it, I shall cease to treat you as my child.' But such characters had a long hold on the popular imagination: Annie Fellows Johnson's *The Little Colonel* (1895) (in

Mary Pickford as
Pollyanna in the 1919
film.

which the heroine wins the heart of the rich, lonely grandfather from whom
her mother is estranged) ran to several sequels, and was eventually filmed,
with Shirley Temple in the leading role, in 1935.

And then there was 'Susan Coolidge's' Katy Carr, who is very much in the
line of Jo March. It has been observed that spinal injuries were a natural haz-
ard of being a children's-book heroine in this period, and although Katy tends
towards the ideally pious girl, her approach to suffering was refreshingly
human. The 'Katy' books, and especially *What Katy Did at School* (1873),
were better known and far more influential in Britain than they were in the
USA, and their influence can be traced in the whole genre of the girls' school
story.

Realism is, of course, highly relative. Alice Hegan Rice's *Mrs Wiggs of the
Cabbage Patch* (1901), which went though seventeen printings in 1902, featured the determined struggles of a working-class optimist who lives beside
the railway tracks in Louisville, Kentucky. Just as natural as a family, but far
more fortunate, were Margaret Sidney's *The Five Little Peppers and How they
Grew* (serialized in *Wide Awake* in 1878, book form 1881); despite the chil-

234

dren's being fatherless and poor, the 'sustained euphoria' of the book (as Gillian Avery has put it) saves them from approaching too near to reality. But they can be very closely linked to Alcott's family stories, a tradition that runs through to Eleanor Estes's 'Moffats'. Perhaps *The Five Little Peppers* would not have been written by a British author, because it does not keep the working classes in their place; the American Dream still had some life in it.

Gradually the heroines became more human, however stereotyped the dead father or the crabby aunts. Kate Douglas Wiggin's *Rebecca of Sunnybrook Farm* (1903)—another role for Shirley Temple (in 1938)—is rewarded for her unflagging good nature (which, naturally, wins over her Aunt Miranda) by inheriting property and having a rich suitor just offstage. Wiggin, who was a follower of the educational reformer Friedrich Froebel, wrote more serious books which focus on children's problems, such as *Timothy's Quest* (1890) and *Polly Oliver's Problem* (1893), which are now almost forgotten. Rather more melodramatic and sentimental was Gene Stratton Porter's *A Girl of the Limberlost* (1909), which has a strong regional setting.

Perhaps the most robust survivor is Jean Webster's epistolary *Daddy-Long-Legs* (1912), in which Jerusha Abbott rises from chief orphan to college graduate and (we assume) marries the rich trustee. Eleanor Gates's more fanciful *Poor Little Rich Girl* (1912), which is rather more of a parable, has not worn so well. Other examples, perhaps less dramatic, were produced by Jacob Abbott and Horace Scudder.

But the apotheosis of this fashion is undoubtedly Eleanor H. Porter's *Pollyanna* (1913) complete with dead parents, a bitter aunt, a rich benefactor, a life-threatening injury, and satisfyingly easy confrontations. Pollyanna's innocent formula, that we should be 'glad, glad, glad' about everything, had world-wide success; 'Glad Clubs' flourished throughout the USA, and after Porter's death the 'glad' books went on, with titles like *Pollyanna in Hollywood*. Perhaps the essence of the genre was summed up in the comic strip *Little Orphan Annie*, which ran for over fifty years from 1924.

The relation of these domestic tales to melodrama and popular literature is clear, and is perhaps best summed up in the work of Frances Hodgson Burnett, whose own life was like an improbable romance. She was born in 1849 in Manchester, England, and moved to Knoxville, Tennessee, in 1865, becoming a

Linking two cultures and setting a fashion. Reginald Birch's rendition of *Little Lord Fauntleroy* (1886).

hack writer to support her family. Of her three great best sellers, *Little Lord Fauntleroy* (1886) crossed both national and age boundaries most thoroughly. The hero, a dispossessed English lord brought up in the democratic streets of New York, was responsible for many small boys—such as A. A. Milne—suffering a childhood of long ringlets and velvet suits. Cedric Erroll, the little lord, has in the manner of Pollyanna or the Canadian Anne Shirley (of Green Gables) a talent for subduing the savage adult by innocent reason. Both *Sara Crewe* (1888, later revised, expanded, and somewhat coarsened as *A Little Princess* (1905)) and *The Secret Garden* (serialized 1910–11) rely for their effects upon the power of wish-fulfilment, and both melodramatic plots and melodramatic settings: the one in the line of Dickens, the other in that of the Brontës. *The Secret Garden*, which first appeared in the *American Magazine* ('the first instance I have ever known of a child's story being published in an adult's magazine', as Burnett observed), derives some of its universality from its closeness to the fairy-tale.

Frances Hodgson Burnett (1849–1924).

One notable oddity of the period, and one of the earliest examples of nonsense in American children's books, was Lucretia Hale's *The Peterkin Papers* (1880) and its less successful sequel *The Last of the Peterkins* (1886). These books are in the tradition of the 'beloved fools' (as well as satirizing Boston life). Each absurd situation is resolved by the omniscient 'Lady from Philadelphia'; she is, for example, the only person who sees that the way to get an obdurate carriage-horse to move is to unchain him from the hitching post. Another satire, which became a children's book, was Gellett F. Burgess's stories of naughty children, *Goops and How to Be Them* (1900).

Humour has been described as probably America's most popular creative achievement, and it was to feature in much imaginative writing for children. Frank Stockton's exuberant fairy-stories (*The Bee-Man of Orn and Other Fanciful Tales* (1887)) were written for the most part in the spirit of burlesque and farce. Palmer Cox's immensely popular Brownies were comic, not fairy, beings; their elaborately illustrated adventures began in *The Brownies: Their Book* in 1887 and continued through twelve sequels. (Cox was actually a Cana-

**Mrs. Peterkin puts salt into her coffee**

dian, who returned to Canada after his success.) The humour in Albert Bigelow Paine's *The Arkansas Bear* (1898) is more subtle, and turns on the pact that Horatio, a roving fiddle-playing bear, makes with his boy patron to overlook 'that sort o' personal supper I was planning on'.

A new vein of comic exaggeration: Lucretia Hale's *The Peterkin Papers* (1880).

## THE AMERICAN BOY

Books for boys tended to flourish in series. For example, Harry Castlemon (Charles Austin Fosdick), whose own life had been especially adventurous, wrote some fifty-eight books in series with such names as 'Gunboat', 'Rocky Mountain', 'Roughing It', and 'Go-Ahead'. Elijah Kellogg, a Congregationalist minister, wrote stories (again arranged in series) about the fishermen and farmers of Maine which were very popular with Sunday schools. His values were simple and based on hard work and strong family loyalties; he did not desire great wealth for his characters. This was in marked contrast to 'Oliver Optic', whose influence continued unabated. When Louisa Alcott attacked what she called 'optical delusions' in *Eight Cousins*, she accused him of wanting to make his heroes so rich that in comparison 'Sinbad in the diamond

The comic ebullience of Robert McCloskey's *Homer Price.*

valley is a pauper': 'Even if the hero is an honest boy, trying to get his living, he is not permitted to do so in a natural way, by hard work and years of patient effort, but he is suddenly adopted by a millionaire whose pocket-book he has returned; or a rich uncle appears from the sea, just in the nick of time.' 'Optic' did not let this attack go by without a riposte in his magazine. However, his work, and Horatio Alger's, is perhaps a little surprising in the American context, as it seems to undercut the democratic myth, although the 'Log Cabin to White House' approach had always involved luck as well as pluck.

But, far more important for boys' books as they developed through the century was the appearance in *Our Young Folks* in 1868 of Thomas Bailey Aldrich's reminiscences of his boyhood, *The Story of a Bad Boy*; it is intrinsically engaging, but it also established the genre of the 'bad boy' as lovable scamp. There were many books that took up the theme, including John Habberton's *The Worst Boy in Town* (1880) and George Wilbur Peck's *Peck's Bad Boy and his Pa* (1883). In the twentieth century we have Booth Tarkington's *Penrod* (1914) and its two sequels, which feature an 11-year-old with a boundless capacity for creating mayhem, and a settled conviction that the cards are stacked against him. Robert McCloskey's *Homer Price* (1943) describes, in more fantastic vein, the exploits of another accident-prone small boy growing up in Hamilton, Ohio, the town William Dean Howells had wistfully recalled in *A Boy's Town* (1890). But Tom Sawyer was to be the most famous bad boy of all.

The status of *The Adventures of Tom Sawyer* (1876), which, as Lee Clark Mitchell has suggested, 'lays claim to being America's most popular novel', may have been cast in doubt by the mischievous and habitual irony of its author, 'Mark Twain' (Samuel Clemens). He wrote to William Dean Howells, 'It is *not* a boy's book, at all . . . It is only written for adults', but in the Preface he said: 'Although my book is intended mainly for the entertainment of boys and girls, I hope it will not be shunned by men and women on that account, for part of my plan has been to try to pleasantly remind adults of what they once were themselves.' Howells's view that it 'is a wonderful study of the boy-mind, which inhabits a world quite distinct from that in which he is bodily present with his elders' is reflected in the fact that it has been considered as the quintessential children's book. There are, however, some interesting parallels

An early depiction of an innocent-looking Tom Saywer.

with contemporary developments in Britain, where Richard Jefferies's *Bevis* (1882) portrays a similar amorality, although that book is linked to the tradition of the empire-building novel, whereas *Tom Sawyer* has at least shades of the melodramatic. *Tom Sawyer* can stand on its own as a remarkably complex work, and not merely as a prelude to its sequel, which has been called, more than once, the 'great American novel'. *The Adventures of Huckleberry Finn (Tom Sawyer's Comrade)* (1884) must be, in the depth of experience that it posits in its reader, outside the scope of this book.

It may well be that Twain, an inveterate 'manufacturer' of fiction, was in *Huckleberry Finn* exploiting the fashion for Southern dialect set by the journalist Joel Chandler Harris in *Uncle Remus: His Songs and his Sayings* (1881), *Nights with Uncle Remus* (1883), and *Uncle Remus and his Friends* (1892), which brought Brer Rabbit, Brer Fox, and the rest into world folklore. (Twain's biographer Albert Bigelow Paine produced similar kinds of stories with his 'Hollow Tree' series.) It is

attractive to suppose that the 'Uncle Remus' collections preserve African and African-American folk-tales, while the presence of teller and (white) listener within the books may increase their immediacy. But Harris's position has been shown to be equivocal, and the problem for later generations is to decide how far he was demeaning African-American culture by his use of dialect, and invading a tradition rather than sustaining it. (The tales have been retold in innumerable versions, and in the 1980s Julius Lester produced versions which use contemporary Black English.)

### ILLUSTRATORS AND OZ

Howard Pyle in characteristic medieval mood in *The Wonder Clock* (1887).

While some nineteenth-century illustrators such as A. B. Frost or E. Boyd Smith acquired modest reputations, it was not until Howard Pyle began his career that a major figure emerged. Pyle was an enthusiastic medievalist and a disciple of Albrecht Dürer. His first book, *The Merry Adventures of Robin Hood of Great Renown, in Nottinghamshire* (1883), is unquestionably the most famous American rendition of the tales. Although his prose is encumbered with the most unlikely 'tushery' his pictures and, still more, the illustrations for his own fairy-tales, *Pepper and Salt; or, Seasoning for Young Folk* (1886) and *The Wonder Clock* (1888) (which use folk materials somewhat in the manner of Andersen), are forceful as well as ornate, and often brilliantly composed. He illustrated what is probably his best book, *Otto of the Silver Hand* (1888), a powerful historical tale about medieval Germany, in the same style. But his most personal work, *The Garden behind the Moon* (1895), has plates in wash and line which are markedly original and often moving; he was admired by the Pre-Raphaelites.

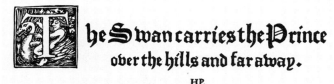

Even more original was the work of his pupil Maxfield Parrish, which used wash, line, and stipple, which, as Maurice Sendak said, have a 'photo-graphic realism [which] combines fact and fancy in a meticulously depicted dream world' (*Caldecott & Co.*).

Another of Pyle's pupils was N. C. Wyeth, who produced some of the most striking illustrations ever for children's books. The huge canvases which became the pictures for the 1911 edition of *Treasure Island* can rarely have been surpassed for their drama.

The century began with a book which some commentators have suggested owed its initial success to its illustrations. It is generally agreed to be no more than workmanlike in its prose, and pedestrian—not to say utilitarian—in its invention. But, like other great myths, it refuses to lie down. In 1900 W. W. Denslow illustrated a book written by a man who had done everything from editing *Poultry Record*, founding the National Association of Window Trimmers, and collaborating with Maxfield Parrish on the book that made that artist famous, *Mother Goose in Prose* (1897).

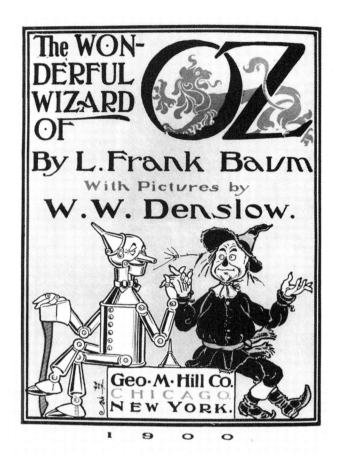

The man was L. Frank Baum and the book was *The Wonderful Wizard of Oz*. Its many sequels, by Baum and other hands, are very uneven in quality, and have been variously regarded as a new kind of fairy-tale, or merely the best that could be achieved by mechanistic minds. Despite its quite remarkable neglect by the critical establishment, Oz (named after a drawer in a filing cabinet) has endured, much helped by the 1939 film and Harold Arlen's songs, which seem to have blended the same ingredients, although the books were sometimes not allowed on to library shelves because they were thought to be 'poorly written'.

Denslow's designs were thought to be an essential part of the book's success. They certainly influenced the film version.

## BETWEEN THE WORLD WARS

American children's books, like their counterparts in Britain, responded only obliquely to the social and political events of a period that saw the great Depression, the Wall Street crash, the 'roaring 20s', the New Deal, and Sinclair

*Facing, above*: cheerful doggerel supported the cheerful pictures of Bernard and Elinor Darwin's *The Tale of Mr Tootleoo* (1925), the first of a popular series.

*Below, left*: colour lithography typical of the 1930s: Amrid Johnson's *Pigwiggen: His Dashing Career* from 1938.

*Below, right*: Angela Brazil, pioneer of the girls' school story, in full flow; she wrote fourteen of her fifty-three books between 1918 and 1923. *A Harum-Scarum Schoolgirl* dates from 1919.

Lewis's attack on Middle-American values in *Main Street* (1920), or H. L. Mencken's *Prejudices*. The image of America in children's books clung on to ideals—notably of family life—that were being eroded.

Two straws in the wind were the work of Willy Pogány from (about) 1914, one of the earliest of the European-born illustrators (he was Hungarian) who came to dominate American illustration in the 1930s, and a book that looked forward to modern 'teenage' fiction: Dorothy Canfield Fisher's *Understood Betsy* (1916), in which the wholesome Vermont rural life transforms the city girl. (Fisher equally challenged the orthodoxy of marriage as the only route by which women could fulfil themselves in *The Homemaker* (1924), in which husband and wife swap roles.) There was also a strand of internationalism running through the books from the turn of the century until the Second World War. Good examples are Lucy Fitch Perkins's twenty-six 'Twins' books, published between 1911 and 1935. Having watched the treatment of immigrants at Ellis Island, and observing that in the Chicago schools twenty-seven nationalities were being taught, she felt a need for 'mutual respect and understanding between people of different nationalities if we are ever to live in peace'.

If reading declined between the wars with the growth of cinema and radio, the literate and educated population grew rapidly, and mainstream publishers demonstrated their commitment to children's books by establishing juvenile departments. Louise Seaman (later Bechtel) was appointed head of their Children's Department by Macmillan in 1920, and her first catalogue contained around 250 titles, of which, significantly, about half were imported from Britain. (Around 400 new titles were being published for children each year.) Women were appointed to similar posts at Dutton, Longmans Green, Stokes, and Little, Brown in the next four years; the most famous were perhaps May Massee at Doubleday Page (1922) and Virginia Kirkus at Harper Brothers (1926).

Their work was encouraged by the founding of Children's Book Week in 1919; this had been suggested by Franklin J. Mathiews, Chief Librarian of the Boy Scouts, and promoted by Frederick G. Melcher (who had just become managing editor of *Publishers Weekly*), and the American Booksellers Association. In 1922 Melcher donated the Newbery Medal, administered by the ALA, for 'the most distinguished contribution to American literature for children written and published in America . . . by an American *resident or citizen*'—a proviso that allowed Hugh Lofting and, later, Susan Cooper to appear on the lists of winners. The first winner was Hendrik Van Loon's *The Story of Mankind*. (Melcher donated the Caldecott Medal for illustration in 1937, and it might well be that the fact that both these medals are named after (or for) British citizens demonstrates the respect that remained for British children's literature.) There was also a growing interest in children's books in

A·HARUM-
SCARUM
SCHOOL-
GIRL

By
Angela
Brazil

the newspapers—the librarian Anne Carroll Moore wrote columns in the *Bookman* and the *New York Herald Tribune*—and the first critical journal, the *Horn Book Magazine*, was founded in 1924, edited by Bertha Mahony. The Junior Book-of-the-Month Club began in 1928, and the Junior Literary Guild was founded in 1929.

The Newbery Medal lists for the 1920s show a bias towards non-fiction, traditional tales, or naturalistic tales, notably Will James's *Smoky, the Cow-Horse* (1926; Newbery Medal, 1927). Like Black Beauty, Smoky is mistreated; he is stolen, found, and returned by his owner to freedom on the range. The language is colloquial, and the treatment occasionally bathetic, but the story shows contrasts between the cruelty of rodeos and affectionate owners, along with accurate details of range life (the author, whose real name was Joseph E. N. Dufault, had experience of range life). Only in the 1930s did the Newbery begin to tend more towards fiction.

If this was a utilitarian period, there were some examples of fantasy; perhaps most important being the poet Carl Sandburg's *Rootabaga Stories* (1922) and its two sequels. These are poetic nonsense fantasies, although they have a touch of the distinctively American 'tall story' about them (they are relatively little known in Britain). Sandburg was a lover of the American landscape (as well as being something of a social activist in Chicago), and his concerns subtly pervade his stories, and the illustrations by Maud and Miska Petersham. Sandburg's biography *Abe Lincoln Grows Up* (an adaptation of his adult book *The Prairie Years*) has remained famous.

And, of course, the series continued to thrive, with such notables as Gertrude Chandler Warner's *The Boxcar Children* (1924), and Howard Pease's 'Tod Moran' series beginning with *The Tattooed Man* (1926). But perhaps the most lasting book of the decade was one which harked back to an older tradition exemplified by R. H. Horne's *Adventures of a London Doll*: Rachel Field's *Hitty: Her First Hundred Years* (1929).

In the years following the onset of the Depression in 1929, children's book departments were slimmed down—including that at Harper; Virginia Kirkus left the company the year after she published one of the most distinctive books of the 1930s, *Little House in the Big Woods* (1932). In the era of the dustbowls and President F. D. Roosevelt, of John Dos Passos's pessimistic *U.S.A.* (1930–6), Steinbeck's *The Grapes of Wrath* (1939), and Margaret Mitchell's *Gone with the Wind* (1936), Laura Ingalls Wilder's book and its sequels struck a popular chord. In the figure of Pa the best of the pioneering spirit is reasserted, in a period when, in real life, the authority of the father had been considerably reduced. Going westwards through Minnesota to the Dakotas is a matter of moving away from the 'crowded' woods of Wisconsin out to the endless prairie; it is a matter of stoic self-sufficiency, a closely knit family, good-neighbourliness. In a sense, this is the best of the American

*Facing*: muralist and illustrator Maxfield Parrish was noted for the strong colours and dramatic composition exemplified in this painting from the third tale of 'Sinbad the Voyager' from the 1909 edition of *The Arabian Nights: The Best-Known Tales*.

The resourcefulness of the pioneer families is shown in this picture of a sod hose and well in Custer County, Nebraska, *c.*1890.

dream, and the telling is modest—and remarkable in its fidelity to growing up, both for characters and readers.

There were other examples, such as Florence Crannell Means's *A Candle in the Mist* (1931) and, more famously, Carol Ryrie Brink's *Caddie Woodlawn* (1935). This begins in Wisconsin after the Civil War, and on one level is about pioneering life and the treatment of native Americans, but it also has wider themes of growing up, raising daughters, and the choice between freedom and wealth.

The prolific Elizabeth Coatsworth's best work of this period looks back to the American Revolution, with a sequence of books in which a large family of adults raise an orphaned niece. In *Away Goes Sally* (1934) the interplay of family relationships is intriguing, as Uncle Joseph finds a way to overcome his sister's refusal to leave her fireside and move from Massachusetts to Maine: he builds a house on a sledge. Louise Seaman Bechtel said of this book: 'Here . . . the weaving of story and poems seems perfect, the combination of meticulous detail of old ways of living with vigorous character and story interest, most complete. Bertha Mahony once said of it, "A book like this makes me 'go up' like the flame of a candle." '

The domestic themes that had dominated at the turn of the century resurfaced in several successful series. Maud Hart Lovelace epitomizes the evocation of small-town America. The ten Betsy-Tacy novels, a reminiscence of girlhood in Mankato, Minnesota, are the antithesis of Mark Twain's sardonic vision of childhood. Like Laura in Wilder's novels, Betsy nudges the rules governing proper behaviour, but the parents are always understanding, even when meting out punishment. Like the 'little House' books, Lovelace's novels provide pictures of families at home in the evenings—an image of safety which, in the war years, appealed at a time when even Middle America feared invasion. With *The Moffats* (1941) Eleanor Estes reasserted this strong strain of domestic books—the 'poor but cheerful' school, which again breathes the spirit of a perhaps idealized Middle America: another kind of tract for the times, set around the previous war. Independence and self-sufficiency are still the watchwords.

Jane clanked her feet against the hollow hitching post. For the hundredth time she was thinking that the yellow house was the best house to be living in in the whole block because it was the only house from which you could see all the way to both corners. You could see every inch of the way down New Dollar Street to Elm Street where the trolley ran. When mama went to town for provisions, you could see her when she got off the trolley, arms laden with bundles and surely a bag of peanuts among them, and run to meet her. In the other direction you could see every inch of the way to Wood Street along which the railroad tracks ran like a river.

In a rather more seriously realistic vein, Elizabeth Enright's *Thimble Summer* (1938)—Wisconsin again—catches perhaps the mood of the period's drought and rains more accurately, while Lois Lenski, in a series of novels which self-consciously and authentically tackled regionalism, included the poor, the share-croppers, and the immigrant workers. *Bayou Suzette* (1943) set in Louisiana and *Strawberry Girl* (1945) are characteristic.

There were exceptions to the rural and historical novels, notably Ruth Sawyer's autobiographical *Roller Skates* (1936), set in late nineteenth-century New York, in which the bright and curious 10-year-old Lucinda meets a cross-section of immigrants from different classes. It presents the same kind of problem to the modern reader as Garnett's *The Family from One End Street*: how far is its portrait of the lower classes patronizing? An interesting comparison is with another New York novel of a different generation, *Harriet the Spy* (1964). A sophistication similar to the metropolitan Harriet's is also found in Elizabeth Enright's 'Melendy' books, beginning with *The Saturdays* (1940), which looks at eight Saturdays in the lives of New York children with notably cultured tastes—on the last of which they go on holiday to the sea.

Most books published for children were directed at the middle years or written for older children, but one very popular exception was the 'Raggedy Ann' stories from 1920, initially by Johnny Gruelle, which ran through to the

1960s. Here too the trend (despite the frequently expressed opinions of the librarians) was towards realism. Carolyn Haywood wrote short novels for independent readers in the primary grades, and both her 'Betsy' series (from 'B' is for Betsy (1939)) and the 'Eddie' books (*Little Eddie* (1947)) reflect everyday events (school, play, pets, family, friends) in a universalized middle-class suburban setting, unlike the Lovelace books which stress the small-town milieu.

Lucy Sprague Mitchell was similarly down-to-earth—positively opposed to fantasy, in fact—with her picture-books of short stories. She had pointed out in 1921 in her *Here and Now Story Book* that very few books for young children reflected the contemporary scene and this she industriously supplied: the 'putt, purr, pat, pat school of writing', as one critic called it. These books filled a very real need, and were particularly influential for one of Mitchell's students at the experimental Bank Street College of Education in New York, Margaret Wise Brown. She began with a series of 'noisy' books. The first was *The Noisy Book* (1939), written under the pseudonym of 'Golden Macdonald', and it was books of this kind that were referred to by May Hill Arbuthnot as 'a kind of pernicious anaemia of theme and plot, with language experiences in place of stories and pitter-patter in place of events'. (Arbuthnot was one of the most influential of critics, who has become a standard authority.) Lois Lenski, similarly, produced series such as the 'little' books— *The Little Family* (1932), *The Little Auto* (1934), and others.

Rachel Field's *American Folk and Fairy Tales* (1929) was a pioneering example of the growing interest in folklore. The Federal Writers' Project (funded by the national government 1935–42) led to a series of 'state guidebooks', the American Guide Series, which explored the 'real' America—not only the geography, but the folklore and 'folkways'. This bore fruit in books like Eula Duncan's *Big Road Walker* (1940), a collection of 'negro' folk-tales, and Richard Chase's *The Jack Tales* (1943) and *Grandfather Tales* (1948), which were collections of Appalachian folk-tales. The American legendary heroes were sustained by books such as Leigh Peck's *Pecos Bill and Lightning* (1940), Esther Shephard's *Paul Bunyan* (1941), Irwin Shapiro's *Yankee Thunder: The Legendary Life of Davy Crockett* (1941), and Walter Blair's *Tall Tale America: A Legendary History of our Humorous Heroes* (1944). Actually, of course, many of the tales are variants of traditional European tale types.

One unusual collection of native American stories was Charles Edward Gilliam's *Beyond the Clapping Mountains: Eskimo Stories from Alaska* (1943), which has illustrations by an Eskimo girl.

As always, it is not clear where the line should be drawn between poetry for adults and poetry for children: Emily Dickinson and Robert Frost have often been published in children's editions. Other major writers also wrote poetry for children, such as Vachel Lindsay with *Johnny Appleseed and Other Poems*

1928) and Carl Sandburg with *Early Moon* (1930), while writers like Rachel Field and Elizabeth Coatsworth also contributed.

## ILLUSTRATORS: THE EUROPEAN INFLUENCE

Looking at the inter-war years, Whalley and Chester, in their *A History of Children's Book Illustration*, wrote:

Over in America, illustrative styles were still being strongly influenced by 19th and early 20th-century English artists such as Crane, Caldecott, Greenaway, Nicholson and Potter, although other elements can be seen in work stemming from Boutet de Monvel in France, Busch in Germany, and Japanese artists and prints.

One of the first to make use of a different, European, background was Wanda Gág, whose *Millions of Cats* (1928) has the air of a folk-tale, as well as making a strong flowing use of black and white. Many European-born illustrators were absorbed into American culture in this period, such as Boris Artzybasheff, Fritz Eichenberg, and Ingri and Edgar Parin d'Aulaire (*The Magic Rug* (1931) ), who were notable for their renditions of folklore, and whose work on large stones for lithography was sumptuous. Kate Seredy's story of the Hungarian tomboy Kate, *The Good Master* (1935), was a good deal more popular than her Newbery Medal book *The White Stag* (1937). Another Hungarian, Miska Petersham (Mihály Petrezselyen), with his American wife Maud illustrated the work of many authors before they produced their own books, beginning with the fanciful *Miki* in 1929. Their most distinguished work was very American: *An American ABC* (1941) and *The Rooster Crows: A Book of American Rhymes and Jingles* (Caldecott Medal, 1946). Two immigrants from Germany, Kurt Wiese and H. A. Rey, produced classic American books— Wiese with his pictures for Phil Stong's *Honk: The Story of a Moose* (1935) and Marjorie Flack's *The Story about Ping* (1933), a model of picture-book dynamics, and Rey with the highly successful series beginning with *Curious George* (1941), which escaped in manuscript form, with its author, from Paris. Ludwig Bemelmans, originally from Austria, is best known for the subtly anarchic *Madeline* (1939) and its sequels, while 'Françoise', with her books about 'Jeanne-Marie' and her sheep Patapon, had some success in Britain in the 1950s and 1960s.

Marjorie Flack herself was no mean artist, witness the perennial 'Angus' books (beginning with *Angus and the Ducks* (1930) ), which give, literally, a portrait of suburban America. America was celebrated in other ways by three American-trained illustrators in a field largely dominated by European-born and/or -educated illustrators. Virginia Lee Burton, a successful printmaker, established herself as an illustrator and writer with a book that epitomizes the flowing style of the 1930s, *Mike Mulligan and his Steam Shovel*

*Facing*: Burroughs's archetypal hero, of whom he wrote: 'His appeal to an audience is so tremendous that it never ceases to be a source of amazement to me'. Tarzan by Burne Hogarth (1939).

(1939). Less well known outside America was another classic, *The Little House* (1942, and Caldecott Medal), a book which is ahead of its time in speaking out against the encroachment of urban blight.

Also outstanding was Robert McCloskey, whose sepia drawings of a duck family settling in central Boston, *Make Way for Ducklings* (1941, Caldecott Medal), set new standards: the pictures range from the comic—the police-man stopping the traffic to let the ducks cross the road—to the architec-turally accurate aerial views of the city. Some critics would claim that *Blueberries for Sal* (1949), printed in blueberry blue on cream paper, is his masterpiece. (McCloskey won a second Caldecott Medal for his first full-colour book, an account of a childhood vacation on the coast of Maine, *Time of Wonder* (1958), a celebration of childhood, perhaps, rather than a book for children.)

Equally distinctive was Robert Lawson, whose delicate, ironic drawings of the gentle young bull who prefers sniffing flowers to fighting for Munro Leaf's *The Story of Ferdinand* (1936) were followed by several fictional bio-graphies of American figures, the best of which was *Ben and Me*, and the Newbery Medal winner *Rabbit Hill* (1945). He also illustrated the highly suc-cessful comedy by Richard Atwater, a comparatively rare fantasy for the decade (although rooted in naturalistic settings), *Mr Popper's Penguins* (1938).

Perhaps the most famous cat in children's literature, as created by 'Dr Seuss'.

## AND MORE CHANGING TIMES

The late 1930s saw the first books by a remarkably original artist, who has be-come a world best seller: 'Dr Seuss's' anarchic *And to Think that I Saw it on Mulberry Street* (1937) and *The 500 Hats of Bartholomew Cubbins* (1938). With their apparently scarcely controlled and brash cartoons they look forward to the post-war 'Beginner Books' series of readers, led by *The Cat in the Hat* (1957). As Dr Seuss (Theodor Seuss Giesel) remarked: 'I would not call my work a "celebration of idiocy". I think of it rather as "logical nonsense". It seems logical to me and children, being strange, find it logical.' This mixture of the homely and the outlandish was also seen in James Daugherty's contemporary version of the Androcles tale, *Andy and the Lion* (1938), with Andy in overalls with a pair of pliers in his pocket.

But the new heroes belonged to new media, for the 1930s also produced the comic book as we know it today. After a false start in the Depres-sion year of 1929—the unsuccessful *The Funnies* (published by Dell)—Max Gaines produced a full-colour reprint mag-azine *Famous Funnies* (1934), which ran for over 200 edi-tions. Then, in 1938, two teenagers, Jerry Siegel and Joe Shuster, created 'Superman' for *Action Comics*; although their per-

sonal reward was meagre compared with the success of the publishers. In 1941 it was estimated that over 90 per cent of American children between 6 and 11 read comic books. The reaction was predictable: just as the Religious Tract Society had produced the *Boy's Own Paper* to beat the devil at his own game, so *True Comics* was produced by *Parents' Magazine*, but they were no match for Superman, Batman (1939), and the surprisingly feminist Wonder Woman (1941). These characters lived in the very ambivalent world of the city, and were soon caught up in the even more problematical world of the war.

The Second World War brought radio listening to the fore, and it soon became a matter of concern such as the cinema had been a generation before, and TV was soon to become. Voices were raised against explicit violence (on radio!), and there were many popular serials such as *Captain Midnight, Jack Armstrong—All American Boy, Don Winslow of the Navy*, and, of course, *Superman.* Just as children were invited to join the war effort in Britain by writers such as Enid Blyton, so the Jack Armstrong 'Write-a-Fighter Corps' recruited a million children. Films entered the war: Minnie Mouse was used for public information films, Donald Duck starred in a somewhat scatological squib *Der Fuhrer's Face* (1942); and the superheroes fought spies.

By the end of the 1930s the numbers of children's books published annually had passed the 1,000 mark, although by 1944 wartime conditions had reduced this figure to just over 600. There were some notable successes: the 25c. 'Golden Books' introduced in 1942 achieved huge sales.

But, as in Britain, not many serious books dealt with the war. The Stratemeyer syndicate continued to produce series fodder, and other notables were John R. Tunis's sports stories, Rutherford Montgomery's 'Yankee Flier' series, and Glen Rounds's 'Whitey' cowboy series (from 1942). Horse stories also had a vogue, notably Mary O'Hara's *My Friend Flicka* (1941), filmed in 1942, with two sequels; Walter Farley's *The Black Stallion* (1941); and Glen Rounds's *The Blind Colt* (1941). Elizabeth Enright's *Then There were Five* (1944) has the Melendy children living in the country while their father works in Washington. Rush, the eldest child, comments that beavers 'had teeth like a Japanese general's', and Rush and Randy collect scrap for the war effort.

But it is generally agreed that the most important book of the war was a historical novel, Esther Forbes's *Johnny Tremain* (1943), which not only has a firm historical background, but is human, and draws on very old themes of pride and initiation and development.

Children's books were also starting to take on issues that had been avoided for many years. Eleanor Estes's *The Hundred Dresses* (1944) has some claim to be the first story to deal with prejudice, and is all the more distinguished by its downbeat ending. After the persecuted Polish girl Wanda Petrowski moves away, Maddie is left considering whether she will be feeling guilty about her behaviour 'forever'. Treatment of blacks remained generally stereotyped, as in

Inez Hogan's *Nicodemus and the Gang* (1939); not until 1945 did books like *Two is Team* by Lorraine and Jerrold Beim and Jesse Jackson's *Call Me Charley* begin to address the question.

From the domestic solidarity of *Little Women*, American children's books were about to launch into new and radical areas. Robert A. Heinlein's *Rocket Ship Galileo*, which revolutionized science fiction for children, was only two years away; the series book was soon to explore unthought-of subject areas; commercialism was to become a fine art—and, in academic circles, the children's book was soon to be taken seriously.

# 10 INTERNATIONALISM, FANTASY, AND REALISM

## 1945–1970

*Peter Hollindale* and *Zena Sutherland*

SINCE the Second World War, the traditions of British and American children's literature have tended to converge, although the cultural colonization by the USA has been more visible. But for many years it was clear that the preoccupations of the two countries were different—possibly because of economic conditions, and the differing impact of the war. Certainly writing in the USA seems to have been more sensitive to social and technological change. Thus the great strength of British post-war publishing was fantasy, whereas in the USA the tradition of historical realism was continued by revisionist history and a new growth of social realism, often multi-cultural. This realism was often expressed in very distinctive humour (notably for younger children). If fantasy in Britain generally involved what Tolkien called 'secondary worlds', in the USA it was at least as often rooted in the pragmatic form of science fiction.

### A CHANGING WORLD OF CHILDHOOD

Twenty-five years is a human generation. Children who were 10 or 11 at the end of the Second World War, in 1945, had 10- or 11-year-olds of their own by 1970. Few generations in human history can have witnessed more dramatic changes than this one, and the 1970 children, growing up in a smaller Britain set in a dangerous world, enjoyed living conditions unimaginable a quarter-century earlier. Implementation of the 1944 Education Act had created a new school system, itself being supplanted by a change to comprehensive schools, which indicated the new political importance of the young and the value placed on education. The school leaving age had risen first to 15, then to 16, and higher education greatly expanded. The age of the private car had come: in 1948 there were 2 million cars and vans; in 1970 almost 12 million. Package holidays abroad were flourishing. In 1951 Britons took 2 million foreign holidays; in 1971, 7 million. Ordinary families enjoyed unprecedented provision for their health and security through the post-war establishment of the welfare state, especially the National Health Service. The material conditions of living had changed enormously since 1945, but for children the most obvious daily fact of life which marked the change was the arrival of television. In the early 1950s few families had television in their homes; by 1971, 91 per cent of households owned a set, and children without access to it were socially illiterate among their peers.

After 1970 Britain entered a new period of unease. Problems of race, following the mass immigration of the post-war years, and of class and gender, and of industrial unrest, troubled the country and affected children's lives. But 1945–70 marks a cohesive period of change, of gains and losses, and not a few of its general historical features can be found reflected in the world of the children's book.

By 1945 it was clear that rising sale figures would permit more promotion of children's books in the United States, and it was expected that increased publicity would lead to increased profits. There was ferment in the children's book world, because of the improvement in the quality and quantity of books and because there was a heightened interest in books from abroad.

The outstanding figure in the encouragement of this interest was unquestionably Jella Lepman, whose zeal in promoting international exchange led to the establishment of the International Board on Books for Young People (IBBY). In 1953, at its first general assembly, IBBY established the Hans Christian Andersen Medal, given for the body of an author's (and later, an illustrator's) work; since then, its jury has chosen winners from over twenty countries. IBBY has been a catalyst for translation exchanges; both the awards and the speeches delivered at the congresses have brought participants a better understanding of other peoples. In America it deepened awareness of the fact that children in other parts of the world often spoke several languages. It

## Riddles

RIDDLE me, riddle me ree,
A little man in a tree;
A stick in his hand,
A stone in his throat,
If you read me this riddle
I'll give you a groat.

LITTLE Billy Breek
Sits by the reek,
He has more horns
Than all the king's sheep.

HIGHER than a house,
Higher than a tree;
Oh, whatever can that be?

OLD Mother Twitchett has but one eye,
And a long tail which she can let fly,
And every time she goes over a gap,
She leaves a bit of her tail in a trap.

BLACK within, and red without,
Four corners round about.

FLOUR of England, fruit of Spain,
Met together in a shower of rain;
Put in a bag, tied round with a string;
If you tell me this riddle,
I'll give you a ring.

147

In picture-books the illustration often provides the answer to hints and questions in the text. The riddles in Iona and Peter Opie's *Oxford Nursery Rhyme Book* (1952) have neat pictorial solutions on this beautifully designed page.

253

Television in America: the shape of things to come in 1953.

was, as Lepman had hoped, a bridge of understanding, a bridge for which she had felt there was an urgent need after the divisive chaos of the Second World War.

There was other evidence of bridges built: the founding of the International Youth Library in Munich and the establishment of the Bologna Children's Book Fair. The Children's Services division of the American Library Association was much concerned with co-operative publishing and translation (the American Library Association's Children's Book Translation Award is named in honour of the Division's executive secretary at this period, Mildred Batchelder). The Children's Book Council, founded in 1945 by the publishers—there were at that point more than thirty children's book editors—

254

began to promote international activity. The titles of the Children's Book Week posters for 1945 and 1946 were, significantly, 'United Through Books' and 'Books are Bridges'.

This activity was reflected in a strong vein of books that dealt with multi-culturalism.

Marguerite de Angeli began her writing career in 1935 with short, simple books based on the everyday activities of her own children: *Ted and Nina Go to the Grocery Store* was the first. She was one of the first authors of her time to show a concern for various ethnic groups, focusing on those who had settled near her Philadelphia home. The stories are slight, but the affection shown both in text and in her own pictures for Amish, Quaker, and Dutch children in *Henner's Lydia* (1936), *Skippack School* (1939), *Thee, Hannah!* (1940), and *Yonie Wondernose* (1944) made her pioneer work in this field valuable. It was not until after the Second World War, however, that she produced her best-remembered books. The first was *Bright April* (1946), one of the earliest books to focus on the problems of a black child. The youngest in a prosperous middle-class family, April copes with the prejudice of a white child. In all her books the pictures have a quiet, happy quality, and in *The Door in the Wall*, which won the 1950 Newbery Medal, de Angeli creates—in pictures and text—vivid images of thirteenth-century England and of the handicapped boy who becomes a modest hero.

Meindert DeJong was the first American to receive, in 1962, the Hans Christian Andersen Medal. As a child, he had come from Holland and be-
came a full-time children's book writer in the 1930s. Many of his early books attested to his love for animals and were written for younger children, like his first, *The Big Goose and the Little White Duck* (1938), or like one of his last, *The Easter Cat* (1971), the story of a child whose mother's allergy makes it impossible to have a kitten in the house. It was his writing for older children, however, that garnered most of the formal recognition of his work, in books of compassion and humour. The first was *The Wheel on the School*, which won the 1955 Newbery Medal; it gives a remarkably detailed picture of life in a Dutch fishing village and at the same time tells a simple, well-crafted story. The next is also set in Holland, and won the National Book

Margaret Tempest, illustrator of the 'Little Grey Rabbit' stories, considered the characters as much her own creation as Alison Uttley's. The artistic standard was high. From *Little Grey Rabbit's Party* (1936).

Award for Children's Literature in the first year it was given: *Journey from Peppermint Street* (1968). Before, between, and after those landmarks were many other books, among them the compelling story of a Chinese boy during the Second World War who searches for his lost family in *The House of Sixty Fathers* (1956) and the particularly percipient *Shadrach* (1957). Whatever the plot and wherever the setting, DeJong's characters have nuance and inner grace.

### A 'GOLDEN AGE' OF CHILDREN'S LITERATURE

This transitional quarter of a century produced in the 1950s and 1960s what is still widely regarded as a second 'golden age' of children's literature in Britain. In these decades a succession of major children's writers came to prominence, among them Lucy Boston, Philippa Pearce, William Mayne, Alan Garner, Rosemary Sutcliff, Leon Garfield, Joan Aiken, Jill Paton Walsh, and Peter Dickinson. We may ask why children's literature came to flourish

Visits to schools by children's authors became an important means of stimulating interest in reading. Here Philippa Pearce, author of *Tom's Midnight Garden*, talks to students at King John School, Thrapston.

so prolifically in these decades. Were the social and literary conditions of the time peculiarly hospitable to children's books? It seems curious that such a flowering came at the very time when television was newly threatening to usurp the children's novel in its claims on leisure time. It seems equally pertinent to ask why in the 1970s the golden age, if not extinguished altogether, at any rate fell into twilight. After the early 1970s fewer new authors of obvious gifts appeared, and some of those who produced such distinguished work in the 1950s and 1960s, while continuing to write, failed to match their earlier achievements. Some blend of circumstances seems to set these two decades apart.

Developments in education were clearly important. Teacher training was expanded, drawing into the profession many men returned from war service, and teaching methods began to change. Gradually the teaching of English in secondary schools began to find a place for the children's book. Until the end of the war, children's literature was perceived by English teachers as purely recreational and no affair of the curriculum or school library. In the post-war climate there was a marked change. The educational world, especially teacher training institutions, was beginning to take children's literature seriously and to see its place in classrooms and school libraries. For junior schools this was nothing new, but for children over 11 in secondary schools it formed a major change of practice. The reinvigorated market for the children's book in schools had the additional effect of closing the gap between 'official' literature and easy narrative entertainment for children. However, in the early post-war years even writers who wrote children's books were at some pains to disclaim any taste for actually reading them. Geoffrey Trease, whose book *Tales out of School* (1949) is one of the landmarks of post-war criticism in the field, declared with firmness verging on asperity:

Adults do not normally read children's books. It would be unnatural if they did. Years ago, if a friend mentioned one to me, assuming that I should know all about it, I felt mildly irritated. 'My dear chap,' I would say, 'I *write* children's books—I don't read them.' This was not arrogance, but a normal adult reaction . . .

But there was a post-war shift away from Trease's 'normal adult reaction' and towards the one expressed by C. S. Lewis in his essay 'On Three Ways of Writing for Children' (1952):

Critics who treat *adult* as a term of approval, instead of as a merely descriptive term, cannot be adult themselves . . . When I was ten, I read fairy tales in secret and would have been ashamed if I had been found doing so. Now that I am fifty I read them openly. When I became a man I put away childish things, including the fear of childishness and the desire to be very grownup.

The post-war years brought a growing realization that if the storehouse of

Denys Watkins-Pitchford was an original and atmospheric illustrator of the natural world. His own stories, written as 'BB', lovingly create the British countryside, as here in his novel *Brendon Chase*.

myth and legend and the classic children's stories could be taken seriously as literature, there was no reason why contemporary writing should not be, or why the adult reader should not openly enjoy it. People came increasingly to agree with Lewis that 'a children's story which is enjoyed only by children is a bad children's story'. For the children's writer this was imaginatively liberating. It brought freedom to exercise imaginative integrity when writing for children, and recognition that a book which is accessible to and enjoyable for children may also work on levels which few children are likely to appreciate. Another of Lewis's dicta in the same important essay came to win widespread practical acceptance, namely his way of writing for children which 'consists in writing a children's story because a children's story is the best art-form for something you have to say'. As publishers, schools, librarians, and ordinary adult readers in the post-war years became increasingly receptive to this view, the conditions existed for children's literature to prosper.

A sure sign of the rising status of work for children in these decades was the growth of critical activity. Before the war there had been surveys of children's reading habits and manuals of advice for would-be authors, but Roger Lancelyn Green noted that before his *Tellers of Tales* was published (1946) the only serious critical work in the field had been F. J. Harvey Darton's classic work of scholarship *Children's Books in England* (1932). After the war there was a steady growth of critical interest; by 1970 there was a small but useful working library available for the specialist.

A lively critical environment is nourished by the existence of good periodicals, which provide a forum for debate and respond to new developments with an immediacy that books alone cannot produce. For many years *Junior Bookshelf* (1936– ), like the *Horn Book Magazine* (1924– ) in the USA, was virtually alone in the field, but in 1962 Margery Fisher founded *Growing Point*, a regular review of new publications; it was not, however, exactly a forum for debate, since Fisher astonishingly wrote nearly all of it herself. The gap was finally closed in 1970 with the foundation of two new journals: *Chil-*

*dren's Literature in Education*, established as an offshoot of the Exeter Conference on children's literature (1969), and the independent *Signal*.

If literary and educational conditions largely explain the 'golden age' of these two decades, they do not account for it completely. There are two other factors which seem to have played their part. One was the advent of television. Usually seen as a negative influence on children's reading because of its easier pleasures, television may have had the paradoxical effect of supplanting books as the lowest level of escapist entertainment for the young, and thereby raising their prestige. Reading, even reading Enid Blyton, was no longer the easiest option. With growing awareness of the importance of regular casual reading in the development of literacy, the status of the story-book in general was steadily enhanced. Concern for reading fostered concern for quality in the things read, and writers for whom children's literature was the appropriate art-form found themselves welcomed, esteemed, and bought. While many publishers promoted higher standards, the particular influence of Puffin Books can hardly be overestimated. Founded in 1941 as the children's paperback imprint of Penguin Books, Puffin prospered under the gifted editorship first of Eleanor Graham and then, from 1961 to 1979, of Kaye Webb.

More speculatively, one might suggest that the 1950s and 1960s were a period of exceptional artistic licence for the children's author. Of course the usual constraints persisted, in ways that subsequent decades would slacken: for the most part sex was still taboo, and teenage sexual feelings at best a matter of polite and euphemistic hints and nudges. An early instance of later trends towards sexual explicitness was Josephine Kamm's *Young Mother* (1965), a stolid and instructive work of 'faction' which attracted many imitators in the following two decades. Death was taboo also, except in history and war, and to dispose of inconvenient parents. But this period, while acquiescing easily in traditional morality, was singularly free of prescriptive ideologies. Pre-war literature was heavily influenced by the values of the British imperial mission and by domestic norms of social class and sexual roles: the unwritten national rule-book demanded propagation of its values and beliefs. From the 1970s onwards another rule-book gained authority, prescribing a new agenda of political correctness in matters of sex and gender, class and race, faithfully reflecting tensions and divisions in the adult political world. Although it would be naïve to suppose that books of the 'golden age' were somehow free of ideology, since no story ever written is born into a value-sterilized environment, it is probably true that this period was unusually free of pressures to promote approved conformities. Britain was a country sure of its identity but unsure of its role; undergoing radical though non-violent social change; immensely concerned for children's welfare but unsure how best to achieve it. And it was also an age which valued literature more highly as it came to seem threatened by the rival attractions of film, tele-

Kaye Webb, the long-standing editor of Puffin Books, seen launching the Junior Puffin Club with a pirate party. The comedian and singer Harry Secombe was the club's president in autumn 1979.

vision, and popular music. In retrospect, the 'golden age' seems a less surprising event.

### EVERY CHILD'S WORLD: THE COMICS

'No one', said the novelist Peter Dickinson in 1970, 'who has not spent a whole sunny afternoon under his bed rereading a pile of comics left over from the previous holidays has any real idea of the meaning of intellectual freedom'. In the years after 1945 such freedom was widely available to the young, little changed from what it had been before the war. Children are conservative in their tastes, and so was their main supplier of comics, the firm of D. C. Thomson in Dundee. *Beano* and *Dandy* continued with few signs of change into the post-war period, as did the most popular comics for older boy readers, *Wizard*, *Hotspur*, *Rover*, and *Adventure*.

Over the years, however, there came changes in response to new commercial realities, and the most important of these was the decline of the long prose story which had been staple fare in comics such as *Hotspur*. By the end of the 1960s verbal content had greatly declined and visual material predominated. *Jackie*, a vastly successful new comic for older girls, contained roughly 16,000 words of fragmentary prose, and *Bunty*, aimed at younger girls, much less than that. By 1970 the comic across all age groups had demoted the word in favour of the picture.

The most imaginative and interesting new venture in these years was the founding of *Eagle* (for boys) in 1950, and its companion *Girl* in 1951. Published by Hulton Press on the initiative of the Revd Marcus Morris, these were major efforts to raise standards of content and production in comics, with a careful and intelligent balance of cartoon and story, fiction and fact. In some ways *Girl* was the more interesting of the two. At first Morris and his colleagues set out to blur gender boundaries and modernize the self-image of girls with stories of female pilots, captains, and detectives. Morris invited reader response, and duly got it. Dennis Gifford, introducing *The Best of Girl Annual 1952–1959* (1990), notes: 'Readers responded in their thousands, proving that what your young female mind of the fifties wanted was not high-flying pilotesses, teenage 'tecs and girl skippers, but the traditional schoolgirls' fiction that they had hitherto been reading in *Girls' Crystal* and *School Friend*. In came schoolgirls Wendy and Jinx, Chums of the Fourth Form; Robbie of Red Hall, orphan heiress among the highland heather; Jala the Jungle Girl, Belle of the Ballet, Susan of St. Bride's—junior soap-opera starring boarders, dancers, nurses and ponies.' Whether such tastes are the sinister product of gender conditioning, or simply evidence of what girls like, is a controversy that rages fiercely in the 1990s but, as the history of *Girl* demonstrates, is nothing new.

*Eagle* and *Girl* survived in their original form until 1959, when a change of management brought Morris's departure and new editorial policy; and the brave experiment with quality ended in 1969 when publication ceased. High standards and strong verbal content were not, it seemed, compatible with commercial success for the comics of 1970; but the 'intellectual freedom' and the fun are testified by the continuing popularity of those that survived.

The USA has had a very different history in terms of comics, with a much greater emphasis on the newspaper strip which has tended to appeal equally to children and to adults. The 1950s, however, saw much innovative artwork, notably in 'westerns'. One notorious trend was the 'horror comic'—the perhaps less horrific but no less disturbing descendants of which have acquired the status of high art over fifty years. In Britain, their importation led in 1955 to the Children and Young Persons (Harmful Publications) Act, and a voluntary 'Comics Code' in the USA. In both countries the superheroes, following

'Superman' and 'Batman', prospered amid a welter of lawsuits, notably over 'Captain Marvel'.

### HISTORY ANCIENT AND MODERN

The time-scale of childhood meant that the Second World War quickly receded for most children into a dimly remembered past, and became a historical event like any other. In the years following, surprisingly few novels of quality for children took the war as their theme. Perhaps writers too were exhausted by the claustrophobia and all-consuming reality of the war years, and seized the opportunity of peace to broaden imaginative horizons of space and time. Only towards the end of this period did major children's novels appear which explored war experience. Most of the best war novels, such as Robert Westall's *The Machine-Gunners* (1975) and Nina Bawden's *Carrie's War* (1973) and, in the USA, Bette Greene's *Summer of my German Soldier* (1973), were written by authors who had been children or adolescents during the war years.

Popular fiction for children was slower to discard the ready-made contest between goodies and baddies supplied by the fight against Germany. Apart from Enid Blyton, the most prolific and commercially successful writer of the immediate post-war period was Captain W. E. Johns, whose fictional hero was the daring aviator, Biggles. Although Biggles diversified his activities world-wide after 1945, the war with Germany remained the centre-piece of his exploits. The novels were translated into many languages and sold hugely. But amongst professionals such as teachers and librarians the mood of the peacetime years was hostile to many features of the 'Biggles' books: their military values, cult of heroism, and propagation of racial stereotypes—as well as their unquestionably modest literary qualities. The books appeared to educated adult readers to be out of tune with the egalitarian, internationalist, post-colonial mood of the new Britain. Boys, who were Johns's target readership, responded enthusiastically to his narrative excitements and heady if simplistic values, outvoting the civilized disapproval of their 'elders and betters', and the books enjoyed a popularity which continues to bring good paperback sales even now. The books are a testament to the durability of imperial attitudes and values, if only as nostalgic chauvinist myth, in the changed world of contemporary Britain, and their vigorous survival points to children's ability to adjust in their reading to the co-existent, contradictory attitudes embedded in their national culture.

A very different view of war was impressively presented in Ian Serraillier's *The Silver Sword* (1956), one of the first novels of substantial literary merit to take the war as its subject, and one which has proved enduringly popular both in schools and as part of children's voluntary reading. Set in Poland, *The Sil-*

*ver Sword* is the story of three children who are separated from their parents by Nazi oppression in Warsaw, and resourcefully survive a dangerous, hand-to-mouth existence in their ruined country both during and after the German occupation until they are finally reunited with their parents in Switzerland. Exciting as the story is, its lasting merit lies in the steady documentary tone of the writing, the residual note of factual reportage which underlies even the most dramatic incidents, and the prevalent sense of endangered community which makes the children's ordeal convincingly a part of a whole world in crisis. The fairy-tale element, the archetypal story of the lost child found, is authentically rooted in political reality.

Novels of exile, alienation, and displacement were part of the fictional treatment of war for children, and continued into the Cold War years. The Danish author Anne Holm wrote the popular *I Am David* (1963 Denmark; 1965 Britain), about the escape of a Danish boy from imprisonment in a concentration camp in an unspecified Balkan Communist country, and his perilous journey across Europe to his home-

land. Though sentimental to a fault, this story powerfully conveyed the terrible anonymity of refugees and political outcasts, and broadened the sympathies of young readers safely rooted in national identity. *I Am David* was one of relatively few European children's books which were successfully translated into English at this time.

Domestic settings rather than the European battleground have provided the backdrop for the best British novels about the war. Real-life experiences undergone by many children, especially of evacuation and the Blitz, underpinned the more distinguished stories such as Jill Paton Walsh's *Fireweed* (1969). Paton Walsh is a writer of great distinction whose subsequent work, which is broad in range and imaginatively profound, is rooted in a poetic sense of time and history. Her two novels about the war, *Fireweed* and *The Dolphin Crossing* (1967), are among her earliest books, more documentary and naturalistic in style and technique than most of her later work, but they too are underpinned by a sense of history in the making and cut no emotional corners.

Another writer of subsequent distinction to take the war as setting for an early book was Jane Gardam. *A Long Way from Verona* (1971) was only the author's second book, following a collection of lively short stories for younger children called *A Few Fair Days* (1971), but already it shows the gift for ruth-

British enthusiasm for steam locomotives is reflected in the continuing popularity of the Revd W. Awdry's little books, which first appeared in 1945. Engines with expressive faces and strong personalities are the key to their success. (This was published in the US in 1965 as *North to Freedom*.)

less social comedy, the sense of arbitrariness in human experience, and the finely tuned alertness to distress that would ultimately dispatch this author through the transfer zone of teenage fiction into the adult novel. *A Long Way from Verona* is one of the books which make nonsense of distinctions between literature for adults and for children. Its background is Teesside at war, its foreground the early adolescent life of a spirited, wayward, and highly intelligent girl. This is a significant book, pointing not only to the imaginative resources of receding wartime memories but more generally to the potential interests and strengths of the newly burgeoning 'teenage novel'.

Some children's books of the period are now prized more for their illustrations than their text. The distinguished artist C. F. Tunnicliffe illustrated all the 'Nomad' books, which blended natural history and fiction.

A glance at the list of Newbery prize-winners between 1945 and 1970 shows how strong the tradition of historical writing was in the USA. No less than ten were historical novels (and it might be useful to observe at this point that of the others, eleven had broadly 'realistic' settings and themes); nearly half the winners were concerned with multi-cultural issues.

In the social context, it is interesting to note the tendency to reconsider history, and the Civil War and the slave trade in particular. Elizabeth Yates's

*Amos Fortune, Free Man* (1951) was followed by writers like Jean Fritz (*Brady*, 1960) deals with the slave escape-route, the 'underground railway'), and, perhaps most notably, Irene Hunt in her obliquely told Civil War novel, *Across Five Aprils* (1964). Many of these books have been controversial, dealing as they do with areas where political correctness is at a premium. William Armstrong's bleak 'black man's story' (written by a white man) *Sounder* (1970), the story of poor sharecroppers, never names the characters. Whether the implied dehumanizing denigrates the black community or makes a political point more strongly can be debated, but the book (like others in the genre, notably the work of Virginia Hamilton) has a merciless impact. After the father dies ('So tuckered out he fell asleep') the boy predicts that Sounder, the dog, will die too.

And the boy was right. Two weeks before he came home for Christmas, Sounder crawled under the cabin and died. The boy's mother told him all there was to tell.

'He just crawled up under the house and died,' she said.

Elizabeth George Speare, who won the prestigious Laura Ingalls Wilder Medal for a lasting contribution to children's literature in 1989, produced a small number of distinctive books. The first was *Calico Captive* (1957), which dealt with a captured New Hampshire girl taken prisoner in the days of the French and Indian War and marched to Montreal. Both of Speare's succeeding books won the Newbery Medal; in *The Witch of Blackbird Pond* (1959) a young girl comes from Barbados to stay with her Puritan relatives, scandalizing them by making friends with the 'witch', an elderly Quaker woman; *The Bronze Bow* (1962) is set in Israel during the time of Jesus, and provides a vivid socio-political context to the biblical account.

Scott O'Dell had written several novels for adults when he learned of a young native American girl who had remained alone on a coastal island when her people fled. That became the story of Karana, in *Island of the Blue Dolphins* (1960), and it not only won a Newbery Medal and became a minor film classic but moved its author into a firm niche among the best exponents of historical fiction. O'Dell never wrote a weak book, and almost every one addresses some inequity in our social history; he was particularly sensitive to the problems of native Americans and Mexican Americans, although several books were devoted to American history, like *Sarah Bishop* (1980). All of O'Dell's books were poignant and powerful, including the last, finished by his wife Elizabeth Hall after his death, *Thunder Rolling in the Mountains* (1992). In 1972 he received the Hans Christian Andersen Medal.

Ferdinand Monjo had years of experience as an editor of children's books before he produced his first book, *Indian Summer*, in 1968. It was historical fiction for primary-grade independent readers, and Monjo the editor knew what a void such a book could fill; but it was not until his next book, *The Drinking Gourd* (1970), that Monjo the writer came into his own, for he had achieved an unusual synthesis of simply written historical fiction and a narrative appropriate to younger readers whose concepts of time were not yet sophisticated. The story focuses on a child's participation in helping escaped slaves on a station of the Underground Railroad. Many other stories appeared, as did some biographical sketches, the most entertaining of which is *The One Bad Thing about Father* (1970); the narrator is Theodore Roosevelt's son Quentin, who in an invented and very funny diary complains that his father is too busy to play with his children. In *Letters to Horseface* (1975) Monjo addressed older readers, basing his text on real letters, but inventing teasing, ebullient missives from Mozart to his sister during the time he was on tour as a child prodigy.

Jean Fritz, a remarkably diverse author, has also produced easy-to-read biographies of historical figures of the Revolutionary War period; she also wrote an unusual book of fiction that has a sturdy story-line yet is an exemplar of research methods: *George Washington's Breakfast* (1969). By then she had written over a dozen other books, including fine historical novels for older readers such as *Early Thunder* (1967), which is set in New England just before the Civil War. All her historical books show the results of Fritz's impeccable scholarship; this is also evident in her later biographies, like *Bully for You, Teddy Roosevelt!* (1991). And somewhere Fritz found time to write a fantasy about a boggart, *Magic to Burn* (1964), and two autobiographical accounts of her coming to the United States after a childhood spent in China: *Homesick: My Own Story* (1982) and *China Homecoming* (1985), which describes her visit to China forty years later. In 1986, Fritz won the Laura Ingalls Wilder Medal.

Another writer who has contributed to children's understanding of their country's past is Yoshiko Uchida who, in addition to three excellent stories about the Depression, wrote of the experiences of many Japanese-American families who were sent to internment camps in *Journey to Topaz* (1971) and *Journey Home* (1978). Uchida, who began her career as a writer in 1949, has produced realistic stories set in feudal and in contemporary Japan and also compiled outstanding adaptations of folk-tales in *The Dancing Kettle and Other Japanese Folk Tales* (1949) and *The Sea of Gold and Other Tales from Japan* (1965).

The historical novel is not the most popular of subgenres with child readers in Britain, but nevertheless it flourished in the post-war years and enjoyed high critical esteem. This period was marked by a welcome decline in the 'gadzooksery' of speech and the pseudo-chivalric activities of earlier stories, and a growth of reconstructive realism based on meticulous research. Typical of the new taste and practice was the work of Ronald Welch, whose series of novels about the Carey family is rooted in detailed military history. History in fiction was no longer a matter of violent fancy-dress games; it was more a matter of recognizable human behaviour in politically true environments.

Some of the period's most gifted authors chose the historical novel as their sole or main activity. Geoffrey Trease, whose *Bows against the Barons* had fundamentally recast the form in the 1930s, continued to produce readable, well-researched novels such as *The Crown of Violet* (1952) and *The Hills of Varna* (1948), which brilliantly illuminated historical process. Barbara Willard began her 'Mantlemass' series, set in late medieval and Tudor England, with *The Lark and the Laurel* (1970). The gap between fiction and social history was at its narrowest in the work of Cynthia Harnett, whose novels such as *The Woolpack* (1951) and *The Load of Unicorn* (1959) are narratives of everyday life in medieval England. There is no high political drama here, instead a convincing sense of the texture of ordinary existences. The problem is that Harnett's books smack of the 'textbook', perhaps an estimable overreaction to the lax sensationalism of earlier books. At the opposite extreme is *The Dream-*

Cynthia Harnett illustrated her own historical stories, with stress on meticulous period accuracy. Here she provides a visual aid to the inconvenience of medieval dress. From *The Woolpack* (1951).

*Time* (1967), the last novel by Henry Treece, who had previously published a number of admirable novels about the Vikings. It is a brilliant work of historical impressionism, an innovative book which in some respects anticipates such later experimental fiction as Alan Garner's *Red Shift* (1973). The advantage of the historical novel for children lies in placing a child protagonist in the key role of simultaneous participant and witness, combining the dangerousness of power politics with the maturing effects of trial and responsibility on the child character. (*The Dolphin Crossing* is a historical novel in just this sense.)

Charles Keeping, one of the finest children's artists of the period, was a regular illustrator for the novels of Rosemary Sutcliff, and in this immaculate pairing of writer and artist we can see the true resources and potential of the historical story. In the work of Sutcliff, displacement and handicap of various kinds are crucial. Sutcliff herself suffered from Still's disease, an arthritic condition which she contracted at the age of 2 and which disabled her for life. In her autobiography, *Blue Remembered Hills*, she wrote that 'disabled children often have an odd unawareness or only partial awareness of how it is with them. They know that they cannot do certain things which other children can do. They know, as it were, in theory, but they have not yet got the full impact. Soon, all too soon, they become aware of subtle social barriers, the full implication and likely effect on their lives, the loneliness.' This, she says, is the plight of Drem, the young hero of *Warrior Scarlet* (1958), a novel set in prehistoric Britain which is probably Sutcliff's finest achievement. In Drem's society the rite of passage which admits boys to the male adult world is the single-handed slaying of a wolf. Drem's withered right arm makes it improbable that he can ever achieve this, and so win his place as a warrior.

## HISTORICAL FANTASY AND TIME TRAVEL

If history as costume fiction gave way to a new kind of psychological novel in such work as Rosemary Sutcliff's, it also gave place to fantasy. Two strands of fiction in particular can be seen to emerge in the post-war years, one of which belongs characteristically to the 'golden age', while the other has retained its vitality and perhaps deepened in seriousness to the present day. The first strand is that of historical fantasy, in which history is raided, ransacked, and rewritten in the service of a unique imaginative vision. The major proponents of this form, two of the finest talents of the period, are Leon Garfield and Joan Aiken. The second strand is that of time travel, which has its roots in the work of Nesbit. Major fantasies of interaction between past and present were produced in the 'golden age' by Lucy M. Boston, Philippa Pearce, Penelope Lively, William Mayne, and Penelope Farmer, and all of them, directly or indirectly, owe something to Nesbit's example.

The Manor at
Hemingford Grey,
near Cambridge.
Reputedly the oldest
inhabited house in
England, it was for half
a century the home of
Lucy Boston and the
inspiration for her
classic 'Green Knowe'
stories.

Like Nesbit herself, several of these writers also owe a debt to Dickens. Indeed Dickens himself, notably in such a novel as *Barnaby Rudge*, is a revisionary historical novelist of genius, in just such forms as writers in this period found congenial. In Leon Garfield and Joan Aiken alike, the line of descent from Dickens is manifest, although their own best work is wholly original and distinctive. Dickensian qualities of wit and verbal exuberance, of macabre comedy, of caricature so inspired that to ask for depth of psychological portraiture is irrelevant and pointless, and above all of an underlying humanitarian indignation, are plain to see. Like their great predecessor, these are writers of formidable zest and energy.

Leon Garfield's *Devil-in-the-Fog* (1966) is an example of his early writing at its characteristic best. Set in the eighteenth century (Garfield's favourite territory) it is the story of George Treet, the eldest son in a family of strolling players, who in an eccentric business contract is first 'rented' and then purchased outright to serve the machinations of a crazed nobleman bent on cheating and punishing a brother he detests. Such grimly polarized family feuds, especially between good and evil brothers, are characteristic of Garfield's melodramatic world of deception, illusion, and trustlessness. Yet the fog-bound horrors of malevolent deceit are offset by the feckless charm of the players, professionally histrionic people in a compulsively histrionic world, which brings reminders of the Crummles family in *Nicholas Nickleby*. The compost for Garfield's extravagant historical locale is the social reality of eighteenth-century England, but it nurtures some exotic blooms. Underlying the hectic narrative surface, however, there is a deep, consistent, understated quest for integrity on the part of his young heroes, and to maintain it in the world of illusions they inhabit is a resounding act of courage. In recent

Pat Marriott's illustration for Joan Aiken's *Night Birds of Nantucket* (1966). Children's books can find rich comedy in parody of adult classics. Captain Casket's search for the pink whale recalls Captain Ahab in *Moby-Dick*.

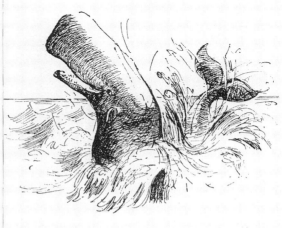

breakfast on the beach? Those ruffians are not likely to come back while *she's* out there. And it's not a sight to miss.''

So Pen fetched the food from the cart while Dido and Nate prospected for a path down the cliff, and then the whole party descended to the beach. Captain Casket made straight for the edge of the ocean, and Pen had much ado to prevent his wading in, so eager was he to approach as close as possible to the pink whale—who, luckily, saw his intention and swam in near to the land; and so these two friends gazed at one another with the utmost delight and mutual satisfaction.

"Could you give her a hint not to come too close, sir?" Nate said anxiously. "It'd be the devil to pay dragging her years Garfield has gone on experimenting, but the early tales such as *Devil-in-the-Fog*, *Smith* (1967), and *Black Jack* (1968) may well prove his enduring achievement.

Joan Aiken rewrote history still more radically, creating an alternative scenario in which the Stuart dynasty is still on the throne, and England is beset by Hanoverian plotters. Starting with *The Wolves of Willoughby Chase* (1962), Aiken's books are a series of comic pseudo-historical melodramas, profusely inventive and witty, about an England that in almost all political respects did not exist. Her ingenuity knows no bounds but despite the zestful hyperbole of action, not everything is gothic-imaginary. The lives of the enslaved pauper-children in *The Wolves of Willoughby Chase* are identical in many respects with those suffered by children of the Industrial Revolution, and the dark satanic mills of her industrial town Blastburn had all too actual counterparts—something which Aiken's imagination seems to assimilate fully in the later, altogether darker novel, *Midnight is a Place* (1974). Like Garfield, Aiken is a highly original and probably a classic writer of this period.

The other main strand, that of time travel, also produced some major achievements. The earliest to appear in these years was Lucy M. Boston's *The*

'Every picture tells a story', but few more simply and graphically than Antony Maitland's illustration of Mrs Cockle's first encounter with the sea. From Philippa Pearce's *Mrs Cockle's Cat* (1961).

*Children of Green Knowe* (1954), the first of six novels about the Norman manorhouse modelled exactly on the author's own home, the Manor at Hemingford Grey in Cambridgeshire. *The Children of Green Knowe* is the story of a Christmas visit by a small boy, Tolly, to his great-grandmother at a time when the house is islanded by a flooded river. Through a series of inset narratives—part stories told by the great-grandmother, part dreams and intuitions and ghostly emanations of ancient wood and stone— Tolly encounters a family of ancestors who lived in seventeenth-century England. The spirit of place, the living continuity of the house, conquers time, making past and present one. In later books, and later visits, Tolly enters further into the past of Green Knowe: united by a kind of spatial telepathy, all those who have venerated the house are in a sense contemporary.

The 'Green Knowe' stories are a composite work of collective distinction, and not far removed from them in spirit is Philippa Pearce's *Tom's Midnight Garden* (1958). Although Pearce's delightful earlier story of holiday treasure-hunt, *Minnow on the Say* (1955), is seriously underrated, she has not since equalled the extraordinary imaginative quality of *Tom's Midnight Garden*, which is widely regarded as the outstanding single book of the period. It is the story of a boy who finds the past at night in the garden of a Victorian house, to which he is admitted for a magic hour when the clock strikes thirteen. The legend of the clock, and for the novel, is 'Time no longer', and the story's vindication of this claim as truth is a triumph of imagination's power to subsume and outreach the reductive strictness of explanatory rationalism such as Tom's uncle Alan stands for. Attempts to explain events as supernatural are discredited by narrative evidence, but so are efforts to account for them through psychological phenomena. Only by discarding our notions of linear time can we make sense of the book's events, and yet in the moving close they do indeed make sense, irresistibly. *Tom's Midnight Garden* is at once a very complex and very simple book, which can be intuitively understood by quite young children.

Such stories of slippages in time, involving modern children with the people and especially the children of the past, are essentially a development from the historical novel. In their modern form they begin with Alison Uttley's *A Traveller in Time* (1939); other major achievements of this kind are

Inspired by her Derbyshire childhood at the end of the nineteenth century, Alison Uttley (1884–1976), was a prolific writer for children, best known for *A Traveller in Time* and the 'Little Grey Rabbit' stories.

Alan Garner at home in his native Cheshire, which supplies the setting for several of his best-known stories, including *The Weird-stone of Brisingamen* and *Red Shift*.

William Mayne's *Earthfasts* (1966), Penelope Farmer's *Charlotte Sometimes* (1969), and the novels of Penelope Lively, whose first book, *Astercote*, was published in 1970. Perhaps it is no accident that fictions of time gained such vitality in the aftermath of a war which seemed paradoxically to have both consummated a history of national greatness and suddenly brought it to a close.

A sense of more than national unease was widespread in the post-war years, as military technology reached new and frightening levels. Fictions of time can look to imagined futures as well as recreate the past, and this period saw the beginning of a dystopian futurist literature for children which has pessimistically flourished ever since. Conventional science fiction, like conventional historical novels, continued to be written, but a sizeable and distinguished modern literature was essentially to combine the two. Writers for children began to engage sceptically with myths of progress, drawing on historical evidence of primitive existences and regimes of superstitious bigotry to project such societies into imagined futures on the far side of nuclear war or other global disasters.

Science fiction flourished particularly in the USA, where the work of Robert A. Heinlein (beginning with *Rocket Ship Galileo*, 1947) and Andre Norton (beginning with *Star Man's Son, 2250 A.D.*, 1952) helped to break down prejudices against the form. *Podkayne of Mars: Her Life and Times* (1963) was significant in having one of the first female protagonists in science fiction. Heinlein's twelve 'juveniles' have been underestimated, probably because of guilt-by-association with the comic book, but science fiction necessarily has links with older forms, and just as Heinlein incorporates themes from myth and legend in his books, so Norton later used native American legend in hers. The science fiction series for young readers issued by the publishers John C. Winston (twenty-six volumes by 1960) was also influential.

Eleanor Cameron's first book was *The Wonderful Flight to the Mushroom Planet* (1954) and it was the first of a series of fantasy novels that were lively, well written, and dear to the hearts of young readers who had developed a hard-to-fill appetite for science fiction. The books that made a greater impression on adult critics, however, were *Court of the Stone Children* (1973), a blend of fantasy and realism which won the National Book Award, and the several stories about Julia Redfern—a remarkably sensitive exploration of maturation and the creative instinct, beginning with *A Room Made of Windows* (1972).

Madeleine L'Engle's first book for children, *And Both Were Young*, appeared in 1949 to restrained applause; it was quite otherwise when critics evaluated her realistic family story *Meet the Austins* (1960). The opening of her next book, *A Wrinkle in Time* (1962), which won the Newbery Medal, suggested that it would be a similar story, but readers were led into a most inventive fantasy, complicated in its intricate weaving of science, philosophy, religion, and familial relationships. The sequels to this space fantasy, *A Wind in the Door* (1973) and *A Swiftly Tilting Planet* (1978), are among the best of L'Engle's other books and are characteristic of the blending of the fantastic and mystic (as well as the mythical) with science fiction characteristic of the 1970s. By comparison with later books, however, the science fiction of this period seems to be very optimistic.

An early example of the new order was David Severn's *The Future Took Us* (1957). Severn had begun his career with conventional holiday adventure stories such as *A Cabin for Crusoe* (1943), but later wrote an excellent fantasy based on simultaneous dreaming, *Dream Gold* (1952), a splendid story in the Mowgli tradition, *Foxy-Boy* (1959), and an interesting forerunner of the adolescent novel, *The Girl in the Grove* (1974). As this suggests, he is a writer whose output is a reliable miniature of more general tendencies in children's fiction. *The Future Took Us*, for all its limitations, is certainly the fictional shape of things to come. It is the story of two boys transported across a millennium to a post-holocaust Britain, where life for ordinary people is primitive, and where power is ruthlessly exercised by a privileged priesthood of mathematicians.

Only since 1970 have variations on this theme come to dominate children's literature, and they coincide with the rise of the 'young adult' novel. The first really major achievement in this field is Peter Dickinson's trilogy *The Weathermonger* (1968), *Heartsease* (1969), and *The Devil's Children* (1970), known collectively as *The Changes*. These too depict a cruel and repressive Britain in which all machines are banned, but their nightmare vision has moved closer to the present day. By the end of this quarter-century, therefore, history, fantasy, and science fiction had merged to create a new and powerful composite genre which was to form the core achievement of the teenage novel on both sides of the Atlantic.

SECONDARY WORLDS, AND MARVELS NEAR AT HAND

The 1950s and 1960s were a heyday for fantasy books in Britain and once again the circumstances of the time seem sympathetic to them. The post-war

273

*Facing*: the flowering of the coloured comic in the 1960s: a selection from the Opie collection.

Pauline Baynes's illustrations have become inseparable from C. S. Lewis's 'Narnia' stories. Here Eustace, Lucy, and Edmund are drawn through the picture-frame to join *The Voyage of the 'Dawn Treader'* (1952).

years were increasingly a period of moral relativism and uncertainty, in which old and seemingly unquestionable values came under scrutiny. In Britain there was a steady decline in church attendance and Christian worship. Pragmatic social morality was substituted for the absolute sanctions of right and wrong which had hitherto been part of the national culture if not necessarily of daily conduct. It is one thing to defy the rules, quite another to repudiate the rule-makers. In these conditions one can see in fictions a nostalgia for ancient clarities, the need to dramatize a superhuman polarization of right and wrong. Again and again in fantasies of the period we see the opposition between the Light and the Dark, as in Susan Cooper's sequence *The Dark is Rising*, which began in 1965 with *Over Sea, Under Stone* and was developed in the 1970s. In the most celebrated fantasies of the period the contrast was memorably personified in central antagonists: the wizard Cadellin Silverbrow and his evil brother in Alan Garner's *The Weirdstone of Brisingamen* (1960), or Aslan and the White Witch in C. S. Lewis's *The Lion, the Witch and the Wardrobe* (1950).

Allusion to Arthurian romance was widespread. In Dickinson's *The Weathermonger* the magician Merlin had turned out to be the source of all the trouble, but more typically the Arthurian knights and their kind were potential saviours of a land fallen prey to evil. In Alan Garner's *The Weirdstone of Brisingamen* the knights are sleeping under Alderley Edge in Cheshire, awaiting the call to arms: this is the 'legend of Alderley' which introduces the battle between two contemporary children and the dark forces of ancient magic.

Something of the period's nostalgia for a lost world of safe absolutes, mingled with desire for clear and inspiriting codes of conduct, is conveyed more explicitly than usual in C. S. Lewis's *The Voyage of the 'Dawn Treader'* (1952), when two of the Pevensie children enter the 'secondary world' of Narnia for the third time. The narrator observes: 'when the Pevensie children had returned to Narnia for their second visit, it was (for the Narnians) as if King Arthur came back to Britain, as some

Tom's Midnight Garden
Philippa Pearce
Oxford
Tom's Midnight Garden
Philippa Pearce

people say he will. And I say the sooner the better.' And in fact the seven-volume Chronicles of Narnia, published at yearly intervals between 1950 and 1956, form perhaps the most complete revival of Arthurian legend in modern children's literature. Even though Arthurian stories and characters are scarcely mentioned, their ideals and values are transposed. The action takes place in the land of Narnia, where the noble lion Aslan takes the place of Christ (being 'crucified' in *The Lion, the Witch and the Wardrobe* to redeem the 'sons of Adam and daughters of Eve') and the White Witch is the Satan figure. Magically transported to Narnia, an imaginary parallel world alongside Earth, the four Pevensie children, joined or replaced in later episodes by two other children, Eustace Scrubb and Jill Pole, become kings and potentates in the new world, joining native figures to fight with noble and violent chivalry against the forces of evil. Many aspects of the books are deeply questionable—their glorification of conflict and retribution, their legitimizing of cruelty, their elements of racism and sexism and their active debasement of adulthood—and have caused the books to be attacked by a number of critics and by some fellow writers such as Penelope Lively and Alan Garner. However, there is no denying the enormous popularity of the series and commentators such as Roger Lancelyn Green defend it with messianic zeal. The elements of Christian allegory (which vary in importance and precision from book to book) are probably unnoticed by most young readers, except in so far as they supply an absolute moral sanction for partisanship, vengeance, punishment, and reward. The books are treasured as adventures in chivalry, where ordinary children are legitimized in power and status, ennobled in a fixed hierarchy of obedience and authority.

Several notable books have arisen out of American interest in these legends. Lloyd Alexander, a master of the picaresque, has written biographies like *Border Hawk: August Bondi* (1958), the story of a Jewish immigrant, and books for young children like *Time Cat* (1963) and the truly beautiful story *The Fortune-Tellers* (1992). It is, however, for his books of fantasy or adventure for older readers that Alexander has been most lauded; of those the finest are the five books in the 'Prydain' cycle, rich fantasies based on the *Mabinogi*: the first was *The Book of Three* (1966); the last, *The High King* (1979), won the Newbery Medal. They incorporate wit and humour, memorable characterization, and engrossing action. Typical of Alexander's adventure tales is *The Marvelous Misadventures of Sebastian* (1970), winner of the National Book Award, which is the story of an eighteenth-century musician. (Alexander also wrote a series of novels about a feisty young heiress who twists her guardian around her little finger as she drags him off all over the world on one wild adventure after another; the first was *The Illyrian Adventure* (1986).)

It might almost be possible to identify an American subgenre springing from the New World's fascination with the mythology of the Old, from Mark

*Facing*: the book that has some claim to be the most distinguished fantasy in a period of distinguished fantasy writing: Peter Farmer's cover for the 1970 paperback edition of Philippa Pearce's *Tom's Midnight Garden* (1958).

Twain and Howard Pyle onwards. Certainly a distinguished contribution is Nancy Bond's *A String in the Harp* (1977) which used material from the *Mabinogi*, and had the distinction of winning the Welsh Tir na n-Óg award as the best English-language book with an authentic Welsh background. But the definitive blending of the ancient and modern had been written ten years before.

Using Arthurian and Nordic legend as a starting-point, Alan Garner's early books were conventional but popular. With *Elidor* (1965) he moved towards a more confident originality with an effective interchange of magic between a threatened secondary world and an ordinary family in present-day Manchester. However, Garner's first truly major achievement was *The Owl Service* (1967) in which he drew again on established legend, this time the Welsh *Mabinogi*. The power of this extraordinary book lies in the precise and concrete social realism of the modern setting in which the ancient tragic legend is replayed. Stresses and tensions of modern Britain—between Wales and England, working class and middle class, parent and child, together with the unchanging trials of adolescent sexuality—combine to substantiate the fundamental human truths of ancient story. With astonishing vividness and a

Two versions of Ted Hughes's *Iron Man*. Despite his more obvious size, George Adamson's 1968 version is an innocent large-scale toy compared with the humanized technical menace of Andrew Davidson's (1986). Compare the eyes and hands in the two figures.

*The Return of the Iron Man*

The Iron Man!
  Hogarth's father put on speed, he aimed his car at the foot.
  Crash! He knocked the foot out of the way.
  He drove on, faster and faster. And behind

22

denouement of remarkable narrative courage (few children's writers have so impressively kept their nerve, and blended remorseless logic with surprise), Garner shows how the clarity of legend can produce a structural framework for our understanding of the complexities and confusions of modern social conflict.

This indeed seems to be a governing principle of fantasy in the period. There are major neo-mythic achievements such as Ted Hughes's evolution-cum-creation fable in *How the Whale Became and Other Stories* (1961). The same writer's magnificent, brief story *The Iron Man* (1968) is in part an allegory of humankind's option to employ its technological resource in order to harness and defeat its self-destructive urge to militant cannibalism. The space-bat-angel-dragon encompasses even in his ambivalent name many of our species' fundamental choices between what is and might be true for us.

Similarly existential as well as ecological questions on a smaller scale (literally rather than metaphorically, perhaps) were asked in Mary Norton's meticulously realized *The Borrowers* (1952) and its sequels. Although perhaps overburdened with its narrative frame, the series is highly original, for all that it is in the tradition of *Gulliver's Travels*, T. H. White's near-masterpiece *Mistress Masham's Repose* (1947), and innumerable fantasies for young children. Equally individualistic and well worked out—and influential—although firmly in the world of myth was the Finnish Tove Jansson's 'Moomintroll' series, beginning with *Comet in Moominland* (1946; English translation, 1951).

Such works of startling originality stand beside other smaller but real achievements, such as Catherine Storr's *Marianne Dreams* (1958), a fable of illness and convalescence which couples fantasy with psychological logic and causes them to meet in the common psychic ground of dream. Writers such as Barbara Leonie Picard remade folk-tale in fresh narratives, as in the fine *The Faun and the Woodcutter's Daughter* (1951), while Mollie Hunter replayed Celtic legend in the world of modern Scotland, in such books as *The Kelpie's Pearls* (1964). Whether refashioning existing legends or extending the store, the achievements in fantasy of this period mark a prevalent sense that perspectives of magic and the supernatural are needed to articulate a new and unfamiliar world. In these years, realism alone was not enough.

Illustration by Diana Stanley for Mary Norton's *The Borrowers* (1952). Pod reclines on Great Aunt Sophy's dressing-table, while she drinks her daily decanter of Fine Old Pale Madeira. '"She thinks my father comes out of the decanter," said Arrietty.'

## SCHOOLDAYS AND HOLIDAYS

Like the historical novel, the school story changed and evolved in this period. It also contracted, occupying a smaller share of the popular market.

The lives and exploits of privileged children at expensive residential schools continued to produce occasional works of distinction by serious writers, and foremost among them in the post-war years were Antonia Forest's novels about the Marlow family, such as *Autumn Term* (1948) and *End of Term* (1959). Finely characterized, beautifully written, guided by a civilized insularity of social values, these are late masterpieces of a vanishing form. Strangely, the school years of the Marlow family match the period of almost thirty years it took to write them.

Geoffrey Trease: *Under Black Banner.* Competitive sports and games figured prominently in the school stories of the period. Richard Kennedy's illustration achieves something of a mismatch between young athlete and small boy.

Amongst many writers, however, there was a growing impatience with the gulf between fictional schools and the actual lives of home and day school lived by the vast majority of children, and a number of important efforts were made to supply what was so obviously missing. William Mayne, a writer of idiosyncratic brilliance and awesome productivity, wrote about real school lives for very young readers, for example in *No More School* (1965), but his lasting contribution to the school story is the splendid quartet about choir school life, *A Swarm in May, Cathedral Wednesday, Chorister's Cake,* and *Words and Music* (1955–63): stories of boarding-school with a difference, rooted in the musical professionalism which links adult and child in the common service of cathedral worship. Even so, this was still as separate a world as that of Anthony Buckeridge's Jennings at his 'prep' school. (Jennings began his career on BBC radio in 1948; *Jennings Goes to School* was published in 1950.)

New departures were made, however, aimed at finding a voice for day school life. Again Geoffrey Trease was an innovative figure. His contribution was the series of 'Bannermere' stories, beginning with *No Boats on Bannermere* (1949), which follow the fortunes of a group of school friends growing up in the Lake District. They are a small and inadvertent document of social history, and they pushed the school story into modern times: no mean achievement.

Perhaps the best single example of the new school story, however, was C. Day Lewis's *The Otterbury Incident* (1948), which stands out with the same mixture of popular appeal and imaginative distinction that made *The Silver Sword* uniquely successful as a war

Suddenly I saw the cluster of figures quite close in front.

story. *The Otterbury Incident* is rooted in the post-war world of small-town spivs and racketeers, whose misdeeds are exposed by the zany enterprise of schoolboys. The book is told as first-person narrative by one of the boys involved, but it makes no unrealistic claims for child status. For all its Englishness, *The Otterbury Incident* is based on a French film, *Nous les gosses*, and in many respects its closest equivalents in children's fiction at this time are the novels of the distinguished French writer Paul Berna, notably *A Hundred Million Francs* (1957), which set ground rules for later stories of believable adventure and suspense such as David Line's *Run for your Life* (1966). For girls, who tend in any case to be more mature and willing readers, there was far more on offer in these years, such as K. M. Peyton's 'Flambards' quartet (1967–9, and *Flambards Divided*, 1982)—which later drifted up the age ranges to become, at least on television, adult fare. Even the no-

torious pony story frequently escaped its formulaic stereotypes through such books as Primrose Cummings's *Four Rode Home* (1951) and K. M. Peyton's *Fly-by-Night* (1968).

It was K. M. Peyton amongst others who brought the modern school story into meaningful contact with the lives of working-class and disadvantaged children in her novel *Pennington's Seventeenth Summer* (1970), a book which accurately signals not only the broadened base of school fiction but the shift towards teenage readers and their world at the end of this quarter-century of writing.

The pony story was popular throughout the post-war years. Lionel Edwards's racing picture is from *Sabre: The Horse from the Sea*, written as a teenager by Kathleen Herald, better-known in later years as K. M. Peyton.

## REALISM AND THE BEGINNINGS OF THE 'TEENAGE' NOVEL

More and more, that world began to include the urban working-class child, and even to make tentative engagements with the newly conspicuous fact of multi-ethnic, multi-cultural life in British towns and cities. Again there are representative prophetic texts which achieved great popularity at the time and also set precedents for a far greater output of such writing in the quarter-century that followed. John Rowe Townsend's *Gumble's Yard* (1961) is set in derelict areas of Manchester and concerns the resourcefulness of urban children abandoned by their feckless parents. Not only the topographical, economic, and social setting but also the systematic demythologizing of parental adequacy, the ruptured cliché of familial harmony, point the way to a more observant, sceptical, and candid social fiction for young children. Sylvia Sherry's *A Pair of Jesus-Boots* (1969) takes the process further. Her young hero, Rocky O'Rourke, is a streetwise urban survivor in a run-down city environment (Liverpool). Rocky's gang is unselfconsciously multi-racial in ways that pointed forward (with no little optimism) to more general urban futures.

But it was the USA that led the way in 'realistic' writing, bringing together the traditions of the domestic or family novel and the 'romance' and blending them with social realism and the story-telling pace (and, perhaps, depth) of television. This highly potent and commercial mixture dominated the world market after 1970 with genres of 'teenage' romances and problem novels, as well as stories for younger children that had considerably more edge and bite than their equivalents of one or two generations before, such as Eleanor Estes's 'Moffat' series, or, in Britain, Joyce Lankester Brisley's 'Milly-Molly-Mandy' stories.

Perhaps most characteristic of the period was Beverly Cleary, whose *Fifteen* (1956) provides an instructive contrast with Judy Blume's *Forever* (1975). The first begins, 'Today I'm going to meet a boy, Jane Purdy told herself', and ends: 'She was Stan's girl. That was all that really mattered.' The second begins: 'Sybil Davison has a genius I.Q. and has been laid by at least six different guys.' Cleary is an adept at family stories for the young, with the cosy Americana of the 'Henry Huggins' and 'Ramona' series—although her work became more serious with the Newbery Medal winner the epistolary *Dear Mr Henshaw* in 1984.

And yet things were changing: Paul Zindel's *The Pigman* (1968) and *My Darling, My Hamburger* (1969) were among the earliest examples of rather bleak novels in which children are let down, more than anything else, by their parents. The subject-matter was treated sensitively by writers like Betsy Byars. Her sixth book, *The Midnight Fox* (1968), impressed critics, although the earlier ones had been adequately received; in this story of a child's protective love for an animal, there is a fore-

Robert Burch's realistic stories of the rural South are epitomized by *Queenie Peavy* (1966).

shadowing of the tender love a girl feels for her retarded brother in *The Summer of the Swans*. Some of Byars's best work was done in the 1970s and 1980s, when she became, as it were, the bench-mark for the middle-range writer: sometimes predictable, but producing highly competent social comedy or sensitive but not too taxing social drama.

Robert Burch wrote for an extended age range, from *Joey's Cat* (1969), a pleasant story for pre-school children, and *Renfroe's Christmas* (1958), which tells a warm and credible tale of a child who learns the pleasure of giving, to *Queenie Peavy* (1966), a thoughtful, percipient book about a child who is doughty and courageous in coping with a father who comes out of prison and breaks his parole. Of Burch's many other books, *Ida Comes over the Mountain* (1980) and its sequel *Christmas with Ida Early* (1983) are two of the best examples of his appealing combination of cheerful humour and a sentiment that never descends to sentimentality.

Another writer whose humour was an outstanding quality was Keith Robertson; he had begun writing for children in 1948 but it was not until 1958 that he produced the hilarious *Henry Reed, Inc.* A sophisticated, inventive lad, Henry advertises himself as dealing in pure and applied research. There is incessant application but not a great deal of purity, as Henry muddles through.

Elaine Konigsburg's highly intelligent humour has crossed the Atlantic successfully enough, although her British publishers have had some trouble with titles. Her *Jennifer, Hecate, Macbeth, William McKinley, and Me, Elizabeth* (1967) appeared as *Jennifer, Hecate, Macbeth and Me*; her study of child schizophrenia, *(George)* (1970), became *Benjamin Dickinson Carr and his (George)*, and *Journey to an 800 Number* (1983)—which contains the memorable exchange: ' "My father and mother are divorced" . . . "Aren't everybody's?" '—became *Journey by First Class Camel*. Her *annus mirabilis* was 1967 when *From the Mixed-up Files of Mrs Basil E. Frankweiler* won the Newbery Medal, and *Jennifer* . . . was runner-up. The former is an imaginative story of two children who briefly and illegally reside in New York's Metropolitan Museum of Art, while the latter is a story of interracial friendship between two girls. Konigsburg is often funny, but her humour is incidental to the protagonists' problems and to the momentum of strong story-lines.

A writer of perhaps equal wit, which belies her serious concerns, was Louise Fitzhugh, who startled and delighted readers with *Harriet the Spy* (1964) and its sequel *The Long Secret* (1965), both of which were controversial because of their inclusion of such activities as the protagonist's prying and her

Louise Fitzhugh's *Harriet the Spy* (1964), a remarkably innovative—and continuingly popular—portrait of urban childhood.

James Earl Jones and the author Virginia Hamilton recording Hamilton's collection of American black folk-tales, *The People Could Fly* (1985).

parents' quarrelling in the first and the discussion of menstruation and some jet-set foibles in the second. The books were sophisticated and funny, and 'Harriet the Spy Fan Clubs' were formed across the United States. In *Nobody's Family is Going to Change* (1974) an African-American father scoffs at the daughter who wants to be a lawyer like him, but 11-year-old Emma will not change her mind. All of Fitzhugh's stories reveal a clear vision of the child's point of view and a quirky humour that lightens the narrative.

Among the numerous awards that Virginia Hamilton has received is the 1975 Newbery Medal for *M. C. Higgins the Great*, which also won the National Book Award; in 1992 she was given the Hans Christian Andersen Medal, never before awarded to an African-American writer. She has produced an impressive body of highly acclaimed work that includes realistic fiction, fantasy, folklore, and biography. *Zeely* (1967), her first book, is a spell-binding story, rich in atmosphere and imagination. It was not until her third book, *The Time-Ago Tales of Jahdu* (1969), that the fluency and inventiveness of Hamilton's writing became apparent. *The Planet of Junior Brown* (1971) is a modern classic, a story of strength and courage, set in New York City and featuring two original, memorable characters. The influences of the oral tradition inform her novels *A Little Love* (1984) as well as the 'Justice' fantasy trilogy and such poetic adaptations of traditional material as *The People Could Fly: American Black Folk Tales* (1985) and *The Dark Way: Stories from the Spirit World* (1990). Even in her biographies, Hamilton writes with a compelling narrative flow.

Like Hamilton, Paula Fox is a novelist of distinction; in fact, they are probably the two great stylists writing for children in the United States in this period. Fox's first book, *Maurice's Room* (1966), focuses with clarity on a mother–child relationship—the boy's room is a collector's joy but a mother's despair. Each succeeding book won critical approbation and the affection of its intended audience, younger children, but it was not until the publication of *Portrait of Ivan* (1969), *Blowfish Live in the Sea* (1970), and the 1974 Newbery Award winner *The Slave Dancer*, that the full potency and insight of Fox's art were seen. In each of these, as in other books, she deals with a young person's problems in personal relationships with compassion, and part of the impact of her books is due to the fact that she lets the characters grow and change rather than tell readers that this is happening. For the body of her work Fox received the Hans Christian Andersen Award in 1978.

Many of these books were straws in the wind, but no such breezes blew on Enid Blyton. The dominant figure in British children's books for two generations, and perhaps the writer for a lost type of childhood, she died in 1968. (Interestingly, she has had virtually no influence in the USA.) After the war she sustained her astonishing output for many years. Only in the 1960s did it decline, and even then in quality rather than quantity. It is unusual to speak of 'quality' where Blyton is concerned. Although she was and is still immensely popular with children, and although she has probably created more habitual recreational readers than any other writer in history, she is routinely despised and vilified by many professional commentators, teachers, and librarians. Undoubtedly she has major shortcomings. Her vocabulary is usually (but not always) very limited, her sentence structures usually (but not always) simple, her attitudes too often aligned with relish with those of the pre-socialized child, and therefore all too enthusiastically welcomed by her target audience. Undoubtedly her plots are often formulaic and predictable. Undoubtedly her social, sexual, and racial values often reflect uncritically the unwholesome standard prejudices of British life in her time. But there is a positive side, which is consistently suppressed in much commentary. Her prose is clear and precise, her sense of narrative sequence immensely skilful and compelling, her wit and psychological shrewdness far greater than she is given credit for, her frequent spiteful intolerances based as often on sane principles of conduct as they are on objectionable snobbery. And her graphic observation of the natural world is gravely underrated. These qualities can be seen at their best in her non-fiction, such as *Enid Blyton's Animal Lover's Book* (1952), and in stories such as *Six Cousins at Mistletoe Farm* (1948). She is in fact a very considerable writer, a complex phenomenon for critics, and a delight for children. As with C. S. Lewis, and as with Roald Dahl, whose equally phenomenal success began in this period with the controversial *Charlie and the Chocolate Factory* (1964), she is a writer whose reputation permits no easy verdict.

The core of Blyton's work lay in school and holiday adventures in contemporary settings for the years of middle childhood. Such stories formed the bread-and-butter writing of the period, attracting other prolific and highly popular authors such as Malcolm Saville. Saville's 'Lone Pine' series extended over more than thirty years, from *Mystery at Witchend* (1943) to *Home to Witchend* (1978), and for many children of this period his powerfully evoked Shropshire and Sussex backgrounds to adventure are some of the most durable fictional images of childhood. Even so, with occasional exceptions the finest literary achievements of these years lay not in the realistic novel but in fantasy and history, and above all at their interface. The dominant child age group, however, was the same regardless of the writer's stance or the subgenre involved. The 'golden age' of children's literature in the 1950s and 1960s lay in work for middle childhood.

## POETRY AND PICTURES

New British poetry was sparse in the immediate post-war period, but what there was ranged widely across the childhood years in its expectations of linguistic and emotional maturity. Eleanor Farjeon remained active and *The Starry Floor* (1949), an attractive series of linked poems, is reminiscent of her earlier work. Ian Serraillier was especially notable in linking his poems to topical events and providing children with an image of verse-writing as something contemporary and fresh. Successful examples of such work include his *The Ballad of Kon-Tiki and Other Verses* (1952) and *Everest Climbed* (1955). Gifts of an altogether more substantial kind are apparent in the work of James Reeves, whose first collection of poems for children, *The Wandering Moon*, appeared in 1950. Reeves is a master of humour and nonsense, and of inventive lyric fantasy, and his best work has remarkable lightness and energy of rhythm and diction—an imagination which appeals uncondescendingly to children is expressed with diverse technical accomplishment. Beyond question, however, the major achievements in children's poetry at this time were those of Ted Hughes and Charles Causley. Hughes's first book of poems for children, *Meet My Folks!*, appeared in 1961, an exuberant, mischievous, and witty assembly of verse-portraits. Imaginative and technically playful, *Meet My Folks!* is uneven in achievement but rich in promise—the fine apprentice-work for children of a poet whose later work includes such varied classics as *Season Songs* (1976) and *The Cat and the Cuckoo* (1987). Causley, whose imagination is deeply entrenched in his native Cornwall, is probably the greatest exponent of the modern ballad. *Figgie Hobbin* (1970) is an outstanding achievement, justly described by Brian Morse as 'a book no childhood should be without'.

Among the American poets who made major contributions in the 1950s and 1960s were David McCord, Karla Kuskin, Myra Cohn Livingston, John Ciardi, and—even earlier—Aileen Fisher. Fisher's poems (*Feathered Ones and Furry*, 1971) were distinctive for their lilt and simplicity, and most of them particularly appealed to children who loved animals. McCord delighted in word-play, and many of his poems had to do with poetry itself, exemplifying types of poetic form; his humour may be seen in the title of his first book of children's poetry, *Far and Few: Rhymes of the Never Was and Always Is* (1952). Livingston is distinguished as an anthologist as well as a poet, and she established her command of form and imagery with her first book, *Whispers and*

*Other Poems* (1958). Ciardi was a master of nonsense and often-caustic humour, as exemplified by *The Man Who Sang the Sillies* (1961). Kuskin is a prolific writer relying on humour and imagination to capture childhood's point of view, as she does in *Alexander Soames: His Poems* (1962) and many other books.

In Britain, the picture-book for very young children was slow to get moving after the war. Distinguished work was done by Edward Ardizzone, notably the 'Tim' books (1951–6), by V. H. Drummond, and by William Stobbs, and the 1960s saw the emergence of new artists such as Raymond Briggs, Victor Ambrus, Brian Wildsmith, John Burningham, and Pat Hutchins, whose most original work still lay ahead. Some of the best work in these years was European, notably the simple and colourful books of the Dutch artist Dick Bruna, and the series which is still the apotheosis of the comic strip, Hergé's *Tintin*.

In contrast, in the USA, the proliferation of fine picture-books, immeasurably enriched by the contributions of European illustrators, had already begun. The work of Roger Duvoisin, who had come to the United States from Switzerland, became known before the war, but it was with his 1948 Caldecott Medal book, *White Snow, Bright Snow*, written by Alvin Tresselt, that he gained a wide audience. Although he used a variety of techniques, most of his work was done in wash with an unfailing sense of design. Usually executed in sunny pastels, Duvoisin's pictures were adapted to the material he was illustrating, so that in the paintings for Gian-Carlo Menotti's *Amahl and the Night Visitors* (1952) he used a range of rich, dark colours that were stunningly appropriate for the dramatic story.

As do many illustrators, Barbara Cooney contributed the art for many books by other people before she became an author as well as an illustrator. Her first work was done in black and white, strong in detail and outstanding for its draughtsmanship. When she turned to colour for the pictures in Lee Kingman's *Peter's Long Walk* (1953), she was already an established artist but won new praise for the softness and delicacy of her colour work. She has won

A tailor, who sailed from Quebec,
In a storm ventured once upon deck;
But the waves of the sea
Were as strong as could be,
And he tumbled in up to his neck.

41

An air of incongruous festivity in the picture brings out the absurdity of the verse in Brian Wildsmith's illustration from *Mother Goose: A Collection of Nursery Rhymes* (1964).

the Caldecott Medal twice, first for her restrainedly styled scratchboard illustrations with brilliant colour, for *Chanticleer and the Fox* in 1959, a deftly adapted variant on Chaucer, and in 1979 for the bucolic pictures, faithful in historical detail, for Donald Hall's *Ox-Cart Man.*

Diverse both in her choices of artistic media and in her style or mood, Marcia Brown began her career with *The Little Carousel* in 1946, gaining almost as much distinction for her articles and lectures on illustrations as she has for her books. No artist in the children's book field has been so catholic in style; her work is always beautifully adapted to the story she is illustrating. She has won the Caldecott Medal three times: first for *Cinderella* in 1955, with its misty pinks and blues echoing Perrault's fairy-tale mood; second for *Once a Mouse* in 1962, in which the stylized coloured woodcuts fit the drama of a tale set in the jungle; third, in 1983 for Blaise Cendrars's *Shadow*, an African poem illustrated with stark silhouettes superimposed on strong colours. In 1992 she was given the Laura Ingalls Wilder Medal for 'a substantial and lasting contribution to literature for children'.

Another artist distinguished for his diversity is Arnold Lobel, who believed that an illustrator should have a wide repertory of styles at his or her command, and whose work showed this range, whether he used wash, pencil, or pen and ink, his favourite medium. His first book, which he wrote and illustrated, was *A Zoo for Mr. Muster* (1962), but most of his work in the 1960s was devoted to illustrating books by other authors. His success with *Frog and Toad are Friends* (1970) was international, and *Frog and Toad Together* was a 1973 Newbery Honour Book, a recognition of the high standard of a first 'chapter book' for beginning independent readers.

Garth Williams had already received honours including the Prix de Rome for sculpture, when he was asked to illustrate his first children's book, E. B. White's *Stuart Little* (1945); he has also distinctively illustrated White's *Charlotte's Web*, the reissue of the Wilder 'Little House' series, Russell Hoban's *Bedtime for Frances* (1960), and George Selden's *The Cricket in Times Square*. Williams's work is always characterized by vigorous composition and authenticity of detail, and it is, perhaps, his ability to instil personality into his characters that is most impressive; no pig could look more complacently smug than Wilbur in *Charlotte's Web*, no father more exasperated by bedtime stalling than the father of Frances, the badger.

The American tradition has used a striking range of techniques, from Ezra Jack Keats's collage and gouache in his urban landscapes for *The Snowy Day* (1962) and *Whistle for Willie* (1964) to the subtle water-colours of Alice and Martin Provensen (perhaps the American equivalents of the British Ahlbergs). They began their partnership in 1952 with *The Animal Fair*, although some of their best work was *The Year at Maple Hill Farm* (1978) and *Glorious Flight: Across the Channel with Louis Blériot* which won the 1984

286

Caldecott Medal. Uri Shulevitz's ink and wash work was also remarkable, notably with *One Monday Morning* (1967), but he used brilliant colours for a cross-cultural and cross-time success, the 1969 Caldecott Medal-winning *The Fool of the World and the Flying Ship* with text taken from Arthur Ransome's *Old Peter's Russian Tales*.

Some of Maurice Sendak's early illustrations were for humorous books like Ruth Krauss's *A Hole is to Dig* (1952) or Sesyle Joslin's *What do You Say, Dear?* (1958), which were showcases for his humour and the lovably absurd children he could create. At the same time, Sendak was showing the sensitivity and compassion that have been persistent characteristics of his art, both in illustrations for other people's stories (Meindert DeJong's books and Else Minarik's *Little Bear*, and a gesture towards Samuel Goodrich, *Higglety Pigglety Pop!* 1967), and for the books he wrote himself, the first of which was *Kenny's Window* (1956). Versatile in interpretation of stories, Sendak used colour and vigour in Charlotte Zolotow's *Mr. Rabbit and the Lovely Present* (1962), gravely beautiful and sophisticated black-and-white pictures for a collection of Grimm tales, *The Juniper Tree* (1973), and bold symbolism in his own *In the Night Kitchen* (1970). The last of these was controversial, as was his abidingly popular *Where the Wild Things Are*, which won the 1964 Caldecott Medal, and the opulently beautiful *Outside Over There* (1981). All of the last three books (Sendak's self-styled trilogy) disturbed some adults because of their frankness or their symbolism, the very qualities that pleased other adult readers.

Maurice Sendak, considered by many to be the greatest twentieth-century American illustrator.

It is rare for an illustrator of children's books to win a Newbery Medal, although William Pène du Bois is not the only artist to achieve this, but even more rare is to have such an artist represented in the Museum of Modern Art. Although he has illustrated the books of other authors, it is for his own work as author/artist that Pène du Bois was most admired, since his stories show a felicitous originality and harmony not often achieved in children's books. The 1948 Newbery Medal was awarded to him for *The Twenty-One Balloons*, a delightfully improbable tale about an arithmetic teacher who is rescued from the Atlantic Ocean, tenaciously clinging to the remains of the balloons.

Since the 1930s William Steig had been known as a humorous artist, particularly for his cartoons in the *New Yorker* magazine. In 1968 he produced two books that delighted children: *Roland the Minstrel Pig* and *CDB!*, which challenged the reader to interpret sentences consisting of only letters. There is a sort of blithe madness in his drawings that is offset by the sweet reasonableness of his text, as in his 1970 Caldecott Medal winner, *Sylvester and the Magic Pebble*. Steig makes it seem perfectly natural that the hero, a young donkey, should turn into a rock because he wished (on a magic pebble) to escape a hungry lion by being a rock—and it seems perfectly natural and eminently satisfying that his lonely parents should just happen to sit on that rock and pick up the pebble just as Sylvester is wishing he could be a donkey again.

In children's literature up to 1970 there was then a subtle balance between new freedoms and old conflicts. In some areas, the United States was unique: Britain had no equivalent to the 'tall tales', of which the post-1945 master was Sid Fleischman, with his Wild West tale of a magician's family travelling by covered wagon, *Mr. Mysterious and Company* (1962). Even more ebullient are the McBroom stories, the first of which appeared in 1966; it is mendaciously entitled *McBroom Tells the Truth*, the story of a farm in which the rich soil produced four crops a day. *The Whipping Boy* won the 1987 Newbery Award and was a picaresque tale of a prince and his whipping boy who ran away together.

Equally, it is difficult to find a writer as sardonic as the *New Yorker*'s E. B. White, whose *Elements of Style* is a standard work. His first children's book, *Stuart Little* (1945), evoked mixed response; there was no dispute over his humour or writing style, but some adults were disturbed by the idea of a mouse being born to human parents. His great classic was and is *Charlotte's Web* (1952), an ambiguous text that moves from realism to fantasy to moral tale, and which can be read on many levels; it has become virtually required reading for every American schoolchild. In E. B. White's third and last book, *The Trumpet of the Swan* (1970), there is a deft meshing of realistic and fanciful details in the story of a mute swan who learns to play the trumpet so that he may woo and win a mate.

And in any literary culture there will be the unclassifiable writers; such as E. B. White, Jane Gardam, T. H. White—and Russell Hoban, whose place as a distinguished writer for adults is secure with books such as *Riddley Walker* (1980). But with his series of six small domestic dramas concerning Frances the badger (from *Bedtime for Frances* (1960)), his inspired collaborations with Quentin Blake (notably *How Tom Beat Captain Najork and his Hired Sportsmen* (1974)), Hoban established himself as not only a good children's writer but (perhaps a natural concomitant) a good commentator on his times. A book like *The Mouse and his Child* (1967) is, classically, appealing to both audiences—deeply existential and moving, very witty and entertaining.

In both Britain and the USA the second 'golden age' established children's literature beyond question as a potent literary force.

# 11 CONTEMPORARY CHILDREN'S LITERATURE

1970–present

*Tony Watkins and Zena Sutherland*

CONTEMPORARY children's literature is a series of paradoxes. There have been several major achievements, but relatively few new writers in Britain; hardback production has declined, paperbacks have boomed; there has been an overproduction of some kinds of books—notably picture-books—and a general underfunding of education; some boundaries have been pushed back with metafictional novels and postmodernist picture-books—and yet internationalism has led to bland commercialism.

Britain suffered economically throughout the first half of the 1970s. The decade began with what was called economic 'stagflation'; spending on books by schools had been low even in 1971 and the education and library budgets were cut steadily throughout the period 1970–5.

Yet, paradoxically, the number of titles of children's books rose steadily during this period, from 2,001 titles in 1971 to 2,688 in 1975. It was not until 1976 that there was a 5 per cent reduction to 2,565. However, the increases conceal the fact that each title had a shorter print run than earlier in the decade: because of cash flow problems, publishers were, as one commentator observed, 'driven inexorably towards shorter print runs, fast selling lines, or both', with the danger that the quality of writing for children would suffer. There was another implication: short print runs affected the structure of roy-alties to children's authors who traditionally relied on their books being re-tained in publishers' lists over several years; by 1977 the Society of Authors was pressing for changes in the contracts offered.

The rise in the cost of block-making, printing, and paper meant that there were fewer illustrations in children's novels and the general inflationary

*Facing, above*: story-telling is alive and well on television. BBC-TV's *Jackanory* began in 1965 and over 650 books had been read by 1990. Here the record holder, Bernard Cribbins (111 programmes by 1992), is on location for *The Wind in the Willows*.

*Below*: *The Chronicles of Narnia*. The Kings and Queens of Narnia with Aslan from C. S. Lewis's *The Lion, the Witch and the Wardrobe* produced by Paul Stone for BBC-TV in 1988. The book had been televised in 1963, by Associated Rediffusion.

pressure throughout the 1970s resulted in a very steep rise in the general cost of hardbound books. Consequently, there was a surge in paperback publishing of children's literature with some originals being published in paperback and others simultaneously in hardback and paperback.

Following some economic recovery in the later 1970s, 3,214 titles were published in 1979, but fears remained that presentation mattered more than content; that the boom in pop-up books of the time, 'whose pages flap and slide and rotate and creak', was 'a tribute to designers' ingenuity, printers' sophistication, publishers' business acumen—and bookbuyers' gullibility'; and that, 'apart from the subliminal message to children that things shaped as books can be fun, they have nothing to do with the magic of the word' (*Children's Books of the Year*, 1979).

The economic trends and anxieties continued into the 1980s. Cuts in money for public libraries, where children's books accounted for 20 per cent of all borrowings, were said to be out of all proportion to the overall cut in Local Authority expenditure. At the same time, the price of children's books rose inexorably.

Librarians were still concerned about the fact that many children's books went out of print before they and other professionals were fully aware of their existence. As the critic Julia Eccleshare noted in 1985:

The result of this policy will be a profound change in our literature. Books, except for an exceptional few, will not pass from generation to generation. They will hardly pass from one school to another, as they will simply not be available. The sharing of books across the years and the common core of a shared reading experience will be lost. (*Children's Books of the Year*)

The commercial ethic fostered by the government in the 1980s brought opportunities for new imprints of children's books, but mergers and take-overs radically changed the structure of children's publishing. The number of titles of children's books went on rising, to the point that in 1991 the number of children's titles published in the United Kingdom (6,154) exceeded by more than 1,000 the number published in the USA (5,111), yet the USA had five times the population. As Alan Giles, managing director of a major chain of bookshops, observed in the *Bookseller* (May 1993):

How can we possibly justify creating 7000 additional children's books each year? What booksellers can hope adequately to display more than a mere handful of these—and often then at the expense of much more saleable backlist titles with greater literary and commercial credentials?

However, others, notably the author Robert Leeson, argued that constantly publishing new titles was the only way to encourage new writers and to compete with the attractions of the electronic media.

Indeed, one of the main concerns in 1993 was for the future of the children's book as such, with the development of 'interactive multimedia', seen by promoters as the 'logical projection of the publishing technology of Gutenberg into the modern digital age'. The interactive books of the future would be electronic with full-colour, full-motion pictures with accompanying soundtrack to support the text and children were seen as one of the biggest markets for such multimedia. Equally, the implementation of a 'National Curriculum'—including lists of books that all state-school children had to read—had implications for book-buying.

Education was a matter of the gravest concern in the USA, but for a different reason. Responding in part to the grim explanation of Rudolf Flesch in *Why Johnny Can't Read* and to a fear that Russian children were far ahead of American children in science education, the United States government in the 1960s passed several bills that made federal money available to libraries: the Library Services and Construction Act, the National Defense Education Act, and the Elementary and Secondary Education Act; both school and public libraries were affected. Since the majority of children's book sales in the 1960s involved the institutional market, publishers responded joyfully to the new budgets of their best customers, expanding their lists and increasing the size of their print runs.

Had the funding continued, it might have affected the literacy levels and reading patterns of a generation. When, in the 1970s, President Nixon dropped the programmes, most publishers had to cut back their staffs and their lists. The adjustment was difficult for librarians, the principal buyers. The brief period of affluence, however, had encouraged some publishers to take risks; one result was that an increasing amount of poetry was published, since financially risky projects could be compensated for by sure sellers. This trend in turn, led to the establishment in 1977 of an award for a poet's body of work by the National Council of Teachers of English. Certainly the successful new paperback market was related to the general economic situation; what began as a tentative programme of buying paperback rights, on the part of a few publishers, led to the frenzied publication of series and reprints that has been called the paperback revolution; this convinced many publishers whose prognosis had been 'a passing fad' to start their own paperback lines.

The same kinds of mergers that took place in Britain occurred in the USA, sometimes resulting in the demise of a children's book department; but another effect was the increased effort to get booksellers to expand stock and publicize children's books. This was so successful that sales to stores have become a much larger percentage of total sales, and many new stores specializing in children's books have been established. In addition to economic factors, several other societal influences made a marked impact on the world of children's books. One was the civil rights movement and the emergent

*Facing*: Fiona French's *King of Another Country* (1992).

291

'black pride', which brought an awareness of the lack of books for or about African-American children; this was emphasized by the appearance in the *Saturday Review* (11 September 1965) of Nancy Larrick's influential article 'The All-White World of Children's Books'. Another was the spectrum of changes in social mores and in language, with a consequent sophistication in young readers (and even more in young adult readers) and the publication of books that broke taboos in non-fiction and especially in fiction, engendering the term 'problem novel'.

Other changes, some of which preceded the 1970s but were most evident in its early and middle years, had to do with new patterns in publishing. One of them was the development of beginning-to-read books that had far more vitality than the 'Up, Spot, up' monotony of curricular material. The pioneers were Dr Seuss, with his *The Cat in the Hat* (1957), and in the same year Harper, with the 'I Can Read' books.

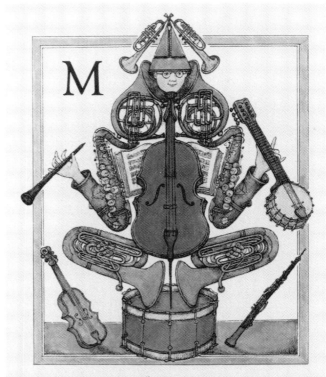

*musical instruments,*

Crowell also began a series of non-fiction with the 'Let's Read and Find Out' books. Another new pattern was the proliferation of folk-tale adaptations, most of them in single-tale picture-books, such as Penelope Proddow's translation of *Dionysos and the Pirates*, illustrated by Barbara Cooney (1970). Some of the folk-tale anthologies incorporated societal issues as well; for example, several compilers reflected the feminist viewpoint, such as Rosemary Minard in *Womenfolk and Fairy Tales* (1975) or Alison Lurie in *Clever Gretchen and Other Forgotten Folktales* (1980).

Children's literature was also being recognized as part of the mainstream of literature, and its study in colleges and universities grew rapidly. Although this was initially in library schools and education departments, children's literature increasingly became a normal feature of English Literature departments. In 1992, the Children's Literature Association issued a *Directory of Graduate Studies in Children's Literature* which listed courses at over 200 institutions. Landmarks included the establishment of the critical and scholarly journals *The Lion and the Unicorn* (Johns Hopkins University Press) and

*Above*: Anita Lobel's ingenuity as shown in the *On Market Street* alphabet book (1981).

*Facing*: Anthony Browne, renowed as the author-illustrator of works such as *Gorilla* (1985) and *Changes* (1990), catches the surreal quality of Carroll's classic in the award-winning illustrations to *Alice in Wonderland* (1988).

*Children's Literature* (Yale University Press), and the Children's Literature Division of a prestigious academic organization in the humanities, the Modern Language Association. A growing corpus of serious literary criticism has emerged and established authors of adult books have chosen to write also for children. A stellar example is Isaac Bashevis Singer, with autobiography (*A Day of Pleasure: Stories of a Boy Growing Up in Warsaw*, 1969) and retold folk-stories (*The Fools of Chelm and their History*, 1973).

Although academic recognition has taken longer in Britain, there are now established postgraduate courses, and the period from 1970 has been one of extraordinary activity in the discussion of the subject. Debate has developed about whether the evaluation of children's books should be carried out according to purely literary criteria or whether social criteria, in particular the representation of gender and ethnicity, should be taken into account and, if so, to what extent.

During the 1980s this trend continued, bringing the full range of literary theory to bear on children's literature as a discipline.

### VERSIONS OF HISTORY

If the period 1945–70 was a very rich time for historical fiction in the USA, the period since 1970 has seen some notable British work in this field. Like Kipling, Rosemary Sutcliff believed that the disintegration of the Roman empire and the onset of the Dark Ages 'contain truths for our own time' because 'we have the same uncertainty the Romans must have had whether the light would show up again at the end of the tunnel'. The emphasis in her novels is on the continuity of history and the values of honour, loyalty, and sacrifice. In 1977 she published *Sun Horse, Moon Horse*, set around the Iron Age making of the White Horse on the Berkshire Downs. As in her earlier novels, what stands out is the superb evocation of landscape and the rhetorical flourish of the language which, in this case, endows the final death with transcendent significance. In *Song for a Dark Queen* (1978), she focused on a female hero in telling the tragic story of Boudicca, who must seek revenge for the treatment she receives from the Romans. One of her last books, *The Shining Company* (1990), is a story of the heroic defeat of the 'Companions' against the Saxons.

In 1972 Jill Paton Walsh launched an attack upon those who would dismiss the historical novel for children in the name of the 'cult of contemporaneity' by vigorously arguing that 'any writer interpreting the past uses nearly the whole of his knowledge of the present'; thus, 'a novel is a historical novel when it is wholly or partly about the public events and social conditions which are the material of history, regardless of the time at which it is written'. But what the novel says about history must be through character and event, not merely setting. Further, she argued, the work of the novelist and that of

294

the historian are closely related, for both impose narrative coherence upon the flux of experience. Her own historical novels include the award-winning *The Emperor's Winding-Sheet* (1974). This is set in Constantinople at the time of the fall of the Byzantine empire, but, seen from the perspective of an English boy, the history of the society and the individual come to be closely interwoven. *A Chance Child* (1978) is a strange mixture of genres: part historical fiction set among the suffering of children during the Industrial Revolution, and part time fantasy. *A Parcel of Patterns* (1983) is the story of a Derbyshire village which heroically accepted isolation during the plague of 1665 to save other communities. It is simultaneously a novel of public events, meticulously researched, and, on the personal level, a tragic and moving love story. *Grace* (1991) retells the heroic act of Grace Darling but examines the resentment from the local community, who would have been paid for carrying out the rescue from the shipwreck.

Writers of historical fiction, according to Robert Leeson, may look back to the past from two different motives: one is 'to seek consciously or unconsciously the stability that is not ours today. The other is to seek the movement and development *then* which is the essence of our *now*.' He is clearly more sympathetic to the latter approach, which he relates to the novels of Geoffrey Trease. His own preoccupations in writing the historical trilogy *Maroon Boy* (1974), *Bess* (1975), and *The White Horse* (1977) were '20th century ones, the fight against the oppression of black people, of women, of working people', but the problem he recognized was the problem of all historical fiction: how to illuminate the past by seeking 'recognizable elements', without imposing a '20th century view'.

Barbara Willard's 'recognizable element' is the family, in her series of eight novels published between 1970 and 1980 which make up the Mantlemass saga. *The Lark and the Laurel* (1970) takes place towards the end of the Wars of the Roses; *A Cold Wind Blowing* (1973), which shows how the

Robin Jacques's humorous drawing adorns the cover of one of Ruth Manning-Sanders's vigorous retelling of traditional stories.

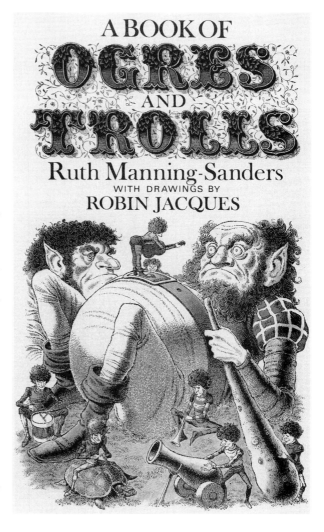

A BOOK OF OGRES AND TROLLS

Ruth Manning-Sanders

WITH DRAWINGS BY ROBIN JACQUES

dissolution of the monasteries affected the lives of ordinary men and women, is generally regarded as the best of the books, and the saga ends in the Civil War. The strength of Willard's work lies in its evocation of the Sussex countryside and in the way she shows how major historical events impinge on the lives of ordinary people.

In contrast, Leon Garfield's is an art of exaggeration, and he has argued that, for most of his novels, the eighteenth-century setting is more of a locality than a time, in which he can represent quite contemporary characters more vividly than he could otherwise: thus his 'historical romances' are not attempts to escape from contemporary life, but attempts 'to view certain aspects of it more clearly and with less clutter'. Placing familiar things in an unfamiliar context allows us to see them and ourselves afresh and thus enlarge our imagination. But there is a didactic purpose too: 'If the young discover that in the past they have been governed, led, abused, and slaughtered by fools and knaves, then perhaps they will look about them and see that matters have not greatly changed, and possibly they will do so before they vote.'

Thus, as the protagonists of *John Diamond* (1980) or *The December Rose* (1986) or *The Empty Sleeve* (1988) pursue their adventure quests for friendship, love, truth, and identity, in a world of mystery and deception, where good and evil are frequently disguised as each other, his novels represent, in fiction, our own contemporary ideological uncertainties about belief and value. But humour in one form or another is present in all of Garfield's novels, and is exemplified most clearly in the hilarious plot convolutions of *The Strange Affair of Adelaide Harris* (1971) and of the sequel, *Bostock and Harris; or, The Night of the Comet* (1979), set in the Regency period.

Joan Aiken believes in the blending of humour and history by 'using the past as a kind of flexible medium, or springboard, adhering to the spirit of history, and to the letter only as much as may be convenient', and her series of 'gothic fantasies' which began with *The Wolves of Willoughby Chase* continued after 1970 with the complexities

Jan Pieńkowski is a versatile author and illustrator. Creator of the popular *Meg and Mog* series, he also won an award for illustrations such as this to Joan Aiken's *The Kingdom Under the Sea* (1971).

of *The Cuckoo Tree* (1971) and *The Stolen Lake* (1981), in the first of which the resourceful Dido Twite outwits a Hanoverian plot to roll St Paul's Cathedral into the Thames during the coronation of the new king, Richard IV.

Penelope Lively has a mistrust of the historical novel because of the danger of didacticism. Her particular preoccupation as a writer is, she says, 'with memory. Both with memory in the wide historical sense and memory in the personal sense.' She draws a distinction between history ('linear and chronological and public') and memory ('that marvellous process of recollection interspersed with oblivion that goes on inside our heads'). Her novels often use fantasy because, to her, memory itself is a kind of fantasy and because, in one sense, we make up our past. Similarly, the fascination with landscape in her novels is related to her interest in memory and her work as a novelist: layers of the landscape are layers of memory and a good novel for children, she argues, should operate in a similar way—through layers of meaning. All her novels are subtle explorations of complex but important themes for children. Her first novel for children, *Astercote* (1970), is about the remains of a medieval village that somehow retains a memory of the plague that once afflicted it. In *The Driftway* (1972) she tries to explore the notion of landscape as a channel for historical memory by setting the novel on a road that is simultaneously modern and ancient. The Carnegie Medal-winning *The Ghost of Thomas Kempe* (1973) is a light-hearted ghost story with the serious concern of encouraging children to become aware of the 'layers of memory of which people are composed'. *The House in Norham Gardens* (1974) is where Clare lives with her great-aunts and their relics, including a ceremonial shield that her anthropologist great-grandfather brought back from New Guinea. Clare dreams of the people to whom the shield once belonged and sees in her dreams how time and place and object are related in their culture and in ours.

There is an argument for grouping together historical fiction and science fiction for children. Writing historical fiction, says Leon Garfield, is like 'science fiction in reverse: you take a moral problem out of context to observe it better; you have the reality of the past to latch on to', and Patrick Parrinder has observed that 'the "other worlds" of science fiction must always be positively or negatively valued in relation to our own' because the essential purpose of science fiction is the 'presentation of a "distancing" vision, leading to social criticism' (*Science Fiction, Its Criticism and Teaching*, 1980). Thus John Christopher, Britain's most notable writer in the genre, calls himself a writer of 'historical novels set in the future'. In *The Guardians* (1970) he followed H. G. Wells in extrapolating the existing class system: Britain is divided into two halves: the Conurb, a nightmare projection of modern cities, and the County, a rural paradise of Edwardian houses and carriages.

The form has attracted one of the major contemporary 'realist' writers, Jan Mark, whose trilogy *The Ennead* (1978), *Divide and Rule* (1979), and

*Aquarius* (1982) was written around the central idea of manipulation, and the novels have been called 'metaphysical thrillers'.

## CONTEMPORARY LIVES

As the 'teenager' emerged during the 1970s as a distinct cultural category, so the debates increased about what kind of books were suitable for these 'older children' or 'young adults'. What kind of stories were best for an age group which experienced particular kinds of emotional and maturational changes? Did they need fantasy or realism? Publishers responded with series specifically written for Young Adults or New Adults, some of which were intended to address the 'problems of adolescence' under the influence of the 'bibliotherapy' movement in the USA.

As we have seen, the groundwork for the 'teenage novel' had been laid by writers like Paul Zindel and Louise Fitzhugh; after 1970, this genre flourished, the most common form being the demotic first-person narrative, often—but unfairly—traced to the huge success of J. D. Salinger's *The Catcher in the Rye* (1951). John Donovan's *I'll Get There, It had Better be Worth the Trip* (1969) was controversial because of its treatment of homosexuality, although some critics thought it an act of courage on the part of both author and editor and felt that the subject was handled with dignity. Whether he wrote realistic stories (*Wild in the World*, 1971) or moved into fantasy (*Family*, 1976) Donovan wrote with clear vision and a remarkably powerful style.

Even the title of M. E. Kerr's first book caused a stir: *Dinky Hocker Shoots Smack!* (1972). In fact, Dinky is not interested in drugs, but only in having her mother pay attention to her. Kerr won readers and praise for her wit and humour, her perceptive characterization, and her ear for dialogue. All of these qualities and a flair for narrative development are also found in other Kerr books: *I'll Love You When You're More Like Me* (1977) or *Little Little* (1981), a sensitive story of 'little people', often called dwarfs, or the most sober of her books, *Gentlehands* (1978), the story of a teenager distraught because his grandfather is reputed to have helped run a German concentration camp.

An author of great variety, Richard Peck published his first book in 1972, a story about premarital pregnancy, *Don't Look and It Won't Hurt. Are You in the House Alone?* (1976) is the story of a babysitter raped by one of the most respectable boys in town. Peck is astute in his perspectives and a polished writer, whether he is presenting problem novels or humorous ghost stories like *Blossom Culp and the Sleep of Death* (1986) or a story of rites of passage like *Unfinished Portrait of Jessica* (1991).

With a background in clinical psychology, it is not surprising that Jan Slepian writes authoritatively about children with disabilities. With her first two books, *The Alfred Summer* (1980) and its 1981 sequel, *Lester's Turn*, which deal with the relationship between a victim of cerebral palsy and his retarded friend, Slepian also shows a gift for percipient characterization, a quiet humour, and a silky-smooth writing style. She uses a literary device successfully in *The Broccoli Tapes* (1989), telling the story through transcriptions of tapes sent to a teacher; in *Back to Before* (1993) Slepian blends time travel with the opportunity it gives two children to obliterate circumstances that have changed their lives.

Lois Lowry won the prize given annually to a first-time author by the International Reading Association for *A Summer to Die* (1977), a poignant story of a girl's adjustment to her sister's terminal illness. *Autumn Street* (1980) is a candid and memorable story of an interracial friendship, but between these two Lowry produced the first of a series of humorous books about a wonderfully precocious character—*Anastasia Krupnik* (1979)—that are as effervescent as champagne. To prove her diversity, Lowry won the 1990 Newbery Medal for a historical novel, *Number the Stars*, a taut story based on the rescue operation mounted by their friends to save Danish Jews from a Nazi roundup. (In 1993 Lowry broke new ground with a chilling and challenging utopian novel, *The Giver*.)

The books that Walter Myers has written for younger readers have been well received, but he is best known for books for and about adolescents. Many of his books are humorous although they deal with matters of substance; in *The Young Landlords* (1979) he gives a positive picture of an African-American neighbourhood as a group of teenagers acquires and renovates a slum building. *Motown and Didi: A Love Story* (1984) is a tender story despite its grim milieu, and in *Somewhere in Darkness* (1992) Myers reaches new depths of characterization and nuances in relationships in a trenchant novel about a boy's painful realization that he cannot achieve a bonding with his just-out-of-prison father. *Fallen Angels* (1988) is probably the most powerful young adult novel about Vietnam to date.

Many books in this genre have been unfairly dismissed because of what they *appear* to be. One underrated writer is Norma Klein, who in *Mom, the Wolf Man, and Me* (1972) introduces an illegitimate child who is perfectly happy with her lot and hopes that Mom does not marry. A 14-year-old adjusts to the separation of her parents in *It's Not What You Expect* (1973), and in *Learning How to Fall* (1989) Klein examines the concept that what you want may not be best for you.

In *Homecoming* (1981) Cynthia Voigt introduces 13-year-old Dicey, who marches her three younger siblings, all abandoned, from New England to Maryland to join their tough, crusty grandmother. The second book, *Dicey's Song* (1982), won the Newbery Medal and was followed by several other books in which the children mature and cope with difficulties. *A Solitary Blue* (1983) is the most sophisticated of these linked novels. Like this intensely real

In *Amazing Grace* (1991) by Mary Hoffman, illustrated by Caroline Binch, Grace, the girl who loves stories, learns an important lesson: 'If Grace put her mind to it—she can do anything she want.'

fiction, Voigt's fantasy trilogy, which concludes with *The Wings of a Falcon* (1993), comprises books that are beautifully sustained.

Patricia MacLachlan, who has done some excellent writing for young children and who is best known for *Sarah, Plain and Tall* (1985), which won the Newbery Medal, seems destined to produce dependably that rare commodity, good books for the intermediate reader. An atmosphere of family love, a strong element in many of MacLachlan's stories, pervades *Arthur, for the Very First Time* (1980), the story of a shy boy of 10, and also *Unclaimed Treasures* (1984). Familial love and acceptance of a child's death are the focus of *Baby* (1993), and in *The Facts and Fictions of Minna Pratt* (1988) Minna admires the conventional parents of her friend Luke but comes to understand why he enjoys her nonconformist parents.

Katherine Paterson was already well known as the author of three fine historical novels about feudal Japan (*The Sign of the Chrysanthemum*, 1973; *Of*

*Nightingales that Weep*, 1974; and *The Master Puppeteer*, 1976, winner of the National Book Award) when she delighted her fans with *Bridge to Terabithia* (1977), which won the Newbery Medal. This is a classic, both as a story of friendship and as a touching story about adjustment to death. As in *The Great Gilly Hopkins* (1978, another winner of the National Book Award), Paterson's compassion is pervasive, and her language simple but eloquent. For older readers *Jacob Have I Loved*, winner of the 1981 Newbery Medal, is a moving tale of the taut relationship between twin sisters. Paterson's adaptation of a Japanese folk-tale, *The Tale of the Mandarin Ducks* (1990), is as elegant as are the illustrations by Leo and Diane Dillon. If evidence of her versatility were needed it would be provided by *Lyddie* (1991), a smoothly told story of industrial oppression and women's rights, set in a New England mill town in 1843.

Books like these are rather more in the restrained mould of their British counterparts, like Jean Ure. But the greatest controversy has centred on two writers, one accused of exposing older children to a savage, amoral world, the other—among the most successful writers of children's books ever—of pandering to the worst self-indulgent weaknesses of adolescence: Robert Cormier and Judy Blume.

With *The Chocolate War* (1974) Robert Cormier's exploration of human evil and of peer and priest pressure in a Roman Catholic school brought him immediate, if controversial, fame; not until 1985 did the sequel, *Beyond the Chocolate War*, appear. *I Am the Cheese* (1977) attracted just as much attention, although in this case it had more to do with the intricacy of the chronology and the use of interpolated interviews. *After the First Death* (1979) deals with the hijacking by a terrorist of a busload of children, and in *The Bumblebee Flies Anyway* (1983) Cormier describes the courage and desperation of terminally ill adolescents.

Although she had written two books for younger children and later some light and amusing novels like *Tales of a Fourth Grade Nothing* (1972), it was with the publication in 1970 of *Are You There God? It's Me, Margaret* that Judy Blume achieved instant popularity with adolescent readers and instant condemnation from some adults. Right out in the open, there was a teenager fretting about mammary development, menstruation, and religious choice. In *Forever* (1976) young lovers find that passion can end; again, controversy and even censorship resulted. Blume is deeply concerned about young people and their coming-of-age problems: obesity in *Blubber* (1974), parental separation in *Just As Long As We're Together* (1987), and the problems of a gifted child in its companion volume, *Here's to You, Rachel Robinson* (1993).

With the setting up of the *Children's Book Bulletin* and the Children's Rights Workshop Other Award for 'non-biased' books of literary merit Britain became caught up with the debate about whether social and ideological criteria as well as aesthetic and literary criteria should apply in the critical evaluation of children's and adolescents' fiction. The debate was outlined most clearly at the end of the 1970s, when fear was expressed that 'guidelines' would be 'imposed' on writers concerning the use of 'non-sexist' and 'non-racist' language. On the one hand, writers like Jill PatoWalsh argued that, 'With a fervour reminiscent of Christian didacts of the 19th century, some people think it wrong to portray for children the world as it is or was, and believe instead it should be shown only as it ought to be; sanitising reality in order to change it.' On the other, critics like Rosemary Stones replied,

The frequent demand from those in the field, for example, for guidelines to assess racism and sexism in children's books has been hailed with glee as the thin edge of the censorial wedge ('rules for writers!') instead of being understood for what it really is—a request for *tools* for understanding the nature of bias in literature (however laborious and mechanistic such tools may be!).

The question of 'identity' became a crucial one during the period: confusion over national identity, sexual identity, and ethnic identity was often focused on what were perceived as the 'problems' of growing up, particularly during the period of adolescence, and how these were to be represented in literature.

Bernard Ashley's novels draw on his extensive experience as a teacher and each of them tells, in his words, 'of a child's attempt to cope with a crisis point in life, each crisis presenting a problem as serious at the time as any he will later have to face as an adult', and he hopes that 'some children, somewhere, whose stresses may not even have been guessed at, can draw comfort from fictional parallels'. For example, in *The Trouble with Donovan Croft* (1974), a West Indian child loses the power of speech when his mother apparently deserts him and he is fostered by a white family.

Contemporary themes were explored in many books. The troubles in Northern Ireland were the background to a quintet of novels by Joan Lingard: *The Twelfth of July* (1970), *Across the Barricades* (1972), *Into Exile* (1973), *A Proper Place* (1975), and *Hostages to Fortune* (1976); Janni Howker's novel *The Nature of the Beast* (1985) vividly depicted the despair of unemployment in a contemporary Lancashire mill town, and the beast that stalks the community is as much symbolic as it is real; Berlie Doherty's *Dear Nobody* (1991) sensitively explored what could have become a cliché, the experience of teenage pregnancy, through the use of parallel narratives including letters to the unborn child; and Gillian Cross's award-winning *Wolf* (1990) is a complex novel with many layers of meaning which combines an exciting thriller about the IRA with the exploration of the psychological maturation of a 13-year-old girl.

To some writers, like Nina Bawden, too many critics in the 1970s were preoccupied with 'fashionable social problems', and praised books which were 'about poor children, handicapped children, children in one-parent families', assuring that such books showed the world as it is. Instead, she argued for 'emotional realism' in which 'poverty, divorce, and cruelty' would have their place, as in books for adults, as 'part of a fully realized story, not dragged in to satisfy some educational or social theory'. Her own novels bear out the strength of her argument. *Squib* (1971) is ostensibly about an abused and lonely little boy but the focus is on the reactions of the other children, who do not quite understand what is going on. *Carrie's War* (1973) is a sensitive portrayal of two children uprooted by war from their home as evacuees in a Welsh town, and we see the characters from the point of view of the children with their guilty fears. *The Peppermint Pig* (1975), the simple narrative of a year in the life of an Edwardian family whose father has gone off to America to seek his fortune, embodies what one critic has described as 'the painful relationship of happiness, hope and the inexorable passing of time'.

Anne Fine demonstrated that writing for adolescents and depicting contemporary family life could blend humour with a discussion of topics such as

David McKee's illustrations for his postmodern picture-book, *I Hate My Teddy Bear* (1982), are full of mysterious, often bizarre, details.

divorce, nuclear disarmament, and sexual stereotyping. In *Madam Doubtfire* (1987), Daniel, an actor, prevented by his divorced wife from seeing his children as often as he wants, dresses up as Madam Doubtfire and works as housekeeper in his wife's house; and in *Goggle-Eyes* (1989) Anne Fine explores the difficulty of adjusting to a new stepfather in a way which, although comic, does not evade questions of sexuality, divorce, and social responsibility.

As in the USA, the realistic mode has produced some notable and influential books, with sophisticated narratives. Jill Paton Walsh's *Goldengrove* (1972) and *Unleaving* (1976) have been called her tribute to Virginia Woolf. Goldengrove is a house on the Cornish coast which provides the holiday setting for an exploration of Madge's developing adolescent feelings and her relationship with Paul (whom she had always regarded as just a cousin) and Ralph, the blind professor of literature. In the later novel there is a complex interweaving of narrative strands which involves Madge preparing for university and her relationship with Patrick; the tragic experience he has with his mentally handicapped sister; and Madge, sixty years on, ultimately finding fulfilment. *Gaffer Samson's Luck* (1984), by contrast, is a simple but very moving novel set in a Fenland village, of an old dying man, Gaffer Samson, and the young James who comes to love the landscape and the people. Jill Paton Walsh's work as a whole displays a deep commitment to humanist values articulated through a fine sensitive intelligence in both her novels and her discussion of the art and craft of children's literature.

Realism also provided the base for a remarkable sequence of novels about adolescence, independence, and sexual identity which brought postmodernist concepts into the children's novel: Aidan Chambers's *Breaktime* (1978), *Dance on my Grave* (1982), *Now I Know* (1987), and *The Toll Bridge* (1992) in a sense redefine children's literature.

But not all writers who concentrated on the theme of growing up wrote within the realistic mode. Robert Westall's powerful evocation of England during the Second World War, *The Machine-Gunners* (1975), in which an adolescent gang retrieve a machine gun from a crashed German aircraft, did involve a realistic portrayal of growing up in a society of violence. But his later books used fantasy and science-fiction elements and in *Gulf* (1992), a novel about the Gulf War, Westall used the device of a mysterious sharing of minds between an adolescent in England and a young Iraqi soldier.

## THE PROGRESS OF FANTASY

Although many of the important children's novels of the last twenty-five years have used realism as the main mode of writing, some have combined realistic and fantasy elements and there has also been a continuing thread of fantasy itself, some of it serious, some comic.

Susan Cooper's 'Dark is Rising' quintet (or 'pentagram' as one commentator has called it) *Over Sea, under Stone* (1965), *The Dark is Rising* (1973), *Greenwitch* (1974), *The Grey King* (1975), and *Silver on the Tree* (1977) restates the eternal battle between the forces of the Light and the forces of the Dark. The 'high fantasy' sequence, with its reworking of myth and legend and material from the Arthurian cycle, has been criticized for the thinness of characterization and ambiguity in the presentation of good and evil. But the latter is probably quite deliberate in Cooper's attempt to explore the duality of human nature ('the endless coexistence of kindness and cruelty, love and hate, forgiveness and revenge', as she put it), and the relevance of medievalism in the modern world. Cooper is perhaps the paradigm for internationalism in children's books. Born in Buckinghamshire in 1935, she has lived and worked in the USA since 1963: *The Grey King* won the Newbery Medal and the Welsh Arts Council's Tir na n-Óg award. For younger readers she has a lighter, often humorous touch, as in *Jethro and the Jumbie* (1979) and an adaptation of a Celtic legend, *The Selkie Girl* (1986).

The other major achievement in fantasy was Ursula Le Guin's 'Earthsea' quartet, *A Wizard of Earthsea* (1968), *The Tombs of Atuan* (1971), *The Farthest Shore* (1972), and *Tehanu* (1990), which is distinguished from most other secondary-worlds adventures by the dense symbolism and psychological depth of the characters. As Jill Paton Walsh has observed: the books concern 'moral dangers, the moral triumphs of the inner world, seen with a fierce clarity . . . The author's vision is suffused with Jungian psychology.' It is an interesting comment on the development of feminism that the final volume, *Tehanu*, takes a revisionist view of the role of male and female in Earthsea, providing a uniquely female victory. Le Guin's diverse talents are evident in *Very Far Away from Anywhere Else* (1976), a perceptive contemporary story about two adolescents. In *Catwings* (1988) and *Catwings Return* (1989) she writes engagingly for younger children about flying kittens.

There are few fantasy writers who can stand beside Cooper and Le Guin in terms of intelligence and originality, although one is Natalie Babbitt, who adds a benign humour and a relish for word-play; these qualities enliven *Knee-Knock Rise* (1970), in which an entire village is terrified by the non-existent Megrimum, and the short stories of *The Devil's Storybook* (1976). The mood and style of what is undoubtedly her most impressive book, *Tuck Everlasting* (1975), are quite different: it is a story about immortality, so smoothly crafted that the deep implications do not obscure the action.

Prolific writers like Jane Yolen in the USA and Diana Wynne Jones and Helen Cresswell in Britain have added to the variety of fantasy, from Yolen's ingenious *Sleeping Ugly* (1981) to Cresswell's eccentric side-glances at English eccentricities such as *Up the Pier* (1972).

The animal story has maintained its popularity in Britain with the cheer-

*Facing*: Michael Foreman took a four-week trip to India to research his luminous water-colours for Madhur Jaffrey's *Seasons of Splendour* (1985).

ful work of Dick King-Smith and the hugely successful Animals of Farthing Wood sequence by Colin Donn. The most spectacular success of the 1970s was Richard Adams's *Watership Down* (1972). Initially rejected by several leading publishing houses, it was published by the relatively unknown Rex Collings, but later by Puffin and Penguin and it broke the record for the sale of paperback rights in the USA. It is an epic animal adventure story in which rabbits are anthropomorphized with their own history, language, and mythology, but at the same time conform to what is known of rabbit life. The novel is a rich blend of fantasy and realism, combining a striking evocation of the English countryside with traditional, male-dominated ideas of leadership and culture—and its commercial exploitation set a pattern for marketing that is now standard.

But the true international publishing phenomenon of the period is Roald Dahl; already known as a writer of highly intelligent short stories for adults (*Kiss Kiss* (1960) ), he began writing for children in the 1960s and his success in the 1970s and 1980s has outpaced even Enid Blyton. Dahl's first three books (discounting *The Gremlins*, a wartime story that added a new word to the language) were first published in the USA and it took some time (six years in the case of *James and the Giant Peach* (1961) ) for them to get to Britain. Since then, his iconoclastic fantasies (including *Charlie and the Chocolate Factory* (USA 1964, Britain 1967), a moral tale on the lines of *Struwwelpeter*) have become part of world culture.

However, the response among adults to Dahl's writing was very divided:

Roald Dahl, one of the most popular and controversial children's writers of the twentieth century. His grotesquely comic books seem objectionable to some adults, but are read enthusiastically by children.

306

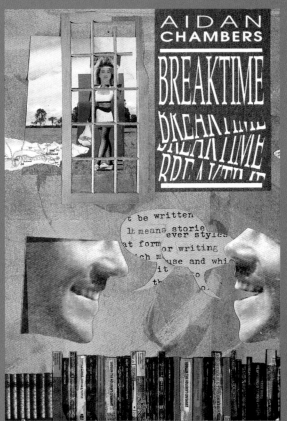

some praised what they called the clear-cut characters, the grotesque villains, the wit, the incidents both dramatic and hilarious; others considered his work bizarre, unethical, sentimental, and nauseating. For example, in *The Twits* (1980) Dahl created in Mr and Mrs Twit one of the most repellent couples in children's fiction; as in other books by Dahl, the adults divide into the stereotypes we find in comic books, and thus there is a strong attraction for children in 'the oppositional culture' of Dahl's work. As Dahl explained, 'Children are terribly rude compared with us snotty grown-ups. They're coarse and crude and rude.' Dahl followed this line of thinking with *Revolting Rhymes* (1982), an irreverent retelling in verse of fairy-tales, and a series of international best sellers such as *The BFG* (1982), which has the temerity to include the Queen of England as a character, *The Witches* (1983), much criticized for apparent misogyny, and *Matilda* (1988), a morality tale which appeals equally to adults of a child prodigy who eventually defeats the sadistic adults in her life. Dahl's autobiographies, *Boy* (1984) and *Going Solo* (1986), have also—perhaps ruthlessly—been marketed for children. Whatever his merits, the case of Roald Dahl is an illuminating one when we consider the status of children's literature today.

There has been interest in both the USA and Britain in retellings: Ashley Bryan and Margaret Hodges's work in the USA being among the best. One instructive comparison is between retellings of the Greek myths in the two countries. Bernard Evslin, who had already blended the sonorous narrative style of traditional story-telling with modern American idiom in *The Green Hero: Early Adventures of Finn McCool* (1975), produced *Greeks Bearing Gifts: The Epics of Achilles and Ulysses* in 1976, with such sentences as 'Screaming like Harpies, Athena and Hera flew back to Olympus, flung themselves before Zeus, and tried to get Aphrodite disqualified for illegal use of hands.' In Britain, Leon Garfield and the critic Edward Blishen tried their hands at the same thing in *The God beneath the Sea* (1970) and *The Golden Shadow* (1973), the first of which won the Carnegie Medal. Lines like 'in a white passion of wings [he] quenched his restless heat' produced varied responses. The Poet Laureate, Ted Hughes, pronounced them 'genuine dramatic retellings', 'an intense, highly coloured, primitive atmosphere'; Alan Garner regarded the prose as 'overblown Victoriana, "fine" writing at its worst, cliché-ridden to the point of satire, falsely poetic', and felt that the only worthwhile thing about the text was Charles Keeping's illustrations.

One of these connections with traditional material has been in the work of the American Robin McKinley, whose retellings—or revisionings—of tales produced a Maid Marian who is the leader of the outlaws, as well as being a better archer than the rather anxious Robin Hood (*The Outlaws of Sherwood* (1988)), and, in *Beauty* (1978), a female hero who finds books by Browning and Kipling in the Beast's library.

*Facing (clockwise from above left)*: covers for Aidan Chambers's *Breaktime* from 1992, 1978, and 1985.

ACROSS THE GENRES

There is obviously a danger in discussing children's literature largely in terms of genres: some writers' work defies classification or else crosses several generic boundaries.

Peter Dickinson's work for children and young adults since 1970 has been quite remarkable for its imaginative range, from *The Dancing Bear* (1972), an adventure story which opens in Byzantium in the sixth century AD, to *Tulku* (1979), set in China at the time of the Boxer rebellion, or *The Blue Hawk* (1976), set in a society resembling ancient Egypt. Dickinson's interest in the imagination and the metaphor of the mask is explored further in *Healer* (1983) and *Eva* (1989). In *Healer*, the girl Pinkie has the gift of healing migraine which is exploited by the false Foundation of Harmony. *Eva* has the extraordinary central metaphor of a girl whose mind is given the body of a chimpanzee and she becomes the first woman of a new race of creatures who will outlive the decay of technocratic civilization. In these novels Dickinson's superb abilities as a story-teller are evident: the surface adventure or science-fiction plot becomes the way to raise important but disturbing questions about psychology or the ethics of technology.

Equally difficult to categorize are Lawrence Yep's books about Chinese-Americans. Yep's second novel *Dragonwings* (1975) gives a vivid picture of the Chinese immigrants' community in California at the turn of the century. *Dragon's Gate* (1993) is set in the Sierra Nevada Mountains in 1867; 14-year-old Otter, the narrator, describes the bitter cold and the harsh working conditions of Chinese labourers. Some of the characters appeared earlier in *The Serpent's Children* (1984) and *Mountain Light* (1985). In addition to this excellent historical fiction, Yep has created an admirable series of fantasies that began in 1982 with *Dragon of the Lost Sea*, narrated by Shimmer, a centuries-old dragon, whose adventures are continued in several additional books. His first book, *Sweetwater* (1973), was a fast-paced, imaginative science-fiction novel, set on the intricately conceived planet of Harmony. In *The Rainbow People* (1989) twenty stories are adapted from a 1930s oral narrative project in Oakland's Chinatown. When Yep turns to contemporary realistic fiction, he is astute in creating characters and situations in which change and interaction are believably paced and psychologically convincing. This is the case in *Sea Glass* (1979), in which Craig and his cousins, Chinese-Americans all, differ in their feelings about their cultural heritage. The same situation is explored in *Child of the Owl* (1977), in which a girl who has not yet adjusted to her Chinese heritage changes when she learns to love the grandmother she has hardly known hitherto.

William Mayne stands as a total contrast to Roald Dahl. He is a prolific writer whose work is considered by some to be admired much more by adult critics and other writers than by children. But, as Edward Blishen put it, 'those who argue that William Mayne is an adult's children's writer and not a children's children's writer are expressing nothing more than guesses'. Mayne's reputation for work of great literary quality was established well before 1970 with novels such as the 'Chorister Quartet', *A Grass Rope* (1957), and *Earthfasts* (1967). In the years since then, he has confirmed that he is a distinguished writer who is able to work in many genres: from the psychological explorations of *A Game of Dark* (1971), to fantasies such as *Antar and the Eagles* (1989). Although his work is firmly rooted in local British landscapes he is an international writer: in *The Jersey Shore* (1973) an American boy learns something of the roots of his family through the memories of his grandfather, who came originally from England. The novel ends with a moving assertion of the boy's ethnic identity and a promise in love of a new life (although the ending of the American edition was changed to play down the boy's mixed ethnic origins). Mayne's ability to explore the importance of other cultures' perceptions of the world and the often limited quality of the European view is exemplified in *Drift* (1985), where a dangerous journey is told first from the point of view

William Mayne, a writer of immense range, whose name is synonymous with high literary quality.

of a white boy, then from that of an Indian girl; in *Low Tide* (1992), which explores Maori and European views of what it means to be cultured and civilized; and in his analysis of Australian city life, *Salt River Times* (1980). Russell Hoban has said of him, 'Mayne is technically unlimited—he can do anything with words', and his facility with language reveals itself through the dialogue, and the word-play of his elliptical, often humorous, style. It is a pity, laments the writer Kevin Crossley-Holland, that there is no Nobel-type award for children's literature: 'not to be given for a single work but for an *œuvre*, a distinguished succession of books written over a number of decades. Such an award would suit William Mayne.'

Landscape and language are two key elements in Alan Garner's work as well. His major works since 1970 have been *Red Shift* (1973) and 'The Stone Book Quartet'. *Red Shift* makes great demands on the reader: three parallel time strands, Britain at the time of the Romans, the seventeenth century, and the present, interweave themselves through the book in an elliptical style: the narrative shifts without warning from one strand to another. What link the three strands are themes of betrayal, jealousy, revenge, and violence. At the end of the novel, the three strands come together in an extraordinary climax of madness, for the novel suggests that all time exists at once: Roman Britain and the My-Lai massacre are now. All three time sequences occur at the same place, in the landscape of north-east Cheshire which forms one of the crucial metaphors in 'The Stone Book Quartet': *The Stone Book* (1976), *Tom Fobble's Day* (1977), *Granny Reardun* (1977), and *The Aimer Gate* (1978). These four short stories of family life are in part Garner's attempt to reconcile himself to an intellectual education which estranged him from his family's line of rural craftsmen. As Margery Fisher has put it, 'The Stone Book Quartet' consists of 'four meticulously linked books about strata (of people and stone), about continuity (of family and buildings) and about change (of occupations and outlooks)' (*Classics for Children and Young People*) expressed in carefully crafted prose. At the end of *Tom Fobble's Day* come words which express something of the quality of these poetic stories: 'The line did hold. Through hand and eye, forge and loom to the hill and all that he owned . . .'

Several writers have used the short story to great effect. James Berry's prize-winning *A Thief in the Village and Other Stories* (1987) is a collection of realistic stories illustrating the cruelty, the poverty, and the joy of Caribbean life told in a style that evokes Jamaican English. If there is an overall theme to the collection, it comes in the story 'The Banana Tree': 'The storm's bad, chil'run. Really bad. But it'll blow off. It'll spen' itself out.' Farrukh Dhondy's *East End at your Feet* (1976) illustrates his realistic approach to the life of Asian teenagers and their relationship with the white community: the story 'KBW' is a powerful ironic exploration of friendship and antagonism between different ethnic groups. And another writer who has produced distinguished work in several genres, Jan Mark, has used the short story brilliantly to explore school life, to mount a critique of the children's book itself, and to capture the true demotic of the teenager (*Hairs in the Palm of the Hand* (1981), *Nothing to Be Afraid Of* (1980), *Enough is Too Much Already* (1988)).

THE EXPANDING WORLD: ILLUSTRATION

In the field of children's book illustration, the technological developments in offset litho and colour separation (for example, Charles Keeping's experiments in the 1960s and Brian Wildsmith's brilliant colours in his books from *ABC* (1962) onwards) led to the superb colour illustrations of the 1970s, 1980s, and 1990s. At the same time, there was increasing recognition in art schools of the importance of illustration and picture-books, combined with the development of academic criticism of children's literature, including the examination of the nature of the illustration and the importance of the relationship between word and image. However, some critics felt that the new technology privileged the illustrations and artistic technique at the expense of the text (as Irene Whalley and Tessa Chester observe, 'though the eye is dazzled, it is not sustained') and that integration of the two is being lost. The development of paper engineering, not universally welcomed because of a similar concern about presentation at the expense of content, nevertheless made possible Jan Pieńkowski's *The Haunted House* (1979), Raymond Briggs's 'plop-up' version of *Fungus the Bogeyman* (1982), and Janet and Allan Ahlbergs' *The Jolly Postman; or, Other People's Letters* (1986) and *The Jolly Christmas Postman* (1991). The picture-book in particular lent itself to the overproduction that was a feature of the 1970s and 1980s: with the development of interna-

tional publishing houses, the pictures could be produced in one large print run and the texts added in the relevant language. The problem was that, given the pressures of time and money, often neither the original author nor the illustrator were consulted about any changes made. But for all that, this has been the richest period of experiment in the history of the picture-book.

Raymond Briggs's comic critique of our civilization created an alternative culture of Bogey people.

In Britain, some of the important author-illustrators of the period had already established their reputations in the 1960s: for example, Raymond Briggs, John Burningham, Charles Keeping, David McKee, and Brian Wildsmith. Some, like Shirley Hughes, were well-established illustrators of others' work who from the 1970s started to write and illustrate their own books. Others have come to prominence during the last twenty-five years: for example, the Ahlbergs, Quentin Blake, Anthony Browne, Patrick Benson, Michael Foreman, Fiona French, Pat Hutchins, Errol Le Cain, Errol Lloyd, Graham Oakley, Jan Ormerod, Helen Oxenbury, and Jan Pieńkowski. Raymond Briggs's work ranges from a gentle wordless fantasy—*The Snowman* (1978)—about a boy and a snowman who together fly over the Sussex South Downs near Briggs's home to Brighton and the Royal Pavilion—to books satirizing aspects of modern society. *Father Christmas* (1973) and *Father*

Fiona French's award-winning *Snow White in New York* (1986) is a retelling of the fairy-tale with a 1920s New York setting and seven jazz musicians playing the roles of the dwarfs.

Fiona French's picture-books are powerful narratives characterized by startling use of colour and pictorial styles ranging from Florentine to Chinese and African.

*Christmas Goes on Holiday* (1975) are creative uses of the comic-strip format in an affectionate attempt to demythologize the institutions of Christmas and the annual summer holiday. The books work on levels which appeal to both children and adults and that is even more true of *Fungus the Bogeyman* (1977), which is an extraordinary creation of an alternative culture of kind, compassionate, and, above all, literate Bogey people that provides a critique of our own civilization. Word-play such as puns, literary allusions, and quotations and misquotations require literate readers. Briggs has written and illustrated biting satires for adults on nuclear war—*When the Wind Blows* (1982)—and aspects of personal and national aggrandizement in the Falklands War—*The Tin-Pot Foreign General and the Old Iron Woman* (1984)—but *The Man* (1992), told entirely in dialogue between a boy and a tiny man who appears one day, returns to a gentler satirical exploitation of aspects of ourselves, in particular, those offered by the two figures' change of roles.

Two artists who have pushed out the boundaries are Charles Keeping and Anthony Browne. Keeping has successfully illustrated for many authors; his own picture-books, such as *Railway Passage* (1974), *Wasteground Circus* (1975), *Sammy Streetsinger* (1984), and *Adam and Paradise Island* (1989), are set in the changing townscape of the streets and the yards of the East End of London. They are peopled with working-class characters who experience poverty, violence, or loneliness in their quest for meaning and hope and Keeping conveys their joy and sadness through a masterly use of colour and line. Anthony Browne consciously works on many levels and often incorporates surrealistic imagery, for example in *A Walk in the Park* (1977), *Bear Hunt* (1979), and *Look What I've Got!* (1988), sometimes combined with super-realistic surface detail, for example in *The Tunnel* (1989), *Changes* (1990), and *Zoo* (1992). The prose text, in contrast, is brief and simple: as Browne puts it, 'I think that picture books work at their best when the words change for the pictures and the pictures change for the words.'

Children's imagination is of central importance too, in John Burningham's *Come away from the Water, Shirley* (1977) and *Time to Get out of the Bath, Shirley* (1978). The fractured narrative satirizes adults' bland reality by placing on the left-hand page the parents' banal admonitions to Shirley, and on the right, the exciting adventures that Shirley can enjoy only in her imagination. His earlier prize-winning *Mr. Gumpy's Outing* (1970) is a classic comic tale displaying Burningham's gentle pictorial style using water-colour and crayon. The same sparse style is used very effectively in *Granpa* (1984), a tale of the close relationship between a child and grandfather and the inevitable loss, where what is said and shown and not said and shown are equally important.

A strange sadness came over the forest. The animals were bewildered. 'What's happening?' they cried. They became so desperate that Lion, the king of beasts, decided to call a meeting of all animals and birds. 'What's happening to our forest?' they all cried. 'It is clear that we are in grave danger,' roared Lion. 'Our forest is being destroyed, and very soon we shall have no place to live in.'

*Above*: one of the most important illustrators of the last half-century, Charles Keeping combined sensitivity and violence in his controversial and wide-ranging work.

*Left*: large and brilliantly painted illustrations are the feature of Brian Wildsmith's *Professor Noah's Spaceship* (1980), a thought-provoking version of the Noah story for our polluted planet.

The Ahlbergs' *Each Peach Pear Plum* (1978), an 'I-Spy' story with a host of familiar nursery characters, is regarded as a 'nursery classic'.

But perhaps the most individual combination of style and form, with texts rooted in the intertextuality, the culture of children's stories, has been achieved by Janet and Allan Ahlberg. They work together on all stages of production of their books, and it is not surprising, therefore, that the written and the visual texts are so well integrated, 'a marriage of words and pictures', as Allan Ahlberg puts it. *Each Peach Pear Plum* (1978) is an 'I-Spy' book in verse of nursery-rhyme and fairy-tale characters set in a nostalgic pastoral landscape. *Peepo!* (1981) evokes another nostalgic period of British history: that of England in the Second World War, with father home on leave. In both books, the atmosphere is enhanced by Janet Ahlberg's use of gentle water-colours. Paper engineering is used most creatively in *The Jolly Postman* (1986), a wonderful fantasy in which the rural postman cycles round uniting a society of modern and fairy-tale characters by delivering letters which satirize modern life—a circular about witch supplies, a solicitor's letter to the Big Bad Wolf, a postcard from Jack to the Giant, a copy of Princess Cinderella's memoirs. The book is envelope-sized and the envelopes and letters are there for the reader to take out and savour. The Ahlbergs repeated their success five years later with the even more elaborate *The Jolly Christmas Postman* (1991).

The American tradition of internationalism in illustration has been very strong, with the intricate work of Peter Spier and Erroll Le Cain, particularly his illustrations for *Beauty and the Beast* (1979), while the Japanese artist Mitsumasa Anno has been particularly influential in the USA. Gerald McDermott's *Arrow to the Sun* (1974) drew on the Pueblo Indian and the team of Leo and Diane Dillon supplied illustrations for Verna Aardema's *Why Mosquitoes Buzz in People's Ears* (which won the Caldecott Medal in 1976), a West African folk-tale they interpreted with highly stylized, almost geometric compositions in soft pastels and watercolours. For *The Hundred Penny Box* by Sharon Bell Mathis (1975) they created gentle pictures that have the blurred sepia quality of old photographs, perfect for the tender story of a child's love for a very old woman. The Dillons won the Caldecott Medal again in 1977, this time for their boldly designed pictures for Margaret Musgrove's *Ashanti to Zulu: African Traditions*. They vary their media and moods: in their illustrations for Leontyne Price's adaptation of *Aida* (1990), a marginal frieze sets off each stately, handsomely composed painting.

Ed Young's interest in the art forms of China, the country of his birth, is evident in many of his books. *Chinese Mother Goose Rhymes* (1968), compiled by Robert Wyndham, includes calligraphy in its illustrations, and Young's adaptation of a Chinese folk-tale, *Lon Po Po: A Red-Ridinghood Story from China*, which won the 1990 Caldecott Medal, contains pictures based on ancient Chinese panel art. In two wordless picture-books, *Up a Tree* (1983) and *The Other Bone* (1984), Young's vigorous pencil drawings tell the stories with antic humour and fluid grace. His interpretation of a classic fable from India, *Seven Blind Mice* (1992), is as deftly told as it is illustrated, with vitality and suspense incorporated into the visual and verbal narration, as each colour-differentiated mouse reports on the amazing creature who turns out to be an elephant.

Diversity in style is, however, predictable from Chris Van Allsburg, who achieved fame with his first book, *The Garden of Abdul Gasazi* (1979). In 1982 he was awarded the Caldecott Medal for *Jumanji* and received it again in 1986 for *The Polar Express*. The bold pencil drawings for the first book reflect the artist's focus on sculpture in his academic studies and have a remarkable solidity of form and chiaroscuro virtuosity. In *Jumanji* he used conté pencil and conté dust for a story of imaginative play, and in *The Polar Express* he used dark, rich colours and misty shapes for an appealing fantasy about Santa Claus. Despite the soft, rounded forms found in *The Sweetest Fig* (1993) and in *The Widow's Broom* (1992), Van Allsburg's pictures have a solidity evident in all his work.

Because of her distinctive line, Trina Schart Hyman's work is also varied yet recognizable. The book she wrote for an autobio-

One of the major prizes in the children's literature world, the Caldecott Medal for 'the most distinguished picture-book' of the year, was first awarded in 1938.

graphical series (*Self-Portrait: Trina Hyman*, 1981) gives evidence of her quirky humour, a facet that often appeared in the several colonial biographies by Jean Fritz that she illustrated—for example, *Will You Sign Here, John Hancock?* (1976). Hyman's black and white pictures balance delicate details and firm line while authentic historical details attest to her careful research. She received the Caldecott Medal in 1985 for her bold, romantic paintings for *Saint George and the Dragon* retold by Margaret Hodges; their talents are combined again in a retelling of *The Kitchen Knight: A Tale of King Arthur* (1990). But none of her work exceeds in beauty the rich colours and the intricate details in her illustrations for Lloyd Alexander's story set in Cameroon, *The Fortune-Tellers* (1992).

But often the most satisfying examples of illustration, on both sides of the Atlantic, have been in books where authors have integrated their own words and pictures for younger children. Rosemary Wells, a pioneer of the small-scale picture-book, has an excellent ear for children's speech patterns and a clear eye for the problems of childhood, from sibling rivalry to misunderstanding parents. *Stanley and Rhoda* (1978) and the Bunny Planet books are among her best books.

James Marshall and Harry Allard's witty *Miss Nelson is Missing* (1977).

Detective McSmogg was assigned to the case.
He listened to their story.
He scratched his chin.
"Hmmmm," he said. "Hmmm."
"I think Miss Nelson is missing."
Detective McSmogg would not be much help.

The special quality that lightens James Marshall's picture-books is a sort of daft innocence, which one finds in the *George and Martha* story of 1972, and which was continued in other books about two friends who may be hippopotamuses but whose behaviour can evoke recognition in any young child. There are many stories about Fox, including *Fox on Stage* (1993), the last in a series notable for the author's ability to make small things humorous.

Quentin Blake's mastery of line and his early professional work as a cartoonist have resulted in his invention of humorous picture-books of eccentric characters such as *Mister Magnolia* (1980). He proved to be the ideal collaborator with Russell Hoban in the creation of Hoban's marvellously comic *How Tom Beat Captain Najork and his Hired Sportsmen* (1974), in which the small boy Tom, the expert in fooling around, outwits his Aunt Fidget Wonkham-Strong ('She wore an iron hat and took no nonsense from any-

316

one. Where she walked the flowers drooped and when she sang the trees all shivered') and beats Captain Najork (and his hired sportsmen) at the incomprehensible games of 'womble, muck and sneedball'. Blake has also collaborated with other writers, most notably Roald Dahl, and with Michael Rosen, in books of poetry such as *Mind your Own Business* (1974), *Wouldn't You Like to Know* (1977), *You Can't Catch Me* (1981), and *Quick, Let's Get out of Here* (1983).

## VERSE: NEW AND TRADITIONAL

In Britain, the colloquial tone of many novels has also found its way into the verse of writers like Kit Wright and Michael Rosen. Rosen draws upon the memory of a wide range of his own childhood experiences to see where they overlap with those of urban children today. He then fashions his poems in a subtle reworking of their language. He sees children using his writing as a catalyst, 'tuning in to its small hurts, jokes and fantasies of everyday life as a means to explore their own'. The power of his verse lies in its ability to point out the significance of the ordinary; for Rosen believes that poetry is 'not simply a separate expressive act but contiguous with hundreds of other kinds of utterance' including 'science reports, newscasts, proverbs, shopping lists', or even railway station announcements. In this way, the definition of poetry for children is widened to include all kinds of voices, even those which may appear trivial. It is poetry which arises out of an oral tradition and which is at its best in performance, as is the poetry of Brian Patten, or of Roger McGough, with whom Rosen collaborated in a joint collection, *You Tell Me* (1979). Like Rosen's, many of McGough's poems are comic, but often, underneath, there are darker preoccupations: pain, loneliness, violence, and death.

Other poems which cry out to be performed are found in John Agard's *I Din Do Nuttin and Other Poems* (1983) and *Laughter is an Egg* (1990) and Grace Nichols's *Come on into my Tropical Garden* (1988), which are aimed at younger children, and James Berry's *When I Dance* (1988), for teenage readers. All three poets can rework the strong rhythms and cadences of Anglo-

"You can't catch me, GRUMBLE PUMP PUMP."
"I'm very, very, very slow but when I'm quick

I'LL GET YOU . . .

I've got you
I've got you
and I'll never let you go."

Michael Rosen and Quentin Blake's award-winning collection of poems, *You Can't Catch Me* (1981), brilliantly represents the child's imaginary world of the everyday.

Back, he spurred like a madman, shouting a curse to the sky,
With the white road smoking behind him and his rapier brandished high
Blood-red were his spurs i' the golden noon; wine-red was his velvet
    coat;

Charles Keeping won the Kate Greenaway Medal in 1981 for his powerful black-and-white illustrations to Alfred Noyes's poem *The Highwayman.*

Caribbean speech in poems which speak directly to children of joy (as in the title poems of Agard's and Nichols's collections) or hurt (as in Berry's 'Dreaming Black Boy').

The American voices of Jack Prelutsky (*New Kid on the Block*, 1984), David Mc-Cord, whose collected poems were published in 1977, Shel Silverstein (*Where the Sidewalk Ends*, 1974), or Karla Kuskin (*Something Sleeping in the Hall*, 1985) are recognizably in the same tradition and there is a growing respect for 'minority' voices, although the more traditional approach of Myra Cohn Livingston or Eve Merriam still has a market. In both countries, poetry is seen increasingly as an interactive business, where children are encouraged to write as well as read poetry.

The work of Charles Causley appears to belong to a different tradition—one more recognizably 'poetic'. Some of his poems are lyrical, some are nonsensical, but many are cast in a form which derives from the same oral tradition, the ballad— a combination of forms which appeal to both children and adults. As he said in an interview, 'a children's poem is a poem that has to work for the adult and the child as well'. His poems, at their best, exemplify his view that 'All poetry is magic. It is a spell against insensitivity, failure of imagination, ignorance and barbarism.' Charles Causley admires in Ted Hughes's work for children 'the qualities of mystery and revelation . . . that celebration in subtly balanced terms, of victor and vanquished, survivor and slain' which are best displayed in the powerful poems of seasonal animals in *Season Songs* (1976).

## THE MEETING OF MEDIA

There should be no apologies for discussing children's television in a history of children's literature. Since the 1960s, children's television has become increasingly important as a source of imaginative fiction for children and the quality of many of the programmes has been very high. In the USA, it has largely been public television stations that have carried 'quality' programming—some of it British. But perceptions of quality shift:

318

It seems that people have always had these feelings, and that in those good old days Muffin was the destroyer of *Children's Hour* on radio and just as evil and subversive as today's television programmes. (Anna Home, *Into the Box of Delights*)

Many children's programmes have become part of contemporary cultural memory and some, like *Blue Peter* or *Sesame Street*, have become almost national institutions. Television has, in some areas, encouraged reading, as well as creating long-running fictional characters, such as Postman Pat, and revitalizing classics, such as *Thomas the Tank Engine*, *The Borrowers*, and C. S. Lewis's 'Narnia' series.

With changes in the structure of families, video-tapes and television have taken over something of the traditional role of the parent. The most famous story-telling programme on British television was probably *Jackanory*, which started in 1965 and was still running twenty-five years later. Its aim was to tell the best possible stories of all kinds from all over the world. By 1990, over 400 well-known actors and actresses had told folk-tales and legends from forty-four different countries and read aloud more than 650 books. The tellings and readings were usually accompanied by illustrations provided by illustrators such as Quentin Blake and Gareth Floyd.

Non-fiction as art. One of David Macaulay's intensely detailed picture-books, *Castle* (1977).

## CONCLUSION

Anyone who writes a historical overview is sadly aware that there are many writers not mentioned because of lack of space. In the USA, in the early 1990s there were 6,000 juvenile titles published per year. It is an amazing success story and the reasons for it are not confined to the world of children's books, a point which applies to both the USA and Britain.

Certainly one factor is the increase in public awareness of the importance of reading and an understanding of the importance of learning in early childhood, an awareness spurred by seminal studies in child psychology and educational theory. More parents, particularly parents of young children, are buying books. Another major influence is the trend toward the use of trade books, rather than textbooks, in

Glen Rounds's publications for children ranged from realistic cowboy stories, and tall tales to this rendition of *The Three Little Pigs and the Big Bad Wolf*.

NOW I'M COMING DOWN THE CHIMNEY, AND I'M GOING TO EAT YOU UP!!!"

schools; the trend is now associated with the catch phrase 'whole language', but it is not a wholly new phenomenon. There is a wider audience for children's books, with people like David Macaulay and Maurice Sendak attracting devoted adult fans as well as young readers. And there is a ripple effect as bookstore and mass market sales increase: the range of books carried in bookstores has broadened, since a healthy sales volume encourages publishers once again to take risks. It is a satisfying spiral.

Despite valiant and continuing efforts to combat censorship, the old struggle has not abated. Controversy over such Sendak books as *In the Night Kitchen* or *We are All in the Dumps with Jack and Guy* gets a great deal of publicity because of the author's fame; less well known are the efforts of organized groups to have books of which they disapprove removed from the shelves of school and public libraries or banned from bookstores. There has always been pressure on publishers to purge their output; with the increased use of trade books in schools this pressure is not likely to decrease.

Influences from within the publishing industry also affect what is published and who is responding to what is published. As the Children's Book Council, the American Booksellers Association, and the National Council of Teachers of English have expanded their activities to include and publicize events in the children's book world, each new audience has been exposed to such issues as cultural literacy, political correctness, multi-ethnic representation in children's books, and the growing status of children's literature as evidenced by the serious attention paid to it in literary criticism.

Among the identifiable trends is the proliferation of 'speciality' books: toy books, board books, books that are merely games, and books created by paper engineering, all of which run the gamut of quality. A contemporary phenomenon is the imbalance in age groups served, with masses of picture-books published, in contrast to the comparative paucity of books for the middle years during which most children do most of their reading. People are also concerned with the amount of time devoted to television; they worry about whether increasing technological sophistication will make printed materials, and their use, rare if not obsolete. They worry about poor reading scores. Yet both sales figures and library circulation figures indicate no reduction; children are buying books, reading books, voting enthusiastically for book awards. They may not all be reading as much as some would like or as well as some would hope, but the fine quality and impressive variety of so many children's books should make all who are concerned with the joy of reading modestly confident that even in a computer age the book will survive, and children's literature will continue in its many complex manifestations.

# 12 COLONIAL AND POST-COLONIAL CHILDREN'S LITERATURE

*Australia, Canada, and New Zealand*

## AUSTRALIA

*Michael Stone*

THE two themes that dominate Australian children's literature in the nineteenth century and which are still influential today are the settlers' reaction to an environment different from Europe and their contact with the Aboriginal population of the new country. These themes were played out in books of adventure which featured the spectacular aspects of landscape (flood, fire, drought, the unusual flora and fauna) and books designed to encourage emigration or help settlers adjust to new conditions and live comfortably in a new land. The boundaries between the two kinds of fiction sometimes merged; settlers' tales made use of the landscape and its unusual features while adventure stories often stressed the bliss and comfort of family life.

The first Australian children's book published in Australia was *A Mother's Offering to her Children* (1841) by 'A Lady Long Resident in New South Wales'. This lady was Charlotte Barton, a governess who arrived in Sydney in 1827. The book is didactic in tone and written in the form of question and answer, a dialogue between a mother and her four children. The mother in the story has a fund of information about colonial life but the manner of telling is sometimes ghoulish, reminiscent of Mrs Sherwood's *The Fairchild Family*. It has stories of cannibals, slaughter, and a description of the horrific death of an Aboriginal child.

William Howitt, the author of *A Boy's Adventures in the Wilds of Australia*

(1854), who with his wife spent two years in Australia, offers a tale of more vigour, and Louisa Anne Meredith's *Tasmanian Friends and Foes: Feathered, Furred and Finned* (1880) mixes a family story with carefully observed nature. The descriptions of Australian life are contained in letters sent to a cousin in England but are read aloud to the family before being posted. This allows the reader to hear family comments and anecdotes which give a sense of ordinary life in a particular Australian community.

Not all books about Australia presented a true picture of the country. As the nineteenth century advanced, the exotic and unusual nature of the country attracted overseas writers, many of whom never left home. Until the 1890s they showed Australia as a place attractive to settlers with promise of sure reward for hard work, as a place for exotic and dangerous adventure and a place which had endless possibilities for missionary zeal in rehabilitating fellow whites or for converting the black man. Often the novels contained all three aspects, with perhaps the adventure theme, often episodic, predominating.

Characteristic were *Alfred Dudley; or, The Australian Settlers* (1830) and *Frank Layton: An Australian Tale* (1865), settler novels in which it is shown that the virtues of hard work and piety are rewarded and the characters are thankful for their decision to settle in Australia; in Mrs Bowman's *The Kangaroo Hunters* (1859) the settlers even convert an Aboriginal girl to Christianity. Otherwise, little interest was shown in the history or spiritual beliefs of the Aboriginal inhabitants. They were portrayed in one of three ways: as heathens, therefore needing to be converted to Christianity; as savages in their sometimes violent clashes with the Europeans; or as faithful retainers in the manner of Robinson Crusoe's Man Friday. Some authors raised issues of moral consciousness pointing out that the Aborigines' livelihood and social structure was being destroyed as settlers intruded further and further into their hunting grounds. E. B. Kennedy's *Blacks and Bushrangers* (1889) tells the story of two brothers shipwrecked off the Queensland coast who are rescued by Aborigines, learn their ways, and are ultimately assimilated. Despite the strength of the adventure theme, Kennedy reveals an admiration for tribal skills and loyalties.

Kate Langloh Parker, a squatter's wife living on a remote station in north-western New South Wales, collected Aboriginal legends which were published as *Australian Legendary Tales* in London and Melbourne in 1896, with

Mickie, Alfred Dudley's faithful Aboriginal servant in borrowed finery, greets his master's family on their arrival from England. Despite a recognizable kangaroo, the atmosphere seems West Indian and the Aborigines look like Negroes. The author had not been to Australia. From Sarah Porter's *Alfred Dudley or The Australian Settlers.*

'Inglewood', in the Sydney suburb of Lindfield where *Seven Little Australians* was written still stands today. The house was extensively renovated about the time of the First World War (1914–18) and the surrounding land has long since been subdivided.

a foreword by Andrew Lang. Another station owner's wife, Mrs Jeannie Gunn, living in the Northern Territory, published in 1905 a children's story, *The Little Black Princess*. The book details the relationship between the 'Missus' and Bett Bett, an 8-year-old black girl. While there is still some condescension, customs and legends are presented to the reader in a way that seeks understanding as the child is portrayed in the context of her tribe and beliefs. Mrs Gunn is better known for her 1908 novel *We of the Never Never*, her attitude towards the Aborigines is sympathetic, one that avoids the stereotypes set up by writers earlier in the century.

By the last decade of the nineteenth century the lure of the exotic frontier was fading; as Australia became an urban society a changing educational philosophy reflected interest in the development of the child and the child's right to be entertained rather than preached at in his or her leisure time. Louise Mack in *Teens: A Story of Australian School Girls* (1890) explored the sensitive relationships of children, especially girls in their teenage years.

The novels of Ethel Turner reflected the imitation of childhood rather than the realization of it. In her lifetime, as well as collections of short stories and anthologies of poetry and fiction, she published twenty-seven full-length novels, the first and most famous, written when she was 21, being *Seven Little*

*Australians* (1894). It has sold more than 1 million copies, has been translated into ten languages, and has been dramatized (1895), filmed (1939), and televised twice (1953 Britain, 1975 Australia). Turner is still the best-known name in Australian children's literature with her first book still in print and regarded as a classic.

Turner drew on the domestic tradition of L. M. Alcott and Charlotte Yonge, investing her children's stories with Australian middle-class characteristics and values. She sent her manuscripts to William Steele, the Melbourne representative of Ward Lock, who urged her to tone down local colour and censor colloquialisms for the English market. Brenda Niall quotes a letter from Steele suggesting that 'a little English experience would help to (excuse me for so putting it) correct the free and easy, somewhat rowdy associations due to atmosphere, climate, environment and the influence of the Bulletin'. The *Bulletin* was a radical magazine, a focal point for Australian nationalist writing.

Ward Lock's other Australian author discovered by William Steele was Mary Grant Bruce. Between 1910 and 1942 Bruce published fifteen books centred upon Billabong Station, a country property which became part of the mythology of outback Australia. It is a timeless place and maps of its buildings and land in some of the editions of the books emphasize its safety and security. From the homestead windows Norah will gaze at the hills 'sometimes purple, sometimes blue, sometimes misty grey, but always beautiful to the child who loved them'. This idealized picture is seen to be the real Australia, the open spaces of the bush.

Mrs Bruce's last book was published just before the Japanese attack on Pearl Harbor, an event which signalled change in the relationship between Britain and Australia. Because of this the books lost their popularity for a time but eventually returned to print. Bruce herself said that her stories grew out of the simple everyday things that happen to Australian children living in the Australian bush and in this way they still present something of the essential mythical view of Australia.

Fantasy in Australian children's books had difficult beginnings and writers felt more comfortable with the realistic mode. Many felt the strangeness of the country and viewed the bush as

Ethel Turner in *Seven Little Australians* (1894), tells her readers that nursery tea is 'more an English institution than an Australian one'. Children usually eat with adults and share in the conversation. In this family separate meals are necessary because of the father's irritability and 'seven children's excellent lungs and tireless tongues'. There is no real nurse; Meg the eldest girl fulfils this role and Pip the teenage son is about to protest about the standard of nursery food, 'bread and melting butter' compared with that provided for adults, 'roast fowl, three veges and four kinds of pudding'.

*Facing*: Blinky Bill's
adventures and scrapes
have been long-time
favourites with
Australian children.

*Below*: Dot's kangaroo
is curious to see the
Corroborree and
believes 'it would be
nice for Dot to see
some other humans
after being so long
amongst bush crea-
tures. Dot is terrified
by the experience but
the kangaroo helps her
to understand human
and animal behaviour'.
*Dot and the Kangaroo*
(1899).

a place of terror where only the black people were at home and where white
people felt isolated and could easily be lost. There were attempts to introduce
the traditional figures of European folklore, mermaids, witches, and dragons,
but these never really took root.

Jessie Whitfield's *The Spirit of the Bushfire and Other Australian Fairy Stories* (1898) reveals an interesting mix of European tradition with Australian
landscape; the first story in the collection tells of a destructive bushfire spirit
who brings a spark to life to start a bushfire, that has to be ultimately extinguished by the Rain Drop Elves.

An obvious source of fantasy was Australian animals, the kangaroo, the
wallaby, and the koala, especially when they were made to speak. In *Dot and
the Kangaroo* (1899) by Ethel C. Pedley, Dot is lost in the bush and finds
refuge and security with a kangaroo. Through eating the berries of understanding she is able to converse with the kangaroo and ultimately is brought
home to safety. There is a strong plea for the preservation of bush life and the
kangaroo points out the destructive habits of humanity.

The best-known and best-loved talking animal (a koala) in Australian children's literature, judging by his sales, appears in Dorothy Wall's *Blinky Bill*
(1933), *Blinky Bill Grows Up* (1934), and
*Blinky Bill and Nutsy* (1937); but the first
creatures invented for the bush were
May Gibbs's Gumnut Babies in *Snugglepot and Cuddlepie* (1918) and its successors. The babies are small and naked
except for a gumnut hat and are constantly threatened by the Banksia Men.
The texts are often complex and are best
suited to reading aloud. The world May
Gibbs provides is the enchanting one of
the bush, peopled with gumnut male
and female heroes, with friends like Mr
Lizard and Mrs Bear, and a villain Mrs
Snake. *Snugglepot and Cuddlepie* is as
important to the imaginative background of Australian children as *The
Wind in the Willows* is to British ones.

Another fantasy story that bears comparison to Grahame's book is *The Magic
Pudding* (1918), a book that appeals to
adults and children alike. Written and
illustrated by Norman Lindsay, it is a
tale of humour and adventure with, as

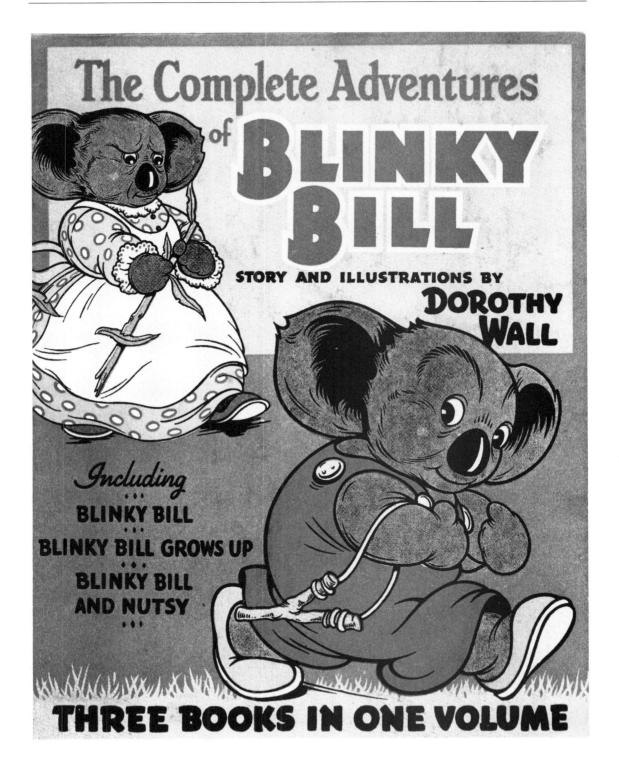

Norman Lindsay's *The Magic Pudding* (1918) has parallels to *Alice* and *The Wind in the Willows*. Part of its lasting appeal is the pleasant life its characters lead; food is on the ready, and though the pleasures of summer give way to the wind and rain of winter it is always snug, aloft in the tree house. The town is in the distance.

hero, a pudding that continually renews itself no matter how much is eaten. The pudding, Albert, is owned by Sam Sawnoff, a penguin, and Bill Barnacle, a sailor. Bunyip Bluegum helps Sam and Bill fight off the professional pudding thieves, Possum and Wombat. The text is strong with satire on society that children would not see; the verse is joyful; the illustrations bold and assertive; and the Australian expressions and speech patterns have helped make the book an Australian classic.

Ethel Turner and Mary Grant Bruce died in 1958 and by this time the early novels of Joan Phipson, Patricia Wrightson, Eleanor Spence, and a little later those of Colin Thiele, were beginning to appear. While these writers' novels were different in mood and characterization they presented traditional images of the Australian family in an idealized landscape.

The pastoral setting with its strong affinity to the natural world created the timeless atmosphere in the novels of Nan Chauncy, a writer who is credited with changing the direction of children's fiction in Australia. Her realistic pictures of childhood and complex characters, the sympathetic presentation of the Aborigine, and her reawakening of commitment to the environment (as in *They Found a Cave*, 1948) were concerns which later writers took up.

Changes in society during the 1960s exposed the values of the pastoral and of family life to questioning, and harsher pictures of family life appeared. There was a move away from the idealized outdoors to an interior world where characters displayed more introspection, with novels like Eleanor Spence's *The Summer in Between* (1959) and *The Green Laurel* (1964).

Other writers reflected the changing nature of the family in Australian society. *The Racketty Street Gang* (1961) by L. H. Evers portrayed the experiences of migrants coming to Australia after the Second World War, while Mavis Thorpe Clark's *The Min-Min* (1966) has her heroine living a life of isolation on the Nullarbor Plain with a depressed mother and angry father. But happy families still exist in books of the 1980s; Thurley Fowler's *The Green Wind* (1985) and *The Wind is Silver* (1991) and Robin Klein's *All in the Blue Unclouded Weather* (1991) present a more innocent time. Robin Klein came to prominence with *Hating Alison Ashley* (1984), a satire on school life told with much humour. Amongst her other works are *People Might Hear You* (1983) and *Came Back to Show You I Could Fly* (1989) which show that no writer of the 1980s could avoid social problems; the earlier novel deals with a girl who must escape from a fanatical sect her mother has married into, while the later one is a sympathetic approach to the problems of drug taking.

The land as an adversary came to prominence in many stories of adventure in the 1960s and 1970s, notably Joan Phipson's *The Way Home* (1973), in which, after a car accident, the boy who is at home with nature survives; his companion, who is not, dies in the bush. Phipson's message is that humanity and nature can be reconciled.

Ivan Southall's *Hills End* (1962) marked a new turn in Australian children's literature. Southall had begun his career with the Simon Black adventure stories, Simon being a character not unlike Biggles. Hills End is a town that is destroyed by storm and flood while the inhabitants are at the picnic races, held out of town. No adults are left to protect a group of children, who are forced to rely on themselves to make order out of chaos. Surrounded by wild mountain and forest country they are threatened by a flooded river, an escaped bull, and a shortage of food. They survive by drawing on strength they did not know they possessed and partly by the determination of a character whom nobody suspects has the qualities of a leader. Southall's later books continue this theme of survival. *Ash Road* (1965) takes place over a day when a bushfire destroys a region. *To the Wild Sky* (1967) has a group of children trapped in an airborne plane with a dead pilot. After the crash on a desert island the children (from country and city backgrounds) go through a bleak ordeal, hoping against hope for rescue. The ending remains open; the reader does not know whether the children live or die. After many requests, indeed pleas, Southall published a sequel, *A City out of Sight* (1984), saying in an Author's Note he had not changed his position but he agreed to go on with the story.

More optimistic is Colin Thiele, whose first book, *The Sun on the Stubble* (1961), is a heart-warming story set in a South Australian farming district in the years between the wars. The story is episodic, dealing with incidents in a boy's life, but held together by the realization at the end that 'the sunny uplands of boyhood' give way 'to the great grey plains of adult life ahead'. Thiele returns to this theme again in *The Valley Between* (1981) with its humour, warmth, and incidents of danger and suspense, but his best exploration of boyhood in isolation is *Storm-Boy* (1963), perhaps Thiele's best-loved book, set on the long finger of sandhills between the Southern Ocean and Coorong.

The leading character of Patricia Wrightson's *I Own the Racecourse!* (1968) is slightly backward; people like him because he has a warm smile and is friendly, but he lives 'behind a closed window' and talks as though 'he was

'Wherever Storm-Boy went Mr Percival followed. Whenever the boy anchored the boat the pelican came gliding in. If Storm-Boy went rowing or fishing, Mr Percival found a good spot to watch from until it was over.'

speaking through glass'. Andy believes he has been sold a racecourse and his friends have to find a way to tell him he has not, without being cruel. Wrightson, Australia's most highly acclaimed children's writer, whose stories have won many international distinctions, began her career in 1955 with a conventional family story *The Crooked Snake*. She moved on to explore Aboriginal characters and motifs and the power of the land to shape its people in such books as *The Rocks of Honey* (1960), *An Older Kind of Magic* (1972), and *The Nargun and the Stars* (1973).

In a note she appended to *An Older Kind of Magic* she wrote: 'It is time we stopped trying to see elves and dragons and unicorns in Australia. They have never belonged here, and no ingenuity can make them real. We need to look for another kind of magic, a kind that must have been shaped by the land itself at the edge of the Australian vision.' Wrightson discovered a rich store of Australian folklore and introduced the native equivalent of elves and goblins into her books, developing these until they reached their peak in her Wirrun trilogy, *The Ice is Coming* (1977), *The Dark Bright Water* (1978), and *Behind the Wind* (1981). In these books the Aboriginal hero, Wirrun, educated in the way of the whites, is called upon to restore harmony to the ancient continent as certain spirits move from their place in nature's scheme to promote chaos.

Some writers have approached the challenge to possess the land for white people through a realistic recreation of the past. One of the most successful writers at doing this was Ruth Park with *Playing Beatie Bow* (1980). Park used the time slip device as Nan Chauncy had done earlier with *Tangara* (1960) to contrast the Sydney of the present with that of 1873. Her warm working-class family of 1873 was contrasted with a present-day more affluent one to show a decrease in community spirit.

Hesba Brinsmead's novels *Long Time Passing* (1971), *Once There was a Swagman* (1979), and *Long Time Dreaming* (1982) create a sense of past with the story of the Truelance family at 'Longtime', their home in the Blue Mountains of New South Wales. Even more forceful is the work of James Aldridge, books, perhaps, for all readers. His *The True Story of Lilli Stubeck* (1984) is set in the 1930s along the banks of the Murray River. While the period setting of the novel is authentic, the values the author brings out centring upon the notion of 'being true to oneself' make it a story that has an appeal for all time. Aldridge wrote other novels with the same background whose appeal is to adults as well as to children. Amongst them *Ride a Wild Pony* (1975), *The Broken Saddle* (1982), and *The True Story of Spit MacPhee* (1986) have particular appeal to children.

During the 1980s and 1990s the subject-matter of children's books widened to include every aspect of life as Australians experienced it. John Marsden in *The Journey* (1988) and *The Great Gatenby* (1989) explored teenage sex, Jenny Pausacher's *What Are Ya?* (1987) portrayed lesbian

331

relationships, while Kate Walker's *Peter* (1991) tells of a 15-year-old youth falling in love with a boy who is gay.

Fantasy as a genre grew considerably in the 1980s. Nadia Wheatley's *The House that was Eureka* (1984) uses an old house where time alternates between two periods, the Depression of the 1930s and the situation of the unemployed of the 1980s. The themes of politics, power, and its use are explored by Wheatley in a radical approach to a serious novel for teenagers. Wheatley is also a historian who gives great attention to the period detail of her book.

However, some of the strongest writers, such as Victor Kelleher and Gillian Rubenstein, did not use Australia as a setting for their fantasy works. Rubenstein is one of the Australian leaders in experimental fiction for children, while perhaps the most impressive achievement in this area has been Gary Crew's novel *Strange Objects* (1990), which has as its background the shipwreck of the *Batavia* off the West Australian coast in 1629 and the horrendous massacre of the survivors by mutineers. Crew tells the story of two survivors, linking their story with a present-day event which makes for an exciting and suspenseful story, with characters not always to be admired. *Strange Objects* has a Jamesian ambiguity where the reader hesitates in deciding how to interpret the novel's events.

Like the novels of Patricia Wrightson and those of Bill Scott, *Boori* (1978) and *Darkness under the Hills* (1980), Gary Crew's work offers positive approaches to the depiction of Aboriginal people by white Australians in children's literature. White writers in the last few years have been anxious to consult with Aboriginal groups for the authenticity of their writing in order to bridge the gap between white and Aboriginal culture. Diana Kidd's *The Fat Juicy Place* (1992) was endorsed by the NSW Aboriginal Education Consultative Group for 'language usage and cultural authenticity'. Jeanie Adams lived among the people of Aurukun for several years before publishing her two books *Pigs and Honey* (1989) and *Going for Oysters* (1991). These publications were endorsed by the elders of the community.

Not only has the increased understanding of Aboriginal spirituality led to books of Aboriginal legend, but the true Aboriginal voice is being heard in autobiographical stories. These stories tell about prejudice, racism, and servitude, and although they are not written for children some, like Sally Morgan's *My Place* (1987), have been made accessible by reissuing them in short volumes which tell individual stories. Glenyse Ward's *Wandering Girl* (1987) and its sequel *Unna You Fellas* (1993) are written simply in a style which is beginning to be recognized as Aboriginal English and is accessible to older children. These stories emphasize a sense of community and tell what it means to be an Aboriginal person living in Australia today.

While there has always been a Chinese, Greek, German, and Italian presence in Australia, the growth of cultural diversity over the last forty years has led to an increasing number of books which reflect the need to establish a harmonious community based on social justice. Notable examples are Nance Donkin's *A Friend for Petros* (1974) and Nadia Wheatley's *Five Times Dizzy* (1982) and *Dancing in the Anzac Deli* (1984). These books look for the common humanity that lies beneath cultural differences and demonstrate the strength of Australian writing for teenagers. New writers are coming forward with new viewpoints and a willingness to write about important issues: children out of the mainstream and children without support. Writers are exploring more the cultural diversity of the country and the differences of race, class, and education, issues that in the past have not been fully confronted.

# CANADA

## *Roderick McGillis*

In 1931, Grosset and Dunlap of New York published one in a series of books about children around the world: *Little Anne of Canada* by Madeline Brandeis. The cover shows a small girl sitting cross-legged in the foreground of an outdoor scene containing fir trees, a log cabin, and snow-covered ground. The girl has dark ringlets under a red wool toque. Her red and black checked jacket is buttoned under her chin. She wears gloves and high boots. Early in the story, the reader learns that Anne is a French Canadian who knows no English, but she also learns that the French and the English waged 'many wars' and that finally 'England won, and now Canada belongs to England'. When this was written, sixty-four years had passed since Confederation.

The Canada imaged in *Little Anne of Canada* is a colonial settlement, dependent largely on its lumber mills, wheat fields, fishing boats, and railways. Americans, the author says, 'feel close to Canada' because 'Canada buys more of our products than does any other country'. The perception is that Canada is both agrarian and wild, consisting of both untouched natural spaces and richly cultivated lands. Canada finds itself caught between England, to which it supposedly 'belongs', and America, which sells its industrial products on the Canadian market. This colonial leviathan slumbering at the top of the North American continent lacked the experience and the confidence to break free of its colonial moorings. This lack of experience and confidence was reflected in the country's small amount of literature for children.

Nearly thirty years ago, Northrop Frye remarked that any criticism of Canadian literature based on evaluative principles 'would become only a debunking project', leaving this literature a 'poor naked *alouette* plucked of every feather of decency and dignity'. Any history of Canadian children's

*The Lucky Old Woman* by Robin Muller (1987), based on Joseph Jacob's *The Hedley Kow*. Muller began his career as a children's illustrator by adapting traditional tales. He uses ink and pencil-crayons to create a cartoon-like effect.

books will have to account both for the scarcity of quality children's books published in Canada by Canadian writers before 1975 and for the sudden explosion in publishing for children that occurred after that date.

The emergence of a distinctly Canadian literature had to await the emergence of a distinctly Canadian sensibility. Only after such powerful cultural events as the celebration of Canada's centenary in 1967, the acquisition of a flag in the 1960s, the acknowledgement through legislation of two official languages in 1969, the important hockey series with the former Soviet Union in 1972, and the repatriation of the constitution in 1982 did Canada's national self-consciousness emerge from its colonial past. Prior to this post-colonial sense of independence and surety, much of Canada's literature reflected either the country's colonial past or the influence of the United States.

Little needs to be said about the early colonial period, from the Proclamation of 1763 to the mid-nineteenth century. Records show few publications for children beyond alphabet books and catechisms. Still in the process of being settled, Canada produced little in the way of fine arts during this period. Several English publications offer views of Canada from travellers: for example, Mrs H. Bayley, *Henry; or, The Juvenile Traveller* (1836), Frederick Marryat, *Settlers in Canada* (1844), and R. M. Ballantyne, *Snowflakes and Sunbeams; or, The Young Furtraders* (1844). By 1847, however, the publishing industry was well enough established for the first children's magazine to appear in Montreal; this was *Snowdrop; or, Juvenile Magazine*. A second magazine, the *Maple Leaf*, appeared from 1852 to 1854, but, as Egoff and Saltman suggest (*The New Republic of Childhood*), the literary works contained in these journals did not differ from similar publications in England. Significantly, however, their Canadian content consisted of information on animals and material on history. Until the watershed year, 1975, Canada's writers for children would make their especial mark in writing about animals and history.

The theme that has marked Canadian literature from the beginning is what Margaret Atwood has succinctly identified as 'survival'. This is the theme of Canada's first children's novel, Catharine Parr Traill's *Canadian Crusoes, A Tale of the Rice Lake Plains* (1852). This novel, drawing as it does upon Defoe's novel, sets the tone for much Canadian writing for children; stories of survival in a harsh and mysterious land are abundant in Canadian children's literature, from James MacDonald Oxley's *Up among the Ice Floes* (1890) to Norman Duncan's *The Adventures of Billy Topsail* (1906) to Roderick Haig-Brown's *Starbuck Valley Winter* (1943) to Farley Mowat's *Lost in the Barrens* (1956) to Jan Truss's *Jasmin* (1982) to Monica Hughes's *Log Jam* (1988). In such books, the Canadian love of and fear of the wilderness is evident, the loneliness and immensity of a huge land in which most people live on a strip some 200 miles wide along the American border. The fact of the land presses on even those books which are not specifically adventures of survival in the wilderness. Novels such as Monica Hughes's *Hunter in the Dark* (1982), Kevin Major's *Hold Fast* (1978), and Morley Callaghan's much earlier *Luke Baldwin's Vow* (1948) represent the recurring necessity of characters to come to terms with the land. Even Canadian fantasy, for example works by Catherine Anthony Clark or Ruth Nichols, manifests the same preoccupation.

In the later part of the nineteenth century, Canadian children's books mirror the concerns and subjects of children's books published in Britain and the United States. For example, James De Mille, described as '[o]ur first major Canadian-born writer' by Egoff and Saltman, wrote several boys' school stories including *The B.O.W.C.* (Brethren of the White Cross; 1869), *Lost in the Fog* (1870), *Fire in the Woods* (1871), and *Picked up Adrift* (1872). De Mille follows the type of story popularized in England by Thomas Hughes and F. W. Farrar, although, as his titles indicate, he sets his stories of schoolboys in the wilderness that demands survival skills familiar to readers of Canadian fiction. The fact of the land takes precedence over all else, including pietistic moralizing or the fabrication of elaborate plots.

Although other books for children did appear in Canada before the end of the century, none was as significant as the ones that began to appear in the 1890s by two writers who remain major innovators in children's literature: Ernest Thompson Seton and Charles G. D. Roberts. Seton and Roberts between them invented the realistic animal story, and in doing so assured Canada a place in the international history of children's books. Even before they began to publish their animal stories, another Canadian prepared the way; this is Margaret Marshall Saunders, who published her dog story *Beautiful Joe* in 1894. Despite the book's realism, *Beautiful Joe* descends into Victorian melodrama familiar to readers of *Black Beauty*.

What Seton and Roberts wanted to do was write stories which remained true to animal nature. Their interest is in the natural world, and their enterprise is to fictionalize true stories from nature. *Red Fox* (1905) sets the pattern for the realistic animal story by taking the typical story of a hero and transferring this to the animal world. Roberts announces a familiar theme: the difference between Canada, a pastoral garden/wilderness, and the United States, a fallen land where violence shatters the innocence of nature. As the title of the last chapter indicates, Red Fox manages to 'triumph' over his enemies.

In creating stories such as *Red Fox,* Roberts (and also Seton) wrote the first works in what Margaret Atwood argues is 'a *genre* which provides a key to an important facet of the Canadian psyche' (*Survival: A Thematic Guide to Canadian Literature*). The Canadian lack of self-confidence is reflected in this literary identification with animals, and it might indicate 'that Canadians themselves feel threatened and nearly extinct as a nation'. Atwood presented her argument in 1972, before the referendum on sovereignty in Quebec and the constitutional wrangles of the 1980s, but her argument might seem more cogent now in the 1990s than it did twenty years ago. Or the Canadian writer's interest in finding heroes in the natural world might simply reflect the Canadian sense of the extraordinary nature of the ordinary, the Canadian or-

*The Shirt of the Happy Man* (1977), illustrated by Laszlo Gal. Hungarian-born Gal also illustrates in full colour; in 1983 he won the Canada Council Award for illustrations to *The Little Mermaid.*

dinary superhero. However one reads the realistic animal story, one thing is certain: Canadian books acknowledge the fact of nature, its inevitable round indifferent to human desire.

If Seton and Roberts present a harsh, post-Darwinian pastoralism, their contemporary Lucy Maud Montgomery presents a more traditional pastoralism in *Anne of Green Gables* (1908) and its eight sequels. In these books, Montgomery depicts the idyllic life of fictional small Canadian towns on Prince Edward Island. She deftly sets out town life with its local gossip, its suspicion of foreigners such as the Italian salesman who sells Anne hair dye, its matriarchal social arrangement, and its expectations for males and females. Tension, of course, does exist in Montgomery's world, but it is always resolvable; what comforts the reader is the sense that human life fits snugly with nature and its rhythms. In this depiction of small-town life, Montgomery looks forward to later Canadian fiction by such writers as Stephen Leacock, Alice Munro, and Isabel Huggan.

Unlike works by these later writers, Montgomery's books reflect the rather sentimental tone of many turn-of-the-century girls' books. Her romances take into account the problems of young people growing up, problems that have to do with relationships, aspirations for the future, community and family ties. In short, Montgomery's novels are early versions of young adult fiction. Canada has excelled in this genre since the late 1970s. Mostly, books of this type eschew fantasy, preferring to give the appearance of real life. The first important modern example of this kind of fiction in Canada is Kevin Major's *Hold Fast* (1978), in which the main character must cope with the death of his parents and his consequent move to a larger town. Later books by Major examine other difficulties faced by adolescents, but they also show a willingness on Major's part to experiment. For example, *Thirty-Six Exposures* (1984) contains thirty-six chapters, each one a snapshot of the main character's life and feelings. Major's attempt here, as in *Far From Shore* (1980) and *Diana: My Autobiography* (1993), is to record the inner world of his characters' lives. The same is true of other examples of the young adult novel: Monica Hughes's *Hunter in the Dark* (1982; a boy comes to terms with terminal illness), Brian Doyle's *Up to Low* (1982; a daughter must forgive her father for a childhood accident), Marilyn Halvorson's *Cowboys Don't Cry* (1984; a boy comes to terms with his mother's death), Mitzi Dale's *Round the Bend* (1988; recovery from suicide attempt), and Diana Wieler's *Bad Boy* (1989; young men confront sexual identities).

Recently fiction for adolescents has begun to focus on Canada's first peoples, a sign that the country is maturing into a post-colonial phase. Prior to the late 1970s, works dealing with Canada's first nations were few and far between. Writers and editors did not, however, ignore these native people completely. In 1918 Cyrus MacMillan published *Canadian Wonder Tales*, the

*Giant or Waiting for the Thursday Boat* by Robert Munsch (1989), illustrated by Gilles Tibo. Writer as well as illustrator, Tibo's reputation is strong in both French and English Canada. His airbrush technique delivers a magical effect.

*Facing*: Mary Durack was one of the earliest Australian writers who tried to make children aware of the lives of aborigines. *The Way of the Whirlwind* (1941).

first of many books to collect and retell for children stories and legends of some of Canada's aboriginal peoples. A second volume of stories appeared in 1922, *Canadian Fairy Tales*. In 1955, MacMillan's stories about the Micmac hero Glooscap were brought together in one volume: *Glooscap's Country and Other Indian Tales*, 'the most significant collection of Indian tales published before the 1960s', according to Egoff and Saltman.

Egoff and Saltman use the word 'Indian' to refer to those of Canada's first peoples who live south of the Northwest Territories and the Yukon. The word is, as they point out, problematic. Not only do the people of the first nations rightly reject this term, but the term misleadingly homogenizes many peoples. In a similar way, the term 'Inuit' is misleading. In an attempt to point out that differences exist between various regions and tribes, collections of native stories for young readers often present stories from various peoples. This is the case in Diamond Jenness's *The Corn Goddess* (1975) or in the earlier collection by Ella Elizabeth Clark, *Indian Legends of Canada* (1960). In the 1960s many books appeared by non-native authors retelling tales of specific peoples across the country: for example, Christie Harris, *Once Upon a Totem*, Dorothy Reid, *Tales of Nanabozho*, and Kay Hill, *Glooscap and his Magic*, all published in 1963. Longer works of fiction also took up legends and cultural practices of the native peoples: for example, Edith Lambert Sharp's *Nkwala* (1958), Roderick Haig-Brown's *The Whale People* (1962), the many books by James Houston, Doris Anderson's *Slave of the Haida* (1974), and Jan Hudson's *Sweetgrass* (1984).

Many non-native Canadian children's writers have taken up the subject of cultural conflict. Books such as Monica Hughes's *The Ghost Dance Caper* (1978) and Brenda Bellingham's *Storm Child* (1985) deal with young people caught between two cultures, one native and the other non-native. For older readers, Cam Hubert's *Dreamspeaker* (1978) offers an uncompromising look at the power of the spirit world as envisaged by the Nookta people of British Columbia.

More recently, books are appearing from native writers themselves. One of

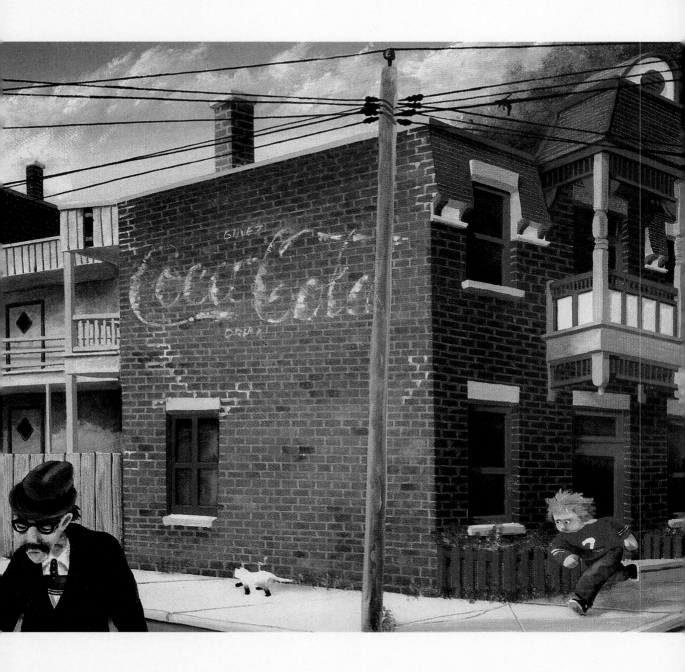

the first of these is George Clutesi's *Son of Raven, Son of Deer: Fables of the Tse-Shaht People* (1967). Collections such as *Tales from the Longhouse* (1973), *Stories from Pangnirtung* (1976), Basil Johnston's *Tales the Elders Told: Ojibway Legends* (1981), and George Elston's *Giving: Ojibwa Stories and Legends from the Children of Curve Lake* (1985) present native stories without the filter of non-native revision.

The sensitivity of native peoples to the words used to describe regional and culturally distinct bands serves as a reminder of another Canadian fact: the country's intense regionalism. In Canada the existence of two literatures, one in French and one in English, simply underlines what exists, with less intensity but no less reality, within Anglophone culture itself. Writers identify with specific places, the windswept prairie of W. O. Mitchell and William Kurelek, the Prince Edward Island of L. M. Montgomery, the British Columbia forests and sea coasts of Ann Blades, the Newfoundland of Kevin Major, the Alberta ranchland of Marilyn Halvorson, the Quebec villages of Roch Carrier. On the other hand, some writers make a concerted effort to embrace all of the country, either through books that tour the country such as Brian Doyle's *Hey, Dad!* (1978) or through a series of books such as Eric Wilson's 'Tom and Liz Austen' mysteries, which are set in various centres across Canada from Ottawa to Winnipeg to Vancouver.

A survey of books for children in Canada reveals little of substance and staying power before the mid-1970s. In the middle of this decade, two books appeared which initiated a boom in the publishing of children's books: Dennis Lee's *Alligator Pie* (1974) and Mordecai Richler's *Jacob Two-Two Meets the Hooded Fang* (1975). Both books show an interest in empowering young readers, Lee by encouraging his readers to play with his rhymes and even add to them, and Richler by focusing on the theme of 'Child Power'. Despite an overt interest in Canadian themes—perhaps more overt in *Alligator Pie*, but apparent in *Jacob Two-Two* as well—these books contain echoes from the sources of Canada's cultural imagery in the two dominating influences on Canada socially, economically, and culturally: for example, references to Bunyan's *Pilgrim's Progress*, Carroll's 'Alice' books, the medieval ballad 'The False Knight and the Little Boy', and American superhero comics appear in *Jacob Two-Two*. *Alligator Pie* contains allusions to traditional nursery rhymes, to A. A. Milne and Peter Rabbit, and to home-grown ghosts such as William Lyon Mackenzie King and the Ookpik who without his hair 'isn't there'.

Whereas Richler's fantasy about Jacob Two-Two, set in England and in Jacob's dream world, served as a catalyst for other writers to turn their attention to fantasies (some of which have settings in the United Kingdom and Ireland: works by O. R. Melling, Elona Malterre, and Welwyn Wilton Katz, for example), Lee's poetry generated a strong sense of the imaginative possibilities of Canada itself. Place-names carry a splendid lyrical potential and Lee

*Facing*: the work of Canadian author-illustrator Stéphane Poulin from his book *Have you seen Josephine?* (1986).

takes wonderful advantage of this: Aklavik, Gatineaus, Kamloops, Kenagami, Kitimat, and on and on. The result of Lee's delight in the sounds of Canadian places and his refashioning of traditional rhymes into a Canadian context is a flood of Canadian poetry for children by poets such as sean o'huigan, bp nichol, Lois Simmie, Robert Heidbreder, and Sherie Fitch. Prior to the publication of *Alligator Pie*, little poetry for children written by Canadians appeared in Canada; perhaps the best-known book of poetry appeared in 1968, *The Wind Has Wings*, edited by Mary Alice Downie and Barbara Robertson, but the poems in this anthology are not specifically written for children. A second result of Lee's celebration of things Canadian is the newly found confidence among Canadian writers to celebrate the country.

Canadian children's literature is haunted by the past, reflecting a colony's need to reconstruct its past in order to understand its present. Notable is the insistence of history in Canadian children's books, even in works of fantasy. One of the better-known Canadian fantasies, Janet Lunn's *The Root Cellar* (1981), explicitly sets the history of the American Civil War against the pastoralism of nineteenth-century Canada, a pastoralism the book claims is still alive and well in the late twentieth century.

What the future brings in Canada is uncertain. Political events indicate a continuing interest in separatism in various regions, especially Quebec. This

*The New Baby Calf* by Edith Newlin Chase (1984), illustrated by Barbara Reid. Reid won the Canada Council Award for illustration in 1986 for *Have You Seen Birds?* She demonstrates a daring and inventive use of her chosen medium, plasticine.

340

might at least partly explain the continuing interest in books that return to Canada's history. At the same time, many recent children's books reflect both a cosmopolitan confidence on the part of Canadian authors and illustrators, and an interest in various cultural groups. The work of Robert Munsch is well known throughout the English-speaking world, and the work of Robin Muller reflects a confidence that Canada too can turn out versions of traditional European stories. Indeed, collections of Canadian fairy-tales such as the well-known volume by Marius Barbeau and Michael Hornyansky, *The Golden Phoenix* (1958), and Eva Martin and Laszlo Gal's *Canadian Fairy Tales* (1984), show clearly the European roots of traditional Canadian tales. The collaboration of Eric Beddows and Tim Wynne-Jones on the 'Zoom' series also shows great confidence in presenting books that are not explicitly 'Canadian' in theme or content.

*The Golden Pine Cone* by Catherine Anthony Clark (1950), illustrated by Clare Bice. Bice was a writer as well as an illustrator. In the 1940s and 1950s he was one of Canada's most important illustrators.

Also writers such as Paul Yee, Joy Kogawa, and Tololwa Mollel bring aspects of minority cultures to young readers.

Traditionally, Canada has been thought of as a country with two cultures, French and English. Even now these two groups constitute the largest cultural regions. Consideration of French Canada's children's literature should be as full as that of English Canada. Space, however, permits only a glance at this literature. In general, the historical observations concerning English Canadian children's books apply to those in French Canada, although the sources of Quebec's literature lie in France (witness the influence of the thirteenth-century *Legenda aurea*). More recently, publishing houses in Quebec—for example, Tundra Books and La Courte Échelle working with Heritage—have released a number of their most successful French books in English translation. Author-illustrators such as Stéphane Poulin and Gilles Tibo, and novelist Suzanne Martel, among others, now have strong reputations in English Canada.

Perhaps Joan Finnigan's *Look! The Land is Growing Giants* (1983; with drawings by Richard Pelham) will serve to sum up the situation in Canada. Finnigan is a specialist in eastern Ontario and especially Ottawa Valley folklore, and in this picture-book she fashions a tall tale around the exploits of a legendary figure, Joe Montferrand. Finnigan attempts to create a truly Canadian myth, one that brings together both French and English culture through her hero's name and his situation between Montreal and Ottawa. But there is more. Timber baron Daniel McLachlin speaks his expletives in French: 'Mon Dieu! Sacre Bleu!' Here a patronizing note rings, and when Joe twice meets

*Zoom Away* by Tim Wynne-Jones (1985), pictures by Eric Beddows. Winner of the Howard-Gibbon Medal for the first two 'Zoom' books, Beddows creates a fantasy of ice and snow for his ordinary cat-hero.

Robert Munsch is Canada's best-known story-teller. From conception to publication, his stories derive from an oral source. He tests all his books with repeated oral tellings before he publishes them.

the monster, the Windigo, on the 'Quebec side of the Ottawa Valley', the association of Quebec with trouble-making is difficult to avoid. Joe defeats the monster and the burning of its corpse 'brought creeds and breeds together in a Melting Pot. And the Ottawa Valley was melded into a separate entity, unique and special as an island.'

It is hard to escape the notion that the defeat of the French has taken place a second time here, and the result is that most Canadian of places—a garrison. Garrisons breed suspicion; they feed the separatist sensibility. On the other hand, Finnigan's use of the 'melting pot' metaphor cannot but remind adult readers of Canada's neighbour to the south. Perhaps the destiny of the nation lies there. In fact, the end of *Look! The Land is Growing Giants* might corroborate this. Joe marries and has six sons. The sons find themselves without employment now that the timber is all gone from the Valley. Wanting to continue their father's work 'in wood' and 'in snow and ice', the boys become the first Montreal Canadiens hockey team. The book ends with a long list of the teams begun by the progeny of Joe's sons, beginning with the Ottawa Silver Seven and moving on to include the Detroit Red Wings, New York Rangers, Los Angeles Kings, and so on. Either we have here another instance of a Canadian 'triumph' south of the border, something akin to what happens in Roberts's *Red Fox*, or the prophecy of Canada's future.

# NEW ZEALAND

## *Betty Gilderdale*

Ever since 1833, when the first book set in New Zealand was published anonymously (*Stories about Many Things: Founded on Facts*), two recurrent themes have dominated New Zealand literature for children. They are a preoccupation with the indigenous Maori people and with the Land itself. Both were totally new experiences for the early—mainly British—settlers. The Maori culture was as alien as the steep forested mountains, the cascading rivers, the smoking volcanoes, and the ever-present danger of earthquakes. This beautiful but wild terrain contrasted sharply with the ancient and largely benign landscape they had left behind them. In this new country vast desolate areas were totally uninhabited and books by early settlers, often assembled from letters 'Home' to Britain, bewailed the inability to reach a doctor in times of crisis and how it took more than six months to receive a reply to a letter sent to England.

The most entertaining early settler writer was Lady Barker, whose account of sheep farming in Canterbury, *Station Life in New Zealand* (1870), has become a classic for adults, but she included stories about New Zealand in her children's books *Stories About* (1870), *A Christmas Cake in Four Quarters* (1871), and *Boys* (1874).

The 'settler' stories often emanated from the South Island and were written by educated women who kept diaries and wrote letters to record their experiences. The early books set in the North Island, however, reveal a greater preoccupation with forging a relationship with the Maori, often expressing the missionaries' point of view. They were generally sympathetic to the Maori, but unfortunately differences between the indigenous people and settlers were to erupt into disputes which later became known as the Land Wars. Overseas writers such as G. A. Henty and Jules Verne were not slow to make capital from the situation in fast-paced adventure stories, but novels written

343

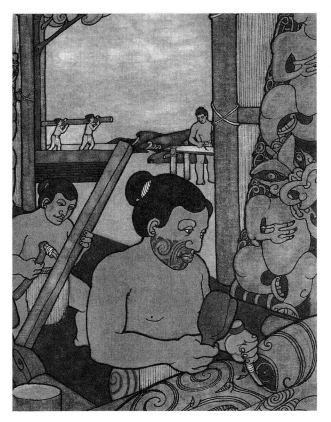

Illustration of R. L. Bacon's *The Home of the Winds* by R. H. Jahnke.

by New Zealanders, most notably William Satchell's *The Greenstone Door* (1914), stressed the poignancy of divided loyalties when friendships between individual Maori and Europeans were at variance with their tribal or national loyalties. The theme was picked up thirteen years later by Mona Tracy in *Rifle and Tomahawk* (1927) and more recently by Anne de Roo in *Jacky Nobody* (1983), and friendship between Maori and European has remained a major component in books for children.

By 1914 local wars were over and the settlers had settled, but there was now a new generation of New Zealand-born children who required stories. Britain's golden age of children's literature had gone unremarked; New Zealand writers were more interested in educating children about the flora and fauna of the land of their birth. Unfortunately they chose to do this through a dismal procession of sentimental fantasy stories which have quite rightly been consigned to obscurity.

One writer, Edith Howes, however, was an excellent story-teller and her 'flower fairy' stories (*The Sun's Babies* (1910) onwards) have a robust sense of narrative. She was a science teacher, determined that children should know more about Nature, and her books received much acclaim both in New Zealand and in England, where they were published by Cassell. In *The Cradle Ship* (1916) she broke new ground by gently explaining the 'facts of life' through the observation of fish, birds, and mammals. It was enormously successful and was translated into French, Italian, and Danish, but to contemporary eyes it is excessively sentimental and it is her later adventure story *Silver Island* (1928) which has stood the test of time.

The fact that many of Edith Howes's books were published in London highlights a dilemma which has plagued New Zealand authors from the outset. In a country with a small population—it is currently only 3 million and was considerably fewer before 1950—royalties are likely to be minimal if a book only has local readership. Aspiring writers have always dispatched their manuscripts to England, where publication would mean wider distribution and higher royalties. An unfortunate consequence of this policy was that New Zealand writers could get swallowed up by the British market and not be recognized in their country of origin, especially as few British publishers had outlets in New Zealand and children's books were never reviewed in newspapers or journals.

A prolific writer of family stories, Isabel Maud Peacocke, whose novels were also published in London (by Ward Lock), complained that her books were often sold out in Britain and never reached New Zealand at all. This loss of indigenous writers in the larger ocean of British publishing may account for the lack of an accumulated literary heritage in New Zealand; relatively few of the best books found their way back into the country and there was no demand for them to be reissued.

During the 1920s a favourable climate for children's literature began to develop. A library conference held in Dunedin ten years earlier in 1910 had advocated the setting up of juvenile libraries and reading rooms in municipal libraries and gradually the decision had been implemented. Not only was reading encouraged, but children were urged to write their own stories and in Christchurch a young journalist, Esther Glen, established a Children's Supplement in the *Christchurch Sun*, where young writers were published. She herself, in answer to Ethel Turner's *Seven Little Australians* (1894), wrote *Six Little New Zealanders* (1917) and its sequel *Uncles Three at Kamahi* (1926).

The books are a natural progression from Lady Barker's depiction of Canterbury as they describe how six city children, unused to life in the country, descend upon their bachelor uncles' Canterbury sheep station. The resulting chaotic and amusing interactions began a tradition of rural stories, later to be developed by Joyce West in the 1950s. Both authors depict a beneficent existence where food is plentiful, family relationships are warm and supportive, and social events centre round point-to-point meetings and the local Agricultural Show.

By contrast the urban novels of Isabel Maud Peacocke, set in Auckland, depict a less happy picture of the period. Disabled ex-servicemen return to unemployment, people die because they cannot afford a doctor, and broken homes result in arguments over guardianship, while the accepting relationships of the country stories are marred in the city by social distinctions and snobbery. Although variable in style and often sentimental the large body of work by Peacocke is nevertheless highly readable and often memorable.

The development of New Zealand children's literature has, unfortunately, been dependent upon a 'boom or bust' economy which seems to lurch between prosperity and poverty over successive twenty-year cycles.

From *Our Street* by Brian Sutton Smith, illustrated by Russell Clark (1950). Russell Clark was a leading illustrator of the period and the Library Association's Illustration Award is named after him.

Advances made in the 1920s and 1930s were quickly eroded first by the Great Depression and then by isolation during the years of the Second World War, and books published during that period suffered from poor editing and production. But when the economy did finally recover in the 1950s, the good writers of the 1920s had been forgotten and it was deemed necessary to start yet again informing children about New Zealand. Well-intentioned authors such as Avis Acres invented flower fairies to introduce children to indigenous flora and fauna, oblivious of the fact that Edith Howes had already done so thirty years earlier. An increasing desire to establish a New Zealand identity, separate and different from the British one, resulted in a proliferation of photographic books with titles such as *David, Boy of the High Country* by Gay Kohlap (1964) and *Kuma is a Maori Girl,* Pat Lawson (1961).

The preoccupation with the land, never far from the New Zealand consciousness, now manifested itself in a number of adventure stories where the protagonists could lose themselves in the bush, be cut off by landslides following earthquakes, or nearly drown in floods. Often during the course of

From *BidiBidi* by Gavin Bishop (1982). Gavin Bishop is a South Island artist and this story of the adventures of a sheep, illustrated with views of the Southern Alps, is quintessential New Zealand.

their adventures they would discover smugglers bent upon illegally exporting either Maori artefacts or rare species such as the paua, the tuatara, or kakapo parrots, and South Island authors Phyl Wardell in the 1960s and Joan de Hamel ten years later have both made conservation and the protection of rare species an integral part of their novels.

The 1960s were also to see a return to 'settler' themes, with Elsie Locke, Ruth Dallas, and Eve Sutton all emphasizing the hardships endured by the less wealthy immigrants who arrived in the country without the financial advantages of the South Island Canterbury settlers. In these later stories widows often had to support their children by taking up either nursing or market gardening and young boys tried to make their way in a hard-headed and largely uncaring society.

There was no place in this spirit of determined didacticism for books which were not specifically about New Zealand, and a young Christchurch librarian, whose stories ran counter to the prevailing search for a national identity, found that no local publisher wanted her work. She was told that her archetypal wizards, witches, and pirates were too international and were not relevant to New Zealand. The young librarian was Margaret Mahy, but fortunately her finely constructed tales were published in the 'School Journals', small magazines distributed as reading material to all schools by the Department of Education. It was when the 'Journals' were sent on exhibition to the United States that Mahy's stories were noticed by an editor of Franklin Watts publishing house, who enthusiastically embraced them, and arranged for them to be illustrated by leading artists. Dent bought the rights for the English market and in 1969 five Margaret Mahy picture-books were launched. They won instant acclaim and her books have since won numerous international and local awards, including the British Carnegie Medal on two occasions. It should, perhaps, also be noted that, like earlier New Zealand writers, she has continued to publish with overseas, and not local, publishers.

Although it is true that most of Mahy's stories are fantasy which transcends national boundaries, there are, nevertheless, strong New Zealand components in her work. Her external landscapes are island landscapes, and the surrounding seas are consistent ingredients in many more stories than the most obvious *The Man Whose Mother was a Pirate* (1972) or *Sailor Jack and the Twenty Orphans* (1970). Earthquakes do not upset libraries in books of other nationalities, as they do in *The Librarian and the Robbers* (1978), nor are there erupting volcanoes like the ones in *Aliens in the Family* (1986).

Many of her stories explore the tensions between the constraints of everyday living and the demands of imaginative freedom. Her characters discard the respectable 'tidy' living demanded in New Zealand suburbia and leave for more adventurous climes, but the nonconformists are not necessarily young, and in the portrayal of unusual and independent elderly characters Mahy is

347

From *Hairy Maclary from Donaldson's Dairy* by Lynley Dodd (1983). 'With tails in the air they trotted on down | Past the shops and the park to the far end of town'. New Zealand's best-known picture-book in which Dodd captures the characters of her animals with no hint of condescension.

following a consistent theme in New Zealand literature. In *The Wind between the Stars* (1976) old Phoebe is willing to go with the wind, the elderly Great Uncle Magnus Pringle in *The Ultra Violet Catastrophe* (1975) resents being cosseted as though he were a pot plant, and in her most brilliant portrayal of old age, *Memory* (1987), Sophie, a sufferer from Alzheimer's disease, although living in outwardly chaotic conditions, is nevertheless imposing what Mahy calls her 'inner society' of order and memory upon a disintegrating 'outer society'.

The New Zealand preoccupation with elderly nonconformists may in part stem from the Maori heritage of respect for grandparents in the extended family situation and the 1970s witnessed a considerable revival of interest in the Maori. This coincided with the development of locally produced picture-books, the result of a number of multinational publishers becoming established in Auckland who were familiar with the complicated processes of colour reproduction, seldom before attempted by local publishers in children's books. One of the first picture-books in full colour on a Maori theme was Jill Bagnall's *Crayfishing with Grandmother* (1973), which was also the first picture-book with both Maori and English texts, a feature which is now an established practice in many contemporary picture-books.

An Auckland teacher, R. L. Bacon, was a major influence in reviving an interest in Maori legends and he insisted that his poetic and economical retellings should be complemented by a high standard of illustration from

348

Maori artists. His three books *The House of the People* (1977), *The Fish of our Fathers* (1984), and *The Home of the Winds* (1986), which explain how the first Maori Meeting House, War Canoe, and fortified 'pa' were constructed, are all finely interpreted by R. H. Jahnke's stylized pictures, which broke new ground in illustration.

By the 1970s a very favourable climate for children's literature was being established on the North Shore of Auckland. A Children's Literature Association had been formed, supported by a nearby enterprising bookseller, Dorothy Butler, one of whose staff, Ronda Armitage, was later to write one of New Zealand's most acclaimed picture-books, *The Lighthouse Keeper's Lunch* (1977).

During the 1970s and 1980s the work of Dr Marie Clay of the University of Auckland was attracting world-wide attention as she insisted that children learnt to read better by reading 'real books', than artificially graded 'readers'. As a result, authors of the calibre of Margaret Mahy, Joy Cowley, and R. L. Bacon were commissioned by New Zealand publishers to write short stories to be produced in picture-book form for the school market. The success of these books as tools for learning to read has led to large export orders and to a phenomenal increase in the production of picture-books in New Zealand.

Quantity, however, has not always meant quality. The lack of courses in illustration and book design in art schools, added to world-wide demise in training in figure drawing, has meant that the pictorial component of New Zealand picture-books has not always matched what are frequently good and appropriate verbal texts. It is no accident that two of the best-known picture-book authors, Ronda Armitage and Pamela Allen, have been published in Britain or Australia, rather than locally.

One New Zealand author-illustrator who has always been initially published locally but who has become internationally famous is Lynley Dodd, whose *Hairy Maclary* series introduces a memorable gallery of canine and feline characters. Dodd's cumulative rhythmical texts are totally at one with the pictures.

Since the 1980s the obsessive desire to produce books with 'Life in New Zealand' as their obvious aim has diminished. Those which have held up the mirror to New Zealand society have done so less self-consciously. In her *Alex* (1987) series Tessa Duder portrays the stresses and strains of a young woman who enters the world of competitive swimming, while the New Zealand preoccupation with sport is satirized in William Taylor's *The Worst Soccer Team Ever* (1987).

Although the Maori component in New Zealand literature remains an important one, there have been few attempts to merge Maori and European literary traditions and Gaylene Gordon is one of the few authors to have placed Maori folklore within modern fantasy settings for older readers. In general

Maori subject-matter is treated in picture-books for younger children or in straightforward retellings of legends.

The interest in the Land which so characterizes New Zealand literature, having first provided material for settler dismay, then having acted as a challenge in adventure stories, has more recently become the province of science-fiction writers. Some of the most accomplished contemporary authors, Maurice Gee, Barry Faville, Caroline Macdonald, Jack Lasenby, and Sherryl Jordan, depict a future in which New Zealand has suffered some holocaust, either war, pollution, or volcanic eruption. Their imagined scenarios often explore alternative methods of government in new and unpredictable circumstances but the ultimate message is usually hopeful—New Zealand will be saved from Armageddon by its isolation, although it must not repeat mistakes of the past if the land is to be restored to its former glory.

The theme of the land itself suffering from human greed is central to the work of Anthony Holcroft, who, in his short stories, explores archetypal themes set in a deeply felt and penetratingly observed South Island landscape where impoverishment of the human spirit results in barren soil. Joy Cowley's numerous books for young children also use fantasy to depict human failings but often with splendid solutions. A duck in a gun succeeds in preventing a war in *The Duck in the Gun* (1969), while a fierce little woman discovers that a bullying pirate is, in fact, afraid of the dark in *The Fierce Little Woman and the Wicked Pirate*, (1984).

Illustration by Robyn Belton from *The Duck in the Gun* by Joy Cowley. Robyn Belton is one of New Zealand's most highly respected illustrators and has charmingly interpreted Joy Cowley's story of how a war was prevented by a duck laying its eggs in a gun. 'The General and the Gunner went out to where the gun had been set.'

Joy Cowley, Anthony Holcroft, and Margaret Mahy are all considerable stylists and are never condescending to young readers. But an overview of language in children's books from 1833 to the present cannot help but reveal a deterioration in vocabulary, particularly over the past ten years. Earlier writers such as Howes, Peacocke, and Glen expected their readers to be literate, but in the past decade books purporting to have been written by 13-year-olds use first-person narration to bewail their problems in the current teenage vernacular.

The variety of style and subject-matter in New Zealand writing for children over the past twenty years has, nevertheless, contributed to a rich tapestry of literature which is out of all proportion to the size of the population. In spite of advances, however, there are worrying signs that books for children are again suffering from a prolonged economic downturn. Cuts in education spending have meant that there are now no university courses in children's literature and those colleges of education which formerly showed a strength in the area have been hampered by staff cuts and short-term employment contracts. The consequence of these measures is that there is very little academic study of the genre, while the unwillingness of publishers to risk reissuing classic books is again leading to the loss of a literary heritage. In an ironic twist of fate authors, like their predecessors in the 1920s, are once again forced on to an overseas publishing market where any specific reference to local New Zealand conditions or vocabulary is strongly discouraged and the hard-won New Zealand literary identity is once again in danger of being lost in the wider world. It is, however, a world where many New Zealand authors are universally known and respected, even if their nationality often remains unrecognized.

# CHRONOLOGY

The items in this chronology are listed generally by short title and by their first publication in book form. Also included are literary and historical events which place these items in their wider context.

| | |
|---|---|
| c.1005 | Ælfric, *Colloquium* |
| c.1138 | Geoffrey of Monmouth, *History of the Kings of Britain* |
| 1382 | William of Wykeham founds Winchester college and grammar school |
| 1391 | Geoffrey Chaucer, *Tretis of the Astrolabie* |
| 1473 | Caxton, *History of Troy*, first book printed in English |
| 1477 | [William Caxton] *The Book of Curtesye* |
| 1483/4 | [William Caxton] Aesop's *Fables* |
| 1547 | Death of Henry VIII |
| 1549 | William Lily, *Short Introduction to Grammar*; *Book of Common Prayer* |
| 1570 | Roger Ascham, *The Scholemaster* |
| 1580 | Jost Amman, *Book of Art and Instruction for Young People* |
| 1607 | Virginia colony founded at Jamestown |
| 1611 | King James's *Bible* (Authorized Version) |
| 1621 | *The History of Tom Thumbe* (earliest surviving edition) |
| 1642 | English Civil War; NZ discovered by Tasman |
| 1644 | Milton, *On Education* |
| 1647 | Massachusetts law makes school provision compulsory |
| 1659 | Comenius, *Orbis sensualium pictus* (trans. Charles Hoole) |
| 1671? | Thomas White, *A Little Book for Little Children* |
| 1671–2 | James Janeway, *A Token for the Children*, parts 1 and 2 |
| 1678 | John Bunyan, *The Pilgrim's Progress* |
| 1686 | John Bunyan, *A Book for Boys and Girls; or, Country Rhymes for Children* |
| 1686–90? | *The New England Primer* |
| 1693 | John Locke, *Some Thoughts Concerning Education* |
| 1700 | Cotton Mather, *A Token for Children of New England* |
| 1706–8 | First English translation of the *Arabian Nights Entertainment* (Grub Street version from French translation, 1704) |
| 1707 | Countess d'Aulnoy, *Tales of the Fairies in Three Parts Compleat* [*Contes des fées*, 1698; part trans. into English in 1699]; Union of Scotland and England |
| 1712 | William Ronksley, *The Child's Weeks-Work*; Pope, *The Rape of the Lock* |
| 1715 | Isaac Watts, *Divine Songs*; Jacobite Rebellion |
| 1729 | Charles Perrault, *Histories, or Tales of Past Times. Told by Mother Goose* [1697] |
| 1744 | [Mary Cooper], *Tommy Thumb's Pretty Song Book Vol. 2*; [John Newbery], *A Little Pretty Pocket Book* |

1749    Sarah Fielding, *The Governess; or, The Little Female Academy*

1751–2    *Lilliputian Magazine*

1756    [Samuel Richardson] *The Paths of Virtue Delineated* (children's versions of *Pamela, Clarissa*, and *Sir Charles Grandison*)

1765    [John Newbery] *The History of Little Goody Two-Shoes*

1769    NZ surveyed by Cook; Goldsmith, *The Deserted Village*

1770    Cook 'discovers' Australia

1776    American Declaration of Independence

1778    Anna Laetitia Barbauld, *Lessons for Children* (and 1794, 1803)

1786    Sarah Trimmer, *Fabulous Histories* [*The History of the Robins*]

1787    Mary Wollstonecraft, *Thoughts on the Education of Daughters*

1788    Mary Wollstonecraft, *Original Stories from Real Life*

1789    French Revolution; Blake, *Songs of Innocence*

1792    Salem Witch trials

1795–8    Hannah More, *Cheap Repository Tracts*

1798    Wordsworth and Coleridge, *Lyrical Ballads*

1800    Union with Ireland; Maria Edgeworth, *Castle Rackrent*

1801    Maria Edgeworth, *Early Lessons*

1802–6    Sarah Trimmer, *The Guardian of Education*

1804    Jane and Ann Taylor, *Original Poems for Infant Minds*

1805    [Sarah Catharine Martin] *The Comic Adventures of Old Mother Hubbard*

1806    [dated 1807] Charles and Mary Lamb, *Tales from Shakespeare*

1807    William Roscoe, *The Butterfly's Ball*; abolition of Slave Trade in British Empire

1811    Jane Austen, *Sense and Sensibility*

1812    American war with England

1814    Johann Wyss (trans. Godwin), *The Family Robinson Crusoe* [*Der Schweizerische Robinson*, 1812–13]; Stephenson's steam locomotive

1815    Battle of Waterloo

1818    Mary Martha Sherwood, *The History of the Fairchild Family* (II, 1842; III, 1847)

1823–6    Edgar Taylor publishes first English version of Brothers Grimm as *German Popular Stories*; Clement Clarke Moore, 'A Visit from St Nicholas'

1823    Fenimore Cooper, *The Spy*

1824    *Children's Friend* (–1882) and *Child's Companion* (–1932)

1827    'Peter Parley', *Tales of Peter Parley about America*

1830    Henry Savery, *Quintus Servitor* (first novel in Australian pub. in book form)

1830s    Jacob Abbott, 'Rollo' books

1836    Dickens, *Sketches by Boz*; Charles Darwin visits Australia

1837    Sara Coleridge, *Phantasmion*; accession of Victoria to English throne

1838    Charles Dickens, *Oliver Twist; or, The Parish Boy's Progress*

1839    Monthly publication of *Peter Parley's Magazine* begins in Britain (–1863); Catherine Sinclair, *Holiday House*

1840 Charlotte Barton, *A Mother's Offering to her Children* (Australia's first children's book)

1841 Harriet Martineau, *The Playfellow*, including *Feats on the Fiord* and *The Crofton Boys*; Captain Marryat, *Masterman Ready* (1841–2)

1842 James Orchard Halliwell, *The Nursery Rhymes of England*; Robert Browning, 'The Pied Piper of Hamelin'; Chartist Riots

1843 'Felix Summerley', *The Home Treasury*; Ruskin, *Modern Painters*; Dickens, *A Christmas Carol*

1844 F. E. Paget, *The Hope of the Katzekopfs*

1845 'Ambrose Merton', *Gammer Gurton's Story Books*

1846 Hans Andersen, *A Danish Story Book*, *Danish Fairy Legends and Tales*, *Wonderful Stories for Children*; R. H. Horne, *Memoirs of a London Doll*; Edward Lear, *A Book of Nonsense.*

1847 Emily Brontë, *Wuthering Heights*; Thackeray, *Vanity Fair*

1848 Mrs Alexander, *Hymns for Little Children*; Heinrich Hoffmann, *The English Struwwelpeter*

1850 North London Collegiate School for Girls founded; Public Libraries Act

1851 W. H. G. Kingston, *Peter the Whaler*; Nathaniel Hawthorne, *The House of the Seven Gables*; Melville, *Moby Dick*; Stowe, *Uncle Tom's Cabin*; Great Exhibition

1852 Captain Mayne Reid, *The Desert Home*; John Ruskin, *King of the Golden River*; Catharine Parr Traill, *The Canadian Crusoes: A Tale of the Rice Lake Plains* (possibly the first Canadian Children's book); NZ granted self-government

1854 'Oliver Optic', *The Boat Club*

1854–6 Crimean War

1855 Mrs Molesworth, *The Carved Lions*; Charles Kingsley, *Westward Ho!*; W. M. Thackeray, *The Rose and the Ring*; Longfellow, *Hiawatha*

1856 R. M. Ballantyne, *Snowflakes and Sunbeams: or The Young Fur Traders*; Charlotte Yonge, *The Daisy Chain, or Aspirations: A Family Chronicle*

1857 Thomas Hughes, *Tom Brown's Schooldays*; Indian Mutiny

1858 Frederick Farrar, *Eric, or, Little by Little*; India transferred to British Crown

1859–72 Tennyson, *Idylls of the King*

1861–5 American Civil War

1863 Charles Kingsley, *The Water Babies*

1865 'Lewis Carroll', *Alice's Adventures in Wonderland*; Walter Crane, *Sing a Song of Sixpence*; Mary Mapes Dodge, *Hans Brinker; or, The Silver Skates*; *Our Young Folks* (–1873); assassination of Lincoln; Slavery prohibited in US

1866 Mrs Gatty (ed.), *Aunt Judy's Magazine* (–1885); *The Chatterbox* (–1946); *Boys of England* (–1899)

1867 'Hesba Stretton', *Jessica's First Prayer*; George Emmett, *Boys of Bircham School*; Dominion of Canada formed

1868 Louisa May Alcott, *Little Women*; Horatio Alger, Jr., *Ragged Dick*; Charles Dickens, *A Holiday Romance*

1869　Jean Ingelow, *Mopsa the Fairy*; *Good Words for the Young* (–1877); Emily Davies founds Girton College, Cambridge

1870　Thomas Adrich, *The Story of a Bad Boy*; Mrs Ewing, *The Brownies and Other Tales*; Education Act (UK) provides education for all children between 5–12 years

1871　'Lewis Carroll', *Through the Looking Glass*; 'Susan Coolidge', *What Katy Did*; G. A. Henty, *Out on the Pampas; or, The Young Settlers*; George MacDonald, *At the Back of the North Wind*; George Eliot, *Middlemarch*

1872　Christina Rossetti, *Sing-Song*

1873　Mary Mapes Dodge becomes editor of *St Nicholas* magazine.

1875　'Brenda', *Froggy's Little Brother*

1876　'Mark Twain', *The Adventures of Tom Sawyer*; *Young Folks* (–1897, variant titles)

1877　Mrs Molesworth, *The Cuckoo Clock*; Anna Sewell, *Black Beauty*

1878　Randolph Caldecott, *The Diverting History of John Gilpin*

1879　*The Boy's Own Paper* (–1967); Kate Greenaway, *Under the Window*

1880　*The Girl's Own Paper* (–1965); Lucretia Hale, *The Peterkin Papers*; Joel Chandler Harris, *Uncle Remus*; *The Union Jack* (–1883)

1881　James, *Portrait of a Lady*

1882　Richard Jefferies, *Bevis: The Story of a Boy*

1883　Thomas Hardy writes *Our Exploits at West Poley* (pub. 1892/3); Robert Louis Stevenson, *Treasure Island*

1884　Johanna Spyri, *Heidi* (1881) (first English translation); Twain, *The Adventures of Huckleberry Finn*

1885　H. Rider Haggard, *King Solomon's Mines*; Robert Louis Stevenson, *A Child's Garden of Verses*; Internal Combustion Engine

1886　Frances Hodgson Burnett, *Little Lord Fauntleroy*; L. T. Meade, *A World of Girls: The Story of a School*; National Society for the Prevention of Cruelty to Children founded (UK)

1887　Talbot Baines Reed, *The Fifth Form at St Dominic's*

1888　Oscar Wilde, *The Happy Prince*

1889　Andrew Lang (ed.), *The Blue Fairy Book*; Wilde, *The Importance of Being Earnest*

1890　Alfred Harmsworth *Comic Cuts* (–1953); Joseph Jacobs, *English Fairy Tales*

1891　'C. Collodi', *Pinocchio* (1883) (first English translation)

1894　Rudyard Kipling, *The Jungle Book*; Ethel Turner, *Seven Little Australians*

1895　Kenneth Grahame, *The Golden Age*; Bertha and Florence Upton, *The Adventures of Two Dutch Dolls—and a Golliwogg*

1898　J. Meade Faulkner, *Moonfleet*; Ernest Thompson Seton, *Wild Animals I have Known*

1899　Helen Bannerman, *The Story of Little Black Sambo*; Kenneth Grahame, *Dream Days*; Rudyard Kipling, *Stalky & Co.*; E. Nesbit, *The Story of the Treasure Seekers*; Ethel Pedley, *Dot and the Kangaroo*; Board of Education est. (UK)

1900　L. Frank Baum, *The Wonderful Wizard of Oz*; Commonwealth of Australia formed

| | |
|---|---|
| 1902 | Walter de la Mare, *Songs of Childhood*; Rudyard Kipling, *Just So Stories*; E. Nesbit, *Five Children and It*; Beatrix Potter, *The Tale of Peter Rabbit* |
| 1903 | L. Leslie Brooke, *Johnny Crow's Garden*; Kate Douglas Wiggin, *Rebecca of Sunnybrook Farm* |
| 1904 | J. M. Barrie, *Peter Pan* (first performance); Laura Lee Hope, *The Bobbsey Twins; or, Merry Days Indoors and Out* |
| 1905 | Frances Hodgson Burnett, *A Little Princess* |
| 1906 | Angela Brazil, *The Fortunes of Philippa*; Rudyard Kipling, *Puck of Pook's Hill* |
| 1907–39 | *Gem* |
| 1908 | Kenneth Grahame, *The Wind in the Willows*; L. M. Montgomery, *Anne of Green Gables*; *Magnet* (–1940); Children's Act ('Charter') UK |
| 1909–10 | First Junior High Schools in USA |
| 1909 | Gene Stratton Porter, *A Girl of the Limberlost* |
| 1910 | Rudyard Kipling, *Rewards and Fairies*; Mary Grant Bruce, *A Little Bush Maid*; E.M. Forster, *Howard's End* |
| 1911 | Mary Grant Bruce, *Mates at Billabong*; Frances Hodgson Burnett, *The Secret Garden*; John Masefield, *Jim Davis* |
| 1912 | Howard Garis, *Uncle Wiggly's Adventures*; Jean Webster, *Daddy-Long-Legs* |
| 1913 | Eleanor H. Porter, *Pollyanna*; Arthur Rackham, *Mother Goose*; D. H. Lawrence, *Sons and Lovers* |
| 1914 | Edgar Rice Burroughs, *Tarzan of the Apes*; Henry Ford installs automobile assembly line |
| 1916 | Dorothy Canfield Fisher, *Understood Betsy*; Edmund Dulac, *Fairy Book*; Eleanor Farjeon, *Nursery Rhymes of London Town*; Arthur Ransome, *Old Peter's Russian Tales* |
| 1917 | Esther Glen, *Six Little New Zealanders*; Eliot, *Prufrock and other Observations* |
| 1918 | May Gibbs, *Snugglepot and Cuddlepie*; Norman Lindsay, *The Magic Pudding*; Rose Fyleman, *Fairies and Chimneys* |
| 1919 | Flight across Atlantic |
| 1919–29 | *School Friend* |
| 1920 | Constance Heward, *Ameliaranne and the Green Umbrella*; Hugh Lofting, *The Story of Dr Dolittle*; Elsie J. Oxenham, *The Abbey Girls*; 'Rupert Bear' appears in the *Daily Express* |
| 1922 | Margery Williams, *The Velveteen Rabbit*; Richmal Crompton, *Just—William*; Carl Sandberg, *The Rootabaga Stories*; first Newbery Medal Awarded by the American Library Association to Hendrik Van Loon's *The Story of Mankind*; *Children's Hour*, BBC (–1963); Joyce, *Ulysses* |
| 1923 | Enid Blyton, *Child Whispers*; e.e. cummings, *Tulips and Chimneys* |
| 1924 | A. A. Milne, *When We were Very Young*; first Labour Govt. (UK) |
| 1925 | Elinor M. Brent-Dyer, *The School at the Chalet*; Woolf, *Mrs Dalloway* |
| 1926 | Will James, *Smoky, the Cow-Horse*; A. A. Milne, *Winnie-the-Pooh* |
| 1927 | 'Franklin W. Dixon', *The Tower Treasure* (first Hardy Boys book); John Masefield, *The Midnight Folk*; A. A. Milne, *Now We are Six* |

1928    'Felix Saltern', *Bambi* , (1923) (first English translation); Wanda Gág, *Millions of Cats*; S. G. Hulme Beaman, *Tales of Toytown*; A. A. Milne, *The House at
Pooh Corner*; William Nicholson, *Clever Bill*

1929    Alison Uttley, *The Squirrel, the Hare, and the Little
Grey Rabbit*; Stock Market crash; Faulkner, *The
Sound and the Fury*

1930    'Carolyn Keene', *The Hidden Staircase* (the first
Nancy Drew book); Arthur Ransome, *Swallows and Amazons*

1931    Eric Kästner, *Emil and the Detectives* (1929) (first English translation)

1932    Capt. W. E. Johns, 'The White Fokker' (first 'Biggles' story in *Popular Flying*);
Laura Ingalls Wilder, *Little House in the Big Woods*; F. J. Harvey Darton, *Children's Books in England*

1933    Marjorie Flack, *The Story about Ping* (illustrated by Kurt Wiese); Dorothy Wall,
*Blinky Bill: The Quaint Little Australian*; Prohibition repealed (US)

1934    P. L. Travers, *Mary Poppins*; Geoffrey Trease, *Bows against the Barons*; Jean de
Brunhoff, *The Story of Barbar* (1931) (first English translation)

1935    Enid Bagnold, *National Velvet*; Carol Rylie Brink, *Caddie Woodlawn*; John
Masefield, *The Box of Delights*

1936    Edward Ardizzone, *Little Tim and the Brave Sea Captain*; Munro Leaf, *The Story
of Ferdinand*; Barbara Euphan Todd, *Worzel Gummidge; or, The Scarecrow of
Scatterbrook*; first British Library Association Carnegie Medal awarded to Arthur
Ransome for *Pigeon Post*; Noel Streatfield, *Ballet Shoes*; Spanish Civil War begins

1937    Enid Blyton, *Adventures of the Wishing Chair*; Eve Garnett, *The Family from One
End Street*; J. B. S. Haldane, *My Friend Mr. Leakey*; Katharine Hull and Pamela
Whitlock, *The Far-Distant Oxus*; 'Dr Seuss', *And to Think that I Saw it on Mul-
berry Street*; J. R. R. Tolkien, *The Hobbit; or, There and Back Again*; [Walt Disney]
*Snow White and the Seven Dwarfs*

1938    Elizabeth Enright, *The Thimble Summer*; Marjorie Kinnan Rawlings, *The Year-
ling*; Caldecott medal established; Kathleen Hale, *Orlando the Marmalade Cat*

1939    Ludwig Bemelmans, *Madeline*; T. S. Eliot, *Old Possum's Book of Practical Cats*;
Robert L. May, *Rudolph the Red-Nosed Reindeer*

1940    Maud Hart Lovelace, *Betsy-Tacy*; Eric Knight, *Lassie Come-Home*

1941    Eleanor Estes, *The Moffats*; Robert McClosky, *Make Way for Ducklings*; H. A.
Rey, *Curious George*; Mary Treadgold, *We Couldn't Leave Dinah*; André Maurois,
*Fattipuffs and Thinifers* (*Patapoufs et Filifers*, 1941) (first English translation);
American Lend-Lease Act; Pearl Harbor

1942    'BB', *The Little Grey Men*; Enid Blyton, *Five on a Treasure Island*; Virginia Lee
Burton, *The Little House*; Diana Ross, *The Little Red Engine Gets A Name*

1943    Esther Forbes, *Johnny Tremain*

1944    Education Act, separating primary, secondary and further education in Britain

1945    Revd W. Awdrey, *The Three Railway Engines*; Australian Children's Book Council formed; N Z Esther Glen Award to Stella Morice, *The Book of Wiremu*; Orwell,
*Animal Farm*; Hiroshima bombed

1946    Graham Greene, *The Little Train*; National Health Service (UK)

1947    William Pène du Bois, *Twenty-One Balloons*; first Canadian Library Association Book of the Year Award for Children

1948    C. Day Lewis, *The Otterbury Incident*; Spock, *Baby and Child Care*

1950    Roger Duvoisin, *Petunia*; C. S. Lewis, *The Lion, The Witch, and the Wardrobe*; *Eagle* (–1969); Elizabeth Yates, *Amos Fortune, Free Man*

1951    Cynthia Harnett, *The Wool-Pack*

1952    Ben Lucien Burman, *High Water at Catfish Bend*; Mary Norton, *The Borrowers*; E. B. White, *Charlotte's Web*

1953    William Mayne, *Follow the Footprints*; Meindert DeJong, *The Wheel on the School*

1954    Lucy M. Boston, *The Children of Green Knowe*; Rosemary Sutcliff, *The Eagle of the Ninth*; J. R. R. Tolkien, *The Fellowship of the Ring*; Kingsley Amis, *Lucky Jim*

1955    Philippa Pearce, *Minnow on the Say*

1956    Ian Serraillier, *The Silver Sword*; Beverly Cleary, *Fifteen*

1958    Philippa Pearce, *Tom's Midnight Garden*; Rosemary Sutcliff, *Warrior Scarlet*; Catherine Storr, *Marianne Dreams*

1959    Iona and Peter Opie, *The Language and Lore of Schoolchildren*

1960    Shirley Hughes, *Lucy and Tom's Day*; Alan Garner, *The Weirdstone of Brisingamen*

1961    Ted Hughes, *How the Whale Became and Other Stories*

1962    Joan Aiken, *The Wolves of Willoughby Chase*; Ivan Southall, *Hills End*; Madeleine L'Engle, *A Wrinkle in Time*

1963    Maurice Sendak, *Where the Wild Things Are*; J. F. Kennedy assassinated

1964    Louise Fitzhugh, *Harriet the Spy*; Lloyd Alexander, *The Book of Three*; Roald Dahl, *Charlie and the Chocolate Factory*; Irene Hunt, *Across Five Aprils*; Vietnam War

1965    Susan Cooper, *Over Sea, under Stone*; BBC TV *Jackanory* begins; Ivan Southall, *Ash Road*

1966    Leon Garfield, *Devil-in-the-Fog*; Stoppard, *Rosencrantz and Guildenstern are Dead*

1967    Alan Garner, *The Owl Service*; Russell Hoban, *The Mouse and his Child*; E. A. Konigsburg, *From the Mixed-up Files of Mrs Basil E. Frankweiler*; K. M. Peyton, *Flambards*; S. A. Wakefield, *Bottersnikes and Gumbles*; George Clutesi, *Son of Raven, Son of Deer: Fables of the Tse-Shant People* (first book of Canadian native legends written for children by a member of the First Nations); *Reading Time*, journal of Australian Children's Book Council

1968    Ted Hughes, *The Iron Man*; Patricia Wrightson, *I Own the Racecourse!*; Paul Zindel, *The Pigman*; Ursula Le Guin, *A Wizard of Earthsea*; Peter Dickinson, *The Weathermonger*

1969    William H. Armstrong, *Sounder*; Margaret Mahy, *The Lion in the Meadow*; first Moon landing

1970    Judy Blume, *Are You there, God? It's Me, Margaret*; Leon Garfield and Edward Blishen, *The God beneath the Sea*; Maurice Sendak, *In the Night Kitchen*; Charles Causley, *Figgie Hobbin*

1971    Virginia Hamilton, *The Planet of Junior Brown*; 'Robert C. O'Brien', *Mrs Frisby and the Rats of NIMH*

1972    Richard Adams, *Watership Down*; Norman Klein, *Mom, the Wolfman, and Me*

1973    Raymond Briggs, *Father Christmas*; Nina Bawden, *Carrie's War*; Alan Garner, *Red Shift*; Britain joins EEC; Nixon resigns

1974    Robert Cormier, *The Chocolate War*; establishment of 'Dromkeen' Australian centre for children's literature

1975    Judy Blume, *Forever*; Alan Garner, *The Stone Book*; Mordecai Richler, *Jacob Two-Two Meets the Hooded Fang*; first issue of *Canadian Children's Literature/Littérature canadienne pour la jeunesse*; Robert Westall, *The Machine-Gunners*

1976    First Pacific Rim Conference on Children's Lit. (Vancouver)

1977    Ronda Armitage, *The Lighthouse Keeper's Lunch*; Anthony Browne, *A Walk in the Park*; John Burningham, *Come away from the Water, Shirley*; Gene Kemp, *The Turbulent Term of Tyke Tyler*; Katherine Paterson, *Bridge to Terabithia*; Jan Mark, *Thunder and Lightnings*; Jenny Wagner (illustrated by Ron Brooks) *John Brown, Rose and the Midnight Cat*

1978    Janet and Allan Ahlberg, *Each Peach Pear Plum*; Aidan Chambers, *Breaktime*; Rosemary Wells, *Stanley and Rhoda*; Russell Clarke Award to N Z illustration

1979    Chris Van Allsburg, *The Garden of Abdul Gasazi*; Anthony Browne, *Bear Hunt*; Shirley Hughes, *Up and Up*

1980    Quentin Blake, *Mister Magnolia*; Robert M. Munsch, *The Paper Bag Princess*; William Mayne, *Salt River Times*; David McKee, *Not Now, Bernard*

1981    Maurice Sendak, *Outside over there*; Michael Rosen and Quentin Blake, *You Can't Catch Me!*

1982    David McKee, *I Hate my Teddy Bear*; Dromkeen Medal established; Aidan Chambers, *Dance on my Grave*; Roald Dahl, *The BFG*; Falklands War

1983    Anthony Browne, *Gorilla*; Lynley Dodd, *Hairy Maclary from Donaldson's Dairy*; Mem Fox (illustrated by Julie Vivas), *Possum Magic*

1984    James Aldridge, *The True Story of Lilli Stubeck*; John Burningham, *Granpa*; 'Advance Australia Fair' new Australian National Anthem; Miner's strike in UK

1985    Janni Howker, *The Nature of the Beast*; Patricia MacLachlan, *Sarah, Plain and Tall*

1986    Janet and Allan Ahlberg, *The Jolly Postman*; Fiona French, *Snow White in New York*; Berlie Doherty, *Granny was a Buffer Girl*

1987    James Berry, *A Thief in the Village*

1988    Geraldine McCaughrean, *A Pack of Lies*

1989    Anne Fine, *Goggle-Eyes*; Michael Rosen and Helen Oxenbury, *We're Going on a Bear Hunt*

1990    Gillian Cross, *Wolf*

1991    Berlie Doherty, *Dear Nobody*; David Wiesner, *Tuesday*

1992    William Mayne, *Low Tide*

# FURTHER READING

## GENERAL SOCIAL HISTORY

Peter Coveney, *The Image of Childhood* (Harmondsworth, rev. edn., 1967) [first published as *Poor Monkey*, 1957].

H. Cunningham, *The Children of the Poor: Representations of Childhood since the Seventeenth Century* (Oxford, 1991).

A. Digby, *Children, School and Society in 19th Century England* (London, 1981).

K. and M. Fawdry, *Pollock's History of English Dolls and Toys* (London, 1979).

Monica Kiefer, *American Children through their Books, 1700–1835* (Philadelphia, 1970).

T. W. Laqueur, *Religion and Respectability: Sunday Schools and Working Class Culture 1780–1850* (New Haven, Conn., 1976).

Ivy Pinchbeck and M. Hewitt, *Children in English Society* (2 vols., London, 1969).

Linda Pollock, *A Lasting Relationship: Parents and Children over Three Centuries* (London, 1987).

J. Springhall, *Youth, Empire and Society: British Youth Movements 1883–1940* (London, 1977).

Elliott West and Paula Petrik, *Small Worlds: Children and Adolescents in America, 1850–1950* (Lawrence, Kan., 1992).

## THEORY AND CRITICISM OF CHILDREN'S LITERATURE

Gillian Avery and Julia Briggs (eds.), *Children and their Books: A Celebration of the Work of Iona and Peter Opie* (Oxford, 1989).

Robert Bator (ed.), *Signposts to the Criticism of Children's Literature* (Chicago, 1983).

Dennis Butts (ed.), *Stories and Society: Children's Literature in its Social Context* (London, 1992).

Eleanor Cameron, *The Green and Burning Tree: On the Writing and Enjoyment of Children's Books* (Boston, 1969).

Tessa Rose Chester, *Sources of Information about Children's Books* (South Woodchester, 1989).

Juliet Dusinberre, *Alice to the Lighthouse: Children's Books and Radical Experiments in Art* (London, 1987).

Sheila Egoff, *Worlds Within: Children's Fantasy from the Middle Ages to Today* (Chicago, 1988).

——G. T. Stubbs, and L. F. Ashley (eds.), *Only Connect: Readings on Children's Literature* (2nd edn., Toronto, 1980).

Margery Fisher, *The Bright Face of Danger* (London, 1986).

—— *Who's Who in Children's Books: A Treasury of the Familiar Characters of Childhood* (London, 1975).

James H. Fraser (ed.), *Society and Children's Literature* (Boston, 1978).

Barbara Harrison and Gregory Maguire (eds.), *Innocence and Experience: Essays and Conversations on Children's Literature* (New York, 1987).

Virginia Haviland (ed.), *Children and Literature: Views and Reviews* (New York, 1973).

Peter Hunt (ed.), *Children's Literature: The Development of Criticism* (London, 1990).

—— *Criticism, Theory and Children's Literature* (Oxford, 1991).

—— (ed.), *Literature for Children: Contemporary Criticism* (London, 1992).

Fred Inglis, *The Promise of Happiness: Value and Meaning in Children's Fiction* (Cambridge, 1981).

Karín Lesnik-Oberstein, *Children's Literature: Criticism and the Fictional Child* (Oxford 1994).

Perry Nodelman (ed.), *Touchstones: Reflections on the Best in Children's Literature* (West Lafayette, Ind., 3 vols., 1985–9).

—— *The Pleasures of Children's Literature* (White Plains, NY, 1992).

Maurice Saxby and Gordon Winch (eds.), *Give Them Wings: The Experience of Children's Literature* (South Melbourne, 1987).

John Stephens, *Language and Ideology in Children's Fiction* (London, 1992).

Michael Stone (ed.), *Children's Literature and Contemporary Theory* (Wollongong, 1991).

C. W. Sullivan III (ed.), *Science Fiction for Young Readers* (Westport, Conn., 1993).

Zena Sutherland, *Children and Books* (8th edn., New York, 1990).

Marina Tatar, *Off With Their Heads! Fairy Tales and the Culture of Childhood* (Princeton, NJ, 1992).

Barbara Wall, *The Narrator's Voice: The Dilemma of Children's Literature* (London, 1990).

## GENERAL HISTORY OF CHILDREN'S LITERATURE

Rosemary Auchmuty, *The World of Girls* (London, 1992).

Gillian Avery, *Childhood's Pattern: A Study of the Heroes and Heroines of Children's Fiction 1770–1900* (London, 1975).

Bruno Bettelheim, *The Uses of Enchantment: The Meaning and Importance of Fairy Tales* (New York, 1976).

Jane M. Bingham (ed.), *Writers for Children: Critical Studies of Major Authors since the Seventeenth Century* (New York, 1988).

Mary Cadogan and Patricia Craig, *You're a Brick, Angela! A New Look at Girls' Fiction from 1839–1975* (London, 1976).

Humphrey Carpenter and Mari Prichard, *The Oxford Companion to Children's Literature* (Oxford, 1984).

Kevin Carpenter (ed.), *Penny Dreadfuls and Comics* (London, 1983).

Tracy Chevalier (ed.), *Twentieth Century Children's Writers* (London and Chicago, 4th edn., 1989).

F. J. Harvey Darton, *Children's Books in England: Five Centuries of Social Life* (Cambridge, 3rd edn., rev. Brian Alderson, 1982).

Patricia Demers and Gordon Moyles (eds.), *From Instruction to Delight: An Anthology of Children's Literature to 1850* (Toronto, 1982).

Alec A. Ellis, *A History of Children's Reading and Literature* (Oxford, 1968).

Roger Lancelyn Green, *Tellers of Tales: Children's Books and their Authors from 1800–1964* (London, rev. edn., 1964).

Peter Hunt, *An Introduction to Children's Literature* (Oxford, 1994).

Bettina Hürlimann (trans. Brian Alderson), *Three Centuries of Children's Books in Europe* [*Europäische Kinderbücher in drei Jahrhunderten*] (London, 1967).

Mary V. Jackson, *Engines of Instruction, Mischief and Magic: Children's Literature in England from its Puritan Beginnings to 1839* (Aldershot, 1989).

Percy H. Muir, *English Children's Books 1600–1900* (London, 1954).

P. W. Musgrave, *From Brown to Bunter: The Life and Death of the School Story* (London, 1985).

Iona and Peter Opie, *The Oxford Dictionary of Nursery Rhymes* (Oxford, 1951).

George Perry (and Alan Aldridge), *The Penguin Book of Comics: A Slight History* (London, rev. edn., 1971).

Pierpont Morgan Library, *Early Children's Books and their Illustration*, chosen and discussed by Gerald Gottlieb (Toronto, 1975).

Eric Quayle, *Early Children's Books: A Collector's Guide* (Newton Abbot, 1983).

Isabel Quigly, *The Heirs of Tom Brown: The English School Story* (London, 1982).

Jeffrey Richards *Happiest Days: The Public Schools in English Fiction* (Manchester, 1988).

—— (ed.), *Imperialism and Juvenile Literature* (Manchester, 1989).

Roger Sale, *Fairy Tales and After: From Snow White to E. B. White* (Cambridge, Mass., 1978).

William Targ (ed.), *Bibliophile in the Nursery: A Bookman's Treasury of Collector's Lore on Old and Rare Children's Books* (Cleveland, 1957).

Mary F. Thwaite, *From Primer to Pleasure in Reading: An Introduction to the History of Children's Books in England from the Invention of Printing to 1914 . . .* (London, 2nd edn., 1972).

John Rowe Townsend, *Written for Children: An Outline of English Language Children's Literature* (London, 5th edn., 1990).

Geoffrey Trease, *Tales out of School* (London, new edn., 1964).

## BRITISH CHILDREN'S LITERATURE

### Early Writings (to 1700)

T. W. Baldwin, *Small Latine and Lesse Greek* (Urbana, Ill., 1944).

Clifton Johnson, *Old Time Schools and School-Books* (New York, 1904).

Paul Sangster, *Pity my Simplicity: The Evangelical Revival and the Religious Education of Children 1738–1800* (London, 1963).

William Sloane, *Children's Books in England and America in the Seventeenth Century* (New York, 1955).

C. John Sommerville, *The Discovery of Childhood in Puritan England* (Athens, Ga., 1992).

Margaret Spufford, *Small Books and Pleasant Histories: Popular Readership in Seventeenth Century England* (Cambridge, 1981).

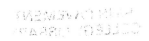

### The Eighteenth Century

M. Nancy Cutt, *Mrs Sherwood and her Books for Children* (London, 1974).

Victor Neuburg, *Chapbooks: A Guide to Reference Material on English and American Chapbook Literature of the Eighteenth and Nineteenth Centuries* (London, 1964).

—— *The Penny Histories: A Study of Chapbooks for Young Readers over Two Centuries* (London, 1968).

Samuel F. Pickering, *John Locke and Children's Books in Eighteenth Century England* (Knoxville, Tenn., 1981).
——— , *Moral Instruction and Fiction for Children 1749–1820* (Athens, Ga, 1993).
S. Roscoe, *John Newbery and his Successors 1740–1814* (Wormley, 1973).
———and R. A. Brimmell, *James Lumsden and Son of Glasgow: Their Juvenile Books and Chapbooks* (Pinner, 1981).
Geoffrey Summerfield, *Fantasy and Reason: Children's Literature in the Eighteenth Century* (London, 1984).
John Rowe Townsend (ed.), *Trade and Plumb-Cake for Ever, Huzza! The Life and Works of John Newbery 1713–1767* (Cambridge, 1994).

## The Nineteenth Century

Guy Arnold, *Held Fast for England: G. A. Henty, Imperialist Boys' Writer* (London, 1980).
Nina Auerbach and U. C. Knoepflmacher (eds.), *Forbidden Journeys: Fairy Tales and Fantasies by Victorian Women Writers* (Chicago, 1992).
Gillian Avery, *Childhood's Pattern; A Study of the Heroes and Heroines of Children's Fiction, 1770–1950* (London, 1975).
Georgina Battiscombe and Marghanita Laski (eds.), *A Chaplet for Charlotte Yonge* (London, 1965).
J. S. Bratton, *The Impact of Victorian Children's Fiction* (London, 1981).
Elias Bredsdorff, *Hans Christian Andersen: The Story of his Life and Works 1805–75* (London, 1975).
Julia Briggs, *A Woman of Passion: The Life of E. Nesbit 1858–1924* (London, 1984).
Joseph Bristow, *Empire Boys: Adventures in a Man's World* (London, 1991).
Dennis Butts, *Mistress of our Tears: A Literary and Biographical Study of Barbara Hofland* (Aldershot, 1992).
——— *Robert Louis Stevenson* (London, 1964).
Humphrey Carpenter, *Secret Gardens: A Study of the Golden Age of Children's Literature* (London, 1985).
Susan Chitty, *The Beast and the Monk: A Life of Charles Kingsley* (London, 1974).
Margaret Nancy Cutt, *Ministering Angels: A Study of Nineteenth-Century Evangelical Writing for Children* (Wormley, 1979).
Patricia Demers (ed.), *A Garland from the Golden Age: An Anthology of Children's Literature from 1850 to 1900* (Toronto, 1983).
Kirsten Drotner, *English Children and their Magazines 1751–1945* (New Haven, Conn., 1988).
Rodney Engen, *Kate Greenaway: A Biography* (London, 1981).
Wendy Forrester, *Great Grandmamma's Weekly: A Celebration of the 'Girl's Own Paper' 1880–1901* (Guildford, 1980).
David Grylls, *Guardians and Angels: Parents and Children in Nineteenth Century Literature* (London, 1976).
D. S. Higgins, *Rider Haggard: The Great Storyteller* (London, 1981).
M. R. Kingsford, *The Life, Work and Influence of William Henry Giles Kingston* (Toronto, 1947).
Marghanita Laski, *Mrs Ewing, Mrs Molesworth and Mrs Hodgson Burnett* (London, 1930).
James Holt McGavran, Jr. (ed.), *Romanticism and Children's Literature in Nineteenth-Century England* (Athens, Ga., 1991).

Edward C. Mack and W. H. G. Armytage, *Thomas Hughes* (London, 1952).

Ruth Michaelis-Jen, *The Brothers Grimm* (London, 1970).

Marjorie Moon, *John Harris's Books for Youth 1801–1843* (Winchester, 2nd edn., 1987).

Stanley Morison, *Talbot Baines Reed: Author, Bibliographer, Typefounder* (Cambridge, 1960).

Iona and Peter Opie, *The Classic Fairy Tales* (Oxford, 1974).

S. W. Patterson, *Rousseau's Émile and Early Children's Literature* (Metuchen, NJ, 1971).

Robert Phillips (ed.), *Aspects of Alice: Lewis Carroll's Dreamchild as Seen through the Critics' Looking Glasses 1865–1971* (New York, 1971).

Eric Quayle, *Ballantyne the Brave: A Victorian Writer and his Family* (London, 1967).

William Raeper, *The Gold Thread: Essays on George MacDonald* (Edinburgh, 1990).

Kimberley Reynolds, *Girls Only? Gender and Popular Fiction in Britain 1880–1910* (Hemel Hempstead, 1990).

Judith Rowbotham, *Good Girls Make Good Wives: Guidance for Girls in Victorian Fiction* (Oxford, 1989).

Lance Salway, *A Peculiar Gift: Nineteenth Century Writings on Books for Children* (Harmondsworth, 1976).

Valerie Sanders, *Reason over Passion: Harriet Martineau and the Victorian Novel* (Brighton, 1986).

Isobel Spencer, *Walter Crane* (London, 1975).

Joan Steele, *Captain Mayne Reid* (Boston, 1978).

E. S. Turner, *Boys Will be Boys: The Story of Sweeny Todd, Deadwood Dick, Sexton Blake, Billy Bunter, et al.* (Harmondsworth, 3rd edn., 1976).

Jack Zipes, *The Brothers Grimm: From Enchanted Forests to the Modern World* (London, 1988).

—— *Victorian Fairy Tales: The Revolt of the Fairies and Elves* (London, 1987).

*The Twentieth Century*

Marcus Crouch, *Treasure Seekers and Borrowers* (London, 1962).

—— *The Nesbit Tradition: The Children's Novel in England, 1945–70* (London, 1972).

Frank Eyre, *British Children's Books in the Twentieth Century* (London, 1971).

Dennis Gifford, *Happy Days: A Century of Comics* (London, 1975).

Peter Green, *Kenneth Grahame, 1859–1932: A Study of his Life, Work and Times* (London, 1959).

Leslie Linder, *A History of the Writings of Beatrix Potter* (London, 1971).

Robert F. Moss, *Rudyard Kipling and the Fiction of Adolescence* (London, 1982).

Neil Philip, *A Fine Anger: A Critical Introduction to the Work of Alan Garner* (London, 1981).

Jacqueline Rose, *The Case of Peter Pan; or, The Impossibility of Children's Fiction* (London, 1984).

Noel Streatfeild, *Magic and the Magician: E. Nesbit and her Children's Books* (London, 1958).

C. W. Sullivan III, *Welsh Celtic Myth in Modern Fantasy* (Westport, Conn., 1989).

Judy Taylor, Joyce Irene Whalley, Anne Stevenson Hobbes, and Elizabeth M. Battrick, *Beatrix Potter 1866–1943: The Artist and her World* (London, 1987).

## ILLUSTRATION

Brian Alderson, *Sing a Song for Sixpence: The English Picture-Book Tradition and Randolph Caldecott* (Cambridge, 1986).

Richard Dalby, *The Golden Age of Children's Book Illustration* (London, 1991).

Jane Doonan, *Looking at Pictures in Picture Books* (South Woodchester, 1992).

William Feaver, *When We were Young: Two Centuries of Children's Book Illustration* (London, 1977).

Bertha E. Mahoney *et al.* (comp.), *Illustrators of Children's Books, 1744–1945* (Boston, 1947).

Douglas Martin, *The Telling Line* (London, 1989).

Perry Nodelman, *Words about Pictures: The Narrative Art of Children's Picture Books* (Athens, Ga., 1988).

Maurice Sendak, *Caldecott & Co.: Notes on Books and Pictures* (New York, 1988).

Janet Adam Smith, *Children's Illustrated Books* (London, 1948).

Joyce Irene Whalley, *Cobwebs to Catch Flies: Illustrated Books for the Nursery and Schoolroom, 1700–1900* (London, 1974).

—— and Tessa Rose Chester, *A History of Children's Book Illustration* (London, 1988).

## CHILDREN'S LITERATURE IN THE USA

May Hill Arbuthnot, *Children and Books* (Chicago, 3rd edn., 1964).

Gillian Avery, *Behold the Child: American Children and their Books* (London, 1994).

Barbara Bader, *American Picturebooks from Noah's Ark to the Beast Within* (New York, 1976).

Louise Seaman Bechtel, *Books in Search of Children*, ed. Virginia Hamilton (New York, 1969).

John Cech (ed.), *American Writers for Children, 1900–1960* (*Dictionary of Literary Biography*, vol. xxii) (Detroit, 1983).

Martin Gardner and Russell B. Nye, *The Wizard of Oz and Who He Was* (Battle Creek, Mich., 1957).

Samuel Griswold Goodrich, *Recollections of a Lifetime* (New York, 1857).

Jerry Griswold, *Audacious Kids: Coming of Age in America's Classic Children's Books* (New York, 1992).

Rosalie Halsey, *Forgotten Books of the American Nursery: A History of the Development of the American Story-Book* (Boston, 1911; New York, 1972).

Virginia Hamilton and Margaret N. Coughlan (eds.), *Yankee Doodle's Literary Sampler of Prose, Poetry and Pictures* (New York, 1974).

Dianne A. Johnson, *Telling Tales: The Pedagogy and Promise of African American Literature for Youth* (Westport, Conn., 1990).

R. Gordon Kelly (ed.), *Children's Periodicals of the United States* (Westport, Conn., 1984).

Mary Lystad, *From Dr Mather to Dr Seuss: 200 Years of American Books for Children* (Cambridge, Mass., 1980).

Anne Scott MacLeod, *American Childhood: Essays on Children's Literature of the Nineteenth and Twentieth Centuries* (Athens, Ga., 1994).

—— *A Moral Tale: Children's Fiction and American Culture, 1820–1860* (Hamden, Conn., 1975).

Barbara Rollock, *Black Authors and Illustrators of Children's Books: A Biographical Dictionary* (2nd edn., New York, 1992).

Ann Thwaite, *Waiting for the Party: The Life of Frances Hodgson Burnett* (London, 1974).

### AUSTRALIAN CHILDREN'S LITERATURE

Walter McVitty, *Authors and Illustrators of Australian Children's Books* (Sydney, 1989).

Marcie Muir, *A History of Australian Children's Book Illustration* (Melbourne, 1982).

Brenda Niall, *Australia through the Looking-Glass: Children's Fiction 1830–1980* (Melbourne, 1984).

—— *Seven Little Billabongs: The World of Ethel Turner and Mary Grant Bruce* (Melbourne, 1979).

Maurice Saxby, *A History of Australian Children's Literature*, i: *1841–1941*; ii: *1941–1970* (Sydney, 1969, 1971).

—— *The Proof of the Puddin': Australian Children's Literature 1970–1990* (Sydney, 1993).

Michael Stone (ed.), *Finding a Voice: Australian Children's Literature* (Wollongong, 1993).

K. White, *Australian Children's Fiction: The Subject Guide* (Milton, 1992).

R. Wighton, *Early Australian Children's Literature* (Surrey Hills, 1979).

### CANADIAN CHILDREN'S LITERATURE

Margaret Atwood, *Survival: A Thematic Guide to Canadian Literature* (Toronto, 1972).

Sheila Egoff and Judith Saltman, *The New Republic of Childhood: A Critical Guide to Canadian Children's Literature in English* (Toronto, 1990).

Judith Saltman, *Modern Canadian Children's Books* (Toronto, 1987).

Jon C. Stott and Raymond Jones, *Canadian Books for Children: A Guide to Authors and Illustrators* (Toronto, 1988).

### NEW ZEALAND CHILDREN'S LITERATURE

Betty Gilderdale, *A Sea Change: 145 Years of New Zealand Junior Fiction* (Auckland, 1982).

—— *Introducing Twenty-One New Zealand Children's Writers* (Auckland, 1991).

J. B. Ringer, *Young Emigrants: New Zealand Juvenile Fiction 1833–1919* (Hamilton, 1980).

Terry Sturm (ed.), *The Oxford History of New Zealand Literature* (Auckland, 1991).

# ILLUSTRATION SOURCES

The editors and publishers wish to thank the following who have kindly given permission to reproduce the illustrations on the following pages:

key: Bodleian = Bodleian Library, University of Oxford; Opie = Opie Collection, Bodleian Library; CUL = Syndics of Cambridge University Library

**x** Mrs Iona Opie. Photo: John Simonds; **2, 10** Bodleian, Mason H35; **3** *above*, **33** Museum of London; **3** *below*, **132, 133, 155, 156** Bodleian; **5** S. Kevill-Davies, *Yesterday's Children*, Antique Collectors' Club, 1991; **6, 32, 34, 35, 51, 52, 53, 55, 73, 88, 89, 90, 95** *below*, **135, 146, 148, 150, 152, 185** *below*, **212, 231, 239, 240, 323, 324, 326, 354** British Library; **8** Bodleian, Douce cc 216; **9** © RCHME Crown Copyright; **13** Opie C183; **14** Opie C680; **15** Opie n P96 (2) vol III; **16, 17** Pierpont Morgan Library, New York. PML 45444; **20** Opie C179; **21, 183** Mary Evans Picture Library; **22, 36, 47, 69** Opie; **24** The Lord Tollemache, Helmingham Hall. Photo: Courtauld Institute of Art; **27** Fitzwilliam Museum, Cambridge; **28, 361** Opie P105; **29, 30** British Museum; **31, 154** The Mansell Collection; **38** Birmingham Museum and Art Gallery; **39, 40** Opie Douce ADDS 298; **42, 365** St Bride Printing Library; **44** Metropolitan Toronto Reference Library, Osborne Collection; **49, 58** © British Museum; **56** Opie Vet A5 f 108; **59** British Library and S. Roscoe, *John Newbery and His Successors 1740-1814*, Five Owls Press. Photo: CUL; **61** Opie A248; **62** *left* Opie N894; **62** *right* Opie C1068; **64, 357** Opie IL56; **65** Opie N1078; **66, vi,** Opie N607; **68** *above* Opie P371; **68** *below* Opie Ms Butterfly's Ball; **70, 97** *left*, **116, 145, 147, 217, 269** CUL; **74** Opie N644; **79** Bodleian, Ms Montagu d 4; **80, 84** Rare Books Library, University of Reading; **87** Bodleian, Douce G160; **92, 93** Opie A247; **94, 144, 164** National Portrait Gallery, London; **95** *above*, **xi** Sotheby's; **96** H.E. the Danish Ambassador; **97** *right*, **xii** Bodleian, 3.C605; **99** Opie A758/1; **103, 104, 105, 106, 107, 108, 110, 127** Rare Book Department, Free Library of Philadelphia; **111** Samuel Colman, *Peter Parley's Christmas Tales*, 1838, illustration by William Croome. The Elizabeth Nesbitt Room, University of Pittsburgh; **112** S. G. Goodrich, *Recollections of a Lifetime* vol 1, 1857. Rare Books Library, University of Reading; **120** *left Our Young Folk*, 1867, British Library; **122** Peter Newark's Western Americana; **123** The Bettmann Archive; **124** Concord Free Public Library; **131** Topham Picture Source; **139, 352** The Pierpont Morgan Library, New York, MA 926; **140** Mrs M. J. StClair and Christ Church, Oxford; **151** The Writers' Museum, Edinburgh City Museums; **165, 190** Illustrated London News Picture Library; **170, 171, 353** reprinted by permission of the Peters Fraser & Dunlop Group Ltd; **172** Mary Evans/ Bruce Castle Museum; **173** The Estate of Kenneth Grahame, *The Golden Age*, The Bodley Head, 1928, illustration by E. H. Shepard; **178** National Trust Bateman's; **181** Line illustration by E. H. Shepard copyright under the Berne Convention. Reproduced by permission of Curtis Brown, London. Reprinted with the permission of Atheneum Books for Young Readers, an imprint of Simon & Schuster Children's Publishing Division from *The Wind in the Willows* by Kenneth Grahame, illustrated by Ernest H. Shepard. Copyright 1933, 1953 Charles Scribner's Sons; copyright renewed © 1961 Ernest H. Shepard; copyright renewed © 1981 Charles Scribner's Sons and Mary Eleanor Jessie Knox; **186, 362, 366** copyright © Frederick Warne & Co, 1946; **194** The Billie Love Historical Collection; **196, 197** Chris Beetles Ltd; **199** *Number One Joy Street*, 1923. CUL; **201** The Society of Authors as literary representative of the Estate of Rose Fyleman; **202** Tony Milne; **203** Quality Family Entertainment Ltd. CUL; **206** © Edward Ardizzone; **209** Hodder & Stoughton Ltd; **214, 363** P.L. Travers, *Mary Poppins*, 1934. CUL; **215** HarperCollins Publishers Ltd; **216** *left* Jane Waller and Michael Vaughan-Rees, *Women in Wartime*, Macdonald Optima, 1987. CUL; **216** *right* Imogen Smallwood; **218** The estate of Eve Garnett, published by Frederick Muller. CUL; **219** Arthur Ransome, *Swallows and Amazons*, 1930. CUL; **220, 221** Joyce L. Brisley, *Milly-Molly-Mandy*, 1928, Chambers Harrap. CUL; **226** MGM (courtesy Kobal); **227, 244** The Bettmann Archive; **228** UPI/Bettmann; **234** United Artists (courtesy Kobal); **235** University of Illinois at Urbana-Champaign; **236** The Huntington Library, San Marino, California; **238** from *Homer Price* by Robert McCloskey. Copyright 1943, renewed © 1971 by Robert McCloskey. Used by permission of Viking Penguin, a division of Penguin Books USA Inc. Print by University of Illinois at Urbana-Champaign; **241** Library of Congress; **248** ™Dr. Seuss Enterprises, L.P. 1958, 1986; **249** © 1972 Edgar Rice Burroughs, Inc. All Rights Reserved. Print by University of Illinois at Urbana-Champaign; **253** I. & P. Opie, *Oxford Nursery Rhyme Book*, 1955, illustrated by Joan Hassall; **255** HarperCollins Publishers Ltd. CUL; **256** Northamptonshire Newspapers Ltd; **260** Kaye Webb; **263** Rev W. Awdry, *Thomas the Tank Engine*, Ward, 1946. CUL; **264** C. F. Tunnicliffe, *Wandering with Nomad*, University of London Press (now Hodder & Stoughton); **266** Cynthia Harnett, *The Wool-Pack*, Methuen. CUL; **268** Mrs Diana Boston; photo by A. F. Kersting; **270** Penguin Group and CUL; **271** John Rylands University Library of Manchester; **272** John Cocks; **274** C.S. Lewis, *The Voyage of the Dawn Treader*, HarperCollins Publishers Ltd. CUL; **276** Ted Hughes, *The Iron Man*, Faber and Faber Ltd; **277** Norton, *The Borrowers*, Dent, London, 1952. CUL; **279** published by A & C Black. CUL; **280** from *Queenie Peavy* by Robert Burch, illustrated by Jerry Lazare. Copyright © 1966 by Robert Burch. Used by permission of Viking Penguin, a division of Penguin Books USA Inc. Photo: University of Illinois at Urbana-Champaign; **281** reprinted by permission of HarperCollins Publishers and Victor Gollancz; **282** Random House; **285**, **312** *left*, **312** *right*, **313** Oxford University Press; **287** Sheldon Fogelman; **292** *Alice's Adventures in Wonderland*, illustrations © 1988 Anthony Browne. Published in the UK by Walker Books Ltd and in the US by Alfred A. Knopf; **293** illustration for *Musical Instruments* from *On Market Street* by Arnold Lobel. Text: copyright © 1981 by Arnold Lobel. Ill. copyright © 1981 by Anita Lobel. By permission of Greenwillow, a division of William Morrow & Company, Inc; **295** Ruth Manning-Sanders, *A Book of Ogres and Trolls*, Methuen. CUL; **296** Jonathan Cape. CUL; **300** Frances Lincoln Ltd. CUL; **303** Andersen Press Ltd. CUL; **306** Topham Picture Library; **309** Walker Books Ltd; **311** cover illustration from *Fungus the Bogeyman* by Raymond Briggs, copyright © Raymond Briggs, 1977. First published by Hamish Hamilton Children's Books; **314** Janet and Allan Ahlberg, *Each Peach, Pear, Plum* copyright © Janet Ahlberg 1978. First published by Viking Kestrel. CUL; **315** American Library Association; **316** Harry Allard and James Marshall, *Miss Nelson is Missing*. Illustration copyright © 1977 by James Marshall. Reprinted by permission of Houghton Mifflin Co. All rights reserved. Photo by University of Illinois at Urbana-Champaign; **317**, **ix** Michael Rosen, *You Can't Catch Me*, illustrated by Quentin Blake, Andre Deutsch Children's Books, an imprint of Scholastic Publications Ltd 1981. CUL; **319** *Castle*. 1977 Copyright © 1977 by David Macauley. Reprinted by permission of Houghton Mifflin

Co. All rights reserved; **320** illustration copyright © 1992 by Glen Rounds. Reprinted from *Three Little Pigs and the Big Bad Wolf* by permission of Holiday House, New York; **324** Philippa Poole; **327** Mitchell Library, State Library of New South Wales; **328**, **329** *The Magic Pudding* written and illustrated by Norman Lindsay by permission of HarperCollins Publishers Australia; **330** South Australian Film (courtesy Kobal); **334** Robin Muller; **336** Laszlo Gal; **338** Annick Press 1989; **340** *The New Baby Calf.* Text copyright © by Edith Newlin Chase. Illustrations copyright © by Barbara Reid. All rights reserved. Reprinted by permission of Scholastic Canada Ltd., 123 Newkirk Road, Richmond Hill, Ontario, Canada L4C 3G5; **342** *above* illustration by Eric Beddows from *Zoom Away*. Text copyright © 1985 by Tim Wynne-Jones, illustrations copyright © 1985 by Eric Beddows. A Groundwood Book/Douglas & McIntyre Ltd; **342** *below* Robert Munsch; **344** Waiatarua Publishing Co 1986. CUL; **345** Reed Publishing (NZ) Ltd; **346** Oxford University Press, New Zealand; **348**, **xiii** Mallinson Rendel Publishers Ltd. CUL; **350** Shortland Publications Ltd.

In a few instances we have been unable to trace the copyright holder prior to publication. If notified, the publishers will be pleased to amend the acknowledgements in any future edition.

Picture research by Sandra Assersohn.

# INDEX

This index includes major subjects and genres as well as people. Individual book titles are not listed.

Page references in italics are to captions to illustrations. There are often textual references also on these pages. Sub-entries are in chronological order.